Foreign Relations and Federal States

Studies in Federalism
edited by Murray Forsyth
Centre for Federal Studies
University of Leicester

FOREIGN RELATIONS AND FEDERAL STATES

Edited by
Brian Hocking

Leicester University Press
London and New York
Distributed in the United States and Canada by St. Martin's Press

Leicester University Press
(a division of Pinter Publishers Ltd.)
25 Floral Street, London, WC2E 9DS

First published in 1993

© Editor and contributors, 1993

Distributed in the United States and Canada by St. Martin's Press, Room 400, 175 Fifth
Avenue, New York, NY 10010, USA

British Library Cataloguing in Publication Data
A CIP catalogue record for this book is available from the British Library

ISBN 0 7185 1477 7

Library of Congress Cataloging-in-Publication Data
Foreign relations and federal states / edited by Brian Hocking.
      p.   cm. — (Studies in federalism)
   Includes bibliographical references and index.
   ISBN 0-7185-1477-7
   1. International relations.   2. Federal government.   3. International law.   I. Hocking,
Brian.   II. Series: Studies in federalism (Leicester, England)
K3201.Z9F67   1993
327—dc20   92-44103
                                                                                                 CIP

Typeset by Florencetype Ltd, Kewstoke, Avon
Printed and bound in Great Britain by Biddles Ltd., Guildford and King's Lynn

Contents

Notes on the contributors

Louis Balthazar is Professor of Political Science, Laval University, Montreal, Canada.

Andrew F. Cooper is Professor of Political Science at the University of Waterloo, Canada.

Greg Craven is Reader in Law at the University of Melbourne, Australia.

David K. M. Dyment is a Political Science lecturer at the University of Ottawa and a Ph.D. candidate at the Université de Montreal, Canada.

Earl H. Fry is Professor of Political Science and Director of Canadian Studies at Brigham Young University, USA.

Stuart Harris is Professor of International Relations in the Research School of Pacific Studies, Australian National University and was formerly Permanent Secretary in the Department of Foreign Affairs and Trade, Canberra, Australia.

Christopher Hill is Montague Burton Professor of International Relations at the London School of Economics and Political Science, England.

Brian Hocking is Principal Lecturer in International Relations, Coventry University, England.

John Kincaid is Executive Director of the Advisory Commission on Intergovernmental Relations, Washington, DC, USA.

John M. Kline is a Professor in the School of Foreign Service, Georgetown University, Washington, DC, USA.

Uwe Leonardy is Ministerialrat in the Lower Saxon Mission to the Federation, Bonn, Germany.

George MacLean is a doctoral student at Queen's University, Kingston, Canada.

Kim Richard Nossal is Professor and Chair of the Department of Political Science, McMaster University, Canada.

Michael Smith is Professor of International Relations and Head of the School of International Studies and Law, Coventry University, England.

Patrick J. Smith is Professor of Political Science at Simon Fraser University, Canada.

Derrick G. Wilkinson is Senior Trade Policy Adviser at Alberta House, London, England.

Robert J. Williams is Professor of Political Science at the University of Waterloo, Canada.

Series editor's preface

Each of the last four books in this series has concentrated on a specific federal system—those of Canada, Germany, the Soviet Union and the United States of America respectively. A volume on the constitutional problem in South Africa is due to appear shortly. In the present volume the series turns from the treatment of individual countries to the treatment of a theme common to a number of federal countries, using a comparative approach to sharpen understanding. The theme is that of the management of foreign relations.

It might seem at first sight that this is an area which does not present serious problems for the student of federalism. Foreign relations are traditionally and conventionally regarded as being the exclusive preserve of the central government of a federal system, rather than as being an area shared by the different levels of government and thus subject to typically federal tensions. However, one of the striking phenomena of recent decades has been the developing international interests of regional and local governments, and this development has manifested itself with particular clarity and force within federal systems. It is towards an elucidation of the causes and consequences of this contemporary trend towards multitiered foreign relations that the present volume is primarily directed. It seeks to compare the experience of four established federal systems—those of Australia, Canada, Germany and the United States of America. It also looks at the problem from the other end, so to speak, by examining the experience of the European Community as it struggles to shape the national foreign policies of its members into a common foreign policy.

The book grew out of an international Conference held at Australia House in London in March 1992. The Conference was organised by the Centre for Federal Studies at Leicester University and the Centre for International and European Studies at Coventry University, in cooperation with the Sir Robert Menzies Centre for Australian Studies. The organisers would like to thank the Australian High Commissioner, Mr R.J. Smith, for kindly providing a venue for the Conference, and the staff at Australia

House for their hospitality. We also wish to thank the British Academy and the Nuffield Foundation for their financial support for the Conference.

Murray Forsyth
Series editor

Introduction

Brian Hocking

During the last two decades a considerable literature focusing on the international activities of non-central governments (NCGs), particularly in
federal political systems, has developed. Much of this interest has been
generated by a belief that the phenomenon of the US states, and Canadian
provinces, for example, intervening in the conduct of external policy at the
national level and opening overseas offices in the quest for enhanced trade
and foreign investment signifies a major development in the character of
international politics.

Of course, the trend has by no means been restricted to federations: local
governments in highly centralised states such as France have been equally
motivated to operate outside their national environments as growing trans-
boundary linkages indicate. The processes of European integration have
helped to encourage this as regional authorities recognise the need to influence the policy processes in Brussels as much as in their own national
capitals.

Moreover, just as localities have become increasingly aware of the implications of international economic forces for their own well-being, seeking to
influence them either through their national governments or by direct
action, so foreign governments and non-state actors have become conscious
of the need to exercise influence at the local and regional level if they are to
achieve their objectives. Hence, for example, the dramatic growth of foreign
lobbying at the state level in the United States, particularly by the
Japanese.

The aim of the organisers of the conference on which this book is based
was to provide an opportunity to examine this subject in the light of
research undertaken in recent years. More specifically, the intention was to
adopt a policy-making rather than purely constitutional perspective and to
review the international activities and influence of NCGs in the context of
the emergence of a far more complex diplomatic milieu in which policy-

makers are constrained to weave into a single skein negotiations at both the domestic and international levels. In other words, as the title of the conference and this book suggest, the focus was on the implications of what might be termed the 'localisation' of foreign relations for their management in an era when the boundaries between domestic and international policy appear ever more indeterminate. A key assumption was that such an undertaking was as significant to an understanding of of contemporary federalism as to the character of international relations.

The implications of this approach become a little clearer when considered in the light of the characteristics of existing discussions of NCG international activity. Obviously, generalisations are as dangerous here as in any area, but it is noticeable that a good deal of the literature has tended to focus on the significance of NCGs in terms of their uniqueness as international actors and their separateness from traditional modes of diplomatic intercourse. Such a tendency has been reinforced by those who have seen in the growth of transborder linkages between regions of different nation-states indications of a new international order suggestive of the demise of national governments. As a consequence, rather than attempting to locate NCGs within the foreign policy processes alongside their national governments, there has been a strong presumption that each have incompatible interests and stand in opposition to one another. As John Kincaid points out in his contribution to this volume, this belief ignores processes which are rendering the boundaries demarcating state and non-state actors far more permeable than hitherto and creating ambiguities about the status and characteristics of each.

The picture has been clouded further by the emphasis in the literature of international interdependence on change at the systemic level and—as Karvonen and Sundelius amongst others have noted—the relative inattention to the changing character of the foreign policy processes which is accompanying it.[1] Consequently, the impact of the image of NCG international activity thus created has been to set it apart from the patterns of traditional diplomacy, to seek new terms to describe it (such as 'paradiplomacy' and 'protodiplomacy') which serve to reinforce the distinction, and to emphasise the elements of conflict between national and subnational governments which have accompanied its growth. Furthermore, and somewhat ironically, given the desire of some observers to use this phenomenon as a means of rejecting the distortions of state-centric interpretations of world politics, NCGs themselves have tended to be treated as unitary actors, whereas, in reality, they represent quite complex patterns of relationships both inside and outside their national settings, and embrace a diversity of interests.

More recently, however, the growing literature analysing the complex character of contemporary diplomacy, such as in the trade policy area, has offered a useful corrective to these assumptions.[2] Here, the emphasis is on the interrelatedness of the domestic and international political environments and the need for national policy makers to conduct diplomacy in both theatres simultaneously if they are to succeed in achieving their objectives. Far from being separate diplomatic players, NCGs become integrated into a densely textured web of 'multilayered' diplomacy, in which they are capable of performing a variety of roles at different points in the negotiating process. In so doing, they may become opponents of national objectives; but, equally, they can serve as allies and agents in the pursuit of those objectives.

In this context, as the contributions from Craven and Harris suggest, the problems of managing domestic and external policy intermesh. Once regarded as lying firmly within the jurisdiction of the central government in a federal system, issues relating to the international environment have become matters of jurisdictional dispute. This, of course, reflects the fact that the foreign policy agenda has expanded greatly since the era in which many federal constitutions were drafted, touching on policy issues under the control of the constituent governments. As the Australian example clearly demonstrates, the resultant disputes can strike at the very heart of the balance of powers in a federation. Put in its simplest form, if central government, by virtue of its control over foreign policy, can impinge more and more on the responsibilities of the constituent governments using the argument that the foreign policy agenda has expanded to include a range of issues once assumed to be exclusively domestic in nature, then the logic of a division of powers is endangered.

Quite clearly, then, the contributions in this book reflect a situation in which policy arenas are becoming more permeable. The notion of a hierarchy of political authority, with central government acting as the effective gatekeeper between national communities and their international environment, is outdated. This is so not because it never performs this role, but because its jurisdictional claims and capacity to do so have been weakened by the changes in the domestic and international environments discussed by Fry. Not only are the non-central governments in federal states seeking to exercise influence on external policy, but—as Smith points out in his study of Vancouver and Seattle—the age of the global city has arrived. When this is set alongside Hill's discussion of the implications of constructing what one might term a 'federal' foreign policy for the European Community, then the true breadth of these developments becomes apparent.

Several of the chapters in this volume return to the question of the motivation for NCG international involvement. Not unexpectedly, answers have focused on the consequences of growing transnational relations and economic interdependence. Fry, for example, recognises the forces producing a global economy, but adds to these domestic considerations which have encouraged the US state governments to expand their international concerns, such as falling revenues alongside growing domestic responsibilities.

Yet, in his thoughtful analysis, Kincaid questions the adequacy of the widespread recourse to interdependence as an explanation for the phenomenon. Rather, he suggests, we are witnessing a more profound set of developments which he describes in terms of a conflict between people's needs and demands as citizens on the one hand and consumers on the other. The tensions between these two orientations helps to explain the desire of NCGs to operate in the global arena: indeed, the needs of 'consumership' can be better served by according localities better access to the global economy. In this image, there is no inherent contradiction between the processes of localisation and globalisation; the one goes hand-in-hand with the other.

Several contributors are, however, concerned to demonstrate that broad generalisations regarding the causes and character of NCG international activity can disguise a diversity of factors. Both Kline and Cooper, for example, provide helpful insights here. Cooper's typology, drawing as it does on a wide range of examples, clearly demonstrates the variations in motivation for and—as he terms it—the 'form and intensity' of localised international activity. This is explained by a variety of factors, from the structure of the local economy to political, and even personality, considerations.

Pursuing this theme, Nossal and MacLean suggest that we look beyond the traditional emphasis on the interests of individual NCGs as the key to understanding their international roles. Rather, they suggest, this needs to be understood in the broader context of interactions between subnational, national and international actors. Taking Australian and Canadian relations with China as an example, they explore this triangular relationship. Not only does such a perspective help to overcome the tendency to view NCG international activity as autonomous and something set apart from the broad patterns of world politics; it touches on one of the key themes running through the essays, namely, that of the balance between conflict and cooperation in the relationship between central and non-central authorities where issues touching on foreign relations are involved.

Here, as indicated earlier, there has been a tendency to stress the conflictual dimension and it is interesting to note the extent to which this is qualified in the chapters. Even in the case of Quebec, frequently seen as a paradigm case of conflict with central government over the conduct of foreign policy, Balthazar argues that to stress conflict offers an incomplete picture. Underlying the more headline-grabbing events which have marked relations between Ottawa and Quebec, there exists a considerable element of cooperation. This, suggests Balthazar, reflects the fact that there are two motivations operative in Quebec's desire to develop an international role: on the one hand, a concern with 'status' and, on the other, the pressures of 'adaptation and necessity' which require it to respond to global economic forces, and to do so in conjunction with, rather than in opposition to, Ottawa.

The degree of tension between the levels of government, and the desire to develop an international voice independent of that of the federal government, is a product of the level of asymmetry of interests between the two. This point is picked up by Dyment who, in contrasting the provinces of Ontario and Quebec, argues that there is a far greater symmetry of interest between the former and Ottawa, generally more representative of 'substate paradiplomacy' within federal states.

In differing contexts, the papers by Kline, Smith, Harris and Leonardy reinforce the point that, whilst conflict over access to the international arena may indeed be present, this is balanced by the need for cooperation. This can be seen in terms of the development of modes of cooperation through the creation of what I term 'linkage mechanisms' which reflect the mutual interests of each level in developing structures and processes for cooperation. In the case of the United States, Kline makes the point that 'promoting coordination and cooperation while minimizing potential conflicts' is a major task now confronting policy-makers at the centre. Drawing on his experience as a trade policy adviser for the Alberta government, Wilkinson argues that developments in the trade policy environment have enhanced the province's international interests. Nevertheless, there is no desire to undermine Ottawa's overall responsibility for the conduct of Canada's foreign relations. What is needed, he argues, is a framework capable of ensuring communication between the levels of government and which protects the interests of both.

Looked at in this way, the problems attending the management of foreign relations enter familiar territory in the literature of federalism: that of intergovernmental relations. Given the changing character of domestic and international politics and the interaction between them, this is hardly surprising. The evolution of federal systems has been one in which a growing interdependence between levels of government in the domestic sphere has resulted from an increasingly complex policy environment requiring the development of cooperative mechanisms to manage this complexity. Bearing in mind the enhanced internationalisation of virtually every sector of public policy, it is hardly surprising that the need for intergovernmental cooperation should impinge on the conduct of external relations. Williams demonstrates the point in his discussion of the management of cultural diplomacy in Australia and Canada. In this instance, there is an obvious disparity in the level and form of cooperation which has been achieved, with Australia having established a coordinating body which, to use Williams's term, 'overcomes federalism'.

The problem of cooperation, however, as noted earlier, is not simply one of reconciling the interests of two levels of government. Rather, it is a multilevel problem spanning cities, regions, national governments and, in the case of the European Community, with the prospect of a common foreign and security policy, supranational institutions. The contributions from Hill and Leonardy offer differing but complementary perspectives on the latter dimension of these processes. Hill's discussion of the character of foreign policy cooperation between the member states of the EC is balanced by Leonardy's consideration of regionalisation within the framework of the Community. His argument is that the image of the future is not a decentralised 'Europe *of* the regions' which would result in overcentralisation of power in Brussels, but a 'Europe *with* the regions' in which appropriate powers and functions should be assigned to the respective levels of political authority.

Overall, the chapters in this volume can be approached at two levels. The first—and broader—perspective concerns the operation of political systems, particularly federal states, as the boundaries between domestic and international policy arenas become hazier. Understanding federalism increasingly demands that the international environment in which a given system functions be taken into account. The traditional concern with relationships between central government and the constituent elements of the federation now has to be expanded to embrace the international environment in which both levels of government operate. Nowhere is this more clearly drawn than in the case of the EC, as Leonardy's discussion of Germany illustrates. In this sense, what have in the past been defined (often for political purposes) as 'turf battles' over the right to conduct foreign policy are more accurately seen as jurisdictional disputes produced by twin processes: the localisation of global economic, political and social forces, and the internationalisation of domestic issues. Nevertheless, the resultant constitutional tensions outlined in Craven's chapter are no small matter for the future of federal systems.

The second level, obviously, concerns the conduct of foreign relations. Whatever else the chapters in this volume demonstrate, they underscore the fact that the traditional assumption that foreign relations are the exclusive concern of central governments is no longer valid. Certainly, the international interests of NCGs are more limited in scope than are those of national governments and have a pronounced economic orientation. It would, however, be misleading to dismiss them as second-order actors as a result. The global web of world politics ensures that non-central governments have interests and responsibilities which can often, quite unexpectedly and sometimes against their wishes, project them into the international limelight. Increasingly, the various levels of government have legitimate international interests and these have to be accommodated rather than denied.

This is hardly likely to be achieved by recourse on the part of central governments to constitutional claims regarding their exclusive right to deal with international issues or—as one observer of the growth in the United States of what he terms 'local activism' has advocated—a policy of 'containment' resting, in the final analysis, on legal sanctions.[3] Injunctions to strengthened control by foreign policy agencies, such as the State

Department, not only deny the realities of a vastly more diversified policy-making environment, but fail to recognise the underlying forces that have created the problem which they seek to solve. The management of foreign relations demands cooperation between levels of government and, whilst admitting that conflicts of interest occur, the contributors describe the emergence of a variety of structures and practices intended to achieve this.

One of the frequently quoted statements on the conduct of foreign relations in federal states is Wheare's observation that a 'spirited foreign policy' and federalism sit uneasily together.[4] Quite what characterises this quality in the context of contemporary diplomacy is open to question. Where the intricacies of trade and environmental diplomacy are concerned, for example, the often slow and uncertain development of domestic consensus is as fundamental to success as is 'spirit'. Indeed, the general theme running through this book is that the growing diffuseness characterising the management of foreign relations is a positive feature. Both Kline and Kincaid portray it as a desirable element of democratisation in an area traditionally associated with the dominance of executive power.

Certainly, as Smith and others suggest, the policy environment is far more complex and this affects the policy choices available to national policy-makers. But added complexity need not be equated with paralysis, and the evidence provided by these contributors suggests that strategies of adaptation have emerged at both central and non-central administrative levels. Amongst other things, this should introduce a note of caution into the debate about the demise of foreign ministries as they are challenged by new bureaucratic players. Whereas they are required to respond to new forces and interests, there is considerable evidence that they are able to do so.

The general thrust of the discussion, then, should not be taken as a denial of the fact that the management of the multilayered diplomatic environment, with its domestic and international elements, presents formidable difficulties. However, it does suggest that it poses challenges that demand practical solutions which go beyond simple assertions of the constitutional prerogatives of central governments in the foreign policy sphere. The essence of the problem is not so much the demarcation of areas of responsibility (particularly where this denies the legitimacy of subnational international interests), but in creating the means by which the increasingly diverse policy interests bearing on the international environment which national communities possess can be related one to another and integrated into the overall policy framework. Within the context of federal states, as in the domestic sphere, this has involved overcoming the constraints imposed by constitutional norms through processes of intergovernmental negotiation and collaboration. It is with these processes, where they operate at the points of interface between domestic and international environments, that these chapters are concerned.

The structure of the book

Deciding on an appropriate structure for this collection of essays has proved no easy task. To order them solely according to geographical focus or theme was difficult given the comparative nature of so many. On the other hand, simply to adopt a structure dictated by the initial letters of authors' names seemed unhelpful and would overlook the interchange of ideas that links together a number of the papers. Consequently, the chapters have been ordered with a view to their general perspective on the issue and their geographical point of reference.

Thus the book opens with two rather different chapters, those of Greg Craven and John Kincaid, which set out some key issues from a constitutional and a political science perspective respectively. These are followed by the main block of essays loosely ordered in terms of their thematic and geographical focus. The chapters by Uwe Leonardy, Christopher Hill and Michael Smith, with their predominantly European perspective, bring the volume to a close. Thus whereas the book can be 'dipped into' by those with specific interests, it also provides a developing discussion for those who wish to read it from cover to cover.

Notes

1. See Lauri Karvonen and Bengt Sundelius, 'Interdependence and foreign policy management in Sweden and Finland', *International Studies Quarterly*, 34 (1990), 212.
2. A particularly useful contribution here is to be found in Robert R. Putnam, 'Diplomacy and domestic politics: the logic of two-level games', *International Organization*, 42 (1988). There are a number of studies which illustrate the impact of subnational interests on the diplomatic processes. See, for example: A.F. Cooper, 'Subnational activity and foreign economic policy making in Canada and the United States: perspectives on agriculture', *International Journal*, 41 (1986); Brian Hocking, 'Multilayered diplomacy and the Canada–US Free Trade Negotiations', *British Journal of Canadian Studies*, 5 (1990); Henry R. Nau (ed.), *Domestic Trade Politics and the Uruguay Round*, Columbia University Press, New York (1989); and Gilbert R. Winham, *International Trade and the Tokyo Round Negotiation*, Princeton University Press, Princeton, NJ (1986).
3. Peter J. Spiro, 'The limits of federalism in foreign policymaking', *Intergovernmental Perspective*, 16 (1990), 34.
4. K.C. Wheare, *Federal Government*, Oxford University Press, Oxford (1963), 186.

1 Federal constitutions and external relations

Greg Craven

As indicated by its title, this essay is concerned with the treatment of the question of external relations in federal constitutions. As such, it is a piece directed primarily to constitutional issues and provisions. It does not—except tangentially—deal with the highly conceptual or profoundly practical aspects of the interplay between federalism and external relations which most excite federal theorists or political scientists respectively. Consequently, it is best seen as an attempt to provide a broad constitutional background for the wider-ranging discussion.

The essay is divided into four sections. The first will seek briefly to outline the general problem of external relations within the task of federal constitutional design. This will include a discussion of the real tension facing the framers of a federal constitution in seeking to produce a document which ensures the capacity of the federation concerned effectively to manage its external relations, without as a consequence imperilling the very constitutional division of power which it contains. The second section involves a consideration of the constitutions of a number of federations, with a view to isolating and comparing their provisions relating to the management of external relations. Here, the constitutions of three federations—Canada, the United States and Germany—are given special attention.

The third section comprises a more detailed case-study of the constitutional aspects of external relations in Australia, the author's own federation. There, the whole question of the relationship between external affairs and federalism has been the subject of intense constitutional controversy for over a decade. Finally, the chapter will attempt to draw some tentative conclusions concerning the general treatment of the subject of external affairs in federal constitutions.

External relations, federalism and constitutional design

The starting-point here must be to note that external relations is ordinarily regarded as the paradigm subject which is to be accorded centre stage in any federal division of power. Whenever lists of 'typical' central powers appear in the relevant texts, then along with such matters as 'national defence' and 'currency', 'external relations' or 'foreign affairs' is prominently enshrined. Thus, Wheare characterizes foreign affairs as one of the minimal powers of a federal government,[1] while Davis comments that such matters as foreign relations have always 'formed the core of federal activity'.[2]

The reason for this ready consignment of external relations to the central basket is obvious. Again to refer to Wheare, one of the prime reasons for the creation of a federation will often be the desire to provide for a unified foreign policy.[3] Given this basic imperative, the last thing that is desired is the sound of contending unit voices whenever the subject of a federation's external relations is raised. Such strident disunity is seen as having the potential to disable the federation concerned from effectively taking its place in world affairs. The argument readily is made that the more evidence there is abroad of inconsistency between the official voice of a central government on matters of foreign policy, and the positions of its federal units, the weaker will be a federation's international bargaining position.[4]

Swallowed whole, these types of strictures may tend to promote a superficial understanding of the place of external relations within federal constitutional structures, to the effect that the subject inevitably is one of unconstrained central competence, and that this is the end of the matter. In fact, however, as will be shown in the next section of this essay, the central control of external relations typically accorded by federal constitutions is very far from being as monolithic as some of the more extreme protagonists of unrestrained central power might hope. Not infrequently, whether by specific constitutional provision, pregnant constitutional silence or simple constitutional vagueness, a whole variety of important issues will survive a constituent document's apparent donation to the central government of an 'adequate power to control the basic aspects of foreign relations',[5] so to enliven indefinitely that federation's constitutional debates.

Of these issues, two are among the most obvious and important. The first concerns the continuing capacity of a federation's constituent units to enter into agreements with foreign states. The mere existence of even a primary capacity in the central government is not dispositive here: unless that power is in terms exclusive, the constitutional question as to the residual international capacity of the federal units will remain, and the political question as to the desirability of such a capacity necessarily will follow. The second key issue relates to the capacity of the central government to invade areas which would otherwise fall exclusively within the competence of the units, through its ability to enter into and effectuate international agreements which relate to subject matters falling inside those areas. Can the central government, simply through the exercise of its capacity in the field of external relations, significantly alter what would otherwise be the constitutional balance of power?

Nor are these the only constitutional issues which arise. Around them revolve a host of subsidiary questions for the drafter or interpreter of a federal constitution. If there is to be some residual international capacity in the units, in what policy areas is this to occur? What substantive and procedural restrictions are to be imposed on it in the interests of federal harmony and efficiency? To what extent should such restrictions involve a requirement of central government consent to the international activities of the units? If a concern is felt to protect the units from excessive central government interference via the exercise of its power to enter international agreements, how is this to be achieved? Should a restraint be placed upon the range of agreements that may be made in the first place? Or should the capacity of the central government to implement international agreements—at least within constitutional systems where a concept of treaty 'implementation' is intelligible—be limited to the same end? Should other, less direct safeguards be employed? Whatever, it is abundantly clear that by the simple placement of the words 'external relations' in the list of central powers, the drafter of a federal constitution has far from exhausted the subject.

Realistically, of course, the subject of external relations is always likely to be one of those most vexing to the perceptive federal constitutional architect. There is a general, and largely justified perception that real difficulty is involved in drafting a federal constitution that simultaneously provides for the discharge of an effective national foreign policy, and the careful protection of unit constitutional interests. For present purposes, a single example will suffice.

On the one hand, allowing a central government free rein to enter into and effectuate any international agreement which it chooses may place the federal units in grave danger of the progressive erosion of their constitutional powers. But to hedge the central power about with too many federalist restrictions may hamstring the federation as an international actor.[6] This problem is greatly exacerbated at a time when the expanding scope of international agreements is such that central governments will be subject both to far greater temptations and considerably increased imperatives to use their international capacities to the detriment of their respective federal units.[7] Of course, the spectre of the 'international federal cripple' hawked around the world by anti-federalists is much exaggerated,[8] but the wider general problem is real enough.

External relations in the constitutions of federal states

The keyword in describing the treatment of external relations by federal constitutions is 'diversity'. True it is that virtually all accord a primary responsibility in this connection to the central government. But beneath this overarching general principle clusters a multitude of different constitutional dispositions on a wide variety of subsidiary matters, presenting a rich and somewhat chaotic picture of constitutional invention, particularly when it is recalled that each provision will typically have acquired its own patina of interpretation and extra-constitutional practice.

Switzerland provides a good example of this degree of constitutional intricacy, which clearly demonstrates the limits of the bald proposition that external relations in federations are 'central property'. Certainly, the Swiss Constitution provides that it is within the sole power of the federation to conclude treaties and alliances (Article 8). But it goes on to qualify this position by providing that, 'exceptionally', the cantons may enter into agreements with foreign states on certain specified subjects (e.g. neighbourship and public economy), provided that nothing in such agreements is contrary to the interests of the Confederation or the rights of other Cantons (Article 9). A further layer of complexity is added by the requirement that official communications between cantons and foreign states (but not between cantons and sub-units of foreign states concerning the matters specified in article 9) be made through the federation (Article 10).

The Swiss Constitution thus, far from simply, provides for a broad federal power over external relations; delineates a limited cantonal capacity which operates as an exception to this general position; and subjects the exercise of cantonal power within this delineated sphere to a number of potentially complicated procedural and substantive safeguards. Not surprisingly, there is a continuing controversy in Switzerland concerning a number of aspects of this arrangement, including the scope of both the federal and cantonal treaty-making power.[9]

Other federal constitutions demonstrate an enormous range of possibilities in relation to the management of external relations, from what is (in constitutional terms at least) effectively exclusive central control to far more loosely structured arrangements. Among the federal or quasi-federal states which vest total responsibility for external relations in organs of the central government are India (Constitution, section 246), Pakistan (Constitution, section 142; 4th Schedule) and Mexico (Constitution, Articles 89, 76 and 117). Many other federal constitutions, however, have dealt with the question far less unidimensionally. Some, for example, have included provisions permitting the making of international agreements by federal units in more or less strictly confined circumstances (e.g. the Provisional Constitution of the United Arab Emirates, Article 123; the Constitution of the now defunct

Union of Soviet Socialist Republics, Article 18; Argentina, Constitution of 1853, Article 107).

Other federal constitutions, while not conceding an international capacity to their units, will nevertheless seek to protect those units from the heavy-handed use by the central government of its power respecting external relations. The Austrian Constitution, for example, requires the federal government to consult with the *Länder* before the conclusion of treaties which touch upon areas of their jurisdiction (Article 10 (3)). The Constitution of the Federation of Malaysia requires consultation with the states before the federal government makes laws implementing treaties touching upon such matters as Islamic Law (section 76), while under the old Constitution of the Czechoslovak Socialist Republic, the central government was obliged to seek the cooperation of the Czech and Slovak Republics in negotiating treaties relating to matters falling within their fields of competence (Article 78).

Thus, even without considering any practical arrangements which may in practice modify a constitutionally unrestrained central monopoly over external relations, it is apparent that federal constitutional systems display a far greater diversity in dealing with this subject than is occasionally supposed. It is now appropriate to deal in a little more detail with the pertinent constitutional provisions of some of the federations which are the subject of this book.

Canada

Canada's constitutional provisions dealing with the issue of external relations are, along with those of Australia, the most primitive and vestigial of those appearing in the constituent documents of the four federations focused upon at this conference. Indeed, in the case of Canada, it makes less sense to talk of what its constitution provides in relation to external affairs than to discuss what it fails to provide.

The reason for this apparent neglect is comparatively straightforward. Canada's primary constituent document, the British North America Act 1867, was drafted at a time when it was not anticipated that any indigenous Canadian authority would possess significant international capacity. Rather, responsibility for international relations as they touched upon Canada was to continue to be vested in the imperial government.[10] Logically enough, therefore, the only directly relevant provision inserted into the British North America Act was section 132, which allowed the federal government to make laws implementing in Canada treaties made by the British Empire — legislative implementation of treaties being indispensable in Anglo-Canadian legal theory. But this provision conferred no power upon any Canadian authority to make and implement treaties on its own behalf.

Of course, the burgeoning evolution of Dominion independence during the twentieth century saw the development of a full Canadian treaty-making power, which (at least primarily) came to reside in the executive government of Canada. The most powerful expression of this developed power is to be found in the 1947 Letters Patent constituting the office of Governor-General of Canada, which contains a plenary delegation of the Royal Prerogative (including, presumably, that part of the Prerogative relating to external relations) to the Governor-General.[11] But this slow evolution of Canadian constitutional law in relation to external relations has opened up two potential controversies concerning the operation of Canada as a federal state.

The first relates to the legislative capacity to implement treaties. Even assuming that the Canadian federal authorities have an unlimited power to make treaties, it must be remembered that, according to inherited British constitutional theory, such treaties will not affect rights and obligations within Canada until they are enacted into municipal law by the appropriate legislature. No problem arises where a treaty concerns a matter within federal power, but what if it relates to a matter of provincial competence? Can the Parliament of Canada nevertheless enact the required implementing legislation, with all the consequent grave implications for the federal balance of powers? Or will a series of provincial laws be required, with the corresponding risk that Canada will be unable to fulfil its federal obligations?

The answer currently given by the Canadian courts, as enunciated in the *Labor Conventions Case*,[12] is that the power of the federal government to enter a treaty does not carry with it a power to implement that treaty independently of its other constitutional heads of power. Consequently, in areas of provincial competence, while the Canadian government can make a treaty, it cannot effectuate it through legislative implementation. This position, often criticized by Canadian commentators,[13] represents clearly enough a choice in favour of safeguarding the federal—provincial balance effected under Canada's constitutional settlement, at the possible expense of significant foreign relations considerations.

There has also been some controversy in Canada over the constitutional capacity of the provinces to engage in external relations, and particularly over their ability to enter into international agreements. Once again, Canada's primary constituent documents are, in practical terms, opaque on this point. Some Quebecois writers have argued, not without force, that the capacity to enter into treaties logically must be regarded as concurrent with the power to implement those treaties, and that, accordingly, the responsibility for entering into international agreements is divided in Canada between the central government and those of the provinces.[14] Unsurprisingly, this position is rejected by the federal government, as well as by commentators of a different constitutional viewpoint, who argue that the provinces possess, at best, a very limited capacity in the field of external relations.[15]

Canada thus presents the picture of a federal state whose constitutional documents devote little or no attention to the difficulties presented by the interaction of federalism and external relations. Naturally, this inadvertence has not prevented, but has rather (if anything) exacerbated such difficulties, and it is likely that the issues briefly considered here will continue to be a staple of federal controversy in Canada into the foreseeable future.

United States

The Constitution of the United States of America stands in stark distinction to that of Canada in its treatment of external affairs. Free from the 'imperial twilight' problem that besets the British North America Act, the United States Constitution deals explicitly with the management of external relations within the American federation, and (comparatively at least) in some detail.

Article II, section 2, clause 1 is the key provision which vests in the President the power to make treaties, provided that such treaties receive the concurrence of two-thirds of the Senate present and voting. The effect of this provision is twofold. First, it is manifestly clear that the executive government of the United States has a substantively unrestrained power to enter into a full range of international agreements. Thus, the sorts of questions that may be asked concerning the powers of the Canadian executive concerning external relations simply cannot be raised in the United States.

Secondly, however, the Constitution introduces into the treaty-making process an indispensable element of legislative concurrence, in the form of a positive Senate vote, an element constitutionally unknown in federations like Canada and Australia where, British-fashion, treaty-making (as opposed to treaty implementation) is exclusively the concern of the executive. Moreover, because the Senate is composed of an equal number of senators from each state (Article I, section 3, clause 1; Amendment XVII), and is by constitutional definition a 'States' House', the requirement for its concurrence in the making of any treaty may be understood as imposing some restraint in the interests of federalism upon the central government's use of its power over external relations.[16]

The other crucial provision bearing upon the central government's control of external relations is Article VI, clause 2, which provides that validly concluded treaties, along with the Constitution and laws of the United States, constitute 'the supreme Law of the Land'. This provision eliminates the issues which were seen to arise in Canada in relation to the power of the central government to legislate for the implementation of treaties into which it validly had entered. In the United States, at least where the terms of a treaty are 'self-executing'—that is, are apt to be applied by a court of law as if they were a legislative enactment—the question of a legislative power to implement does not arise.[17] Even where treaties are 'executory', in the sense that they do require 'translation' into legislative form, it is accepted that Congress has full power—subject only to the prohibitions contained in the Constitution—to enact the necessary legislation.[18]

The net effect of these provisions, therefore, is to confer upon the government of the United States a power to enter into and effectuate international agreements which is, as a matter of substance, essentially unconfined. To the extent that federal restraints upon this power are embodied in the United States Constitution, they are comprised in the important procedural requirement that the Senate—the chamber in which the states are represented—give its consent to each treaty made by the Executive.

The international capacity of the states is also the subject of explicit provisions contained in the United States Constitution. Under Article 1, section 10, clause 1, the states are absolutely prohibited from entering into any treaty, alliance or confederation. But clause 3 of the same section goes on to permit lower-level external relations on the part of a state, to the extent that a state may, with the consent of Congress, enter into an 'agreement or compact' with a foreign state. The basic effect is that the Constitution permits 'non-political' external relations by a state, subject to the supervision of Congress.[19]

Of course, none of this is intended to suggest that serious constitutional issues do not arise concerning the federal dimension of external relations in the United States. It may be argued that the capacity of the federal government to usurp the jurisdictions of the states by use of its treaty power is too extensive; the complete effectiveness of the Senate as a federal brake may be questioned, particularly when it is recalled that 'executive agreements' (unlike treaties) are not subject to senatorial consent;[20] on a contrary tack, the Senate's veto may gravely frustrate the Executive's foreign policy; and many other areas of doubt do arise, such as the range of agreements which may be made by states under the 'agreement and compact' dispensation.[21] What is undeniable, however, is that the United States Constitution is both far more specific on the question of external relations than that of Canada, and ultimately much more sympathetic to the claims of central government for a pervasive control in this area.

Germany

In broad terms, the German Basic Law resembles the United States Constitution far more closely than that of Canada in its treatment of external relations. Like the United States document, the Basic Law contains a series of explicit provisions concerning external relations which prevent (or at least limit) the occurrence of most of the constitutional lacunae that have arisen in Canada.

Thus, Article 32 (1) contains a general statement of federal competence in providing that relations with foreign states shall be conducted by the federation. This position is reinforced by Article 73, which places the subjects of foreign affairs and defence in the list of exclusive federal powers, and by Article 87, which makes the foreign service a matter of direct federal administration, rather than an area of federal policy administered by the *Länder*.

Perhaps the most crucial provision is Article 59, which operates both to structure and (at least procedurally) to limit the exercise of federal power. By way of structure, Article 59, paragraph 1 identifies the relevant organ for the discharge of the federation's responsibilities in the area of external relations, by providing that the federal political executive has responsibility for the conduct of foreign affairs.[22] Paragraph 2, whose effect is basically limiting, is more complex.

In essence, it operates to require legislative consent in the case of a wide range of important treaties, by providing that treaties which 'regulate political relations', or which concern matters of federal legislation, must be the subject of a federal law made according to the constitutionally required procedure for the passage of such a law by the constitutionally appropriate bodies.[23] What this means in terms of federalism-inspired restraints upon the central treaty-making power is that the legislative implementation of the relevant class of treaties will require the participation of the Chamber of the German federal legislature in which the *Länder* are represented, the *Bundesrat*.

The nature of this participation will vary according to the subject matter of the law to be passed (which will in turn depend upon the topic of the treaty concerned), and a United States Senate-style veto will not always be involved. But at the very least it will be open to the *Bundesrat* to object to a law, requiring its re-passage through the *Bundestag*, and in the case of laws which will affect such matters as *Länder* rights over taxation and fiscal policy, *Bundesrat* consent must be forthcoming.[24] To this extent, the method adopted under the German Basic Law for the protection of federal interests from the central government's use of its treaty power is broadly similar (though in terms less stringent) to that enshrined in the United States Constitution.

It should also be noted that paragraph 2 of Article 32 places a further restraint upon the federal government's treaty power in requiring that the *Länder* be consulted before the conclusion by the federation of a treaty affecting their special circumstances. This consultative provision is unique among the constitutional documents of the federations considered at this conference. Nevertheless, its practical significance pales beside the extra-constitutional mechanisms of the Lindau Agreement, which are considered elsewhere.

Like the United States Constitution, the German Basic Law makes specific provision for the entering of international agreements by the Federation's component units. Paragraph 3 of Article 32 permits the *Länder* to conclude treaties with foreign states relating to matters within the limits of their legislative competence, but only with the consent of the federal government.

The German Basic Law thus contains a quite detailed regime for the management of external relations within the federation. Like the United States Constitution, and unlike Canada's constitutional system, the provisions of the Basic Law are weighted towards enhancing the central government's capacity to prosecute and effectuate its foreign policy, rather than towards the protection of the federal interests of the units. Despite its comparatively detailed treatment of the subject of external relations, however, this is not to say that federal problems have not arisen in this connection under the Basic Law. Notably, its terms are profoundly unclear as to the power of the central government to implement treaties in areas of *Länder* competence, and it is the Lindau Agreement, rather than the Basic Law, which has in practical terms resolved such questions.[25]

What the preceding very brief constitutional sketches of the Canadian, American and German federations serve to illustrate is the real variability of federal constitutional arrangements in relation to external affairs, a matter which has already been stressed. A fairly wide range is covered by these constitutions in terms of their textual explicitness on the subject of external relations, the degree of central control which they permit, the general complexity of the constitutional arrangements which they contain, and the methods which they adopt to protect the perceived legitimate interests of component units. Interestingly, however, there is a considerable—and indeed inevitable—degree of similarity between the issues which arise for resolution (or non-resolution) under these constitutions. The scope of the central treaty power; issues of legislative implementation; and the capacity of the units to make international agreements are hardy perennials of federal constitutional debate. This paper now passes to a slightly more detailed case-study of the constitutional treatment of external relations in the author's own federation, the Commonwealth of Australia.

External relations and the Australian Constitution

Of the federal constitutions already examined, the one which most closely resembles the Australian Constitution in its treatment of external relations is that of Canada. Like the British North America Act, the Commonwealth of Australia Constitution Act contains only the sketchiest of references to external relations. The predictable result has been that the entire question of the relationship between federalism and the management of external relations has become a major subject of constitutional uncertainty and disputation in the Australian federation.

In order to understand the Australian Constitution's treatment of external relations, it is necessary to know something of the constitutional circumstances and expectations of the Australian colonies in the period leading up to federation in 1900. Prior to federation, these colonies never possessed a significant international competence, although they were occasionally permitted by the imperial authorities to enter into minor agreements with foreign states relating to such matters as postage.[26] These isolated cases aside, however, full power over matters of external relations affecting the colonies was firmly located with the imperial government.[27] Of course, even once the imperial executive had entered into a treaty, that treaty still had to be implemented into the municipal law of its various territories if it was to have legislative effect. Within a particular colony, this could be done by the relevant colonial legislature itself, but in any event, the imperial Parliament reserved the right to alter the laws of the colonies on matters of imperial concern as it saw fit.

The crucial point to grasp is that the framers of Australia's Constitution did not intend that this position would in any way change after federation. At least from the aspect of external relations, the new Commonwealth was to be not an independent nation, but merely a larger, aggregated colony. As a matter of conscious decision by the framers, it was to have no power to enter into treaties, and no such power was accorded by the Constitution.[28] The position pertaining to the implementation of imperial treaties was to continue essentially as before. In accordance with this vision, the only provision of direct relevance to external relations that was inserted into the Australian Constitution as eventually passed was the highly obscure section 51 (29), which gave the Commonwealth Parliament a power to legislate with respect to 'external affairs'. It is unclear exactly what the scope of this power was intended to be, but it may have been directed (at least in part) towards permitting the legislative implementation by the Commonwealth of some Empire treaties. It certainly did not confer any power upon the Commonwealth to enter into treaties in its own right.

As was the case with Canada, however, the gradual transformation of the Empire into a loose community of independent states made Australia's constitutional dispositions (or lack of them) in relation to external affairs almost unintelligible, and certainly unworkable. Inevitably, the recognition by the Imperial Conference of 1926 that each dominion was entitled to make treaties on its own behalf, followed by the general constitutional liberation of the dominions involved in the enactment of the Statute of Westminster in 1931 (adopted by Australia in 1942), had meant that Australia was now mistress of her own external relations whether she liked it or not.[29] The problem was, however, that the practical disappearance of the imperial authorities from the field of external relations undeniably left a major vacuum in Australia's constitutional dispositions on a number of crucial questions, two of which are considered here.

First, and fundamentally, who was now to have the authority to enter into international agreements? Secondly, which legislature was to have the power to implement such agreements by the passage of the requisite municipal legislation? These questions raised similar, vexing issues to those facing Canada during the same period. In relation to entry into international agreements, it was theoretically possible to argue either that the old imperial prerogatives devolved intact upon the national government, as a sort of successor in constitutional title, or that the competence to enter into such agreements would henceforth follow the federal division of power, in which case the states would have acquired significant power over external relations. On the question of implementation, one could maintain either that the Commonwealth Parliament had a more or less general power to implement treaties into which it had entered, by virtue of the external affairs power contained in section 51 (29); or, broadly following the Canadian example, that the power of the federal Parliament to implement legislatively a treaty was again in some way linked to the division of power between the Commonwealth and the states, in which case implementation would be a state matter in relation to a wide range of treaties.

The first question, as to which level of Australian government has responsibility under the Constitution for entry into international agreements, has proved by far the more tractable of the two. It is universally recognized that it is the Commonwealth government that speaks for Australia in international affairs, and upon which the old imperial treaty-making power has devolved. It is accepted that the states may make comparatively low-level arrangements upon various commercial and cultural subjects,[30] but entry into any higher form of international agreement, such as a treaty, would be beyond their constitutional powers.

While this position commands general acceptance, it is not without logical difficulty as a matter of strict constitutional law. The suggested devolution of the imperial treaty-making power is usually based upon section 61 of the Constitution, which vests the executive power of the Commonwealth in the Governor-General.[31] But it is incontestable that when section 61 was drafted it was never intended to convey any such power. The response usually made to this difficulty is that section 61 nevertheless contained a germ of a power, always intended to expand over time, which grew and flowered in the lurid light of imperial devolution (*New South Wales* v. *Commonwealth*).[32] The problem with this argument is that section 2 of the Constitution specifically provides for the assignment by the Monarch of further prerogatives to the Governor-General, and no such assignment has ever been made in relation to treaties, although it has in the case of the appointment of Australian diplomats. It is difficult to see how the extra-constitutional developments relied upon for the expansion of the power contained in section 61 can (at least in strictly constitutional terms) prevail over the specific procedure set out in section 2.⁻

The fairest view, therefore, is that the Australian Constitution has been bludgeoned by judicial interpretation into conceding a power to make treaties to the Commonwealth, rather than that it confers such a power as a matter of textual logic. Perhaps fortunately for the Commonwealth, the states' constitutional case for a treaty-making competence is even weaker than its own. Their authority is enshrined in section 107, which simply continues the powers of the colonies (now States) as they existed at federation. As the states had no treaty-making power at that point, it is difficult to see how one could have emerged thereafter. Moreover, the Commonwealth at least enjoys the benefit of the Constitution's enigmatic reference to 'external affairs' in section 51 (29).

In fact, the real constitutional controversy over external relations in Australia has not concerned the making of treaties. Rather, it has centred around the scope of the power of the Commonwealth Parliament to enact legislation pursuant to section 51 (29) implementing treaties into which it is acknowledged that the Commonwealth executive validly has entered. It will be recalled here that in Australia, as in Canada and the United Kingdom, a treaty must be the subject of legislation if it is to affect rights and obligations in municipal law.

Two quite different views have been taken of the effect of the Australian Constitution's external affairs power in this connection. Broadly, protagonists of the Commonwealth have argued that section 51 (29) confers upon the Commonwealth Parliament a plenary power to legislate in implementation of any treaty (a treaty being itself an 'external affair') into which the Commonwealth executive may have entered. This includes treaties whose subject matter falls within areas otherwise 'reserved' to the states. Federalists, on the other hand, have rejected this view on the basis that it accords to the Commonwealth an ultimately open-ended capacity to rework the federal balance, simply by means of its entry into international agreements. They have tended to argue that the Commonwealth Parliament can legislate in the implementation of a treaty under section 51 (29) only where the subject matter of that treaty is truly 'international' in character, and thus properly to be described as an 'external' affair. One of the concerns behind this view obviously relates to the increasing tendency of modern international agreements to deal with a vast range of matters once regarded as being of purely municipal concern, many of which—under the Australian Constitution—would ordinarily fall within the jurisdiction of the states.

The scope of the external affairs power received surprisingly little judicial attention in Australia through the first seven decades of its constitutional history. For many years, it was supposed that the narrow view was the correct one.[33] But in the early 1980s the Commonwealth, drawing upon a vastly expanded range of international agreements, began to strain against the limits of the traditional interpretation of section 51 (29), which first bent in *Koowarta* v. *Bjelke-Petersen*,[34] and finally broke in *Tasmania* v. *Commonwealth* (the *Dams* case).[35] In practical terms, the *Dams* case established (by a bare majority) that the Commonwealth could legislate to implement treaties generally, at least in so far as such legislation involved the fulfilment of treaty 'obligations'. The subject matter of a treaty was, as such, irrelevant. On the basis of the subsequent case of *Richardson* v. *Forestry Commission*,[36] it would appear that not only have the dissentients in *Dams* reluctantly accepted the broad interpretation of the external affairs power, but that the qualification in relation to treaty 'obligations' has been quietly dropped, so that the power is now a full one of treaty implementation.

This interpretation of section 51 (29) has excited great constitutional controversy, with supporters of the states going so far as to argue that the federal balance achieved by the Constitution is now at the mercy of the treaty-making activities of the federal executive.[37] Defenders of the *Dams* position maintain (in somewhat exaggerated terms) that an unrestrained power of treaty implementation is necessary if the Commonwealth is not to be an 'international cripple',[38] and they point to the existence of suggested federal safeguards, such as the judicially expounded requirement that treaty-based legislation be an 'appropriate and adapted' means of implementing the treaty concerned,[39] an admittedly somewhat limited refuge for the states.

In the wake of this dramatic expansion of the external affairs power, a number of suggestions have been made with a view to better safeguarding areas of state jurisdiction from incursion by the Commonwealth. In 1985, the Australian Constitutional Convention proposed the creation of an Australian Treaties Council along the lines of the German Permanent Treaties Commission, to facilitate the coordination and expression of the views of the States on Commonwealth treaties.[40] This suggestion was endorsed in the 1988 *Report of the Constitutional Commission*, but the proposed body has not been established.

The Australian Constitution clearly presents an unhappy picture of a federal constituent document failing to deal adequately with the complicated issues arising out of the interaction of federalism and external relations. Its provisions, drafted with a vanished empire foremost in mind, are quite inadequate to the task. Certainly, the *Dams* case has introduced an element of certainty into the constitutional picture, but that certainty has been achieved at the cost of raising very real questions as to the future security of the jurisdictions of the various states. Among the federations surveyed here, Australia now stands out as a federal state which, in constitutional terms, possesses a very highly centralized regime for the management of external relations, and in which the demands of a centrally driven foreign policy clearly have been preferred to considerations turning upon any perceived necessity to maintain a federal balance of powers.

Conclusion

An essay of this limited size and range does not permit the drawing of a series of detailed conclusions concerning the treatment of external relations in federal constitutions. A few brief and general points may, however, be made.

The constitutions examined here do all conform to the federal 'paradigm' of confiding primary responsibility for the conduct of external relations to the central government. Nevertheless, there are clearly degrees of constitutional centralization in this context, both with regard to the entry into and implementation of agreements, with Australia—somewhat ironically—standing out as the federation in which central control of external relations is most constitutionally pronounced.

Moreover, as stressed throughout this chapter, the variability of the four federations in terms of constitutional detail on the issue of external relations is indicative of the richness of federal constitutional law generally in this connection. This is particularly true of the approach taken towards the protection of unit interests from the effects of the central treaty-making power. In Canada, constitutional protection is achieved by limiting the power of the centre to implement agreements. In the United States, reliance is placed upon the insertion of the 'States House' of the Federal legislature into the treaty-making process. In Germany, a different version of this legislative intrusion is adopted, as well as a specific requirement of consultation with the Länder in the making of a range of treaties. Only in Australia is there no substantive constitutional protection for the units in this regard. Other obvious differences between the four federal constitutions considered here include the degree of specificity in which they deal with matters of external relations, and the extent to which they authorize, limit or prohibit the making of international agreements by the relevant federal units.

It is, of course, clear from an analysis of the provisions of these constitutions, the issues that they address and the problems that have arisen under them, that the drafter of a federal constitution faces a real challenge in seeking to balance the potentially competing interests involved in the pursuit of a cohesive foreign policy, and the maintenance of a federal balance of power between the central government and those of the units. The natural tendency is that the greater the ability of the central government to enter into and implement international agreements, the greater its ability to invade the jurisdictions of the units. Australia is a clear case of a federation where central power over external relations has a grave potential to disrupt the established division of powers.

Correspondingly, however, it will be argued by centralists that the possession by a central government of an inadequate constitutional power over external relations will cripple its foreign policy. Inadequacy in this sense may be discerned in a lack of power in the central government to implement treaties which it has made (as in Canada), or—more dramatically—in the existence in the constituent units of a federation of an extensive, independent power to make high-level international agreements, a power confided under none of the constitutions considered here. Wherever one stands in a debate like this, the task of the constitution-maker in striking the right balance for a particular federal state is a prodigious one.

One thing that does emerge clearly from this study is that the provisions of federal constitutions dealing with external relations are sometimes, in a purely technical sense, far from adequate as pieces of constitutional drafting. The best examples here are, of course, the Australian and Canadian documents, which effectively fail to make provision in relation to external affairs. Historical factors clearly account for much of this vagueness, but it must be noted that the entire relationship between federalism and external affairs is so fluid, various and complicated that it is exceedingly difficult for any federal constitution to deal with the matter adequately. As was seen, even the vastly more detailed constitutions of the United States and Germany contain their own points of vagueness and confusion in this regard.

Consequently, it is far from surprising that anyone seeking an understanding of the management of external relations within a particular federation must take the constitutional dispositions of that federation merely as the starting-point of enquiry. Given the fluidity of the subject matter, and the frequency of indifferent constitutional drafting, the 'real' regime for the management of external relations will all too often be located outside the constitution concerned.[41] This chapter, directed as it is purely to federal constitutional provisions, is not concerned with such pragmatic solutions to problems arising under those provisions, but it is appropriate to note that anyone relying on the constitutional dispositions of, say, Germany or the United States as giving an accurate idea of the practical interplay between federalism and external relations in those countries would be in for a rude awakening.

What ultimately emerges from all this is a need for the drafters (and re-drafters) of federal constitutions, particularly those who are constitutional lawyers by training, to reflect carefully upon questions of external relations, and to insert the results of their reflections in the form of clear, adequately flexible provisions in the constituent documents which they formulate.[42] This need is particularly apparent when one considers constitutions which are patently inadequate in this regard, such as those of Australia and Canada. Drafters of federal constitutions should approach their task, above all, with a clear idea of the type of federal state that they are trying to create, and a determination to ensure that the constitutional provisions upon which they ultimately determine in the field of external relations accurately reflect their vision.

Notes

1. K. Wheare, *Federal Government*, Oxford University Press, Oxford (1967), 169–70.
2. R. Davis, 'The federal principle reconsidered', in A. Wildavsky (ed.), *American Federalism in Perspective*, Little Brown, Boston (1967), 7.
3. Wheare, op. cit., 169.
4. P. Boyce, 'International relations of federal states: responsibility and control', in M. Wood *et al.* (eds), *Governing Federations*, Hale & Ironmonger, Sydney (1984), 187.
5. L. Sohn and P. Schafer, 'Foreign affairs', in R. Bowie and C. Friedrich (eds), *Studies in Federalism*, Little Brown, Boston (1954), 236.
6. Wheare, op. cit., 183–6.
7. D. Elazar, *American Federalism*, Crowell, New York (1967), 213–14.
8. J. Kincaid, 'Constituent diplomacy in federal polities and the nation state: conflict and co-operation', in H. Michelmann and P. Soldatos (eds), *Federalism and International Relations: The Role of Subnational Units*, Clarendon Press, Oxford (1990), 55.
9. See generally L. Wildhaber, 'Switzerland', in Michelmann and Soldatos, op. cit., 250–3; A. Di Mazzo, *Component Units of Federal States and International Agreements*, Sijthoff & Nordhoff, Alphen ann den Rijn (1980), 26–30.
10. G. Mahler, *New Dimensions of Canadian Federalism*, Fairleigh Dickinson University Press, Rutherford, NJ (1987), 5; P. Hogg, *Constitutional Law of Canada*, Carswell, Toronto (1985), 242.
11. Hogg, op. cit., 242.
12. [1937] AC 326.
13. See e.g. Mahler, op. cit., 113–20.
14. J.-Y. Morin, 'La conclusion d'accords internationaux par les provinces canadiennes à la lumière du droit comparé', *Canadian Yearbook of International Law*, 3 (1967).
15. Hogg, op. cit., 254–5.
16. See e.g. Wheare, op. cit., 180–3.
17. J. Nowak, R. Rotunda and J. Young, *Constitutional Law*, 2nd edn, West Publishing Co., St. Paul's (1983), 205–6.
18. *Missouri* v. *Holland* 252 US416 (1920); E. Fry, 'Sub-national units in an age of complex independence: implications for the international system', in L. Brown-John (ed.), *Centralizing and Decentralizing Trends in Federal States*, University Press of America, Philadelphia (1990), 279–80.
19. Fry, op. cit., 279–81; Di Marzo, op. cit., 40–1.
20. Wheare, op. cit., 182–3; Nowak *et al.*, op. cit., 206–8.
21. Di Mazzo, op. cit., 40–1.
22. H. Michelmann, 'Germany', in Michelmann and Soldatos, op. cit., 215–16.
23. ibid., 215–16.

24. ibid., 216–17.
25. Di Mazzo, op. cit., 34–5; Michelmann, op. cit., 220–1.
26. L. Zines, *The High Court and the Constitution*, 2nd edn, Butterworth, Sydney (1977), 7.
27. J. Ravenhill, 'Australia', in Michelmann and Soldatos, op. cit., 79–80.
28. P. McDermott, 'External affairs and treaties: the founding fathers' perspective', *University of Queensland Law Journal*, 16 (1990).
29. Ravenhill, op. cit., 79–80.
30. ibid., 101–5.
31. See Zines, op. cit., 244–5.
32. (1975) 135 CLR 337, 373 per Barwick C.J.
33. See *R. v. Burgess; ex parte Henry* (1936) 55 CLR 608.
34. (1982) 153 CLR 168.
35. (1983) 158 CLR 1.
36. (1988) 164 CLR 261.
37. M. Crommelin, 'The significance of the Franklin dams case', in Appendix A., *Report of the External Affairs Subcommittee to the Standing Committee of the Australian Constitutional Convention*, Government Printer, Queensland (1984), 21.
38. See e.g. Zines, op. cit., 253–5.
39. See e.g. *Richardson* v. *Forestry Commission* (1988) 164 CLR 261, 315–16 per Deane J.
40. See Australian Constitutional Convention, *Report of the External Affairs Subcommittee*, op. cit.
41. J. Kincaid, op. cit., 68.
42. Sohn and Schafer, op. cit., 260–1.

2 Consumership versus citizenship: is there wiggle room for local regulation in the global economy?

John Kincaid

The management of foreign relations in federal nations is becoming more democratic and polycentric, partly because the emergence of a global economy has induced the peoples of the constituent governments of most federations to assert consumership and citizenship interests internationally. Constituent governments (e.g. states, provinces, *Länder*, and cantons) are seeking a greater voice in foreign relations and a more independent role in global affairs. Such demands, moreover, are not confined to federal nations; they are arising in a growing number of unitary states (e.g. Japan and France). They are likely to become more intense as democratization erodes the monopolization of foreign policy-making by national élites, and as globalization reduces the ability of traditional nation-states to serve the economic and political interests of their constituent regions and localities.

A certain tension, therefore, is developing in the conduct of foreign relations as well as in the conduct of local self-government. That is, while democratization allows and encourages individuals and groups to assert their citizenship interests both locally and nationally, globalization requires citizens to extend assertions of their rights of democratic self-government beyond the nation-state. At the same time, globalization allows and encourages citizens to assert consumership interests, namely, rights to acquire the goods and services that are increasingly produced in a global market. Yet maintenance of a global market characterized by free trade and efficient allocations of resources entails limits on local and national self-governance and, thereby, restrictions on the exercise of historic citizenship interests. Consequently, underlying the centrifugal forces developing in foreign relations is a tension between citizenship and consumership, a tension felt not only by governments but also by persons who want to foster a global marketplace able to satisfy their consumership interests while still maintaining rights of local self-government able to satisfy their citizenship interests.

Mixed signals from the new world order

It is now common, therefore, to observe, among other developments, two trends in the global arena: (1) the simultaneous gravitation of national governance powers toward transnational regimes and toward domestic constituent governments, and (2) the emergence of non-state actors as forces in world politics. The first trend suggests that traditional nation-state sovereignty is being eroded from above and below. The second trend suggests that nation-states increasingly compete with non-state actors (e.g. transnational corporations and environmental interests) in world politics and, indeed, may not always prevail against non-state actors. These trends, especially the first one, do not yet encompass all nation-states, but they do include the leading state actors, and they represent long-run pressures likely to affect all nation-states in the near future.

Whether or how to characterize these developments as a 'new world order' is a puzzle, however. Realists, such as Kenneth Waltz,[1] emphasize continuity in so far as nation-states are still the final, decisive actors, whether their actions be voting in the United Nations Security Council or putting disagreeable non-state actors in jail at home. Others see a profound change occurring in human existence, the kind of change not seen since the discovery of agriculture or the rise of urban civilization.[2] Still others, sometimes called neorealists, see something in between: the emergence of a highly pluralist, interdependent world[3] characterized by 'intermestic' politics[4] or 'a bifurcation in which the state-centric world coexists and interacts with a diffuse multi-centric world consisting of diverse "sovereignty-free" actors who endlessly confront an "autonomy" dilemma that differs significantly from the "security" dilemma of states.'[5]

Each of these views has a certain intuitive validity. The world does seem to be more interdependent; yet interdependence has characterized global relations at least since European circumnavigation of the earth, and intermestic politics extends back to marriages among royal families. Interdependence, therefore, seems to be a weak descriptor of what appears to be a more profound change. The concept of the nation-state as the supreme sovereign no longer seems realistic; yet the nation-state is still the decisive force and organizing principle of world politics. Furthermore, there are puzzling anomalies.

The sovereignization of nations

While incremental de-sovereignization seems to characterize nation-state cessions of power to transnational regimes and domestic constituent governments, there has also been an upsurge in the creation of new nation-states since 1990, thus seeming to reaffirm the nation-state order. This development might be characterized as a 'sovereignization of nations,' that is, the establishment of independent states by secessionist nationalities (formerly known as 'nations' or 'peoples') that have regarded themselves as 'captive nations' and resented their demotion to the status of ethnic groups by their captors.[6] The sovereignization of nations may become a booming business because most nation-states are multinational;[7] many are undemocratic, if not oppressive; and self-perceptions of victimization are expansive.

Many observers view ethnic nationalism with surprise and horror: surprise because modernization was supposed to erode such presumably primitive loyalties, and horror because ethnic nationalism is seen as an anarchic force bound to balkanize the world. Hence, there has been substantial intellectual support for such arguments as Lord Acton's contention that every nation should not have its own state because homogeneous primordial states descend into absolutism. Instead, freedom and the advancement of civilization require 'the co-existence of several nations under the same State'.[8]

What Acton, much like James Madison, had in mind were somewhat federal, democratic states. However, as the Kurds and many other peoples can testify, what emerged in the twentieth century was well over a hundred absolutist nation-states, epitomized by the former USSR, within which different nations were coerced into submission. The count can be taken much higher if one includes the seemingly non-absolutist states, such as the United States, which subdued several hundred nations within its borders, namely, those peoples now known as Native Americans. Hence, ethnic strife, civil war, and secession are as much the order of the day as globalization, regional security and economic arrangements, and interdependence by fax transmission.

Indeed, it is these latter conditions of the late twentieth century that make it both possible and attractive for many of the world's 'separated or suppressed nationalities', for whom Lord Acton had great sympathy, to assert old-style nationalist claims in the new world order. The novel conditions associated with globalization also make this new nationalism different from the old nationalism of only a few years ago. As in the past, many new nations want to ally themselves with a great-power protector, but, more important, they almost invariably want to join international organizations and transnational unions, such as the European Community. As soon as they obtain state sovereignty, they want to cede some of that sovereignty to larger regimes and bring their citizens rather quickly under the aegis of international conventions.

Thus, a condition of 'divided patriotism', which Acton saw as being an essential crosspressure needed to temper the destructive effects of absolutist nationalism on domestic freedom and international peace, seems to be arising, though not from 'the coexistence of several nations under the same State' but from the coexistence of many nations under common, agreed-upon intergovernmental rules. These rules are beginning to give the world a generally federal character, though in a broader sense than envisioned by Lord Acton, because they are based on implicit and explicit covenants that combine self-rule with shared rule.[9]

The governmentalization of non-state actors

Another anamoly, one not usually captured by the realists and neorealists, is the increased governmentalization of non-state actors in the global arena, namely, the transformation of non-states into states (e.g. Ukraine) and the acquisition of governmental attributes by non-governmental actors. For one, a number of previously non-state actors, such as the Slovenians, have become state actors, and more will do so. There has been some movement in the opposite direction as well. At least one state actor, East Germany, has become a non-state actor by being absorbed into the German federal republic, and two state actors—North and South Korea—may become a one-state actor. The boundary between state and non-state actors, therefore, is permeable, and movement across the boundary, one way or the other, no longer necessarily represents modernization.

Second, many non-state actors in both the public and the private spheres are assuming governmental functions and are being given governmental responsibilities by state actors. Thus, in some respects, the European Community, for example, looks like a state actor; in other respects, it is clearly a non-state actor.

Third, not all non-state actors in the global arena are nongovernmental. Many are governmental actors, namely, the constituent governments of nation-states. Although the US government classifies state and local government representatives in international forums as 'nongovernmental', lumping governmental and nongovernmental actors under the label 'non-state actors' obscures important differences in capacities, purposes and public accountability.

Fourth, state actors do not always prevail over non-state actors, and even some non-state, nongovernmental actors, such as environmental organizations, often exercise considerable influence on the domestic and foreign policies of nation-states and on the behavior of international organizations.

In addition, many non-state actors attract loyal supporters from many nation-states, supporters whose loyalty to the transnational enterprise (e.g. Amnesty International) is sometimes stronger than loyalty to their home state. Such loyalty is evident not only among some multinational corporation executives but also among some Eurocrats, employees of other international organizations, members of international pressure groups, and adherents to worldwide religious orders.

Divided patriotism

Thus, the kind of 'divided patriotism' advocated by Lord Acton is being realized, though in more complex ways than he could envision in the 1860s. In turn, the concept of a world bifurcated by state and non-state actors seems increasingly unrealistic as these historic categories are muddled by the density and diversity of global interactions. There is at least a large area of ambiguity between state and non-state actors, much like the ill-defined boundary between the public and private sectors in many industrial democracies.

To the extent that there is a bifurcation, it is occurring not so much out in the world as it is within individuals throughout the world whose self-interests increasingly encompass both state and non-state concerns. This bifurcation, which is more in the nature of a tension, arises from the fact that the average person's place-specific livelihood and loyalties are increasingly enriched by and dependent on the resources and actions of other places and non-place-specific (i.e. global) institutions. This bifurcation, therefore, introduces tensions between autonomy and dependence, and community and individuality, but not necessarily a chasm or zero-sum conflict between two worlds of action.

Consumership versus citizenship

The nature of the tension between state and non-state concerns can be characterized, in large part, as a tension between citizenship and consumership (with the latter being defined to include the acquisition of career opportunities and the tools of self-actualization as well as common goods and services). Most persons wish to be citizens of an identifiable place, ordinarily a state infused with primordial nationality sentiments (e.g. the state of Israel), but they also desire the means and freedom to consume the goods and services available on the world market. Yet the more those persons desire global consumership, the more they weaken the autonomy bases of traditional citizenship, and the more they emphasize individuality as defined by their behavior as autonomous consumers, the more they discount their duties as loyal citizens.

To give a prosaic example, when Americans were asked in a national opinion poll in early 1992 whether they felt guilty about purchasing non-American products, only 14 percent felt very guilty. Some 38 percent felt somewhat guilty, while 43 percent did not feel guilty and 5 percent were not sure.[10] Clearly, there is a tension between citizenship and consumership; yet few Americans feel guilty enough not to purchase foreign products, even though such purchases may increase trade deficits and reduce domestic employment. Consumership is overtaking traditional notions of citizenship as individuals struggle to define what it means to be a good American in a Japanese automobile. Furthermore, the nature of modern production is such that it is increasingly difficult to distinguish between foreign and domestic goods as products themselves become 'intermestic'. Hence, a nationalist who insists on buying wholly domestic products must be either an ascetic or an antique lover.

This tension is being felt throughout the world, including the Third World where modern orientations toward regional and global phenomena are developing among citizens[11] and where citizens are beginning to press against the confines of the nation-state. Virtually everyone, especially with the spreading of television, is aware of the fascinating goods and services available in the larger world; yet most people still have little or no access to them because they live in places where their national government is (or was, until recently) unable or unwilling to afford them access.

The basic problem is that citizenship remains place- and group-specific while consumership is no longer place-specific, although it is still place-dependent. That is, access to global goods occurs from some place, which for nearly all people is their nation-state, and some places afford much better access than other places. Thus, while consumership is characterized by financial mobility, citizenship is still largely characterized by geographic immobility—both the voluntary immobility arising from loyalty to a place and the involuntary immobility arising from continued nation-state monopolization of citizenship.

It is at this point, though, that consumership and citizenship converge to contribute to the sovereignization of nations and the restiveness of regions within previously stable nation-states. If citizenship cannot be made mobile, and it is not likely to be made mobile for the foreseeable future outside of restricted regions, such as the EC, then citizens must transform nation-states in order to mobilize consumership.

Such a transformation, however, leans toward disaggregation of the historic nation-state because, to the extent that consumership is place dependent, it is increasingly dependent on local places rather than on the nation-state. The average person's livelihood and ability to access global goods depend first and foremost on the viability of his or her local community, secondly on the economic region surrounding that community (a region that may encompass communities in neighboring foreign states), and tertiarily on the nation-state. Even in the most free and developed countries, local communities have highly differential access to global goods.

A transformation to mobilize consumership also leans toward disaggregation because the nation-state is more often economically relevant as a rule producer than as a wealth producer. By design or default, many nation-states have been better able to impoverish certain peripheral regions than to produce even and upward development.[12] Consequently, when the national center constrains regional economic development, when the center is controlled by a particular nationality or religious group, and when peripheral regions have little or no voice in central decision-making, it begins to appear quite rational in today's global environment for regions to go it alone through devolution or secession—and all the more so when economic regions correspond with historic nationality homelands, as is the case in many multinational nation-states.

At the same time, the viability of nation-states as economic units is diminishing as states cede power to international entities and are otherwise buffeted by global economic forces. Subnational and transnational regions are becoming the more relevant economic units for citizens; consequently, regions are asserting themselves in the global economy, even in countries where consumers are firmly patriotic.

In these respects, the desire to mobilize consumership complements the desire to reassert primordial citizenship so as to produce a drive for local autonomy involving some form of exit or extrication from traditional nation-state arrangements, followed by entrance into international arrangements that can provide newly autonomous citizens better access to global goods and also give them a greater voice both in their own regional or national affairs and in international affairs. Furthermore, citizens realize that in today's global environment the prospects for the economic viability of small states is increasing, as already demonstrated by such places as Singapore, Taiwan, South Korea, and even Japan—an island not well endowed with natural resources. The improved prospects for small-state viability further undermine the argument that every nation should not have its own state.

Of course, this orientation toward exit is being driven by other factors as well, particularly the spreading consciousness of individual and group rights and the idea of consent as the basis of legitimate governance, but among the rights prominently asserted are those of property and the acquisition of goods, especially among young people who have been exposed to global goods and music. Furthermore, this orientation toward exit combined with local loyalty is not confined to authoritarian states. It has spread to some democracies that have long guaranteed rights of citizenship and consumership, as in Canada and Great Britain. Nationalist aspirations in Quebec and Scotland are being driven by a rights rhetoric that accentuates resentments that are trivial compared to the plight of such peoples as the Kurds, but that assume psychic importance because of the autonomy, individuation and prospects for small-state viability made possible by global consumership.

For the most part, however, in the stable democratic states, regions are asserting rights to participate in the global arena, particularly on economic matters. These rights already exist to varying degrees in the federal democracies. This participation takes the form of cities, states, provinces and other regional entities opening offices abroad and otherwise engaging in activities intended to promote exports and to attract foreign investment and tourism. Additional dimensions include activities intended to enrich the quality of local and regional life, such as cultural and educational exchanges and interregional environmental and transportation agreements.

In the EC, however, there is the additional dimension of regional participation in Community decision-making. The federal members have intergovernmental mechanisms that can help to accommodate regional interests in Community decision-making, but the unitary members do not necessarily possess such mechanisms or have much experience with them. Furthermore, as additional authority is delegated to and assumed by the Community, regions will have stronger incentives to press for a resolution of the EC's 'democratic deficit' and even for the creation of a 'Europe of the Regions'.

It is this prospect that brings back into view the tension between consumership and citizenship, as the drive for universalistic consumership begins to disaggregate the unity of particularistic citizenship into multiple and sometimes competing citizenships (e.g. European, Catalonian and Spanish). Americans have long sought to cope with dual citizenship—state and national—but many Europeans may have to cope with tripartite citizenship.

This condition raises a host of questions about autonomous spheres of competence and intergovernmental relations, which are being addressed in the European Community. Although these issues are most pronounced in the EC, they are emerging everywhere as regions assert their economic and political interests. In terms of managing foreign relations in federal states, where dual citizenship is already implicit if not explicit, these issues raise questions about how to conceptualize the character of constituent governments when they enter the global arena. Are they state actors, semi-autonomous polities engaged in a political enterprise, governmental interest groups, or entrepreneurial firms engaged in economic competition?

The tension between constituent governments behaving as polities or as firms mirrors the tension between citizenship and consumership. The problem is that most people want both. Yet the more that constituent governments behave as polities in the global arena, the more they fragment and retard the development of global consumership, but the more that constituent governments behave as firms, the more they fragment and undermine the autonomy bases of traditional citizenship. This is precisely the dilemma facing the United States, where the emergence of competition from Japan and the prospects of heightened competition from the EC have created considerable pressure to eliminate state barriers to commerce so as to create a uniform national marketplace. As the Secretary of the US Treasury said upon introducing President George Bush's proposals to reform the country's dual (federal and state) banking system in 1991, something is seriously amiss when a bank in California can open a branch in Birmingham, England, but not in Birmingham, Alabama. Yet the people of Alabama, and of other states, want to retain rights of democratic self-government over banking within their borders.

President Bush's complaint has been echoed by many European leaders, most recently, for example, by the EC's ambassador to the United States:

When Europeans look at the United States, we are surprised to find increasing fragmentation of this huge market. We see states establishing differing rules on labeling, air quality, bottled water contents and a wide variety of other health and safety regulations. We also see U.S. competitiveness hampered by skyrocketing federal and state budget deficits and hurt by outdated banking and insurance systems, which states overregulate.[13]

In turn, US states are especially concerned about EC policies governing the harmonization of standards and certification, public procurement, and rules of origin, local content, and common commercial policies.[14] Hence, about twenty-eight states have offices or representatives in EC member-states, thirteen of which are in Brussels.

The pressure for uniform regulation

The tension between constituent governments as polities and as firms is most pronounced in the field of regulation, which is central to both citizenship and consumership. A government without regulatory powers is hardly a polity, but a global or regional marketplace, such as the EC, is hardly a common market without rules of its own that supersede local or national regulation. Given that modern consumership is rivaling traditional citizenship, tremendous pressure is building for uniform regulation (or deregulation) across jurisdictions, whether nation-states in the EC or constituent governments in federal nations.

The spread of uniform regulation is readily evident in the United States and the EC. For example, in the United States, the federal government, under the authority of the supremacy clause of the US Constitution, has enacted since 1789 more than 440 laws pre-empting (i.e. displacing) state and local regulatory powers. What is significant, though, is that over 50 percent of these laws have been enacted only since 1969.[15] These statutes, moreover, do not encompass the full range of mechanisms by which the federal government displaces state and local law. A similar path may be followed in the EC. Pursuant to the Single European Act of 1987, the internal market program sets forth 297 measures to be implemented Community-wide. It is apparently anticipated that 75 percent of national legislation will originate, directly or indirectly, from Community legislation in the near future.[16]

Sources of pressure for uniform regulation

This substantial and growing displacement of local regulatory authority is being driven by a number of forces. One is consumers, who desire regulation in itself in order to protect themselves. Consumers seem willing to delegate more regulatory powers to larger jurisdictions in order to protect their global consumer interests, including such matters as environmental protection.

A second source of pressure for uniform regulation is business, which increasingly sees benefits in a common, uniform marketplace and a single point of government regulation. As some business leaders in the United States put it, they prefer to deal with one 500-pound gorilla in Washington than with fifty monkeys on steroids. As business has come to recognize the political inevitability of regulation, and as states (and many local governments) have become more energetic regulators in the face of consumer pressure, business has increasingly sought federal pre-emption of state and local powers. For example, when the US Supreme Court upheld in 1991 the statutory authority of local governments to enact pesticide regulations more stringent than federal rules, the pesticide industry quickly obtained the introduction in Congress of a bill to overturn the Court's ruling and pre-empt local pesticide regulation.[17]

State and local regulation is said to create a number of problems. It fragments the marketplace, increases the cost of doing business and the complexity of compliance with multiple rules, frustrates the development of company-wide or industry-wide standards and procedures, produces conflicting and inconsistent regulations across jurisdictions, and eventuates in regulatory gridlock. Additional problems develop in particular fields, such as food labeling, where state action produces inconsistent warnings and also confuses language when states give different meanings to the same words or use different words to convey the same warning. As one observer put it, fifty autonomous regulators produce a 'constitutionally questionable tower of regulatory Babel'.[18]

Business leaders also argue that state and local regulation is not always well thought-out, in part because many of these governments lack the ability to regulate effectively and efficiently, and in part because they act on behalf of their own citizens rather than of the nation. At times, state and local regulation is principally anti-competitive, intended to benefit the interests of in-state firms or consumers at the expense of outsiders. These were, for example, among the principal motivations for federal pre-emption of local regulation of cable-television rates in 1984. The legislation, supported by the Reagan administration, deregulated cable-television rates in all localities not having 'effective competition'. A crescendo of consumer complaints about rising rates, however, led the Congress to consider legislation to reregulate cable rates nationally by requiring the Federal Communications Commission to set a nationwide price for basic cable, including local channels and 'superstations'.

State regulation can also be undemocratic in the sense that a few states so dominate the marketplace as to set the pace for all the states. For example, California accounts for 14.7 percent of the US drug market. Together, California, New York and Illinois account for 27.2 percent of that market. Hence, regulations enacted by these states can effectively drive the market and constitute a *de facto* pre-emption of the laws of other states.

State and local regulation may also promote destructive competition and conflict among jurisdictions, driving down regulatory standards and shutting out products from other states. Thus, when California's popularly initiated food-label law, Proposition 65 (1986), was seen as requiring cancer warning labels on products from other states, such as Georgia peanuts and Vermont maple syrup, a number of states advocated federal pre-emption of Proposition 65.

Indeed, another source of pressure for uniform national regulation is state executive officials, mainly governors, who have welcomed federal pre-emption of state regulation in many fields related to economic policy. They have endorsed such pre-emption in the belief that a more uniform national marketplace will render the nation, and thereby each of its fifty states, more competitive in the global marketplace. It is governors primarily who have also led the states into the global arena by opening offices abroad, leading trade missions, and establishing institutions to attract investment and tourism.[19] At first, one might construe these initiatives as assertions of states' rights to behave as co-sovereign polities in the federal system, but governors seem to see themselves more as corporate executives leading a public firm into global competition. In part, this transformation of the gubernatorial role from citizenship to consumership is a matter of political survival. Given the balanced budget requirements in forty-nine states, governors are among the most vulnerable of the country's elected officials when a recession requires them to reduce services and raise taxes.

Pressure for uniform regulation also seems to be emanating from the executive side of government in other political systems. In Australia, for example, state premiers and chief ministers have pressed for mutual recognition of state standards and uniform standards in many fields, as well as Commonwealth legislation to enforce uniformity. In the EC, the incorporation of Community law into national law usually falls to national executives.[20]

The final source of pressure for uniform regulation is the federal government in the United States and the Community in the EC. Constitutional restrictions on the exercise of federal powers, especially over foreign and interstate commerce, have been relaxed considerably by the US Supreme Court, and the Congress and executive agencies increasingly respond to discrete and insular constituent interests. In both the United States and the EC, uniform regulation appears to grow as well because it is only loosely constrained by budget limits. The size of the federal government's regulatory staff grew from less than 70,000 persons in 1970 to about 125,000 in 1992,[21] but the costs of federal regulation are paid primarily by firms, consumers, and state and local governments. In the United States, costs are often passed on to state and local governments in what are called unfunded and underfunded mandates. The city of Columbus, Ohio, for example, estimated that its costs of complying with current federal and state environmental regulations will average $135 million annually from 1996 to 2000, equalling 23.1 percent of the city's total budget (up from 10.6 percent of the city's 1991 budget).[22] In the EC, the European Commission has been rather effective in initiating legislation; member states have gradually accepted the priority of Community laws over national laws asserted by the European Court of Justice in 1964; and Article 235 of the Treaty of Rome has created room for expansive interpretations of EC powers.[23] In addition, the EC, like Australia, is moving away from unanimity rules to majority or qualified majority rules to enact uniform standards across jurisdictions.

Sources of opposition to uniform regulation

In the United States, opposition to uniform regulation more often arises from state legislators, attorneys-general, local governments, and certain citizen groups. Legislators exercise the key power of state sovereignty, namely, law-making; hence, they are less eager than governors to see that power reduced by federal pre-emption. State legislatures have also become more energetic bodies because they have become more professionalized during the past twenty-five years; forty-three of them now meet annually instead of biennially, and high re-election rates have made legislative service a career for many legislators. In addition, because most legislators represent districts with comparatively small populations, and each legislator is one voice among many, they are more vulnerable to voter discipline for regulatory failures than for market failures.

Attorneys-general have also tended to oppose uniform regulation because they are popularly elected in forty-three states; nearly two-thirds of them are Democrats rather than Republicans; and consumer protection is one of their most visible and popular responsibilities. Consequently, state attorneys-general have become aggressive regulators, especially since the

Reagan and Bush administrations were seen as having a *laissez-faire* attitude toward business. Surprisingly, moreover, the US Supreme Court has upheld some locally protective state economic regulation, such as state restrictions on 'hostile' takeovers of in-state corporations.[24]

In turn, local government officials are independently elected within their jurisdictions. Given their limited powers, they generally prefer maximum freedom to respond to their constituents and to position their jurisdiction in the marketplace. In addition, some local governments are captured by consumer and environmental interests, which desire local regulation that is more stringent than state or federal regulation or that otherwise fills regulatory vacuums. Many liberal public-interest groups that once supported federal pre-emption of what they regarded as weak and parochial state and local regulation now oppose federal pre-emption of state and local authority to fill federal regulatory vacuums and to set standards higher than federal standards.

Nevertheless, despite these sources of opposition to uniform regulation, massive displacements of the regulatory powers of constituent governments in several continental economic regions are under way, thus reducing the historic citizenship functions of constituent governments as polities and pushing those governments in the direction of consumership functions, thereby converting them, in effect, into entrepreneurial firms. This transformation is not likely to reduce the international activities of constituent governments, however; instead, it is likely to increase these activities because, like private corporations, constituent governments will find it increasingly necessary to behave like aggressive firms in the global market. For the most part, though, these activities are likely to be largely confined to consumership interests. Indeed, there is some opinion poll evidence in the United States suggesting that the pursuit of citizenship interests by constituent governments in the global arena may not be viewed as proper by the public.[25] Hence, the management of foreign relations is not likely to become overly complicated in the United States by constituent diplomacy, although state and local governments can be expected to assert their economic interests more aggressively in federal decision-making, as was recently the case when state and local governments blocked an effort by the US House of Representatives to restrict the access of certain foreign ships to US ports.

Developments may be more complicated and contentious in the European Community. European nation-states are becoming more like US constituent states; a number of intranational and cross-national regions would like to become more like constituent states in a federalized Community; some regions are expressing secessionist sentiments against their home state; the admission of new member-states will expand the field of conflict as well as cooperation; and the prospect of adopting a common foreign policy is a novelty. Recent reservations about the Maastricht Treaty indicate how difficult it may be to convert historic nation-states into constituent units of a

European quasi-state. Public pressure on national governments to submit major EC questions to the electorate or to the European Parliament, however, suggest that citizens may be more receptive to union if they have a greater voice in its governance. This, though, is likely to undermine the univocal integrity of nation-states.

Wiggle room for local regulation

Although the emergence of uniform regulation in continental regions appears to be largely salutary for consumers and entrepreneurs, it is troublesome for citizens, who find their regulatory voice constricted in local and regional jurisdictions and their voting voice either non-existent or drowned out in the continental pool. Consequently, there are counter-pressures to preserve room for local regulation by constituent governments.

An adequate theory and rationale for local regulation in the global economy has yet to be developed, but the EC has moved in this direction by switching from harmonization in virtually every field to mutual recognition of standards in many fields. After laboring for decades to harmonize standards for jam, toys, lawn-mower noise levels, sausage and many other products, the Community finally succumbed to the message trumpeted in a *Daily Telegraph* headline: 'Hands Off Our Bangers, We Like Them Lousy'.[26]

From the perspective of citizenship interests, mutual recognition has the advantages of not delegating regulatory powers to the EC and of avoiding the contentious difficulty of legislating for very diverse communities. From the perspective of consumership, mutual recognition has the advantages of preserving local preferences and access to diverse products, maintaining competition among local regulators, and allowing common standards to emerge as desired by the process of competition. However, mutual recognition also has disadvantages. It does not work well in every area, such as telecommunications where products must be interconnected, and it can be harmful when it induces jurisdictions to set low standards and engage in competitive deregulation, especially in such areas as drug manufacturing and environmental protection. Mutual recognition also lacks the efficiency and effectiveness of collecting regulatory information Community-wide, and it still requires voluntary recognition of foreign standards. Finally, one could 'argue that mutual recognition is incompatible with the logic of an integrated market, which cannot allow the achievement of the single market to be brought into question by unilateral measures of member states.'[27] Hence, the question of local regulation is not entirely resolved by mutual recognition.

Local regulation and classical rationales for regulation

An adequate theory of local (or national) regulation in the global economy would begin with the classic rationales for regulation: externalities, information asymmetries, monopolization and public goods.

With respect to externalities, the preservation of local regulation is difficult to justify because almost any activity can be said to create spillovers into other jurisdictions. For almost 200 years, for example, the US government understood its authority over water resources to be confined to navigable interstate waterways. Recently, however, recognizing that pollutants enter those waterways from many sources, the federal government has essentially expanded its jurisdiction to encompass all waters and lands within US boundaries upon which rain falls. This logic places the federal government in a position to engage in land-use regulation unprecedented in US history and unstated in the US Constitution.

However, the spillover argument is often exaggerated. Even many types of environmental pollution are localized, and all the more so in large jurisdictions like Texas and California. Where spillovers do require cross-jurisdictional action, there are other options. For one, the US government and the EC can establish minimum standards applicable to all constituent jurisdictions while allowing those jurisdictions to enact more stringent standards. Second, in lieu of overt regulation, fiscal transfers can be employed to provide incentives to laggard jurisdictions. Third, interjurisdictional self-regulation can be encouraged, such as interstate compacts to create river-basin commissions encompassing all jurisdictions located in a basin.

With respect to information, there appears to be more defensible room for local regulation, especially in terms of the manufacture, sale and consumption of products and services. However, this room is limited in so far as certain types of local regulation impose undue burdens on interjurisdictional commerce and fragment a common market. Although technology makes it possible to manufacture products with different labels to meet different local labeling requirements—much like major magazines such as *Time* produce different regional and foreign editions—the cost may be prohibitive, especially for small manufacturers. Furthermore, diverse labeling laws would prevent manufacturers and wholesalers from shipping excess supplies in one jurisdiction to other jurisdictions experiencing shortages. Consequently, local regulation of information for consumer protection is likely to be confined to the labeling of local products, public education and information about extralocal products, and prohibitions on the sale of products deemed harmful by local authorities.

With respect to monopolization, it is possible to conceptualize the fragmenting effects of local regulation as an important barrier to monopolization and concentrations of economic power in a large common market. Leftist critics of the EC have especially voiced this concern and have campaigned, therefore, for more social, economic and environmental regulation by the EC as well as for a stronger European Parliament able to counteract the emergence of more consolidated corporate power.[28] An evisceration of local regulation, moreover, would expose localities to corporate buccaneering in which large enterprises take over local businesses and exact tribute for local investment. Authority to maintain and promote its economic base is a key attribute of a government. Diminutions of this authority, therefore, curtail the exercise of local citizenship and may also undermine local consumership if a jurisdiction cannot protect its economic base. However, the beneficial effects of fragmentation arising from local regulation must be weighed against its anti-competitive and protectionist tendencies.

With respect to public goods and services, there would appear to be substantial room for local autonomy to allow citizens to institutionalize their preferences. At the same time, however, the need to compete in the global market is likely to constrain that autonomy and alter public choices — perhaps, for example, driving down public goods that impede competitiveness, such as certain welfare expenditures, and driving up public goods that enhance competitiveness, such as education and transportation expenditures.[29] Nevertheless, the OECD, for example, has acknowledged that:

In recent years, a new paradigm has emerged for urban service provision in OECD countries. The guiding principles of provision have moved away from ideas of universality and standardization, towards an enhanced awareness of the need for sensitivity and responsiveness to the large variation of urban service needs between citizens.[30]

The extent to which each of these rationales for regulation leaves room for local regulation is likely to vary across industries and sectors of the economy. However, these rationales have come under considerable criticism in recent years for producing regulatory failures as governments become more aggressive in their efforts to correct market failures. Hence, there has been strong pressure for deregulation as well as for denationalization of industries. To the extent that deregulation limits the power of the US government or the EC, then the constituent governments may gain a measure of autonomy. However, if Community-wide deregulation and denationalization are understood to include pre-emption of local authority to fill regulatory vacuums, as has been the case in a number of areas in the United States (e.g. bus and airline deregulation), then the constituent governments lose a substantial measure of autonomy.

Practical and political rationales for local regulation

There are, however, other rationales for local regulation. One is the need for innovation and experimentation. Nothing succeeds like success, and the availability of local regulatory experimentation allows successful innovations to be adopted by other jurisdictions or by the Community-wide government, while failed experiments remain confined to smaller jurisdictions. Local regulation can also spur other jurisdictions and the Community-wide government into action and improve the performance of industries.

Local regulation may also be a necessary concession to fundamental disagreements about regulatory policies. The French, for example, tend to favor industrial policy, while the British tend to be less enthusiastic about industrial policy.[31]

In addition, 'where effective regulation requires detailed and accurate information about' an industry, local regulation may increase 'the effectiveness of monitoring, and thus the credibility of regulation'.[32]

In turn, local regulation may serve a redundancy function to check regulatory failures on the part of Community-wide institutions. Such central failures may be due to a number of factors, including regulatory overload, lax enforcement, industry or bureaucratic capture of regulatory agencies, or oversight. A dramatic example of redundancy occurred in 1990 when laboratory workers in the Department of Environmental Protection in Mecklenburg County, North Carolina, discovered benzene in their Perrier. A month later, Perrier was forced to withdraw 160 million bottles of its sparkling mineral water from worldwide circulation. Another example occurred in 1981, when a Virginia bank regulator called into question the request of the Bank of Credit and Commerce International (BCCI) to take over First American Bank. In this case, however, the Virginia regulator was overruled by the federal government's regulators who, at the time, failed to uncover BCCI's criminal activities.[33]

Related to redundancy is the need to fill regulatory vacuums. Neither the US government nor the EC is likely to be able to occupy every field and to respond in a timely manner to unanticipated needs for regulation arising from new developments or peculiar impacts of economic activity on particular regions. There are, moreover, likely to be some mismatches between uniform regulations and local conditions. Accordingly, responsiveness to local needs can be regarded as an important rationale for local regulation. Such factors as population density and traffic patterns, for example, may require room for local regulation of the transportation and disposition of hazardous materials.

Local regulation may also occur in conjunction with Community-wide regulation. Administration and implementation may be delegated to constituent governments; those governments may assist or supplement

Community-wide regulation; minimum standards may be established for the Community, with local authority to exceed those standards; regulatory exceptions can be made for functions integral to the operation and viability of constituent governments; and those governments might be given veto power over certain forms and procedures of Community regulation.

Finally, cooperative local regulation may occur as an alternative to Community regulation through interjurisdictional compacts and agreements, and voluntary adoptions of uniform laws. Such instruments tend to be fragile, however—although jurisdictions wishing to preserve elements of autonomy may have incentives to employ them.

Conclusion

The centripetal pulls of globalization are having centrifugal effects on the conduct of foreign relations by many nation-states because the citizens of constituent governments and subnational regions are encouraged and compelled to assert their consumership and citizenship interests globally. For federal democracies in which constituent governments enjoy significant domestic self-government, these developments complicate but do not necessarily paralyse the management of foreign relations. In many respects, these developments democratize foreign policy-making by broadening participation in decision-making, requiring national élites to attend to the local effects of foreign policy decisions, and allowing constituent governments some freedom to operate globally. For multinational federations and many unitary states, however, these developments pose less of a problem for the management of foreign relations than for the maintenance of the nation-state itself. Consumer desires for access to the global market and citizen desires for an independent communal identity in the global arena produce pressures for secession or for separation and reaffiliation along the lines of confederation, Quebec's proposed sovereignty-association, or limited functional union—all within the context of larger transnational regimes, such as the EC and the North American Free Trade Agreement.

A key challenge in managing contemporary foreign relations and constructing a pacific world order lies in balancing the tensions between consumership and citizenship. The satisfaction of consumership interests increasingly requires an open, interdependent world market, but the satisfaction of citizenship interests requires a multiplicity of at least semi-independent jurisdictions able to afford citizens meaningful self-government. A multiplicity of too highly independent jurisdictions, however, would fragment a global arena that requires rules of regulation and deregulation that supersede local rules. Yet local governments shorn of their regulatory powers would hardly be polities able to afford persons meaningful citizenship.

The management of foreign relations is further complicated by the temptation of citizens to view their own governments as entrepreneurial firms for purposes of global economic competition in the pursuit of consumership interests while also expecting those governments to perform as polities, or sovereign states, for purposes of local regulation and protection against adverse global intrusions in the pursuit of citizenship interests. At the same time, the emergence of global concerns and authoritative international organizations multiplies the number of actors in the global arena and blurs distinctions between state and non-state actors, thereby encouraging citizens to bypass their home governments in order to assert their citizenship and consumership interests directly in the global arena, sometimes in competition with their home governments. Consequently, the challenges of managing foreign relations in federal democracies, or any democratic nation-state today, arise in part from the fact that citizens themselves are pulled in two directions at once: global consumership and local citizenship.

Notes

1. Kenneth N. Waltz, *Theory of International Politics*, Addison-Wesley, Reading, MA (1979).
2. See e.g. Peter F. Drucker, 'The changed world economy', *Foreign Affairs*, 64 (1986), 768–91; F.E. Emery and E.L. Trist, *Towards a Social Ecology*, Plenum, New York (1975).
3. Robert O. Keohane, 'Realism, neorealism and the study of world politics', in Robert O. Keohane (ed.), *Neorealism and Its Critics*, Columbia University Press, New York (1986), 1–27.
4. Bayliss Manning, 'The Congress, the executive and intermestic affairs: three proposals', *Foreign Affairs*, 55 (1977), 306–24.
5. James N. Rosenau, 'Patterned chaos in global life: structure and process in the two worlds of world politics', *International Political Science Review*, 9 (1988), 327.
6. John Kincaid, 'Constituent diplomacy in federal polities and the nation-state: conflict and co-operation', in Hans J. Michelmann and Panayotis Soldatos (eds), *Federalism and International Relations: The Role of Subnational Units*, Clarendon Press, Oxford (1990), 54–75.
7. Ivo D. Duchacek, *The Territorial Dimension of Politics Within, Among, and Across Nations*, Westview, Boulder, CO (1986).
8. J. Rufus Fears (ed.), *Selected Writings of Lord Acton*, vol. I, *Essays in the History of Liberty*, Liberty Classics, Indianapolis (1985), 425.
9. Daniel J. Elazar (ed.), *Self Rule/Shared Rule*, Turtledove, Ramat Gan (1979); John M. Bryson and Robert C. Einsweiler (eds), *Shared Power*, University Press of America, Lanham, MD (1991); Hurst Hannum, *Autonomy, Sovereignty, and Self-determination: The Accommodation of Conflicting Rights*, University of Pennsylvania Press, Philadelphia (1990).
10. Yankelovich for CNN-*Time*, 'Opinion outlook', *National Journal*, 24 (29 February 1992), 536.

11. Alex Inkeles and David H. Smith, *Becoming Modern: Individual Change in Six Developing Countries*, Harvard University Press, Cambridge (1974).

12. See, for example, Milica Zarkovic Bookman, *The Political Economy of Discontinuous Development: Regional Disparities and Interregional Conflict*, Praeger, New York (1991).

13. Andreas van Agt, 'Trading with the new Europe', *State Government News*, 34 (December 1991), 20.

14. Brandon Roberts, *Competition Across the Atlantic: The States Face Europe '92*, National Conference of State Legislatures, Denver, CO (1991); Stephen Cooney, 'The impact of Europe 1992 on the United States', *Proceedings of the Academy of Political Science*, 38 (1991), 100–12.

15. US Advisory Commission on Intergovernmental Relations, *Federal Statutory Preemption of State and Local Authority*, ACIR, Washington, DC (1992).

16. Theo A.J. Toonen, 'Europe of the administrations: the challenges of '92 (and beyond)', *Public Administration Review*, 52 (March/April 1992), 108–15.

17. John Kincaid, 'Developments in federal–state relations, 1990–91', *The Book of the States, 1992–93*, Council of State Governments, Lexington, KY (1992), 613.

18. Randall Bloomquist, 'Can the states regulate national ads?' *Governing*, 2 (July 1989), 64–5.

19. John Kincaid, 'The American governors in international affairs', *Publius: The Journal of Federalism*, 14 (Fall 1984), 94–114. See also, 'State and local governments in international affairs', *Intergovernmental Perspective*, 16 (Spring 1990), entire issue.

20. Heinrich Siedentopf and Christoph Hausschild, 'The implementation of Community legislation by the member states', in Heinrich Siedentopf and James Ziller (eds), *Making European Policies Work*, vol. 1, Sage Publications, London (1988), 1–87.

21. Melinda Warren and James Lis, 'Regulatory standstill: analysis of the 1993 federal budget', Occasional Paper Number 105, Center for the Study of American Business, Washington University, St. Louis, MO (June 1992), 1.

22. Richard C. Hicks, 'Environmental legislation and the costs of compliance', *Government Finance Review*, 8 (April 1992), 7–10.

23. Giandomenico Majone, 'Cross-national sources of regulatory policymaking in Europe and the United States', *Journal of Public Policy*, 11 (1991), 79–106.

24. Eric S. Rosengren, 'State restrictions of hostile takeovers', *Publius: The Journal of Federalism*, 18 (Summer 1988), 67–79.

25. John Kincaid, 'Rain clouds over municipal diplomacy: dimensions and possible sources of negative public opinion', in Earl H. Fry, Lee H. Radebaugh and Panayotis Soldatos (eds), *The New International Cities Era: The Global Activities of North American Municipal Governments*, David M. Kennedy Center for International Studies, Brigham Young University, Provo, UT (1989), 223–47.

26. Quoted in David Brooks, 'Jam sessions', *The New Republic*, 205 (4 November 1991), 15.

27. Majone, op. cit., 100.

28. Ben Lowe, 'Something rebellious in the state of Denmark', *The Guardian* (USA), 44 (17 June 1992), 14.

29. See various essays in Daphne A. Kenyon and John Kincaid (eds), *Competition Among States and Local Governments: Efficiency and Equity in American Federalism*, The

Urban Institute Press, Washington, DC (1991).
30. OECD, *Managing and Financing Urban Services*, OECD, Paris (1987), 11.
31. J. Pearce and J. Sutton, *Protection and Industrial Policy in Europe*, Routledge & Kegan Paul, London (1985).
32. Konstantine Gatsios and Paul Seabright, 'Regulation in the European Community', *Oxford Review of Economic Policy*, 5 (1989), 54.
33. Howard L. Rosenberg, 'Sheik to sheik: BCCI's Washington connection', *The New Republic*, 205 (2 September 1991), 16–18.

Towards a typology of non-central foreign economic behaviour: the case of agricultural trade

3

Andrew F. Cooper

The purpose of this essay is to try to help further the development of a typology of non-central foreign economic behaviour. In terms of approach, it tries to steer a middle course between the ambitious, and rather abstract, attempts at conceptualisation,[1] and the bulk of the empirically oriented studies which have for the most part concentrated on what may be described as the thick description of various forms of micro-diplomacy.

With respect to subject area, the work focuses on agricultural trade. To a certain extent, this choice of case-studies is problematic in that agriculture has remained exceptional in terms of public policy and the international political economy (IPE). Agriculture has always received special treatment in terms of the multilateral trading system. In the various GATT negotiations, prior to the Uruguay Round presently in train, trade in agricultural products was largely exempt from the rules and regulations governing trade in manufactured goods. These included the prohibition of quantitative import restrictions (Article XI of the GATT), export subsidies (Article XVI) and technical barriers (Article XX).

Agriculture has often been treated as a distinctive case *vis-à-vis* bilateral trade issues (and debates) as well. Up to the beginning of the negotiations on the Canada-US Free Trade Negotiations in the mid-1980s, for example, agriculture was universally considered to be beyond the scope of any continental/bilateral agreement. The 1978 report of the Canadian Senate Committee on Foreign Affairs, which revived the idea of some form of Canada-US Free Trade Agreement, was careful to declare that agriculture would be 'the most notable exception'.[2] Likewise, the 1985 Report of the Royal Commission on the Economic Union and Development Prospects for

Canada (commonly known as the Macdonald Commission), conceded that the agricultural component of the 'leap of faith' might have to be less swiftly taken than in other areas of the economy.[3]

Yet it may be suggested that any methodological disadvantages imposed by agriculture's distinctiveness are more than compensated for by its value in working towards a more systematic study of non-central foreign economic behaviour. The very fact that agriculture is regarded as special to so many actors allows for a breadth of treatment, divergent from the more specialised country-specific studies which have been undertaken. Indeed, the argument can be made that an examination of the agricultural dimension of foreign economic policy may be one of the most appropriate vehicles for meeting the two fundamental needs of an evolving research agenda, as laid out by Earl Fry in a recent article on the international economic relations of federal states.[4] At one level, the force and the extent of the pressures imposed on the agricultural sector from overall trends in the ipe highlight the need for the integration of analysis with respect to the 'domestic' and the 'foreign'. At another level, given the importance of this issue area for the politics in and policy of a wide variety of countries, including those (Canada, the United States, Australia and Germany) examined in this chapter, the need for more rigorous comparative research is demonstrated. What agriculture lacks in representativeness, therefore, it more than makes up for in scope.

Turbulence and the dilemma of interdependence

A full discussion of the change experienced in the global economy since the early 1970s is well beyond the scope of this paper. A number of points relating to the growth of turbulence[5], complex and accentuated interdependence,[6] and the associated innovations in economic statecraft,[7] however, must be made. The first of these is that the post-1970 period has seen a serious decline in the principles and norms that were established as the basis of the post-Second World War liberal international economic order.[8] It is, of course, possible to present empirical evidence that there has been no measurable decrease in the ratio of trade to gross national product.[9] The point of concern for this essay, though, is the degree to which perceptions of both the erosion of the 'rules of the game' and of the extent of uncertainty in the ipe are having a deleterious effect. Secondly, the crisis of liberal internationalism has featured a dynamic process, marked by the impact of a number of traumatic events and challenges in the world economy including the resource shocks associated with OPEC, and the heightened mobility of capital and technology. Thirdly, and most significantly from the perspective of this study, the political impact of these economic changes has been contradictory in nature.

The common assumption about the changes in the ipe is that they have severely weakened the capacity of nation-states to act in any effective fashion. In particular, students of foreign policy and the ipe have taken their cue from R.N. Cooper and other early popularisers of the concept of interdependence, namely that this process 'by joining national markets, erodes the effectiveness of [domestic] policies and hence threatens national autonomy in the determination and pursuit of economic objectives.'[10] Reinforcing this impression that the coherence of national policy *vis-à-vis* the international economy has been undermined, it must be added, has been the ascendancy of a variety of other trends with respect to public policy, ranging from the imperatives of fiscal cutbacks due to budget deficits, and the impetus for deregulation and privatisation. Whether inspired by either a neo-conservative or neo-liberal ideology, or resorted to as part of a pragmatic response to economic realities, these tendencies emphasise markets over statism.

Still, as this array of forces acted to constrain forms of activity at the national level, they also opened up certain windows of necessity and windows of opportunity for local action. On the one hand, the incentives for local action as a response to international conditions were strong. As one observer put it: 'The economic interdependence of the modern world is more than international. It is interlocal . . . Every jiggle in the pattern of the international economy is likely to pinch some local group . . . and convert it immediately into a vocal group.'[11] On the other hand, there was often a political and policy vacuum to fill. As national policies diminished in either form or scope (limiting their effectiveness), non-central actors increasingly took it upon themselves to compensate for this loss (or change in emphasis) through self-help.

It must be emphasised here as well that this response, or, more accurately, set of responses, did not occur across 'a seamless plane'.[12] Rather, this localistic action took on a wide variety of forms and shapes. Broadly speaking, these strategies may be categorised as spanning a broad continuum from adjustment to resistance to change in the ipe. That is to say, they encompassed a spectrum from an outward-looking approach to an inward-looking posture. On a sectoral basis, it is also important to note, the patterns of behaviour may be at odds or contradictory with each other.

Agricultural trade showcases, in a rather exaggerated fashion, many of these changes in and responses to the ipe. As in the case of other sectors, agricultural transactions have become more fully globalised since the 1970s. In the immediate post-1945 period, the international agricultural trading system may be said to have been governed by a broad set of norms and rules, values which included comparative advantage, specialisation, and the free and open exchange of goods and technology. This regime was underpinned in turn by the power of a strong leader (the United States, which championed, although not always practised, these liberal economic values),[13] the diplomatic efforts of what may be termed the main supporters of the system (Canada and Australia),[14] and the acquiescence to the system of potential 'spoilers' (the European Community and Japan)[15] due largely to benefits accruing to them through the importation of cheap, plentiful and secure foodstuffs.

What eventually undercut the stability of the international trading system was the impact of a number of exogenous events in the early 1970s. The most dramatic of these were natural in form and included the failure of crops due to drought in Asia, the Soviet Union, North America and Africa and the impact of other changes in the environment. This type of shock was preceded, nevertheless, by signals that the United States was withdrawing from its commitment to the orderly international marketing of grains and foodstuffs and that it was putting more emphasis on national self-interest. Most dramatically, the Nixon administration took action to place an embargo on soybean and soybean products in mid-1973. Whether this decision was interpreted as a sign of poor crisis management, an indication of the dominance of domestic interest, or a blatant attempt to use American 'food power' in the commodity sector, the credibility of the United States as a reliable supplier of foodstuffs was seriously damaged.

The ultimate consequence of these events was to heighten tension in agricultural trade. The issue of autonomy and self-sufficiency with respect to foodstuffs was placed at the top of the political agenda in the EC and Japan. In the case of the EC, however, the more inward-looking approach gradually took on an important external dimension. As massive 'mountains' of agricultural produce accumulated in the post-crisis period, the EC's Common Agricultural Policy (CAP) was gradually pushed outwards and a new EC agricultural export strategy, based on export subsidies and restitutions, emerged. This effort to 'export' the CAPs problems, in turn, posed a direct challenge to the United States' continued predominance with respect to agricultural transactions, a challenge the United States responded to by a combination of multilateralism (the strengthening of GATT rules), bilateralism (special deals) and unilateralism (fighting fire with fire).[16]

This heightened tension was not restricted, furthermore, to the United States and the EC. A variety of LDCs, since the 1970s, have taken a more aggressive stance *vis-à-vis* the export of agricultural products. These include both diversified, well-positioned actors such as Brazil, Argentina and Thailand and more specialised, but increasingly competitive, countries such as Mexico and Morocco. The impetus to take collective action was of course particularly great in the case of the Latin American debtor countries—as the servicing of that debt required, among other things, an expansion of sales of agricultural goods.[17]

In short, while agricultural trade has always been seen as an exception by the major producers, it has in most nations also come to exhibit many of the worst features of the new ipe and to occupy a position of peculiar political sensitivity that makes it distinct from, although not unconnected to, the other sectors of global trade. Given these problems, it comes as no surprise that the issue of agricultural reform (including domestic restructuring) has come to dominate international trade negotiations in the 1980s and early 1990s.[18] Although on the top of the agenda, however, the issue remains fraught with uncertainty and risk.

The impact of these changes in agriculture, and the potential of a still further acceleration of these processes, has been felt in all of the countries under review in this chapter. The traditionally dominant, as well as the long-subordinate, are affected. As one American study put it: 'The US economy has become more closely linked to foreign economies in the last decade, and American producers and consumers are consequently more sensitive to supply and demand changes outside the United States.'[19] But, as suggested by the discussion above, the impact of turbulence and a new form of complex interdependence has not been felt in a uniform or consistent fashion at the local level in any of these national entities. For some non-central entities the new political sensitivity towards agriculture has had a positive side in that it has provided an impetus towards an improvement in economic efficiency and/or the encouragement for action on a governmental basis to take advantage of the fresh set of circumstances. For others, though, the consequences of change—and possibility of further reform in the agricultural trading arena—was less than benign. Bluntly put, the trends in the ipe raised the level of vulnerability, exposing their farm economies to harmful challenges.

Types of non-central agricultural trade behaviour

In attempting to categorise non-central agricultural trade behaviour, this study tries to depict the broad range of choice available to the actors. To do so, there is a need to go beyond the offensive/defensive mode of analysis which has been the focal point of much of the research in this area up to now.[20] For sure, this dualistic approach outlines the broad geographical features, or terrain, of non-central behaviour. Many interesting and significant contours, however, are left out. Put another way, by a concentration on broad categorisation (often with connotations of 'winners' and 'losers' attached) the nuances of behaviour are lost. What is needed therefore is a schema allowing for some additional elaboration.

This essay tries to map out the agricultural dimension of non-central behaviour in a somewhat different format. Figure 3.1 tries to capture the scope of this behaviour by depicting several broad categories of behaviour. These are liberal adjusters, illiberal adjusters, joiners, mavericks, pragmatic resisters and fundamental resisters. At the same time, by necessity looking at 'ideal' types, the emphasis on behaviour allows this method of analysis to serve as a useful tool in placing selected non-central actors within these broad categories. Again, the advantage of this format lies not only with its

integration of the domestic and the international but its wide-ranging comparative perspective. Examples can be drawn from Australia and Germany
as well as Canada and the United States.

At one end of the continuum are the *liberal adjusters*. In many ways this
grouping constitutes the most clearly identifiable form of non-central foreign
economic behaviour. Actors falling into this category such as California in
the United States and Alberta in Canada have been the most rule-oriented.
Indeed, it is this grouping which has been the most committed to constructing a revamped regime based on non-discrimination and a firm code of
conduct for subsidies, NTBs, as well as the most determined to take advantage of an open trading system in terms of their own exports.
Interdependence for them has not only been a long-standing reality, but a
positive force which should be encouraged.[21]

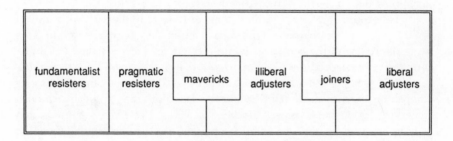

Figure 3.1 Types of non-central agricultural trade behaviour

To term the behaviour of a number of non-central actors as fitting into
this liberal adjuster category is not to claim that there are not considerable
differences between these actors. Significantly, California lacked much of
the 'me-tooism' associated with other non-central actors with regard to
foreign economic activity. California only opened its first official trade
offices in the late 1980s, and even then only did so in London and Tokyo.[22]
In terms of the scope of this sort of effort, therefore, California lagged
behind many other states, including Illinois and Iowa which had opened up
a variety of foreign offices and sister-state arrangements (Brussels, Osaka,
Hong Kong, Sao Paulo, Shen-Yang, Liaoning Province, China; and
Frankfurt, Hong Kong respectively).[23] Organisationally, California relied
heavily on outside consultants[24] and on the work of the California World
Trade Commission, a non-profit corporation, rather than a state agency.

By way of contrast, Alberta may be viewed as an innovator and a catalyst
in terms of foreign economic behaviour generally and agricultural trade
specifically. Indeed, Alberta served as a model both for other Canadian

provinces (most notably, British Columbia) and even some US states.[25] Through the 1970s and early 1980s, Alberta self-consciously built up its own capabilities for export development. Bureaucratically, this push outwards was reflected by the establishment of the Alberta Department of Agriculture, the Alberta Agricultural Development Corporation, and the Foreign Marketing Section of the provincial Department of Industry and Commerce. Diplomatically, Premier Lougheed led a well-publicised official trade mission to Japan (1972), Europe (1974), the north-western US states (1976), the Soviet Union and the Middle East (1977), and the Orient (1983); and Alberta expanded its representation abroad to include not only the presence of offices in London and Tokyo, Hong Kong, New York, Houston and Los Angeles, but the development of sister-state relations (Hokkaido in Japan and Heilonjing in China).

Nor did the generalised 'rules of the game' approach exhibited by California and Alberta signify that these two non-central actors could not play 'hard ball' in terms of trade. In declaratory terms, at least, Californian politicians could threaten to utilise forms of linkage diplomacy with respect to foreign economic relations. One state senator, for example, contemplated using the repeal of the controversial unitary tax as a lever in terms of trade: 'I understand negotiations and you negotiate best when you have something somebody wants. You want unitary relief. We don't have any necessarily compelling need to do that in California. If we're going to do it, we need something.'[26] Others, most notably Lt.-Gov. Leo McCarthy warned California's trading partners about the possibility of the reinstatement of the unitary tax if they did not respond in a positive fashion.[27]

Alberta exhibited an even greater willingness to contemplate linkage diplomacy. Premier Lougheed, for example, was quick to respond to US ambassador Thomas Enders' suggestion in October 1977 of a long-term agreement, or swap, whereby Canada would send an additional supply of natural gas to the United States in return for a more open market for Canadian products. As Lougheed informed the Alberta legislature: 'We've said that we would authorize the approval . . . of accelerated natural gas supplies to the United States beyond our needs here in Alberta, provided we have improved access for agricultural products into the United States.'[28]

Finally, in keeping with the style revealed above, Alberta demonstrated a higher degree of intensity *vis-à-vis* its intergovernmental relations than was the case with California. While California was not entirely satisfied with the record of the federal government, it attempted for the most part to build a better set of cooperative arrangements. One means of achieving this goal was the establishment of a market development programme, parallel to the one established by the US Department of Agriculture, which would grant matching funds for export promotion.[29] Alberta was more forthright, and even confrontational, in its efforts to push Ottawa on the issues of trade promotion and reform. On several occasions Premier Lougheed sharply (and publicly) criticised the Trudeau government's performance on agricultural trade.[30]

Yet, notwithstanding all of these contrasts and anomalies, California and Alberta approached international trade in a fundamentally similar fashion. On the one hand, the approach was largely facilitative in nature. No government-to-government transactions were considered, and politics was seen as subordinate to markets and the activity of the private sector. Alberta, for all its governmental activism, was strongly opposed to any over-regulation of enterprise. California, while 'doing something' to help, was unwilling to move too fast or too far from its tradition of leaving trade promotion to the private sector. As the Californian representative in Japan made it clear to his clientele: 'The assistance you're going to get from this office has a limit.'[31]

On the other hand, the target of much of this diplomatic endeavour was the high-growth markets within Asia-Pacific. Besides upgrading its trade promotion work in the region in the short term,[32] California devoted considerable resources to collecting information and statistics to build up a database on restrictive trade barriers in the longer term.[33] Likewise, Alberta spent a great deal of energy and money not only pursuing sales directly in the region but also building up a cultural/social presence in the area.[34]

The second category constitutes the *illiberal adjusters*. While outward-looking in terms of their focus, these actors were more inclined to manage interdependence by more strategical means. Indeed, the foreign economic diplomacy they pursued had characteristics of what may be termed a relatively benign form of micro neo-mercantilism. Breaking with the orthodoxy of economic liberalism,[35] the actors which fall into this grouping were prepared to experiment with practices which put politics ahead of market forces. Rather than acting merely as facilitators, they took a more interventionist approach to trade as a means of self-enhancement.

Western Australia fits most neatly into this category. This 'Cinderella state'/'state of excitement' had long and consciously accepted the need for government 'to be actively involved as part of an overall strategy for encouraging resource development.'[36] The Liberal government of Sir Charles Court took the lead in forging this strategy. But, far from discarding the model, the pragmatic and business-oriented Labor government of Brian Burke embraced and institutionalised these entrepreneurial practices to the extent that Western Australia was commonly referred to in the 1980s as WA Inc.

In terms of administrative means, the centrepieces of Western Australia's foreign economic activities were the Western Australia Development Corporation and EXIM (originally, the South East Asian Marketing Authority). The focal point of much of Western Australia's strategy was the mineral sector. Certainly, the most ambitious set of transactions undertaken by the Western Australian government were those negotiated with

Romania, in tandem with the giant Hancock mining corporation.[37] Nevertheless, agricultural products played a key role in the overall approach. As one minister in the Burke government put it, many of the originators of WA Inc. 'saw huge agricultural, horticultural and floricultural markets in Asia and believed that an incoming Labor government should set up an agency to foster that export market.'[38]

It would be misleading to suggest that Western Australia was alone in developing an entrepreneurial role. There were signs, for example, that Victoria had taken considerable steps under the Cain government in moving in a similar direction, issuing a document ('Victoria: The Next Decade') that laid out the path for an enhanced international trade policy and establishing the Victorian Trading Corporation.[39] But the main thrust of this state initiative was the establishment of joint ventures in the non-resource sector. The best illustration of another non-central actor attempting to develop a creative approach to the agricultural dimension of foreign economic policy was the province of Saskatchewan. Most notably, the Agricultural Development Corporation of Saskatchewan experimented with non-traditional marketing techniques (such as barter), targeting Eastern European markets from an office in Vienna.

A third category constitutes the *joiners*. The most dynamic (and certainly most publicised) phenomenon of trans-border regional cooperation is the activities of the so-called four motors of Europe. Formed explicitly as a new form of regionalism in Europe,[40] the four motors concept allows Rhône-Alpes, Lombardy, Catalonia and Baden-Württemberg to share knowledge with respect to technology and advanced education. Less known perhaps are the attempts at regional cooperation inside a single nation under review in this chapter. Of these the examples in the United States are particularly worthy of mention because, in addition to the fact that they have an agricultural dimension, they are at a somewhat fragile stage in their development.

This is not to underestimate the import of the more traditional forms of cooperation among American states. These bodies range from the inclusive National Governors' Association, the National Conference of State Legislatures and the National Association of State Development Agencies (NASDA) to the regionally focused Midwestern Governors' Conference, the New England Governors' Conference, the Southern Governors' Association and the Western Governors' Association. But these bodies have concentrated for the most part on information-gathering, agenda-setting and the lobbying of the federal government. To operationalise groupings in the way of cooperative action in terms of foreign economic activity is much harder.[41] This is especially true given the shift towards a more malevolent form of micro neo-mercantilism on the part of many American states since the early 1970s in the pursuit of trade and investment. Commentators have gone so far as to describe this competition as economic warfare.[42]

In these circumstances the progress of groups such as the Mid-South Trade Council, the Council of Great Lake Governors, and the Old West Regional Commission are interesting and significant.[43] All of these bodies have operationalised some forms of cooperative trade activities. The Mid-South Trade Council, a six-state consortium, has tried to share the cost of trade promotion through a regional effort, with joint sponsorship of representative offices overseas and regional trade missions. The Council of Great Lake Governors has promoted trade between Canada and the eight-state Great Lakes region. The Old West Regional Commission has tried to coordinate the international marketing of the area's agricultural commodities and livestock. The purpose of these types of action was to modify the 'beggar thy neighbour' tendencies on the part of the US states. Or as one governor put it, to 'identify common regional interests and actions to encourage regional development rather than pit one state against another.'[44]

A fourth category constitutes the *maverick* non-central actors. These actors are the most difficult to place in any category because their behaviour in trade diplomacy has tended to be unpredictable in nature. As in the case of the illiberal adjusters they have broken with orthodoxy, but they cannot be said to have conducted their foreign economic relations on a strategic basis. Rather their actions have tended to be tactically oriented, with a style that is both extremely emotionally driven and personalistic. Given this impetuousness, the behaviour of these actors can be either inward-looking or outward-looking. Each acts in its own individualistic fashion at different times and on different issues, searching for 'quick fixes'.

Queensland, under Bjelke-Petersen, stands out as an exemplar of this category. The Queensland premier's statement when he opened the state's Tokyo Office and urged his Japanese audience to 'come to Queensland, not to Australia',[45] underscores this idiosyncratic style. For the purposes of this essay, the most salient feature of Queensland's foreign economic approach was its periodic bursts of enthusiasm for resources diplomacy. One case in point was the interjection of the idea of some form of linkage between coal exports and fishing rights with the importation of beef with Japan throughout the 1970s. The Queensland government also attempted to restrict dairy products from New Zealand during the height of the nuclear vessels dispute between the United States and the Lange government.

Queensland, nevertheless, was not alone in acting as a maverick. Reference can be made to at least two US states which acted in this fashion on agriculturally related issues. The first of these was South Dakota, under Governor Janklow, during the early 1980s. Not only did Janklow 'invade' Washington, DC with 103 state legislators to make the case for increased farm aid, he showed he was willing to go to extreme lengths to protect the local agricultural interest. The most controversial episode in this defensive struggle came in 1985, with the decision to keep Canadian hogs from entering the state ostensibly because they contained residues of the drug chloramphenicol. A second, and more recent case, has been the attempt by Texas (with Jim Hightower as Agriculture Commissioner) to go its own way from the national government on the hormone issue. Rather than joining with Washington in its diplomatic efforts to fight the EC's ban on treated beef, Texas attempted to introduce an autonomous certification plan and to sell its produce directly to the Europeans on that basis.[46]

Finally, there is the category of *resisters* among non-central actors. Standing out with the liberal adjusters as the most readily identifiable type, the resisters stress the hurt rather than the help with respect to any reform process in international trade on agricultural products. Rather than a 'springboard' to enhanced economic opportunities, more interdependence and openness in the trading system are seen as an 'obstacle' to the future well-being of their localities.[47] In an effort to safeguard their internal needs and interests, they have fought long and hard against the forces of change.

As in the case of the liberal adjusters there is some variation in the form that this resistance takes. One subcategory within this grouping may be termed the pragmatic resisters. These actors have tended to defend their agricultural interests against the vicissitudes of international trade less on territorial or communalistic grounds and more on an economic or environmental basis. Ontario is a representative case in point. While resisting against dramatic changes in the rules of the game with regard to agricultural trade either in the bilateral (FTA) or multilateral (GATT) domain, the Peterson Liberal and the Rae New Democratic Party governments have tended to downplay the special nature of the farming communities. Instead they have focused more attention on the consequences of these changes on specific subsectors in the agricultural industry (fruit and vegetable, poultry, and dairy) and/or on the loss of valuable land to other forms of production. As such, Ontario has not been totally uncompromising or rejectionist in its bargaining stance concerning trade negotiations. It does what it is possible to resist, not what is necessary to defend its agricultural interests at any and all costs.

The other subcategory may be termed the fundamentalist resisters. This grouping perceives the forces of interdependence, economic integration and competitiveness as being not detrimental to agriculture *per se* but to a national way of life. Indeed, it is because of this nationalistic aspect, that this essay refers to non-central actors rather than sub-national actors.[48] For these actors there is little room for compromise. Not only does agriculture occupy a unique, even a superior, position in communal terms, trade negotiations on this issue are seen in stark realist terms, where actors gain or lose in a zero-sum fashion.[49]

Bavaria and Quebec are the embodiment of this latter subcategory of actors. Both have fiercely defended the needs and interests of their agricultural producers not on the basis of any rational economic argument, but on the basis that any further reduction of farms and farming in these territorial entities would extract a high social and cultural price. The concept of national self-sufficiency has even been invoked in Quebec, as the agriculture and sovereignty question have become more intertwined.[50] At the same time, in both communities, the anti-reform fight in terms of agriculture is seen as one in which almost any means may be utilised. Government leaders in both Bavaria and Quebec have intervened directly in an attempt to thwart reform. F.J. Strauss did so vigorously during the 1984 milk quota controversy, and Premier Bourassa has told Prime Minister Mulroney repeatedly that any GATT deal in the Uruguay Round that erodes or eliminates Article XI will not be acceptable to Quebec.[51]

Explaining the differences

In attempting to explain why the non-central actors examined in this chapter behave as they do, two variables must be taken into account. The first of these focuses on structural position in the ipe. In trade, as in other areas of foreign policy behaviour, it may be asserted that how an actor sits determines to a large extent how it acts. As Gourevitch has lucidly phrased it, 'an account of how the production profile of . . . [an actor] fits into the international division of labour proves instructive.'[52]

The explanatory value of this mode of analysis seems particularly high at either end of the continuum developed in this study. Certainly, it seems clear that the enormous economic strength of California helps shape its approach as a liberal adjuster. At a general level, of course, California is not only strong in manufacturing, high-tech, services, and tourism. It also serves as gateway to the Pacific in terms of port facilities. All in all, California would rank in the top seven if an independent country.[53] Just as materially for the purposes of this chapter, California exports an extremely wide array of specialised agricultural products. If not the leading producer or exporter (ranking behind Illinois and Iowa), California is by far the most diversified. A sophisticated form of agribusiness, research network, irrigation system, and access to abundant labour all contribute to California's comparative advantage.

At the other end of the continuum, Bavarian and Quebec agriculture remains marginal in a strict economic sense. Dependent on an entrenched system of protection and support (through CAP and marketing boards), agriculture remains the preserve of smaller farmers. Especially in Bavaria, many producers work the land on only a part-time basis. In these non-central entities, unlike California, production is neither fully integrated with industry, highly specialised, nor specifically geared to export markets.

Structural characteristics, in some cases, also point to why there are differences in behaviour between non-central actors within the same category. One of the reasons determining the nuances between the approach of

Ontario and Quebec on agricultural trade seems to be the differences in the form of production in the two provinces. In Quebec, farm production is highly concentrated in the dairy subsector. More than 40 per cent of Quebec farms are estimated to have some dairy activity, and milk products contribute to about one-third of farm income. This subsector is, in turn, the most inward-looking. By way of contrast, Ontario's agriculture has a greater range in the type of production. If much of this production is geared towards supplying the internal 'home' market, several subsectors, in particular the red meat industries, are export-oriented.[54] The greater complexity engendered to Ontario's trade approach by this agricultural duality is reinforced, furthermore, by the greater diversification found within the province's economy in aggregate terms.

An emphasis on structure alone, nevertheless, does not provide a complete explanation for non-central foreign economic behaviour. Situational factors have also played a part in conditioning this behaviour. In the Californian case, for instance, a new set of circumstances was instrumental in shifting the thrust of Californian behaviour from a passive to a more activist (albeit facilitative) approach. Whereby traditionally California could leave trade almost entirely to the private sector, a number of factors in the early 1980s stimulated a greater appreciation for non-central trade diplomacy. In terms of markets, California faced mounting difficulties attributable to a combination of a soaring American dollar, the impact of recession and the debt crisis, and well-entrenched restrictive practices via NTBs.[55] In terms of production, it faced new forms of aggressive competition from Mexico and elsewhere.

At least some reference to the political context also has to be introduced, in order to gain a more comprehensive understanding of the variations in terms of style as well as substance of non-central behaviour. To give one illustration, the intensity of Alberta's liberal adjustment approach in the 1970s and early 1980s can only be understood against the background of that province's ongoing wrangle with Ottawa not only with regard to agricultural trade but resources policy generally and energy policy more specifically. Not surprisingly, Alberta's push in terms of foreign economic activity reached its height during the controversy over the National Energy Program.

Western Australia's adoption of an illiberal adjustment strategy in the 1980s buttresses this point concerning the salience of the political dimension. To a considerable extent, the statist approach adopted from the period of the Court government onwards was motivated by its aspiration to catch up with the 'eastern' Australian states in terms of economic development. For despite an abundance of mineral and agricultural wealth, Western Australia lacked investment to exploit those resources. At the same time, though, the aggressiveness with which the Court government pursued this approach reflected the deep-set intergovernmental/partisan tensions which existed between the Court and the Whitlam governments. In effect, the Court government's efforts to go a more autonomous route were hardened by its desire to redress perceived grievances *vis-à-vis* the interference of the ALP federal government into state affairs. Although, not entirely analogous to Court's anti-Canberra stance, it is worth mentioning that Burke also had a strong dislike toward federal ALP politics.[56]

What Gourevitch terms the political sociology of political economy[57] is also important for comprehending the staying power of a particular form of foreign economic behaviour. At one end of the spectrum, the defensive approach of actors such as Bavaria and Quebec in agriculture (although, to reiterate, not in other economic areas) is extremely well entrenched. In large part, this staying power is attributable to the strength of the agricultural interest in the two entities. With all the characteristics said to be conducive for allowing success in a campaign of resistance, namely a high degree of motivation, concentration and organisation,[58] the performance of both of these interests has been impressive. In Quebec, the farming community has been mobilised through a central peak body, the Union des Producteurs Agricoles (UPA). Using its size of membership (over 40,000), its relatively strong financial resources (due to a system of compulsory fees from all accredited farmers in Quebec), and its political clout (exercised through demonstrations and personal lobbying), the UPA has campaigned hard to protect the needs of Quebec agriculture.

In terms of tactics, the UPA has kept all its political options open. At the federal level, the UPA has maintained political pressure not only through the large Quebec caucus of the Mulroney government but also through emergent Bloc Quebecois. At the non-central level, the UPA (in keeping with what Grace Skogstad has termed the 'provincial-producer alliance')[59] has continued to cultivate close ties with both the Liberals and the Parti Quebecois. Alternatively, the UPA has consolidated its ties with other groups within Quebec which are opposed to economic liberalism.

It is not only the clout of the agricultural interest but the viewpoint which that interest embodies that is of importance in determining the UPA's import. For, unlike the rest of Canada, it may be argued that an emotive campaign based on the defence of 'a way of life' in Quebec may be effective in resisting the forces of rationalisation. That is to say, the UPA, through its appeal to La Terre de Chez-nous and local self-sufficiency, has been able to wrap that resistance in a nationalist cloak in a fashion unthinkable in Ontario.[60]

The Bavarian situation is similar in many ways. The Bavarian farming community exerts a considerable degree of influence through the central peak agricultural organisation in Germany, the Deutscher Bauernverband (DBV), an influence exerted through a skilful combination of militancy and access to the decision-making process. At the same time, Bavaria benefits from a number of institutional features in German politics. In particular, the system of proportional representation and multi-party representation has allowed Bavarian politicians to monopolise the agricultural portfolio in the federal Cabinet. Josef Ertl, of the Free Democratic Party, served as Agriculture Minister in the Social Democratic-Free Democratic government from 1969 to 1982, and Ignaz Kiechle from the Christian Socialist Union, the Christian Democratic Union's sister party, became Agriculture Minister after 1982.[61]

Again, however, the position of the Bavarian farming community is strengthened by the association of agriculture in that region with a distinctive Catholic/social way of life. It has become a dominant principle in Bavarian politics, under conservative governments, that a 'corporatist' bargain has been struck between state and society that agriculture will be defended in the interests of national well-being. Any erosion of this principle will, it has been consistently argued, undermine the harmony between progress and traditional structures.[62]

At the other end of the spectrum, illiberal adjusters, joiners and mavericks all seem to have had a more difficult time in maintaining continuity in the pattern of their foreign economic behaviour. With respect to the illiberal adjusters, the key destabilising factor is the large amount of risk contained in an ambitious statist approach. As evidenced by the case of Western Australia and WA Inc., a strategy along these lines can founder on charges of grandstanding, misjudgments and scandal.[63]

The source of instability for the joiners was, conversely, based on the impediments to cooperation because of limited resources. Although with a solid rationale because of the cost-sharing aspects of joint activity in terms of trade promotion, suspicions about control and/or free riding have continued to hamper the operation of these exercises among US states. A go-it-alone approach, to many politicians and officials, still seemed a more reliable choice than cooperation. Hard times merely solidified the bias against experimentation.

Finally, its inherent personalism and impulsiveness have imposed serious limits on the staying power of the mavericks' foreign economic behaviour. Because this sort of approach was identified so strongly with an individual politician, when that politician either left office or lost control of the policy agenda, there was inevitably a sharp change in course. The first scenario was played out when Bjelke-Petersen was replaced as the premier of Queensland. The second scenario is represented to a certain extent by the diminution of the powers of the Texas Agriculture Commissioner, largely prompted by the hormone issue.[64]

Another scenario, not contradictory with the above, is that counter-pressures within the non-central entity will modify the maverick behaviour in a fundamental fashion. Signs of this sort of backlash could be found, most clearly, in South Dakota on the Canadian hogs issue. While able to rally a considerable amount of support for a ban in the short term, Governor

Janklow was criticised as time went by for this type of action. The theme of this criticism, as expressed in the media, was that a state such as South Dakota had to accommodate itself to new international challenges, not fight those forces. As one newspaper expressed the sentiment: 'Shutting down the flow of Canadian hogs is a good idea, if it is meant as a publicity move to call attention to this farm problem. As an economic move [however] it's got to be bad news . . . We feel that free trade is the only long-term solution for the economies of the free world and protecting this or that industry is a short-term solution at best.'[65]

Conclusion

The picture one gets from these snapshots is the broad range in terms of form and intensity of the agricultural dimension of the foreign economic behaviour of non-central actors. By trying to analyse this behaviour in terms of a relatively parsimonious typology it is hoped that some order of this behaviour can be determined. In doing so, this work seems to complement other work done on an issue-specific level.[66]

Further work along these lines needs to concentrate in a more detailed fashion on not only the why but the how of foreign economic behaviour. This task can only be attempted through an examination of both the international context and the domestic politics. In effect, then, what is increasingly needed is a series of two-level analyses in which the non-central actor's interaction with the ipe and national politics is highlighted. By this type of exercise it seems possible to capture both the stability or the volatility of non-central foreign economic behaviour. At the same time, the geographical focus of research needs to remain as all-encompassing as possible. Notwithstanding the metaphors of 'cascades',[67] as Katzenstein suggests, 'strategy and statecraft will remain an essential tool for navigating political currents.'[68] A fundamental task of comparative study, at the non-central level, will be to capture the nature and parameters of issue-specific diplomatic behaviour as the pattern of global architecture changes.

Notes

1. See, most notably, Ivo D. Duchacek, *The Territorial Dimension of Politics Within, Among, and Across Nations*, Westview, Boulder, CO (1986).
2. Canada, Senate, Standing Committee on Foreign Affairs, Canada–United States Relations, vol. 2, *Canada's Trade Relations with the United States*, The Queen's Printer, Ottawa (1978) 2.
3. *Report of the Royal Commission on the Economic Union and Development Prospects for Canada*, The Queen's Printer, Ottawa, vol. 2 (1985) 422–35.

4. Earl H. Fry, 'The impact of federalism on the development of international economic relations: lessons from the United States and Canada', *Australian Outlook: The Australian Journal of International Affairs*, 43 (April 1989), 16–35.
5. See James N. Rosenau, *Turbulence in World Politics*, Princeton University Press, Princeton (1990).
6. For an excellent critique of this concept, see James A. Caporaso, 'Interdependence and the coordination of foreign and domestic politics in the Atlantic world', in Wolfram F. Hanrieder (ed.), *Economic Issues and the Atlantic Community*, Praeger, New York (1982).
7. David Baldwin, *Economic Statecraft*, Princeton University Press, Princeton (1985).
8. For examples of competing explanations, see Robert Keohane, *After Hegemony: Cooperation and Discord in the World Political Economy*, Princeton University Press, Princeton (1984); Robert Gilpin, *The Political Economy of International Relations*, Princeton University Press, Princeton (1987); and Robert Cox, *Power, Production and World Order*, Columbia University Press, New York, (1987).
9. See Michael C. Webb and Stephen D. Krasner, 'Hegemonic stability theory: an empirical assessment', *Review of International Studies*, 15 (Spring 1989), 183–98.
10. Richard N. Cooper, 'Economic interdependence and foreign policy in the seventies', *World Politics*, 24 (January 1972), 164.
11. Bayless Manning, 'The congress, the executive and intermestic affairs: three proposals', *Foreign Affairs*, 55 (January 1977) 309. John Kline has thoroughly explored this theme in his book, *State Government Influence in US International Economic Policy*, D.C. Heath, Lexington, MA (1983).
12. Robert L. Dilenscheider, 'The dark side of globalisation', *New York Times* (28 August 1988), F2.
13. Raymond Hopkins and Donald J. Puchala (eds), *The Global Political Economy of Food*, special issue of *International Organization*, 32 (Spring 1978), 581–880.
14. Richard Higgott and Andrew Fenton Cooper, 'Middle power leadership and coalition building: Australia, the Cairns Group, and the Uruguay Round of trade negotiation', *International Organization*, 44 (Autumn 1990), 589–632; and Andrew F. Cooper, 'Likeminded nations and contrasting diplomatic behaviour: Australian and Canadian approaches to agricultural trade', *Canadian Journal of Political Science*, 25 (June 1992).
15. David Lake, *Power, Protection, and Free Trade: International Sources of US Commercial Strategy, 1887–1939*, Cornell University Press, Ithaca (1988).
16. See, for example, Robert Paarlberg, *Fixing Farm Trade: Policy Options for the United States*, Ballinger, Cambridge, MA (1988).
17. For a good review of these general trends, see Cornelia Butler Flora, 'Rural peoples in a global economy', *Rural Sociology*, 55 (1990), 157–77.
18. See, for example, Dale Hathaway, *Agriculture and the GATT: Rewriting the Rules*, Institute for International Economics, Washington, DC (1987), 2.
19. J. Norman Reid, 'Global economy demands new rural strategies', *State Government News* (September 1986), 10.
20. For an earlier study utilising this perspective, see Andrew Fenton Cooper, 'Subnational activity and foreign economic policy making in Canada and the United States: perspectives on agriculture', special issue on foreign policy in federal states, *International Journal*, XLI (Summer 1986), 655–73.
21. Premier Lougheed's views on Alberta's position have been widely cited: 'We

remain directly affected in Alberta and in Canada by decisions that are made in Riyadh, Geneva, Tokyo, Beijing, Hong Kong, London, or you name it.' in Duchacek, *The Territorial Dimension of Politics*, op. cit., 230, and James N. Rosenau, *Turbulence in World Politics*, Princeton University Press, Princeton, NJ (1990), 416. In similar fashion, the Pacific Rim Task Force Report, conducted by the California Economic Development Corporation, emphasised the fact that increased interdependence will present California with new opportunities as well as new challenges. *California and the Pacific Rim: A Policy Agenda*, Sacramento (May, 1986).

22. 'US governors target trade with Europe', *Journal of Commerce* (14 April 1987), 5A.
23. Iowa had also launched innovative programmes such as Iowa Ambassadors Marketing Program, whereby the state commits funds in return for private sector commitments to market and promotes products from the rural areas of the state. See also Ross Talbot (ed.), *Iowa in the World Economy*, Iowa State University Press, Ames, IO (1985).
24. See, for example, the study by Mentor International on the Feasibility of Overseas Offices for the State of California, 1985.
25. See, for example, Elliot J. Feldman and Lily Gardner Feldman, 'The impact of federalism on the organization of Canadian foreign policy', *Publius* (Fall 1984).
26. State Senator Jim Nielsen, International Agricultural Trade: Negotiations in the mid-1980s, Hearings before the Committee on Agriculture, Nutrition, and Food, US Senate, 2 April 1986, Sacramento, CA, 7.
27. Janet Porter, 'California opens European office', *Journal of Commerce* (15 April 1987).
28. Alberta, *Hansard*, 24 April 1978, 815. See also Henry Giniger, 'Alberta ties more gas for US to wider farm sales', *New York Times* (26 November 1977), 27.
29. John Spitier, 'California program helps farmers break into export market', *Christian Science Monitor* (11 September 1986), 6.
30. See, for example, 'Lougheed demands measures to boost grain', *Calgary Herald* (9 May 1978), A3.
31. Gregory H. Feldberg, 'The trend to trade', *Japan Economic Journal* (29 September 1990).
32. Toshiyuki Yahagi, 'Calif. beefs up efforts to export more wine, agricultural products', *Japan Economic Journal* (21 June 1986), 13.
33. Jean-Mari Peltier, *California Agriculture Barriers to Trade*, no.1, Pacific Rim, California State World Trade Commission (30 June 1986).
34. Andrew F. Cooper, 'Roots and directions: functional and geographical aspects of Canadian cultural diplomacy', in the Association for Canadian Studies, *Culture, Development and Regional Policy, Canadian Issues*, IX, Montreal (1988), 17–32.
35. Peter Gourevitch, 'Breaking with orthodoxy: the politics of economic policy responses to the depression of the 1980s', *International Organization*, 38 (Winter 1989), 95–130.
36. Stuart Harris, 'State and federal objectives and policies for the use and development of resources', Peter Drysdale and Hiofumi Shibata (eds), *Federalism and Resource Development: The Australian Case*, George Allen & Unwin (Australia), Sydney (1985), 74. See also Elizabeth J. Harman and Brian W. Head (eds), *State, Capital and Resources in the North and West of Australia*, University of Western Australia Press, Nedlands, WA (1982).

37. A forty-person-strong joint ministerial task force had visited Romania in 1987. 'WA to exploit Hancock trade tie with Romania', *Australian Financial Review* (30 July 1987), 6.
38. Julian Grill, 'Policy innovation as imagination: political origins of the WADC', *The Business of Government: Western Australia, 1983–1990*. The Federation Press, Annadale (1991), 176–7.
39. Tim Duncan, 'Victoria revives the mercantilist era', *Business Review Weekly* (1 May 1987), 37–8.
40. Lothar Spath, 'Europe's nation states are obsolete', *European Affairs*, 3 (1990), 9.
41. See, for example, Peter K. Eisinger and William Gormley, *The Midwest Response to the New Federalism*, University of Wisconsin Press, Madison (1988), 37.
42. See, for example, 'The second war between the states', *Business Week* (17 May 1976); James Barron, 'Economic development can be a contact sport', *New York Times* (22 June 1986), 5.
43. For an interesting review of these trends, see Kirk Johnson, 'State lines eroding under trade pressure', *Globe & Mail* (29 December 1990), B4.
44. Terry Branstad, 'Farm states must unite to preserve rural America', *State Government News* (September 1986), 4–5.
45. Cited in Brian Hocking, 'Pluralism and foreign policy: the states and the management of Australia's external relations', *Yearbook of World Affairs* (1984), vol. 38, Stevens & Sons, London, under the auspices of the London Institute of World Affairs, 1.
46. Texas populist isn't cowed by Washington', *Financial Post* (Toronto) (9 February 1989), 8; *Inside US Trade* (10 February 1989), 9.
47. On this general point, see Stanley Hoffmann, *Janus and Minerva: Essays in the Theory and Practice of International Politics*, Westview Press, Boulder (1987), 272.
48. On this point, see Kim Richard Nossal, 'The limits of influence: the impact of non-central governments and Canadian foreign policy', paper presented to a seminar on 'The Role of the States and Provinces in the International Economy', University of California, Berkeley, 9–10 November 1990.
49. On this general point, see Gilpin, *The Political Economy of International Relations*, op. cit., 47.
50. See, for example, Jeffrey Simpson, 'Milking the system', *Globe & Mail Report on Business* (November 1990), 110–18.
51. See, for example, Don MacPerson, 'Farmers may yet plow under free trade', *Montreal Gazette* (5 December 1987), B3.
52. Gourevitch, 'Breaking with orthodoxy', op. cit., 99.
53. See Douglas Henton and Steven A.Waldhorn, 'California', and especially chapter 12 'The megastate economy', in R.Scott Fosler (ed), *The New Economic Role of American States: Strategies in a Competitive World Economy*, Oxford University Press, New York (1988).
54. See, for example, Grace Skogstad, 'The farm policy community and public policy in Ontario and Quebec', in William Coleman and Grace Skogstad (eds), *Policy Communities and Public Policy: A Structural Approach*, Copp Clark Pitman, Toronto (1990), 59–90.
55. For a good overview, see *The Other Deficit: A Review of International Trade in California and the US*, prepared by John Griffing, Senate Office of Research (November 1984).

56. See Ronald T.Libby, *Hawke's Law: The Politics of Mining and Aboriginal Land Rights in Australia*, University of Western Australia Press, Nedlands, WA (1989), 2–4.

57. Gourevitch, 'Breaking with orthodoxy', op.cit., 97.

58. Henry R. Nau, 'Domestic trade politics and the Uruguay round: an overview', in Henry R. Nau (ed.), *Domestic Trade Politics and the Uruguay Round*, Columbia University Press, New York (1989).

59. Grace Skogstad, 'Canada: conflicting domestic interests in the MTN', in Grace Skogstad and Andrew Fenton Cooper (eds), *Agricultural Trade: Domestic Pressure and International Tensions*, Institute for Research on Public Policy, Halifax (1990), 48.

60. This nationalist sentiment comes out most strongly in the UPA's submission to the Commission Sur L'Avenir Constitutionnel Du Quebec, 'Elements d'analyse sur les relations actuelles' (November 1990).

61. See, for example, Gisela Hendriks, 'The politics of food: the case of FR Germany', *Food Policy* (February 1987).

62. See, for example, Carole Carl-Sime, 'Bavaria, the CSU and the West German party system', *West European Politics*, 2 (January 1979), 89–107.

63. See Ronald Conway, 'The rise and decline of '80s man', *The Bulletin* (21 May 1991).

64. Robert Suro, 'Texas tory democrats go the way of the armadillo', *New York Times* (1989).

65. *Madison Daily Leader* (16 May 1985).

66. Perhaps the best of these is the work of Peter K.Eisinger, *The Rise of the Entrepreneurial State*, University of Wisconsin Press, Madison (1988).

67. Rosenau, *Turbulence in World Politics*, op.cit.

68. Peter J.Katzenstein, 'International relations theory and the analysis of change', in E.-O.Czempiel and James N.Rosenau (eds) *Global Changes and Theoretical Challenges*, D.C. Heath, Lexington, MA (1989), 301.

4 Managing foreign relations in federal states: linking central and non-central international interests

Brian Hocking

Discussions of the growing international interests and activities of non-central governments (NCGs) in federal systems have tended to underscore their actual or potential role as autonomous international actors and the consequent friction that can develop between them and their central governments. Less attention has been paid to possible modes of bureaucratic adaptation whereby the differing power-centres in federal states seek to develop structures and processes which help to contain, if not resolve, possible tensions resulting from apparent infringements of the centre's constitutional right to act as the conduit through which contacts with the international environment are conducted. The aim of this chapter is to suggest that in the management of foreign relations an increasingly complex 'multilayered diplomacy', embracing actors and interests at both domestic and international levels, places a premium on the creation of forms of consultation and cooperation with domestic constituencies which, at once, desire increasingly to gain access to the international system and are the focus of attention from a range of international actors.

Our point of departure is the recognition that the character of multi-layered diplomatic interactions creates mutual needs between levels of political authority within national communities imposed by the changing agenda of international politics and the enhanced points of interface between those communities and the international system. These needs are not, of course, identical. As one Australian state premier has argued, it is quite possible to acknowledge the federal government's primacy in the conduct of foreign policy whilst, at the same time, recognising that 'the states have a legitimate role in the prosecution of their own interests abroad (that is, of their constituent communities and corporations) as well as supporting the national interest.'[1] From this it follows that the tasks confronting the levels of government within national communities will differ—principally in terms of the scope of their concerns. Whereas central governments are required to develop policies reflecting the diversity of interests within a broad agenda, non-central governments' interests will usually be determined by a narrower range of domestic constituencies with more finely targeted objectives.

The need for linkages

Nevertheless, the achievement of their respective aims within a policy environment marked by a growing confluence of international and domestic pressures requires the establishment of linkage mechanisms capable of providing for each level of government access to resources over which the other has a relative, if not absolute, advantage. In other words, whilst conflictual relations between national and subnational governments are by no means absent, they are but one point on a spectrum of relationships equally characterised by the need for cooperation.

One area in which this reciprocal need is evident is that of bureaucratic expertise. In specific functional areas with a growing international dimension such as education, human rights and the environmental agenda, key repositories of policy-making skills essential to the conduct of diplomacy, both in terms of policy formulation and implementation, reside at the level of subnational government. In part, this is the reason that NCG specialists are included in international delegations relating to issues within their areas of competence. At the same time, policy-making structures at the centre will be able to command resources which lower levels of government will find it difficult to match. Clearly, this is particularly true of the smaller, less wealthy constituent elements of a federation, but even those capable of devoting considerable resources to the pursuit of their international interests will often require access to skills and information that only the centre can provide. To take but one example, the National Governors' Association in the United States, along with individual states including California, have consistently pressed the US Department of Commerce to produce more accurate and comprehensive international trade statistics for the states.[2]

Most obviously, of course, in spite of the growth of their overseas offices, NCGs lack the international information and communications networks that diplomatic services afford national policy-makers. This mutuality of interest in maintaining good and effective working relationships has been stressed by the Director General of the United States and Foreign Commercial Service in a discussion of a recent US&FCS strategic review. On the one hand, she argues, by 'working together with the "wholesalers" or "multipliers" of our information and services, we increase our export development outreach to regions and companies that might not know about or have ready access to US&FC's valuable information.' On the other, local 'partners' in the export development drive

are a supplement to US&FCS services, not a replacement. Our partners' programs and support vary from region to region. Their funding is inconsistent from year to year. They cannot enjoy the economies of scale necessary to collect and disseminate worldwide market information on a timely and regular basis.[3]

A second motivation for the creation of linkage mechanisms lies in the demands that multilayered diplomacy places on access to the different levels of political activity. One of the crucial dimensions of modern diplomacy lies in the interaction between interests located in a number of arenas, successful outcomes depending on the establishment of adequate communications. Moreover, this is likely to be necessary for the duration of negotiations, not simply the initial or concluding phases. Instances such as the Canada–US free trade negotiations have demonstrated how significant the role of NCGs can be as transmitters of information between localities and the centre where complex trade diplomacy is involved.

Thus the advantage that local bureaucracies can offer to central foreign policy managers is the former's access to local interests. On the other hand, national governments can offer NCGs access to the international system and its networks in pursuit of their regional interests. This is not to say that non-central governments are entirely dependent on central government for their overseas activities; international offices are often set up without formal permission from the centre. However, the successful operation of these and other international activities rest most frequently on the cooperation of the federal government and its agencies. Furthermore, international legal norms, the operating principles of international organisations and the attitudes of foreign governments, which may see little advantage and some dangers in dealing with a proliferation of subnational entities, all present obstacles to NCGs wishing to develop their international presence. Instances of foreign governments actively courting NCGs in the face of opposition from the federal authorities appear to be rare. Moreover, it cannot be assumed that such action would be welcomed by an NCG. As Balthazar suggests in his chapter, such attention as Quebec received from de Gaulle in the 1960s was not met with unqualified enthusiasm by the provincial government.

The creation of cooperative mechanisms between levels of government is also prompted by the opportunities that the existence of differing levels of political authority offers for the diversion of pressures that flow from the international part of their overall diplomatic strategies. Sensitive political issues may be redefined in lower-level, quasi-administrative terms by engaging the services of subnational agencies. Not only will this tend to reduce external pressures on central government, but it will also lessen the strains that the conduct of ever more complex policy processes impose on national administrations. Looked at from the perspective of non-central governments, developing close working relationships with central government can be valuable in dealing with growing international forces. Here it has to be recognised that developing an international profile is not a cost-free activity, as the Australian states have discovered in their dealings with Japan, and the Canadian provinces from their proximity to the United States. Where the attentions of international actors become burdensome, then the constituent governments in a federal system may well find it to their advantage to seek the support of the centre, thereby creating a coalition against external pressures.

The coordination problem

This mutuality of interest between central and subnational policy-makers, which balances conflicts of interest arising in specific policy sectors, creates at both levels the need for modes of cooperation and communication. This is, of course, one dimension of the frequently debated problem of coordination in the foreign policy processes resulting from their growing bureaucratisation.[4] The negative consequences of this trend are seen as growing incoherence in policy as a result of increasing diffusion of information amongst government departments and agencies, the danger of a reduced capacity to respond rapidly to changing events, and the greater opportunities provided for external actors to further their objectives by building alliances with actors in other bureaucratic structures. In turn, these developments reduce the capabilities of governments in their operations within their international environments.

The patterns of intergovernmental relations characteristic of federal systems create an additional dimension to these problems. Usually, foreign policy coordination is seen as an issue for central governmental management, depicted by Underdal, for example, in terms of 'vertical disintegration' as the number of departments in the national bureaucracy possessing external policy interests increases.[5] Here, the role of the foreign ministry, and its capacity to act as a coordinating agency in an increasingly fragmented bureaucratic environment—as we shall see later—is crucial to the debate. In reality, it is more useful to view this in terms of a process of 'horizontal' fragmentation between departments at one level of bureaucratic organisation, reserving the term 'vertical disintegration' to refer to the possible consequences of the involvement of subnational levels of bureaucracy in the multilayered diplomatic processes.

In this situation, fragmentation produced by bureaucratic specialisation is likely to be reinforced by locally based domestic interests which are clients of NCG bureaucratic structures. The danger is that policies intended to achieve quite general external policy goals can become redefined, not simply in terms of the perspectives and concerns brought to them by domestic agencies of central government, but also through the emergence of regionally based bureaucratic politics.

As the interaction between domestic and international diplomacy has become more pronounced, and as regional and local authorities' international interests have grown, so have the problems associated with coordination. Matching the complexity of multilayered diplomacy, the coordination of policy on which it rests extends across the totality of political systems and is no longer simply an issue concerning the relative status of foreign ministries and domestic departments at the level of central government.

Moreover, given the mutuality of interests noted above, each level of government has a vested interest in ensuring, to the extent that it can, that the necessary work of coordination is carried out at other levels. In other words, the coordination issue is present both across levels of political authority and within each of those levels. In examining the bureaucratic structures which Ontario has developed to manage its international interests, Dyment points to the range of coordinating tasks that confront NCGs, paralleling—and no less burdensome than—those present at the national level:

— coordination between provincial ministries and agencies;
— coordination of local government international activities;
— liaison with other provincial governments;
— coordination with the federal authorities.[6]

In one sense, then, the coordination problem, long regarded as an issue for national policy-makers, has expanded as the international involvement of subnational agencies and interests has grown. Coordination of external policy becomes increasingly essential, yet harder to achieve as policy-makers seek to (a) balance domestic and international factors impinging on a decision; (b) link issues which may cut across the responsibilities of several horizontal and vertical layers of bureaucracy; (c) weigh the respective priorities of bilateral relationships and those imposed by membership of international organisations; and (d) relate short-term aims to long-term goals.

To a degree, a distinction can be made here in terms of *sectoral* coordination, where the focus is on relatively discrete policy issues, as contrasted with the much broader goal of *strategic* coordination, where the aim is to interrelate the demands which flow from specific policy sectors within the overall fabric of external policy. Whereas it would be convenient to argue that these two areas remain separate, both in the sense that they involve distinct tasks and that one is the peculiar problem of a particular level of government, it would also be misleading.

Firstly, sectoral policy issues can rapidly assume the proportions of a strategic coordination problem for the reasons cited earlier, namely as a result of pressures exerted by domestic constituencies combined with inter-bureaucratic conflicts. Secondly, both central and non-central governments confront each type of problem, but to different degrees since the tasks of strategic coordination presented to national policy-makers are likely to be broader in scope and more intense reflecting the extent of their responsibilities for the general management of external relations.

Linkage mechanisms

Given this situation, it is not surprising that federal systems are witnessing the emergence of a variety of 'linkage mechanisms' intended to overcome these policy-fragmentation problems. Despite the mutual interests that have led to the creation of such mechanisms, it should be stressed that the objectives of each level of government in participating in them are likely to be different. They may well be regarded primarily by foreign ministries as a means of containing subnational international activity, whereas NCGs will be inclined to see them as a route to an enhanced role and influence. As a result, the character and operation of the linkage mechanisms themselves can become a source of contention between the levels of government. Taking one example to which we shall return later, namely the inclusion of NCG representatives in international delegations, it is often the case that the terms and objectives of such a practice are the subject of dispute. For the centre, a major goal is to ensure the acquiescence of affected domestic constituencies in any international agreement by establishing immediate channels of contact with their representatives.

Non-central governments, however, may have as their key objective the shaping of policy outcomes and, consequently, may be dissatisfied with anything which smacks of tokenism on the part of the national authorities. One senior Californian trade policy official identified the differing perspectives of the US federal government and the states in the following terms:

We are involved in a push-pull relationship with Washington in the trade area. The federal authorities are anxious to see the states increasingly involved in trade promotion but not in the trade policy area.[7]

Wilkinson makes a similar point in his discussion of Alberta's trade policy interests in this volume.

Sectoral policy linkages

As one would expect, federal systems utilise the network of consultative and cooperative mechanisms created for the management of domestic policy when dealing with issues of external relations crossing the boundaries of central and regional responsibility. Because subnational international interests normally register a narrower focus than those of the national government, this has been a logical and economical method of dealing with problems resulting from the internationalisation of areas of public policy traditionally regarded as domestic. When dealing with such matters, linkages between centre and region have assumed two forms: consultation prior to and during international negotiations and, second, participation by NCG representatives in the negotiations themselves.

Consultation between the levels of bureaucracy in federal states on international issues is well established, dictated, for example, by the need to ensure regional cooperation in the implementation of International Labour Organisation (ILO) conventions. Here, Australia has developed a three-level machinery of federal–state consultation through which the impact of ILO conventions on labour practices and legislation can be considered, involving meetings of departmental officials, permanent heads, and an annual conference of ministers. The essential task of evaluating the impact of ILO conventions on state practices and the possibilities of adjusting state legislation to allow the ratification of conventions falls to the specialist officers from Canberra and the state departments of labour who, apart from formal twice-yearly meetings to monitor both proposed and existing conventions, maintain continuous contact with each other. Similar consultative practices are to be found in a variety of issue areas which have acquired international significance. One of the most sensitive areas, demanding intensive consultations, has been that of human rights. Since the human rights agenda affects many areas of regional competence, it was inevitable that the Australian states should exhibit a great interest in the processes surrounding the ratification of the International Covenant on Civil and Political Rights. Two years of intensive domestic negotiations preceded the final ratification of the ICCPR, negotiations largely conducted through the consultative networks which have developed between federal and state legal officers.

Similar processes of federal–state/provincial consultations have adapted to the internationalisation of the policy agenda, as Boardman has noted in the case of environmental policy in Australia and Canada.[8] In both cases, subnational governments have established a role for themselves in the framing of international environmental policy issues despite the tensions that have developed on occasions between the two levels of government.

In the Australian case, during the 1970s a federal–state consultative framework evolved, reflected in the establishment of the Australian

Environment Council (AEC) and the Council of Nature Conservation Ministers (CONCOM). Such mechanisms have acted as focuses for both cooperation and conflict between Canberra and the states as the dramas of federal–state politics came to embrace environmental issues. On the one hand, Canberra was able to take advantage of the international dimensions of environmental policy to expand its powers through creative use of the external affairs power granted to it by the constitution, whilst at the same time recognising the need for state cooperation if it was to participate in the development of environmental regimes. Boardman has clearly illuminated the interactions between subnational, national and international levels of political activity that have developed over the last two decades:

State governments varied in the degree of interest they showed in international institutions. Even if they lacked appreciation of how such developments might be relevant to their concerns, however, the federal–state machinery centring on the AEC and CONCOM allowed them access to Australian decision-making in these areas. Some of the more important international programmes to which the Australian government was committed, moreover, required for their effective working some form of active contribution by the states. The MAB [Man and the Biosphere] Programme, for example, had among its objectives the creation of a global network of protected biosphere reserves; Australia could be an active participant in this work only if state authorities were drawn into the process.[9]

The emphasis on an enhanced cooperative relationship between central and subnational governments associated with the assertion of 'new federalism' in various federal systems during the 1970s and 1980s was reflected in the management of external policy. Thus, in the United States, the creation of Intergovernmental Affairs sections (IGAs) in federal departments reflected at once the desire of state governments to gain better access to executive agencies at the centre as well as the avowed ambition of the Reagan administration to devolve power within the political system. The degree to which this arrangement touches on the management of external policy depended, obviously, on the functions of a particular department. In the case of the Department of Commerce, the IGA had, by 1989, come to assume a central role, reflecting the desire to establish a closer cooperative framework in the trade promotion area.[10] The aim of IGA programmes such as the Department of Commerce State Initiative, as described to the author, is to coordinate activities at the respective levels of operation: 'to get the right state people and DOC people together.'[11] Apart from working with the states to coordinate export-assistance programmes, the IGA acts as an information point, monitoring the activities of state organisations such as the National Governors' Association and the Southern Governors' Association. Within the Department, this information is disseminated to various sections through a series of monthly briefings: 'the aim is to let people know what is going on in the states'.[12]

As the policy agenda spanning the domestic–international divide has expanded, so the impetus to establish more regularised procedures for consultation between levels of government has developed. Characteristically, this is manifested in treaty-consultation procedures of which those in Germany are amongst the most well established.[13] As Leonardy's essay later in this book demonstrates, under the Lindau Convention the respective roles of the federal government and the *Länder* have been established depending on the degree to which policy issues fall under *Land* jurisdiction.

In Australia, under the aegis of the 'new federalism' pursued by the Fraser governments of 1975–83, a regularised system of treaty consultation monitored by the Department of Prime Minister and Cabinet in Canberra was developed from discussions held during the 1976 and 1977 Premiers' Conferences. This enhanced mode of communication between Canberra and the states was prompted by both ideological and practical considerations, and symbolised a departure from the confrontationist policy of the Whitlam years which threatened to use the external affairs power vested in the federal government to gain access to policy areas under state control. Several considerations, however, were to ensure that whilst a useful opportunity to involve the states in one dimension of Australia's external relations had been created, at the same time the prospect of intra-bureaucratic tensions had been enhanced.

In part, these tensions reflected the strains that such consultative processes impose on small bureaucratic machines. The smaller states, such as Tasmania, are ill equipped to produce responses to proposals from Canberra which involve consultation with a number of state public service departments. Moreover, since the interests of specific states in issues relating to international agreements vary widely, the incentive to devote time to such an activity can frequently be limited. These factors have produced some disillusionment at both federal and state levels. Indeed, one official in the federal Attorney-General's Department questioned the capacity of state officials to engage in consultative processes:

The States aren't really geared up for the process . . . Much of the material is above the heads of their officials. We might seek information or opinions and ask for responses within two weeks but often they never arrive. When they do, the response is usually to ask for the insertion of a federal reservation.[14]

An equally frustrated legal officer in Queensland pointed out that since the states had never hitherto been encouraged to express opinions in this area, they lacked the necessary expertise in international law and were having to undergo a rapid process of self-education. Some of these tensions seem to be due to the fact that the process focuses on legal officials at both levels of government. In the view of one former federal public servant, there was 'no meeting of minds' between the state and federal law officers. Each issue was redefined as one of constitutional principle by the state lawyer so that, whilst reasonable discussion might be conducted with officials from state functional departments, nothing but the 'most rabid opposition' was forthcoming from those state officials actually operating the consultative processes.

Despite the election of the Hawke Labor government, committed to an active use of the external affairs power afforded Canberra by the constitution, treaty consultation procedures have survived and developed.[15]

However, the suggestion (emerging from the Constitutional Convention in the mid-1980s) that Australia adopt a Treaties Council along the lines of the German system received little support. The need for a greater degree of cooperation and coordination was nevertheless recognised at the Special Premiers' Conference convened in 1991 to consider the future of the federal system. Apart from reviewing the consultation machinery, it was agreed that a standing committee of senior officers be created 'to provide more timely and coordinated assistance to the Commonwealth on the negotiation and implementation of international treaties.'[16]

The nature of linkage mechanisms

The precise character and extent of policy linkage mechanisms will depend on a number of factors, such as the interest expressed by NCGs and the attitudes of particular federal government departments. Taking the first point, the problem for national policy managers becomes not so much one of unwelcome interference by subnational governments and the constituencies they represent, but of encouraging an informed interest and involvement in areas of external policy. For one member of the Office of the United States Trade Representative (USTR), this was a major constraint in formulating a US position within the context of the Canada–US free trade and Uruguay Round negotiations.

The states' interest in trade policy is very patchy and depends very much on resources at the local bureaucratic level. It also varies with the character of the issue. The states quickly grasped the issues that affected them in the case of the free trade negotiations; but it is much more difficult to get them involved in the intricacies of the Single European Market or the MTN. We now need the states' cooperation and advice in the context of the GATT talks, on such questions as services and intellectual property rights. USTR has spent two years getting countries to talk about these issues; at the same time we have been trying to bring the states in. In part, our role has become one of educating the states as to the significance of these issues for them.[17]

Differences deriving from styles of federal culture and attitudes of the federal bureaucracy can be seen in the ways in which Australia and Canada have responded to the need for federal–state/provincial consultation in the trade policy area.

In Canada, recognition of the growing provincial concern with trade policy issues during the GATT Tokyo Round, combined with active lobbying by the provinces themselves, led to the creation of the Canadian Trade and Tariffs Committee (CTTC) as a means of developing communications between the federal government on the one hand, and industry and the provinces on the other.[18] In the field of federal–provincial consultation, the CTTC (intended to serve as a conduit for the transmission of information) conducted negotiations with the provinces on non-tariff barrier issues such as government procurement and subsidies, and received briefs from them on provincial attitudes. Demands by the provinces for a greater input into the negotiations was to result later in the creation of an *ad hoc* federal provincial deputy ministers committee.[19] These processes were greatly expanded in the context of the Canada–US free trade negotiations.

The fact that similar, regularised mechanisms for trade policy discussions have not developed in Australia, where consultation has hitherto occurred on a much more spasmodic basis, reflects in part the tendency for domestic economic interests to intercede directly with Canberra rather than to use the states as intermediaries when seeking to influence the formulation of foreign economic policy. Additionally, the lack of consultation reflects attitudes on the part of both state and federal officials. One federal trade official recalled touring the states to discuss standards codes and government purchasing policies, a venture which he found was not always welcomed by state officials.[20]

Hence it was impossible for an officer in the British Columbia public service to discover the nature of the Australian states' position on non-tariff barrier issues during the Tokyo Round because there were no regularised consultative mechanisms at the centre through which such information might be obtained.[21] Rather, the Australian pattern assumed the form of irregular contacts on specific issues carried out between Canberra and individual states on a bilateral rather than multilateral basis.[22]

A lack of federal–state consultation was apparent to New Zealand diplomats involved in the negotiations with Australia on Closer Economic Relations. At the suggestion of the federal government, the New Zealand trade minister toured the states to discuss government purchasing policies:

We received a reasonably good reception but this was because the States hadn't really thought about the issues involved and we left our proposals regarding government purchasing on the table . . . the replies that eventually emerged from the States were strange, linking all kinds of extraneous issues to the government purchasing issue.[23]

The fact that state reaction to CER issues was not very informed and therefore not very helpful was seen by New Zealand negotiators as symptomatic of the style of Australian diplomacy when confronted with the need to engage in consultation with domestic constituencies:

The New Zealand consensus style of politics involves taking domestic interests into the government's confidence and keeping them informed. But the nature of Australian diplomacy appears to avoid this; in fact one has the impression that there is a contempt for industry in the Department of Trade and that Australian ministers don't want to know what the opinions of industry are.[24]

However, by the early 1990s, stimulated by Australia's declining share of international trade, there were signs that the need for developing linkages was being recognised. In November 1991, the then Minister for Trade and Overseas Development, Dr Blewett, struck a very different note from that which had traditionally characterised federal–state relations in the trade area by launching his national trade strategy.[25] The clear intention here is to bring together industry, the states and the federal government within Australia by, for example, cooperating to set up export centres to provide advice for business, and by establishing an annual trade and investment forum for reviewing trade strategy. Overseas, the stated aim is to rationalise federal and state trade promotion activities under the lead of the federal Trade Commission, Austrade.[26]

Access to negotiations

In the Canadian case, the demand for a greater provincial voice in the shaping of trade policy has, almost inevitably, led to claims for involvement in the negotiating process itself. This has produced pressures for the second kind of sectoral policy linkage, that of participation in international delegations. It is here that the greatest tension between federal and subnational authorities has developed. At one level, demands by NCGs for access to international negotiations may be seen by the centre as a potential threat to the coherence of the national negotiating position and offer negotiating partners the opportunity to exploit domestic differences. At another, bureaucratic level, access for state officials to international forums is likely to be resented by federal public servants who may regard such activity as their own exclusive preserve.

For both reasons, Canadian and Australian federal politicians and public servants have resisted pressures from the regions to include their representatives in negotiating teams. In the case of the Tokyo Round during the 1970s, the Canadian provinces pressed for representation on the negotiating team in Geneva but this was opposed at both the political and bureaucratic levels:

Federal ministers saw this as a breach of the federal government's constitutional responsibilities, while civil servants emphasised that adding provincial representatives to the small negotiating team (five or six persons) would make the team unworkable and would further introduce a partisan note that would detract from the team's ability to serve the best advantage for Canada as a whole.[27]

Similarly, despite considerable pressure, particularly from the larger provinces, for representation in the Canada–US free trade negotiations, Ottawa refused to concede and by June 1986, shortly after the start of the negotiating sessions, it appeared to be accepted that provincial representatives would not be included in the negotiating team.[28] Nevertheless, in trade negotiations with a narrower focus in which specific provincial interests are involved, then both domestic and international imperatives have suggested the wisdom of a provincial presence at the negotiations themselves. During the Atlantic fisheries negotiations in the mid-1970s, provincial representatives were present at certain points in the negotiations.[29] Again, during the dispute between the European Community and Canada over provincial liquor pricing policies (which had been referred by Brussels to a GATT panel), eight provinces were represented in the negotiating team sent during 1988 in an attempt to resolve the problem.

In this case, provincial representatives attended the initial and closing plenary sessions and were fully briefed as the negotiations proceeded: they were not, however, involved in actual negotiating sessions. According to one Department of External Affairs official, a provincial presence was dictated both by constitutional considerations (the need to obtain provincial cooperation in any agreement concluded) and for strategic reasons: demonstrating to the EC the domestic political difficulties confronting Ottawa, and to the provinces, the international implications of the issue. Consequently, this dual negotiating role created a situation where 'the federal government had to act as a quarterback'.[30]

In the Australian case, as suggested above, there appears to be no tradition of state participation in negotiations on trade policy issues. In the words of one official of the federal Department of Trade regarding the CER negotiations: 'no state observers were involved; there is no tradition of this in trade negotiations which are, firmly, a function of the Commonwealth. However, we provided them [the states] with background information and asked for reactions.'

In other areas, however, state representatives have been included in Australian delegations, So, for example, in the case of UNCLOS, a state representative was included in Australian delegations from 1979. Federal public servants, whilst admitting the value of the expertise that some state officials have provided, see this largely in terms of political expediency, 'to sell the Law of the Sea to the States' or (in the words of a DFA legal specialist) 'to provide an educative process for the States and to make them aware of international realities and the effective limitations on our actions.'

Needless to say, the perspective offered by state officials is somewhat different. One state representative present at several UNCLOS sessions maintained that state representation had made a definite impact on the evolution of Australian policy in this area, 'because state expertise problems have been identified that the Commonwealth Government did not even see.' As new issues have been added to the environmental agenda, so the need for state involvement has been recognised in the composition of Australian delegations. State representatives were included in the delegations to the 1989 World Conference on Preparing for Climate Change[31] and the 1991 third preparatory meeting of the United Nations Conference on Environment and Development, in which an official of the South Australian Department of Environment and Planning acted as an adviser.[32]

The existence of expertise at the regional level is, however, unlikely to provide a sufficient condition for the involvement of the regions in international negotiations. Indeed, as already noted, possession of specialist skills may in itself engender resentment and escalate tensions between the two levels of bureaucracy, as in the management of Australian international fisheries negotiations. One state fisheries officer, suggesting that the federal Department of Primary Industry (DPI) had been forced to create consultative mechanisms with the states because of its own lack of practical experience in the fisheries area, noted the limitations on participation imposed by the DPI where international negotiations are involved:

We [the states] are able to influence fisheries negotiations where we are consulted, but the Commonwealth is coy about informing the states and try to control the channels of information. The DPI has taken the view that international issues are its preserve and this reflects the belief of federal bureaucratic empire-builders who believe that they are the only repository of skills.[33]

Not surprisingly, the view from the DPI is somewhat different:

The problem is that the states don't think in terms of the national interest. They are close to the fishermen, they have a constituency and we don't. But this means that their position reflects purely local interests. They are also trying to maximise their control of fisheries by whatever means available. For both reasons, the states will come into conflict with the DPI.[34]

Personnel exchanges

A mode of policy linkage with both an internal and external dimension is that of personnel exchanges between central and subnational governmental departments. Obviously, this can be valuable to both levels of government as a means of acquiring information and expertise together with access to the policy-making processes. One factor seen as underpinning California's influence in the trade policy area has been the use of former federal officials with experience in the area. Thus its Washington-based trade policy adviser in the late 1980s and early 1990s had served with the USTR, a factor which was regarded as valuable by both state and federal trade policy officials.[35]

This practice has extended to exchanges between foreign ministries and NCG departments. In addition to the usual familiarisation programmes intended to provide serving officers of these departments with a knowledge of the domestic constituencies which external policy is intended to serve, it has become quite common to find either former members of the respective foreign ministries serving in state/provincial bureaucracies, often in premiers' departments, or foreign affairs officers on secondment to particular departments.

In Canada, this practice seems to have become far more institutionalised than in Australia. Ontario, for example, developed a series of exchanges with the Department of External Affairs in the 1980s. In 1988, a DEA officer from the trade policy branch on secondment to the International Relations Division of the Ministry of Intergovernmental Affairs had been assigned the task of working on mechanisms for better provincial involvement in the Uruguay Round of GATT negotiations, following the experience of the Canada–US free trade negotiations.[36] Meanwhile, an Ontario official was attached to the DEA working on GATT issues. On the external linkage front, the practice of seconding provincial officials to Canadian embassies has grown in recent years, as has discussion of attaching 'provincial affairs' officers to embassies, either as replacements for, or supplements to, provincial overseas offices.

Strategic policy coordination

As suggested earlier, the task of coordinating the overall thrust of external relations will be far greater than those involved in specific policy sectors. In part, as we have seen, this is because it demands the balancing of interests between a number of those sectors each of which may have implications for a particular bilateral or multilateral set of relationships; and partly because the scope for domestic political and bureaucratic tensions is vastly increased. Immediately, it poses the vexed issue of who, in modern, complex bureaucratic structures can, and should, act as gatekeeper between the domestic and international political environments and, of course, the continuing claims of foreign ministries to perform this role. The quest for coordination can thus easily become—and be perceived within the torrid milieu of bureaucratic politics—a weapon in the interdepartmental power struggle. Karvonen and Sundelius's study of foreign policy management in Sweden and Finland has illustrated the strategies which foreign ministries can pursue in their attempts to reinforce their central role in the conduct of external policy against the claims of bureaucratic actors.[37] These include, for example, the use of planning meetings, chaired by foreign ministry representatives, for the heads of international sections of domestic ministries and the placement of foreign service officers in key positions in domestic agencies.

One form of response to the particular issues posed by growing international activity on the part of subnational authorities is to create units in the foreign ministry specifically charged with the task of developing linkages between the levels of political authority. Here, it is appropriate to restate the point that this is not a problem for federal states alone. In the case of France, for example, Mény has noted the growing international interests of regions and local government which 'contradicts the central and exclusive function of the Ministry of External Relations, already deeply affected by the intervention of specialized ministries in the international sphere.'[38] This concern led, in 1983, to the appointment of a 'delegate', directly responsible to the Secretary-general of the Ministry, charged with the task of ensuring that 'the initiatives of the communes, departments and regions respect the rules of the constitution and the law and do not interfere unfavourably with the foreign policy of France.'[39]

But, of course, the more marked this tendency, the more developed is likely to be the response on the part of a foreign ministry. Taking Belgium as another example, Lejeune has described in some detail the mechanisms of coordination established and intended by the Ministry of External Relations to 'protect its traditional powers and to provide pragmatic responses to the requests of communities and regions.'[40] Amongst these processes of 'concertation' are the Ministerial Coordinating Committee External Relations/Communities/Regions attended by the Minister of Foreign Affairs and his opposite numbers in the communities and regions, and a section within the Ministry of External Relations to oversee relationships between the latter and the ministry. In the case of the well-established federal systems, the Canadian Department of External Affairs appears to have devoted considerable effort to establishing a strategic coordination mechanism in the shape of the Federal Provincial Coordination Division (FPCD).

The role and operation of the FPCD

Created in 1967, partly as a response to the increasing challenge from Quebec, but also with an eye on the growing interests of the provinces in foreign economic policy, the FPCD took over the role of liaising with the provinces from the legal division of the DEA—an indicator of the dominant perspective adopted towards provincial involvement in external policy questions by Ottawa. Its purpose was to act as a channel of communication between Ottawa and the provinces, a transmitter of information from the DEA to provincial capitals, to monitor provincial activities and to serve as advocate of regional interests within the foreign policy processes. One diplomat beginning his tour of duty within the Division in the mid-1980s described his role in the following terms:

I could be regarded as a 'Mr. Fixit', a troubleshooter. We are trying to keep the door open both ways here. There are legitimate provincial interests in external policy and our job is to see that they are heard. It is also our function to give the Provinces the information they require. At the same time we are here to see that the national interest is preserved. For example, when we are asked to provide assistance for provincial ministers travelling overseas, we always want to know why they are going and who they are going to see.[41]

This two-way focus was reflected in the way that a desk officer with responsibility for relations with Quebec perceived his role: 'my job is to check that the federal interest is respected in Quebec and that Quebec's interests are respected in Ottawa.' The growing awareness of the potential impact of provincial activities touching on Canada's external relations underscored the significance of the Division's operations and by 1984 it had expanded to nine officers under a director who was a senior diplomat. Perhaps not surprisingly, attitudes towards the FPCD's work varied.

Certainly, the common perception within the Division was that its role was, at this period, understood and respected. One indicator of this was the fact that it had no problems in attracting experienced officers. Nevertheless, desk officers who had established close working relationships with counterparts in provincial departments, it was recognised, could resent attempts to insert an additional layer of responsibility in the system.

Similarly, attitudes varied at the provincial level. The most positive attitudes came from those responsible for international affairs in ministries of intergovernmental relations. Indeed, in Ontario, officials occupying this position appeared to hold a very high opinion of the FPCD's work, regarding it as meshing in with their own in the pursuit of an overall integrated and coordinated foreign policy machine spanning the levels of governmental interests and activity. The view from provincial line ministries, predictably, was noticeably at variance with this positive attitude. Thus a senior trade development official in Alberta saw the FPCD as 'a filter of information which isn't needed'. Typically, the FPCD was viewed as an obstacle to established channels of communication with Ottawa and the purveyor of outdated and useless information.

Such attitudes help to explain the relative decline of the FPCD by the late 1980s. A senior provincial official in Toronto saw this as a consequence of criticism of the division and the response of the Minister of External Affairs in the Mulroney government to it. Accordingly, the DEA, at least in theory, had been made a more 'open' system with which communication was far easier than in the days when the FPCD was established. Of equal weight, however, was the changed atmosphere of federal–provincial relations in the mid-1980s and the more relaxed atmosphere that this encouraged towards the issue of the provincial impact on foreign relations. Whatever the reasons, interviews conducted during 1988 revealed that the status of the FPCD had dramatically declined. Not only was this reflected in reduced size and the lower status of officers serving in it, but in its responsibilities and attitudes towards it. Thus one DEA officer no longer regarded the FPCD as possessing the influence that it had in the early 1980s nor as the major route to the provinces within the DEA: 'the days have gone when members of the department would actively seek out membership of the FPCD.'

Determinants of strategic linkage patterns

The experience of the FPCD indicates one factor determining the character and extent of strategic coordinating linkages: namely perceived need. Not unexpectedly, where the impact of NCG activity is regarded as having potentially serious consequences for the management of external relations, then the greater the likelihood that attention will be paid to devising methods of coping with the problem. A second factor lies in the character and traditions of the federal system and the attitudes that these produce. There is a clear contrast between Canada and Australia here, indicated in the response given to a Canadian diplomat, then serving in Canberra, when he asked an Australian foreign service officer why the Department of Foreign Affairs (as it then was) had not developed a mechanism similar to the FPCD: 'here we barge ahead and try to remedy the damage afterwards.'

A third consideration is the status of the foreign ministry and, therefore, its capacity to assume a key coordinating role in the overall management of external relations and, particularly, in the crucial interface between domestic interests and foreign policy. Although by no means the only factor, the negative images widely held of the US Department of State help to explain the apparently low-key role of its Intergovernmental Affairs section. The account of its role provided by members of the section to the author emphasised its relative lack of significance compared with the FPCD in Ottawa. Rather than viewing its activities as closely related to policy management, the central functions appear to be of an administrative nature, such as helping to organise state governors' overseas visits.[42] Furthermore, the rationale for its activities seems to relate as much to the need to establish a domestic constituency for the department in the context of intra-bureaucratic battles and the struggle to avoid budgetary cuts as any commitment to enhance the states' input into its work.

Questions of status, together with the more general character of the foreign policy process, have affected the extent to which the Australian Department of Foreign Affairs and Trade has developed mechanisms similar to the Canadian FPCD. One factor here lies in the extent to which the conduct of Australian foreign policy has rested on strong links with the national community. It is hard to point to the kind of fundamental evaluation of the relationship between domestic interests and foreign policy that has occurred at regular intervals in Canada. Consequently, the DFAT has not been encouraged to build bridges within the Australian community. Moreover, traditionally the DFAT has not been regarded as a 'strong' department within the Canberra departmental hierarchy, and attempts to establish it as a 'super-department' coordinating Australia's external relations have met with resistance from other departments. Certainly, the 1987 reorganisation which assigned responsibility for multilateral trade negotiations previously held by the Department of Trade to the then Department of External Affairs can only have strengthened its position in Canberra. Nevertheless, other powerful rivals, particularly the Department of Prime Minister and Cabinet, which has a significant role in both federal–state relations and foreign policy, are likely to act as constraints on attempts by the DFAT to expand its domestic linkages.

Somewhat perversely, the one coordinating mechanism through which state interests in external relations could gain a voice in the policy process—the Japan Secretariat—was abolished in the wake of the DFAT reorganisation. Created in the light of criticisms expressed in the Myer Report on Australia–Japan relations to the effect that a lack of coherence in Australia's dealings with Tokyo (partly due to state interests and activities) was disadvantaging Australia, the Secretariat sought to achieve a degree of coordination in this highly significant relationship from Canberra's viewpoint by establishing a consultative committee comprising representatives of federal public service departments as well as regular consultations with officers from state government departments. Since the Secretariat, although responsible to the permanent head of the DFA, was a separate agency, there was a degree of bureaucratic tension regarding its operations.

Following its disappearance, however, the only formal mechanism for maintaining linkages between the states and the DFAT has been the maintenance of Senior Foreign Affairs Representatives in the state capitals, intended to develop contacts with the business community. However, according to those who have served as SFARs, the system has always suffered from scepticism within the department, a lack of resources and, particularly, the absence of any mechanism at the centre for processing information coming in from the state offices.[43]

Conclusions

The central argument of this essay has been the need to bring NCGs into the mainstream of contemporary, multilayered diplomacy and not to regard them as occupying some position unique amongst the menagerie of non-state actors. Indeed, it can be argued that it is the linkages that tie non-central governments to their respective political systems that endow them with their significance rather than attempts to carve out discrete diplomatic strategies. It should be quickly re-emphasised that this does not mean that the existence of linkages between central and subnational authorities precludes conflict: it does not. But it does reinforce the fact that there exist a number of permutations in these relationships reflecting the diversity of roles and functions that NCGs can perform in the intricate network of interactions characteristic of contemporary diplomacy.

Focusing on the adaptive strategies developed by the foreign policy machinery helps to illustrate the point. We have seen that responses have varied in accordance with a number of factors. Not least amongst these is the position of the foreign ministry within its respective bureaucratic system and the battles for control over the conduct of external policy that the consequences of interdependence have created in modern administrative systems. Some years ago, Raymond Hopkins noted the significance of what he termed 'global management networks' based on domestic bureaucratic linkages.[44] As the agenda of world politics has expanded to include issues—such as global warming—that demand action at all levels of political responsibility from the local to the regional and the international, so these management networks will demand more effective linkage mechanisms and the involvement of representatives of a growing diversity of subnational interests. From the perspective of national policy-makers and negotiators, the resultant multilayered diplomacy demands the creation of multilayered policy management structures and processes. It is in this context that the significance of the international involvement of non-central governments can be viewed.

Notes

1. Wayne Goss, 'Advancing the international interests of the states', *World Review*, 30 (1991), 40.
2. National Governors' Association, *Infoletter*, 1 May 1989.
3. Susan C. Schwab, 'Building a national export development alliance', *Intergovernmental Perspective*, 16 (1990), 19.
4. For a summary of the arguments relating to bureaucratisation of the foreign policy process, see Lloyd Jensen, *Explaining Foreign Policy*, Prentice-Hall, Englewood Cliffs, NJ (1982), 121–9.

5. Arild Underdal, 'What's left for the MFA? Foreign policy and the management of external relations in Norway', *Cooperation and Conflict* 22 (1987), 188.
6. David Dyment, 'Substate para-diplomacy: the international activities of non-sovereign governments: the case of Ontario', *Conference of the Canadian Political Science Association*, University of Victoria, British Columbia (1990), 14.
7. Interview, California Trade and Investment Office, London, September 1989.
8. Robert Boardman, *Global Regimes and Nation-States: Environmental Issues in Australian Politics*, Carleton University Press, Ottawa (1990); and Robert Boardman, 'Approaching regimes: Australia, Canada, and environmental policy', *Australian Journal of Political Science*, 26 (1991), 446–71.
9. Boardman, *Global Regimes*, op.cit., 128–9.
10. Schwab, 'Building a national export development alliance', op.cit., 19–20.
11. Interview, Department of Commerce, Washington, DC, September 1989.
12. ibid.
13. Hans J. Michelmann, 'The Federal Republic of Germany', in Hans J. Michelmann and Panayotis Soldatos (eds), *Federalism and International Relations: the Role of Subnational Units*, Clarendon Press, Oxford (1990), 219–21.
14. Interview, Attorney-General's Department, Canberra, 1983.
15. See Henry Burmester, 'Federalism, the states and international affairs: a legal perspective', in Brian Galligan (ed.), *Australian Federalism*, Longman Cheshire, Melbourne (1989), 208–9.
16. *Communiqué*, Special Premiers' Conference, Sydney (30–1 July 1991), 37.
17. Interview, Office of the United States Special Trade Representative, Washington, DC (September 1989).
18. G.R. Winham, 'Bureaucratic politics and Canadian negotiation', *International Journal*, 34 (1978–79), 73.
19. ibid., 76.
20. Interview, Department of Trade, Canberra (March 1987).
21. Interview, International Economic Relations Branch, Victoria, BC (July 1984).
22. Information provided during interviews in Department of Trade and Resources and Department of Industry and Commerce (July 1983).
23. Interview, New Zealand High Commission, Canberra (August 1983).
24. Ibid.
25. David Lague, 'Government, industry join in export booster', *Australian Financial Review*, 29 November 1991; 'Tiers of government unite on trade', *Canberra Times* (29 November 1991).
26. Guy McKanna, 'Governments trial new trade strategy', *Australian Financial Review* (1 November 1991).
27. Winham, 'Bureaucratic politics', op.cit., 78.
28. Brian Hocking, 'Multilayered diplomacy and the Canada-US free trade negotiations', *British Journal of Canadian Studies*, 5 (1990), 311–12.
29. M. Cohen, 'Some important lessons for Canadian, US negotiators', *Citizen*, Ottawa (16 January 1986).
30. Interview, Trade Policy Group, Department of External Affairs, Ottawa (November 1988).
31. Department of Foreign Affairs and Trade, *News Release*, D51, Canberra (7 December 1989).
32. Department of Foreign Affairs and Trade, *News Release*, D62, Canberra (13

August 1991).
33. Interview, Department of Fisheries, Hobart (July 1983).
34. Interview, Fisheries Division, Department of Primary Industry, Canberra (July 1983).
35. Interviews: California State World Trade Commission, Governor's Office, Washington, DC, and Office of the United States Trade Representative, Washington, DC (September 1989).
36. Interview, International Relations Division, Ministry of Intergovernmental Affairs, Toronto (November 1988).
37. Karvonen and Sundelius, 'Interdependence and foreign policy management in Sweden and Finland', *International Studies Quarterly*, 34 (1990), 222–3.
38. Yves Mény, 'French regions in the European Community', in Michael Keating and Barry Jones (eds), *Regions in the European Community*, Clarendon Press, Oxford (1985), 202.
39. loc.cit.
40. Yves Lejeune, 'Belgium', in Michelmann and Soldatos (eds), *Federalism and International Relations*, op. cit., 148 and 162–7.
41. Interview, Federal Provincial Coordination Division, Department of External Affairs, Ottawa (July 1984).
42. Interview, Intergovernmental Affairs section, Department of State, Washington, DC (May 1990).
43. Information gathered from interviews held with SFARs in Melbourne, Sydney, Brisbane and Perth between 1983 and 1986.
44. Raymond F. Hopkins, 'The international role of "domestic" bureaucracy', *International Organization*, 30 (1976).

5 Federalism and Australian foreign policy

Stuart Harris

Introduction

De Tocqueville's view was that a nation 'that divided its sovereignty when faced by the great military monarchies of Europe would . . . by that single act . . . be abdicating its power, and perhaps its existence and name.'[1] Today he would probably add great economic powers to the list and not limit himself to Europe. Nevertheless, that statement reflects a commonly accepted view of foreign policy as a key central power of any country and an essential attribute of sovereignty, with international law and international organisations being based upon unitary conceptions of a nation. Indeed, in Australia as elsewhere, federalism is often discussed in terms of infringements on the sovereignty of the states or restrictions on the central government's powers.

The growth of global interdependence has meant increasing constraints on the ability of Australian governments to take independent action on matters previously seen as essentially domestic. Some of these constraints emerge from collaborative international arrangements to which Australia adheres more or less voluntarily. Others emerge from developments in the way markets, such as the capital and technology markets, or international actors, such as transnational corporations, have changed. Because interdependence emphasises the importance of coherence and cohesion of national action, both have increased the needs for policy coordination.

From one viewpoint, the existence of state governments in a federal system is judged to complicate the formulation and implementation of foreign policy in such a context in ways not experienced by unitary states. From another perspective, the growth of international involvement and the growing range of international treaty commitments that increases the

Commonwealth's power over what the states regard as their domestic interests are seen as potentially threatening to the sovereignty of the states.

In considering how foreign policy is affected by federalism this chapter starts by asking why we have foreign policy. It then looks at what objectives are normally seen as encompassed in the term federalism and how federalism is affected by international developments. It follows with an analysis of the changes in international and domestic circumstances most relevant to the relationship between the two. It then considers how the two sets of objectives conflict with or complement each other and in particular the mechanisms that exist and have been used to manage the interrelationships between them.

Defining the questions

There is little doubt that the existence of state governments offers potential constraints on the freedom of the Commonwealth government to frame and implement foreign policy in its own terms. Governmental powers and responsibilities in Australia are fragmented. This poses difficulties in coordinating national action in pursuit of national goals and common interests.[2] Federal nations appear disadvantaged with global interdependence because some of the inevitable conflicting pressures that exist in any society have relatively independent options for action. As well as the international constraints on policy-making, therefore, Australian foreign policy faces internal constraints. Yet to consider how important these are in practice and to assess what that implies it is useful to consider, in the first place, why we have foreign policies.

It is common to think in terms of foreign policy dealing with matters beyond Australia's borders, and to a degree that is correct. The reasons for being involved with those matters, however, are to achieve essentially domestic objectives.[3] Thus, strategic, political, economic, immigration and other policies are designed to give domestic security, economic well-being, community cohesion and development, and the like. Some objectives are directly linked—our domestic growth depends upon our international performance. Some objectives have more complex relationships, including various indirect links—increased expenditures on military capacities may mean less can be spent on domestic social services or infrastructures; or more tariff protection to domestic interests may inhibit progress towards other domestic objectives such as economic growth and employment. Some objectives have alternative means to a similar end—foreign aid, political influence or military expenditure are all means of providing greater security but with differing domestic impacts.

It is difficult, in practice, to cite domestic policies which do not have some foreign policy implications, and all foreign policies have some domestic links. In some cases they will be substantial, in others they will be negligible. That the purpose of foreign policy is to achieve domestic objectives is important in the present context because there are few domestic objectives in which the states do not have a valid and significant interest. Before looking at what these interests of state governments mean in foreign policy formulation and implementation terms, we need to question whether constraints that exist on foreign policy-making because of state government activity arise from the existence of state governments themselves.

Many such constraints arise from the concerns of specific economic interests, pressure groups or political activists that are likely, at least in democratic systems, to find a mechanism through which their views can be represented, whether through state governmental machinery or in some other way. Certainly, Australian mayors or heads of Greater London Councils have shown a desire to take independent foreign policy initiatives, whether over Taiwan or Northern Ireland. This suggests that at subnational levels of government, attempts can be made to be involved in foreign policies without the need for federalism to be the culprit.

Similarly, adherence to obligations accepted internationally may be circumscribed by bodies other than state governments even now, such as local fire authorities' reluctance to move to halon substitutes in fire control equipment despite Australian commitments given, endorsed by the states, under the Montreal Protocol on Measures to Reduce Ozone Depleting Substances. Municipal or other forms of local governments would presumably have a wider range of powers and responsibilities in the absence of state governments.

More fundamentally, it raises the broader issue of what we mean by a federal system itself. Federalism can be argued to be not simply a question of which legislation or authority should prevail, or how far the central government's objectives (and legislation) should override those of the states. Federalism can be seen as a system of political interdependence in which responsibilities are shared and outcomes are negotiated. Some, indeed, from Lord Acton on, have pointed to the strong links between federalism and democratic processes. Although this tends to be in terms of protecting local cultural or ethnic diversity, federalism in Australia is less about these objectives, or about political nation-building, than an expression of the physical and social separation of populations, and a means by which regional interests are represented and institutionalised, seeking more direct involvement in decisions, achieving more rapid responses to regional questions and pursuing regional community aspirations against the pressures of central governments or the centres of economic power in south-east Australia.

A strong view of this, sometimes termed 'the Leviathan hypothesis' is that, as Walsh has put it, 'One of the important features of federal constitutions is their role in constraining the ability of governments to use in an exploitative way the coercive powers that are necessarily given them.'[4] Certainly, what policies can be pursued and how they are pursued depends upon community support, or at least lack of community opposition. To a degree at least, states reflect legitimate community interests in the issues which ought to have a voice in decision-making.

Changes in the relationships

Changes are taking place in the underlying factors affecting relations between the states and the Commonwealth government in a variety of ways. These include the legal, economic and political aspects of federal relationships.

There have been important changes in legal interpretations of the constitutional position of the Commonwealth but these have been dealt with extensively in the literature,[5] and there is little to add here. In summary, three successive legal decisions—those on the *Seas and Submerged Lands* (1975), *Koowarta* (1982), and the *Franklin Dam* (1983) cases—have strengthened the Commonwealth government's constitutional position with respect to foreign policy-making and implementation.

An important factor associated with this development, however, was a strong political response. This emerged particularly from the result of the *Franklin Dam* case. The dam proposed by the state government of Tasmania did not proceed in the light of the High Court's decision to support the Commonwealth's use of the treaty-making power (linked to Australia's obligations under the World Heritage Convention). It also became an issue in the subsequent federal election.

The state Labor premiers, from the same party as the Commonwealth government, did not oppose the Commonwealth's action against the Tasmanian government, a government of a different political complexion. They may perhaps have personally favoured preserving the environmentally valuable site. Nevertheless, they made clear their great unease at the extension of the Commonwealth's legal powers. They stressed the political problems generally and within the Labor Party that the Commonwealth would face if it took undue advantage of the new legal interpretation of its international treaty-making power. Since criticism of the Commonwealth government and its remoteness tends to be a feature of most state elections, for a long time made into a fine and effective art in Queensland, the warning was undoubtedly a serious one.

Although Section 51 of the Constitution, which among other things gives the Commonwealth the power to make international treaties, is generally accepted as the basis on which the Commonwealth exercises executive powers relevant to foreign policy,[6] the Commonwealth has significant powers elsewhere in the Constitution which relate to international policy questions. It has power under the Constitution over defence, trade and commerce, territorial waters, fisheries outside territorial waters, migration, foreign corporations and relations with the Pacific Islands.

The significance of some of these powers may seem not to have changed materially in recent years. In one sense, the domestic significance of the defence power, for example, remains the basic objective of protecting Australia's territorial sovereignty. In another sense, security threats have been the major centralising influences in Australia and the decline of external threats of the traditional kind may reduce many of those influences.

An important change, however, is the greater salience of security questions with more specific interests for individual state governments, such as the potential for terrorist attacks on the offshore Bass Strait oil rigs or North-west Shelf gas installations, the need for protection from illegal fishing of trochus shell off Western Australia, from the influx of boat people in northern Australia, or from the import of addictive drugs into eastern Australia.

The states are, of course, concerned with procurement and logistics aspects of defence. States have economic interests in wherever military bases are established and where major defence purchases are made. On these issues, the contentions—at times heated—are nevertheless not in principle federal in their nature. The common Australia federal solution of trying to provide some sops to losers—as with the construction and purchase of submarines—could well occur in a unitary state.

The Commonwealth is not constrained constitutionally in handling the external aspects of foreign policy—concluding treaties, declaring war or appointing diplomats. In other words, the Commonwealth has the power, basically untramelled, to speak for Australia and to deal and negotiate with other international actors.[7]

In the implementation domestically of foreign policy commitments, however, the major area of sensitivity in the Commonwealth–state relationship exists. It is the potential power over domestic issues given to the Commonwealth by the treaty-making power, and the rapidly expanding range of issues seemingly capable of falling within processes of international treaty making, that are seen by the states as threatening to the existing federal system.

In the 1970s, resource issues tended to be central to state–Commonwealth disputes related to foreign policy, notably over export controls and controls on foreign investment, resource security and taxation.[8] In the 1980s, disputes have tended to arise in the environmental field where the Commonwealth in recent years has sought to establish its environmental leadership credentials.

The Commonwealth maintains export controls on mineral sands so that it can have some influence on environmental protection of sand-mining, and has threatened to use export controls on woodchips for similar purposes. Its use of the World Heritage Convention has been particularly contentious with the states, not just with respect to the Franklin Dam but with the World Heritage listing of Queensland tropical rainforest, which the Queensland government tried unsuccessfully to dispute directly with UNESCO.

That environmental groups have also directed their attention increasingly at the Commonwealth level, recognising the latent powers there, has involved the Commonwealth in various state-level resource development issues. This has brought it at times into sharp conflict with the state government affected. On the other hand, industry for its part often sees the states as an alternative way to press its case with the Commonwealth.

The foreign policy of Australia, like that of other countries, has been radically altered by the development of international agreements or understandings on a wide range of relatively new issues in addition to the environment. Growing interdependence and internationalisation of world markets has increased the difficulty (or the cost) for any nation of determining its own economic policy. Now few domestic policy issues have no foreign policy implications and do not lend themselves to some form or other of international agreement—health, education, Aborigines, social services, energy supplies, uranium and nuclear issues, food, technology transfer, international standards, ocean resources, human rights, criminal law (hijacking, terrorism), and private law (international contracts, service of process abroad).

A question for the Australian government, as for the central governments of other federal states in accepting international commitments, is the extent of dependence upon the states for their implementation. Although, in principle, the Commonwealth can use its legislative power to override state executive action if it wishes to do so, usually it will do so only if it judges state actions, or lack of actions, as significantly prejudicial to its foreign policy. Nevertheless, at times it has felt the need to legislate itself, as it did in the case of the domestic legislation supporting the South Pacific Nuclear Free Zone.

In general, however, it tends to rely on state laws. In this sense, the states can be considered to be exercising power concurrently, with implementation often relying on state legislation, as with treaties ranging from migratory birds to ILO conventions, or the delegation to Queensland, under previous international sugar agreements which contained economic provisions, of certain of Australia's international obligations.

The constitutional settlement between the Commonwealth and states regarding jurisdiction over the territorial waters can be seen either as an example of 'cooperative' federalism of this kind or a politically enforced compromise. The control of pollution from ships is essentially an international issue, and therefore falls legally within the powers of the Commonwealth. Under this arrangement, however, the Commonwealth gave title to the territorial waters to the states. Through concurrent legislation, the states regulate activity in the three miles of territorial sea around Australia.

Its reliance on state laws means that Australia's ability or willingness to participate in any international action commonly depends upon the cooperation of the states. To participate in the GATT standards code, for example, the Commonwealth needed to gain the the support of the states for the domestic action required. Moreover, there are other international developments that will require closer coordination of state activities by the central government as part of the international presentation of a federal nation. Achieving state uniformity in their legislation, however, has meant that a substantial number of conventions, notably those of the ILO, have not been ratified.

What Gareth Evans, the Commonwealth Minister for Foreign Affairs and Trade, has called 'the vagaries of the Australia federal system' frustrated for some considerable time the Commonwealth's wish to sign the First Optional Protocol to the International Covenant on Civil and Political Rights, allowing the UN Human Rights Committee to accept complaints from individuals, as it did with a similar jurisdictional declaration under the optional provisions of the Racial Discrimination Convention.[9]

In Australia's case, for some time a federal clause was often inserted into an international treaty to the effect that the commitment was dependent upon the compliance of the federal subunits. This was taken to diminish, and to a degree perhaps did diminish, the obligation under the treaties involved, and these federal clauses became generally unacceptable in international negotiations. Although the states still saw them as valuable, the current Commonwealth government indicated in the 1983 Guidelines that it did not favour such clauses and would not be seeking them.[10] Burmester also doubts their constitutional significance, given the Franklin Dam judgment, since the Commonwealth now clearly has the power to legislate to override any state objections.

Something close to a federal clause in the GATT was part of the overall balance that was accepted by all parties to the GATT in accepting its original formulation. In the Uruguay Round, the EC—partly as a tactical response to the pressure it is under largely from the federal states of the United States, Canada and Australia—has argued that an imbalance exists between the obligations of federal and unitary states because federal states are only obliged to take 'reasonable measures' to achieve compliance by federal subunits. It wants this provision tightened despite, or perhaps because of, issues related to central authority in its own system, which includes federal governments at member-state level.

As well as the strengthened constitutional position of the Commonwealth government with respect to foreign policy-making, changes in the international economy have themselves affected state federal relationships. The global interlocking of economies and, to a degree, societies is leading to a diminished capacity in some contexts of state economic and political interest. Given the growing influence of global forces on issues of interest to state governments, increased interest in the policies that relate to state interests is to be expected. Whether it means that they have to be directly involved is a separate question.

The increasingly blurred distinction between domestic and international issues has, together with the growing concern for public participation, brought the states greater potential for involvement. Yet this has only been exercised in a limited way in practice, and probably can only be so exercised. In the case of trade, for example, the role of the states can be helpful but is normally something that has limited scope for individual state action internationally, since the gain from an individual state's market opening and trade promotion effort might be reaped by other states. Nevertheless, the inaugural national trade strategy meeting of Commonwealth, state and territory ministers held in November 1991 included trade as a target of a major part of the effort to be undertaken, although the primary emphasis seemed to be on investment.

In the case of investment, where states are able to offer competitive differences, and where the Commonwealth has some difficulties in going beyond broad nationwide boosting, state involvement is essential. Without individual state governments delineating clearly the conditions they offer to, or conditions they impose on, investors or producers in specific terms in their states, nationwide Commonwealth boosting may have little impact.

Finally, a further change is that, whether because of the effect of the loss of apparent control of policy that international interdependence implies, or simply as an evolution of democratic processes, the public are anxious to be more effectively informed and consulted on issues affecting them, including foreign policy decisions, and to look, as well, for greater decentralisation of decision-making. These trends would limit the scope for a central government to reduce the role of the states in areas of policy closely affecting them, reinforced perhaps by the general concern to reduce rather than extend the field of government powers.

Management of Commonwealth–state relations

Commonwealth–state relations in the field of foreign policy have been a mix of cooperation and conflict. This is unavoidable. If there were no cooperation, government and foreign policy would be crippled. If there were no conflict it would imply something about the extent to which state governments had sovereignty to exercise or whether the Commonwealth was in fact pursuing Australia's interests internationally.

How, then, have the states and Commonwealth responded? One might

have expected state governments to respond to the changes by more intensive and more competitive international activity. For example, the
Queensland Premier has observed, given that state governments are now
rated individually by the international credit-rating agencies, that the states
have to be able to answer for themselves internationally on their economic
performance and management.[11]

Kincaid notes fears which have been expressed to the effect that the
growing number of international activities undertaken by constituent governments (or subunits of national governments) raise concerns about the
future of the nation-state.[12] He was understandably sceptical and the argument here is that, for various reasons, the constituent units are more likely
to stay as what Millar refers to as fringe participants.[13]

Diplomacy by state governments or their agencies is not insignificant.
Since Ravenhill's survey of state government offices overseas,[14] the range of
their overseas representation has probably grown marginally, although now
relying more on locally appointed representatives. Most states/territories
are represented in London, Tokyo and, increasingly, Hong Kong. Victoria
also has offices in Frankfurt and Los Angeles; Western Australia is represented in Kobe, Kuala Lumpur, Singapore, Surabaya and Seoul; the
Northern Territory in Jakarta, Kuala Lumpur and Singapore; and South
Australia in Bangkok and Singapore. Tasmania shares some tourism representation with Victoria in Singapore and elsewhere, and Queensland's
tourist authority has an office in Taiwan. The states obviously communicate
with foreign governments and conclude agreements either with governments
or more usually their instrumentalities, if only of a 'best endeavours' or
'memorandum of understanding' nature.

Unlike most federal states, Australia does not share land borders with
other countries and the need for international dealings on a state basis is not
therefore very significant. There are limited contacts between the
Queensland state government and Papua-New Guinea with whom a border
is shared. Perhaps more important is the growing relationship between the
Northern Territory and Indonesia and to a lesser extent Brunei. This is
largely a consequence of the proximity of what are important economic
interests to a territory which is, in some respects, closer to Asia than to the
rest of Australia. The limited needs for contacts on a day-to-day basis,
however, means that, unlike some other federal systems, the development of
a limited international competence in constituent units arising from agreements concerned with cross-border or related matters has not been
developed.

Professional, commercial, academic and cultural ties by state
government-linked bodies, including sister-state relationships, although
often not of major substance, are nevertheless numerous. That not all the
constituent diplomacy in Australia's case, however, is at the state government level is shown by the extensive development of sister-city relation-

ships, usually with comparable municipal authorities in Asian countries, particularly Japan and China.

To some extent there was an expansion in state governmental activity overseas in the 1980s in these and other fields. How much this was a response to global interdependence is less clear. The history of state representation overseas has been mixed, with a variety of causal factors having influence from time to time, ranging from clear-cut commercial or legal objectives to the maintenance of offices either for protocol reasons or as a means to reward (or punish) state politicians and provide convenience for visitors. Commercial reasons, however, have generally and increasingly predominated.

Important in the resurgence of interest in the 1980s was the entrepreneurial push of state Labor governments in the industrial policy and export promotion field. Western Australia and Victoria in particular, but they are not alone, created industrial development agencies which saw a role for themselves internationally. These were generally less concerned with traditional relationships—linked to overseas posts in London—than to newer areas such as China and Japan, reflecting changing patterns of trade and, in Japan's case, investment.

Such areas were seen as having economic potential for the state involved and to require government-to-government links to facilitate economic exchanges. They also reflected a desire to parallel broader Commonwealth strategies to go beyond simply responding to foreign investment requests by seeking positively to attract overseas capital and technology. A particular interest was to attract foreign investment for resource development as well as to establish government to government links relevant to resource development and marketing. Consequently, local industry often saw benefit in state government activity of this kind.

The returns from these efforts have probably been limited although the, in some cases thundering, failure of these enterprises in other respects has dwarfed consideration of the financial costs and benefits of their constituent diplomacy. It was not apparent, however, that if sensibly done these efforts need be contrary to the pursuit of the national interest—indeed they are likely to advance it—or a coherent foreign policy. Even if not sensibly done the consequences, although sometimes irritating, will normally be minor.

A range of specific consultation and coordination mechanisms exist or have been introduced to mediate these relationships between state governments and the Commonwealth. In some contexts coordination arrangements have existed for some time between state and Commonwealth governments in relation to international affairs—a long-standing participation by the states in delegations to the UN Food and Agriculture Organisation (FAO), for example, was an outcome of a decision by the Commonwealth and state ministers meeting as an Agricultural Council. More formal arrangements having wider applicability were developed in the

1970s as part of the Fraser government's 'new federalism' to meet the particular state government concerns over the Commonwealth's treaty-making powers. The adoption of the Guidelines on Treaty Cooperation in 1977, subsequently revised in 1983, was seen as a way of meeting state government wishes to have early notice of treaty negotiations, to be involved in discussions and decisions on foreign policy questions where state interests were concerned, and to have state representation on international delegations.[15]

The practice of more effective consultation and wider state representation on international delegations has been maintained on multilateral issues ranging from human rights and commodity negotiations (sugar) to private international law, and as well to bilateral issues such as negotiations on fisheries (with Japan) and maritime boundaries (with Indonesia).

Trade-related and other international policy-related interests have been tied more specifically to specialist state–Commonwealth ministerial councils. There are well over twenty of these councils which normally meet once or, in some cases, twice a year, with counterpart meetings of senior officials at least as frequent. As well as the Agricultural Council, those with major international interests deal with minerals and energy, with environment and conservation matters, with industry and technology and with tourism, but few of the other councils—from health and transport to legal matters—do not have significant international linkages. New Zealand ministers participate in many of these councils and, in the case of government procurement, arrangements under CER have led to state governments giving non-discriminatory access not just to each other's enterprises but also to those of New Zealand, nominally a foreign government.

Since 1990, the special premiers' conference process has been dealing with a variety of microeconomic reform issues, most of which have substantial indirect, if not direct international policy implications. Specific coordination arrangements were developed in 1987 to deal with foreign investment in Australia. The Investment Promotion Program meets at least annually, with coordination between the Commonwealth and the states and territories being a prime objective.

On trade-related questions, informal contact has also been sustained as, for example, on GATT Uruguay Round matters. In the development of a national trade strategy, specific processes of consultation have recently been established to coordinate, and make more effective, trade (including trade in services) and investment promotion policies and their implementation and, as well, industry policy as it affects trade and investment. These processes include State Coordinating Committees to work with Trade Centres established by Austrade, the Commonwealth government's trade promotion body, and an annual Trade and Investment Forum of senior state, territory and Commonwealth officials,[16] with the first meeting of this forum in April 1992.

Among other things, Commonwealth and state/territory ministers agreed to pursue a cooperative and coordinated approach in overseas trade and investment offices. Arrangements have also been established which should improve liaison between state and territory ministerial visits overseas and Australia's diplomatic posts.

These various mechanisms and the way they are used might be said to have reflected both the attitudes and the effectiveness of policies of 'new federalism', the initiatives first of Malcolm Fraser's government in the 1970s to decentralise policies and funding in many areas (influenced by earlier US approaches in this direction under President Nixon) and then the Hawke government's new 'new federalism' of the 1980s. These developments have mainly emerged in the context of the regular premiers' conferences and the special premiers' conferences dealing with microeconomic reform.

Among the mechanisms for managing federal relationships is, of course, parliamentary discussion and consideration, particularly in the Senate, which was developed constitutionally, following the US pattern, as a states house. There is a degree to which the existence of the Senate has provided some safeguards to the domestic interests of the states in the Commonwealth's pursuit of its foreign policy. Its existence may also have reduced pressure to have greater public or parliamentary discussion of international treaties, which in Australia do not require legislative approval before acceptance, although it is not evident that discussion in the Senate on treaty issues has been substantial in the past.

The constraints that Senate consideration might offer have probably become more important with the increased acceptance that governments with majorities in the lower house will commonly not have majorities in the Senate. This tends to mean that for legislation generally, including any legislation needed to implement international obligations under the treaty powers of the Commonwealth, a more negotiated outcome is necessary. In this sense the emergence of a cooperative federalism process can be looked at in part as a recognition by the Commonwealth of the reality of shared powers.

At the same time, there seems to have been a general acceptance by the states as well as by the Commonwealth that, for whatever reason, the responses that Australia was making to the changes occurring internationally were too slow and that the persistence of short-term conflicts over the use of the shared responsibilities and powers was a major factor. Perhaps also a third factor, reflecting Duchacek's conclusion that 'uniformity needs diversity to be effective',[17] was important. This would reflect an acceptance by the Commonwealth that reliance on familiarity with local possibilities and local limitations, and on local pride in participation and responsibility, could increase policy efficiency and effectiveness.

Specific suggestions for managing the relationships between Commonwealth and state governments have included proposals for a Treaties

Council, comparable to that in the Federal Republic of Germany, for constitutional change to limit the powers of the Commonwealth to legislate to
implement treaty obligations, as well as for greater parliamentary scrutiny
of treaties and their implications. None of these suggestions, even though
gaining a degree of support at the 1984 constitutional convention, has been
acted upon. In the case of the proposed constitutional amendment, this may
be in part because of the poor record of achieving constitutional amendments in the past, but for all of them the failure to proceed is probably due
more to the lack of political enthusiasm at the Commonwealth level for
action beyond that already in place. It may also be due to a belief that
existing arrangements already provide 'a continuing restraint on unilateral
assertion of power over matters of traditional concern of the states'.[18]

Conclusion

In the case of the external affairs power, one question is whether it has the
potential to overshadow all other sources of constraint upon the independence
of the states. Collins suggests that 'it is upon this ground that the most
intensive battles of Australian federalism are likely to be fought' in the coming
years.[19] Reinforcement for this view is likely to come from the
Commonwealth's current involvement in UNCED with its hopes of moving
towards international agreements on global climate change, biodiversity and
possibly forestry, each of which leads to very sensitive areas of state interest.
This has been doubted by others who see the financial powers as more
important. Walsh, for example, has argued that, compared with the financial
powers which are largely hidden, 'the use of the Commonwealth's trade or
external affairs powers are inevitably selective, well publicised, subject ultimately to public opinion and open to legal challenge.'[20]

Clearly political solutions are likely to be the main form in which the
relationship problems will be resolved in the future. In that respect, the legal
position is less important, in the sense that the outcomes will not be determined primarily by legal provisions. Nevertheless, the fact of ultimate power
of the Commonwealth cannot do other than influence the negotiated
outcome.

There can be little doubt that there will be continuing debates, and at
times strong arguments, about the exercise of Commonwealth powers over
foreign policy. State governments often have genuine differences of economic
and political interests, not just with the Commonwealth but with each other.
These reflect, among other things, their differences of resource endowment,
management policies, and efficiency equity or other objectives, many of
which—such as resource security, development or environmental
protection—impinge on international policies.

Their responses will also reflect differences of understanding, viewpoints and priorities—what is seen as an effort to achieve uniformity from one viewpoint will be seen as interference from another. Political allegiances will always remain an important factor and the predominance of state governments of the same political complexion as the Commonwealth Labor government for much of the last decade has undoubtedly made cooperation easier. On the other hand, many of the moves to cooperate were by New South Wales under a non-Labor government.

The process of change in Australia, however, has reflected a degree of mutual accommodation in the process of adjustment of overlapping boundaries, a movement towards a smaller direct international role for the states but towards a greater involvement in cooperative participation. The traditional arguments supporting the need for a nation to speak with one voice in its international dealings remain strong, although it is more difficult, conceptually and practically, now that the dividing line between domestic and foreign policy has become blurred. Nevertheless, despite occasional anomalies and minor exceptions from time to time, there is no general sense in which the present Australian state governments seek to differ from that, although there will undoubtedly be continuing and at times heated arguments about the way the Commonwealth makes use of its powers to be involved in domestic issues in response to what develops internationally. Nevertheless, while speaking with one voice remains critical, to achieve the objectives of federalism, cooperation and coordination with the states on what that one voice should be saying on national issues is unavoidable.

Acknowledgements

Help and comments on an earlier draft from Jacques Grinberg, Joan Hird, John McCarthy and Mike Smith are gratefully acknowledged.

Notes

1. Alexis de Tocqueville, *Democracy in America*, Phillips Bradley (ed.), vol. I, Alfred Knopf, New York (1945), 172.
2. Hugh Collins, 'Political factors', in Paul Dibb (ed.), *Australia's External Relations in the 1980s: The Interaction of Economic, Political and Strategic Factors*, Croom Helm, Canberra (1983), 216.
3. Stuart Harris, *Review of Australia's Overseas Representation*, AGPS, Canberra (1986), 2ff.
4. Cliff Walsh, 'An economic perspective', in Brian Galligan (ed.), *Australian Federalism*, Longman Cheshire, Melbourne (1989), 219.
5. See, for example, Henry Burmester, 'A legal perspective', in Brian Galligan, op.cit., 192–216; John Ravenhill, 'Australia', in H. Michelmann and P. Soldatos (eds), *Federalism and International Relations*, Oxford University Press, Oxford

(1991), 76–123; also, Greg Craven's discussion in Chapter 1 of this book.

6. Burmester, op.cit., 196.

7. ibid.

8. Stuart Harris, 'State and federal objectives and policies for the use and development of resources', in Peter Drysdale and Hirofumi Shibata (eds), *Federalism and Resource Development: The Australian Case*, Allen & Unwin, Sydney (1985), 70–2; Ravenhill, op.cit., 77ff.

9. Gareth Evans and Bruce Grant, *Australia's Foreign Relations: In the World of the 1990s*, Melbourne University Press, Melbourne (1991), 146.

10. Burmester, op.cit., 214.

11. Wayne Goss, 'Advancing the international interests of the states', *World Review*, 30 (1991), 43.

12. John Kincaid, 'Constituent diplomacy in federal politics and the nation-state: conflict and cooperation', in Michelmann and Soldatos, op.cit., 54.

13. Tom Millar, *Australia in Peace and War*, Hurst & Company, London (1978), 402.

14. Ravenhill, op.cit., 99.

15. Burmester, op.cit., 206.

16. Neil Blewett, Minister for Trade and Overseas Development, *Press Statement* (28 November 1991).

17. Ivo Duchacek, *Comparative Federalism: The Territorial Dimension of Federalism*, University Press of America, Lanham, MD (1987), 351.

18. Burmester, op.cit., 209.

19. Hugh Collins, 'A political science perspective', in Brian Galligan, op.cit., 185.

20. Walsh, op.cit., 219.

6 Managing intergovernmental tensions: shaping a state and local role in US foreign relations

John M. Kline

Central governments have dominated foreign relations since the emergence of the nation-state system, including countries which chose federal structures. The United States Constitution designates the President to manage foreign relations while the Congress gives its advice, consent and money. US states are denied traditional foreign relations powers in principle and (until recently) in practice. As the nation celebrated its constitutional bicentennial, however, many states and some localities were expanding international programs initiated a decade or two earlier. These activities have caused periodic intergovernmental tensions, posing both legal and political issues regarding the role of non-central governments (NCGs) in foreign relations. A central challenge for the 1990s is how to manage these tensions and shape future NCG participation in foreign relations during the federal system's third century.

Intrusion, integration and irritation

Global interdependence is the primary stimulus to NCG participation in foreign relations. The flow of people, information and commerce among nations increased sharply over the past several decades. Technological revolutions in communications, transportation and information systems ripped broad holes in the walls of ignorance and isolation that marked separate and sovereign national jurisdictions. This transition affected political institutions at all levels of governance, including NCGs which had previously been protected from external influences by effective national boundaries.

Growing local impacts from global interdependence result in a mixture of intrusion, integration and irritation that affects relationships among federal system entities.

International commerce can no longer be channeled through narrow border checkpoints closely monitored and regulated by central government authorities. Foreign direct investment penetrates into a nation's heartland, spreading transnational business influence throughout the economy. Increased cross-listings on world stock exchanges distribute corporate shareholdings worldwide, along with the results of those firms' fortunes and misfortunes. Real-time images appear simultaneously on living-room televisions around the world, bringing shared information, awareness and a sense of personal involvement in dramatic and sometimes tragic events taking place in faraway lands. These changes and many others heighten general public interest in international issues. Suddenly, the somewhat mystical realm of foreign affairs takes on a more decidedly domestic face, in the process drawing NCGs into matters where international forces directly and visibly affect local constituencies.

For the United States, NCG involvement in foreign relations underwent a quantitative and qualitative transformation beginning in the mid-1960s. Prior to that time, state governors occasionally acted to support a presidential foreign policy initiative, usually in response to a White House appeal. This involvement dealt more with the governors' personal prestige than with direct and immediate state interests. Not since the Republic's early decades, when the practical boundaries of federal powers were still being determined, had states attempted to engage directly and actively in foreign affairs in order to advance individualistic policy positions.[1]

Global economic interdependence provided the initial impetus for change. Foreign trade nearly doubled its share of US GNP over the 1970s. The following decade, foreign direct investment reversed historical trends as record inflows made the United States the largest host as well as home nation for foreign investors. State governments developed a stake in this international economic activity, attempting to spur growth and create jobs by expanding overseas markets for local exporters and attracting new foreign investment. Both the average and median state budget for trade promotion surpassed one million dollars as state spending on international programs tripled over the mid-1980s, nearly equaling in the aggregate national government expenditures on trade promotion activities.[2]

The international dimension of state economic development programs emerged unevenly across the country but initially was oriented toward a seemingly natural geographic extension of state interests. Early state government innovators appeared along the Atlantic seaboard and in the industrial heartland of the Midwest. North and South Carolina, Georgia, New York and Illinois built programs that initially focused on expanding economic ties with European nations. As state efforts spread, Florida looked south to Latin America, Texas and Arizona concentrated on dealings with Mexico, New England and upper-tier Midwestern states focused on Canada, while Oregon and Washington turned westward to seek enhanced relationships across the Pacific. The state-nation of California, whose economy would rank among the largest in the world if measured separately, at first disdained organized promotional efforts, but finally, in 1983, it launched one of the most extensive and expensive of state international programs.

These developments proceeded in cascading fashion, with successful experiments in one state adopted and adapted for use in other jurisdictions as states sought to exploit their own particular strengths. Programs expanded from the first sponsored trade missions to the establishment of overseas offices, trade-lead dissemination, export financing support, and a wide range of investment incentive packages. During the 1980s, a number of larger metropolitan areas devised their own promotional campaigns. The early emphasis on trade, founded on the activities of local port authorities and foreign trade zones, later expanded to include more aggressive efforts to attract foreign investment.[3] After all, an investor's ultimate locational choice depends on local factors as much as or more than on the surrounding state's general business environment.

These developments gave most states and many localities an immediate and tangible stake in international economics. NCGs acquired a vested interest in the formulation and implementation of US foreign economic policy at the same time that they expanded their direct contacts with overseas business executives and foreign government officials. State governments did not directly seek to usurp national government powers over foreign relations, but the impact of international economics on the health and well-being of domestic jurisdictions led NCGs into the foreign policy arena.

The intrusion of foreign economic influence fostered an integration of domestic and international interests that overlapped areas of traditional NCG jurisdiction in the United States. Resulting NCG attempts to influence US policy and to pursue their expanding overseas interests interjected the states into US foreign relations. The irritation factor developed as national and state efforts began to intersect, usually unexpectedly and without a clear definition of the proper boundaries of federal powers. Relatively insulated from overseas forces, the United States had not previously confronted situations of this nature and therefore lacked both experience and precedents for dealing with them. Intergovernmental tensions were bound to arise as national, state and local jurisdictions sorted out their foreign relations involvements within the federal structure.

Evolving NCG interests and activities

With an economic impetus to involvement in foreign relations, it is not surprising that core state government activities revolved around trade and investment promotion. The trade efforts had clear parallels in national export expansion programs while state investment actions broke new public policy ground in the United States. Other policy initiatives ventured into more unexpected areas as international economic interests drew NCGs closer to intersecting political issues. Special interest groups recognized the potential to use the NCGs' federal system leverage to influence national policy and foreign relations. These groups promoted enhanced awareness of how foreign relations affects state and local welfare, encouraging NCG activism on foreign policy issues, particularly concentrating on metropolitan areas where policy campaigns could be focused most intensely.

NCG trade and investment interests

Trade promotion initiatives were the most extensive programmatic elements introduced by state governments in the international field. Directed at expanding exports, these activities both complemented and supplemented national government efforts, taking on added importance as budget deficits constrained national programs. State and national authorities largely overcame potential rivalries as the NCG role developed. Compatible policy objectives permit coordinated activities such as information-sharing networks and joint assistance offices. Despite occasional squabbles over resource and responsibility allocations, the various parties forged the basis for a working intergovernmental partnership on trade promotion.

Current cooperation did not evolve without some initial tensions, however. National government officials welcomed the additional state resources committed to export promotion and recognized that NCGs have certain relative advantages; for example, in contacting and assisting small, new-to-export companies. Nevertheless, state enthusiasm for trade promotion threatened to run afoul of multilateral agreements when the states moved from sponsoring simple trade missions to providing benefits such as export financing support.

The United States backed the so-called 'Gentlemen's Agreement' in the Organization for Economic Cooperation and Development (OECD) that restricted subsidies offered by national export financing facilities. As US states formulated their own financing mechanisms in the early 1980s, the NCGs appeared both uninformed and unconcerned about such multilateral agreements. Largely in response to this situation, the US Commerce Department established an advisory center on state export finance and staffed district offices with specialists ready to promote model programs that would not conflict with US trade policy while offering assistance designed to facilitate coordination with existing Commerce Department resources.[4]

Export financing facilities involve substantial administrative costs, long-term commitments, and hold out the possibility for competition with private sector institutions. To surmount these obstacles, the US Export–Import Bank (Eximbank) developed a pilot program for a sharing of tasks with NCG authorities. Beginning in 1987 with three states and three cities, agreements were reached that allow NCGs to prepare trade financing applications for expedited approval at the Eximbank. Some twenty-two NCGs (mainly states) now participate in this program, with proposals to permit regional multistate groupings and to enable NCGs to commit Eximbank support for financing guarantees for certain types of export projects.[5] This program helps Eximbank reach more small enterprises while local and state governments handle much of the export financing assessment and preparation process in tandem with local banks as part of their general trade promotion efforts. Policy coordination has become programmatic cooperation, enhancing comparative intergovernmental advantages while minimizing duplication and resource wastage.

NCG investment activities raise different challenges because there are no similar national efforts to attract foreign investment. Official US policy endorses an essentially neutral foreign investment policy based on non-discriminatory national treatment, an 'open door' to investment in most sectors, and the absence of incentive or performance requirements for foreign investors.[6] State and local governments, on the other hand, operate aggressive business promotion programs. Historically focused on aiding local business growth and enticing investment from companies in other states and regions, these efforts encompass a range of benefits such as tax reductions, worker training assistance, and infrastructure improvements for roads, railways, and water and sewerage facilities.[7]

A few states courted foreign investors in the late 1960s and 1970s, but these efforts rapidly proliferated during the 1980s when foreign investment in the United States outpaced US investment abroad for the first time since early in the century. State overseas offices took on dual missions as trade promotion and investment attraction outposts. State and local government leaders combined public assistance benefits into incentive packages designed to entice specific investors, sometimes finding themselves locked in bidding wars with other NCGs for particularly attractive investments such as new Japanese automobile plants.[8]

This competitive bidding is wasteful from a national perspective because most potential investors have already decided to establish operations in the United States and the public largess only influences the specific local site within the country. State incentives also proved a bit embarrassing to national authorities who were objecting to investment incentives used by foreign governments and pressing for a multilateral accord to constrain their distortionary effect on foreign investment flows.

Nevertheless, NCGs were exercising a fundamental right to promote economic development within their jurisdiction. Limiting incentives for foreign investment without similarly restricting domestic business promotion would prove very difficult (especially without also violating the national treatment principle). Facing these differences of opinion on the desirability and utility of investment incentives, national officials have apparently deferred potential policy battles, at least until the achievement of concrete multilateral accords may force the issue.

Tensions rose a bit higher over NCG efforts to restrict trade and investment flows. Investment limitations were directed mainly against foreign acquisition of agricultural land, recreational areas and certain metropolitan office complexes. These restrictions proved sporadic, occurring within emotional national debates in the mid-1970s and again in the mid-1980s over growing concern with investment from the Middle East and Japan. Overall, however, the general NCG desire for investment far outweighed the few cases of restrictive actions and major intergovernmental problems did not arise.

More serious difficulties sprang from NCG actions to discriminate against imports by providing preferential treatment for local products through 'buy-American' regulations and procedures. Procurement by NCG authorities for public works projects such as roads, schools and urban transportation systems placed foreign exporters at a serious disadvantage in bidding for billions of dollars in annual sales. On numerous occasions the US State Department has contacted state officials, communicating protests from foreign governments and urging the defeat of discriminatory trade proposals. Sometimes these entreaties helped generate a governor's veto of pending legislation; other times they were ignored. Nearly two-thirds of the states now have some type of buy-American law.[9]

Potential versus practical power

Instances of discordant policies point up the difference between the US government's potential versus its practical power over NCG trade and investment activities. The national government has generally declined to attempt to impose direct controls on state actions where global economic integration brings international principles into conflict with traditional state prerogatives. For example, the government procurement code agreed to in the previous round of negotiations conducted under the General Agreement on Tariffs and Trade (GATT) does not extend to NCGs. The same limitation faces current negotiations on extending this code, as well as talks aimed at formulating multilateral accords that cover trade in services and limitations on the use of investment incentives.

NCGs can be constrained in these areas through congressional approval of agreed international restraints or by direct national legislation that removes the states' current authority, such as in the regulation of insurance industries. The nation's constitutional struggles over interstate commerce and foreign relations powers affirmed the national government's supremacy in such matters, but past judicial precedents do not necessarily translate into current political power. The potential for constitutional pre-emption does not imply an easy choice for its use. Congress has been loath to restrict states' rights in cases where international priorities are argued to be more important than traditional NCG prerogatives.

The continuing importance of states' rights traditions in the face of foreign policy interests is demonstrated in the multi-decade battle over state unitary taxation practices. Despite Executive Branch efforts to enact legislative restrictions and pass overriding treaty commitments to meet international obligations, NCGs and their supporters have successfully stymied these efforts. The US failure to deliver on initialed commitments under a US–UK Tax Treaty and to bring state practices fully into conformance with accepted international 'arm's length' accounting standards perpetuates commercial frictions with important trading partners.[10]

Congressional reluctance to restrict NCG prerogatives also extends to some issues involving more overtly political foreign policy positions. For example, over one-half the states and nearly three times as many localities acted during the 1980s to exert pressure against South Africa. Initially using stock divestment actions and later (even more effective) selective public procurement and contracting restrictions, these NCGs penalized companies doing business in or with South Africa. For some firms, being excluded from contracts with major metropolitan jurisdictions such as San Francisco, Boston, Houston, New York, Chicago and Los Angeles could more than offset profits accruing from their South African operations. Through their actions, these NCGs inflicted damage on the South African economy using the medium of US multinational corporations. These actions ran counter to official US foreign policy which for many years called for 'constructive engagement' with South Africa rather than withdrawal.[11]

The NCG impact on US relations with South Africa should not be underestimated. The US government eventually imposed its own South African sanctions, lifting them in July 1991. Despite warnings that the US Justice Department might sue local jurisdictions that did not follow the national lead, virtually all NCG restrictions remain in force. Numerous corporations cite the continuing NCG restrictions as a major reason why they have not considered renewed investment in the region. Congress considered a pre-emption proposal in the debate over national sanctions that would have overridden state and local actions, but the amendment was defeated. NCGs remain free to use their economic leverage, exercised through the channels of global integration and the multinational corporation, to engage in foreign relations.[12]

Congressional sympathy for state prerogatives is not without limits, however. When several governors mounted a frontal assault on presidential authority to order state national guard units to participate in training exercises in Central America, the Congress affirmatively supported the President's powers and this decision was upheld in the courts.[13] In this case, economic issues and instruments were not directly involved as much as political disagreements over prevailing US foreign policy designed to bring pressure to bear on the Sandinista government in Nicaragua.

Local government involvement in foreign relations

Metropolitan governments have proven even more aggressive than the states in adopting policy positions on foreign relations issues. With regard to South Africa, metropolitan selective procurement and contracting regulations became the most effective tool for anti-apartheid forces in pressuring corporations to withdraw from South Africa. In recent years, city council resolutions have also addressed foreign policy matters ranging from the Tiananmen Square massacre to aid to El Salvador and US policy towards the Palestinians. Hortatory declarations generally do not provoke any measurable response from the national government, but local NCG efforts to translate words into actions do raise concerns and have led to intergovernmental friction.

For example, a number of cities declared themselves 'nuclear free zones', a position that provoked conflict with the national authorities over the operations at nearby military bases, particularly homeport facilities for naval vessels that may carry nuclear weaponry. On this issue, the US government chose to challenge the legality of the local action and won a court test in April 1990 against an Oakland, California ordinance. The judgment has not yet proven definitive, however, as other jurisdictions continue to pass nuclear free statutes and express support for similar actions by foreign municipalities, including cities in the former Soviet Union.[14]

Local government leaders have also become increasingly vocal in their criticism of general US defense policy, viewing massive military expenditures as drawing away money that could be used for urban infrastructure and social welfare needs. These officials note that resource transfers to states and localities were reduced at the same time that 'new federalism' initiatives decentralized more programs and shifted additional responsibilities to the NCGs. This frustration over federal resource allocations led some NCGs to oppose US military assistance to Central America, argue against large expenditures on the 'Desert Storm' operation against Iraq, and call for applying the 'peace dividend' from the end of the Cold War to domestic program needs, including assistance for local economic readjustment in areas that move away from a defense industrial base.[15]

NCGs utilize the framework provided by the sister city program to engage even more directly in foreign relations activities. This long-established program began with a goal of developing greater intercultural understanding and appreciation through decentralized international contacts. During the 1980s, sister city and sister state relationships added a decidedly economic dimension as both the selection of new international 'relatives' and the design of follow-on programs were influenced by NCG trade and investment objectives.

Also in the late 1980s, political objectives emerged more overtly in the development of US sister city relationships as some NCGs established or expanded ties to local government leaders in politically troubled regions of the world. Among the areas chosen for sister city relationships were black townships in South Africa, small rural communities on the edge of conflict areas in El Salvador and Nicaragua, Palestinian towns in the Israeli-occupied West Bank, cities in the former Soviet Union where dramatic transformations were under way, and communities in China where future changes were uncertain.

These direct ties with local leaders overseas gave foreign communities a communications channel to NCG officials in the United States that bypassed national government establishments in both countries. At times this connection led to publicity and political pressure on US officials to address allegations of human rights violations or other injustices in the foreign communities. Occasionally the US city aided its foreign counterpart directly, providing financial and material assistance as well as sponsoring trips by NCG representatives to show their support or assist in tasks such as monitoring voting during elections.[16]

Emerging patterns of NCG action

Increased NCG involvement in US foreign relations thus encompasses several dimensions involving local as well as state government authorities and covering a range of economic and political issues. Most state activities are grounded solidly in jurisdictional economic interests. The growing impact of global commerce on state economies captured the attention of state officials, motivating their creation of programs to promote exports and attract investment beneficial to the state's economy. This economic interest generates both policy and programmatic actions that can have an impact on intergovernmental relationships.

In several instances, states attempted to use economics as a lever to influence more distinctly political elements of US foreign relations. In addition to the South African divestment actions, nearly a dozen states in the mid-1970s attempted with some success to influence US policy regarding the Arab boycott of Israel.[17] More recently, a few NCGs are exploring bringing pressure to bear on US corporate employment practices in Northern Ireland.[18] These types of actions generally emanate from the state legislature. On rarer occasions states will directly challenge national government authority on political issues, as illustrated by the National Guard dispute. These instances are likely to be centered in the state's executive branch rather than the legislature.

Local government involvement in foreign relations also exhibits a strong economic component. At the core are port authorities engaged in international commerce and business development units seeking new job- and tax-generating investments from abroad. Local NCG activity on matters such as defense policy is often tied to economic interests. Developing this economic connection is part substance and part strategy. On the macro level, defense allocations can constrain spending on social programs of interest to local leaders. Specific communities do need funds to help support the conversion of local economies from a defense industry concentration. However, anecdotal evidence and polling data suggest public support is weak for city government involvement in foreign relations matters unless there is a clear tie to local economic welfare.[19] Hence, these issues are often strategically framed in terms of alternative uses for federal revenue.

Political process realities may explain the generally greater local as compared to state government activism on foreign relations issues with a stronger political component. It is easier for special interests to win official approval for actions in a narrower political forum than in a broader one. At least a few of the fifty states may offer political demographics favorable enough to gain NCG support on a given issue even if victory is (at least temporarily) unattainable in the Congress or through White House action. City governments present a multitude of even narrower political targets where precedent-setting cases can be carefully selected for the most politically sympathetic constituencies, recognizing that general public attention is less specifically engaged in and interest group efforts can be concentrated on the chosen local campaign.

The result of these developments is an emerging pattern of multilayered diplomacy that is slowly breaking the national government's monopolistic grip on the management of foreign relations. A cauldron of incipient foreign relations activity has begun to boil in scattered local jurisdictions, with state governments adding to the brew occasionally when a broad enough political constituency is mobilized and well-placed leadership resources are activated. This potential for NCG involvement in foreign relations has existed for some time; it was the NCGs' stake in the international economy that drew attention to it. The blending of economic and political issues overlaps traditional NCG prerogatives on economic matters, giving these governments both the interest and the ability to participate in foreign policy matters. Lacking recent useful historical precedents for managing intergovernmental relationships of this nature, federal system leaders are faced with the task of promoting coordination and cooperation while minimizing potential conflicts.

Coordination, cooperation and conflict

For the United States, it is already too late for the national government to force a return to the status quo ante in terms of federal control over foreign relations. The US economy's integration with an interdependent global system dictates that NCGs will have a growing stake in foreign affairs, and the structure of the federal system guarantees them an influence where foreign relations and domestic interests overlap. What remains to be determined is what type of role NCGs will play and how intergovernmental relationships will be managed.

The national government holds a strong primary position based on constitutional powers, but it cannot afford to squander its resources nor generate bitterness and resentment among other federal system players. Thus far most parties have emphasized attempts at coordination and cooperation while carefully selecting issues and forums for controlled conflict. The relationship is still fraught with tensions, but process mechanisms and institutional channels are emerging as possible avenues to improve communication and facilitate occasional conflict resolution.

Factors shaping intergovernmental relations

Intergovernmental responses in cases of NCG involvement in US foreign relations could be arrayed along a continuum running from cooperation through coordination to conflict. Several interrelated yet identifiable factors emerge from past cases that appear to have determined the type of response generated. The most important elements are issue content, the adjudicating forum used to resolve disputes, and the relative priority and resource commitment to particular issues.

Although the dividing line is often blurred, issue content can still usually be classified by objectives that are primarily political or economic in nature. Economic matters can be subdivided further into trade and investment categories, and into promotional and restrictive effects. Intergovernmental cooperation is most complete on issues dealing with trade expansion where NCG activities promote national as well as state and local welfare. Here the intergovernmental challenge is to minimize duplication and resource wastage, promote beneficial multiplier effects through cooperative programming, and assure NCG actions do not overstep agreed international bounds of fair competition.

Investment promotion issues do not offer the same potential for programmatic cooperation because the national government maintains an essentially neutral stance toward foreign investment flows and eschews efforts similar to the NCGs' investment attraction campaigns. Since international accords do not yet seriously constrain investment promotion actions, NCGs are unlikely to run afoul of firm multilateral obligations although their activities may complicate US goals to negotiate such agreements.

Trade and investment restrictions present more potentially troublesome problems for intergovernmental relations. Except for state buy-American provisions, most restrictive NCG activity has been limited, however, appearing sporadically around the country without a sustained impact large enough to generate a major conflict. National officials have used information dissemination to argue for the benefits from freer trade and investment flows, relying on progression persuasion over time. Of course, these officials have also been increasingly occupied by a direct challenge in the Congress to the country's general free trade posture. Without a strong and more unified political position on general US trade policy, national leaders are unlikely to challenge state practices directly. (For example, US negotiators are seeking a GATT formula that would broaden the government procurement code coverage only to those NCGs that agree to the regulations in their own self-interest.)

Foreign policy issues with a more predominant political content provide less room for debate about jurisdictional prerogatives whenever NCG actions conflict with official US policy. Some ambiguity may exist on when and how political positions become official US policy, and opinions can differ on whether particular NCG actions actually interfere with conduct of US foreign policy rather than express legitimate political differences of opinion. Nevertheless, NCGs have less freedom for initiative on political matters, which explains the attempt to redefine many efforts to highlight their associated economic component and to use economic means to pursue political ends.

These issue content factors seemingly leave a broad scope for potential conflicts to arise regarding NCG involvement in foreign relations, with a strong basis for close cooperation evident only on trade promotion programs. When disputes do occur, issue content can also provide a useful guide as to the adjudicating forum that will likely be called upon to resolve the matter. Intergovernmental conflicts involving overtly political issues are likely to be decided in the courts on the basis of constitutional precedents that favor the national government. Issues with a larger economic content face a more uncertain future in the courts where states have greater legal standing on such issues and precedents appear less clearly applicable to the complexities of interdependent economic processes.

These considerations mean that many if not most potential intergovernmental conflicts over NCG foreign relations activities will be addressed by the Congress rather than the courts. The presumption of an Executive Branch victory in this adjudicating forum is far less certain. The federal system and the separation of powers principle embodied in the US governmental structure combine to make legislative pre-emption a difficult task. The White House can anticipate a bruising and potentially unsuccessful political battle virtually any time it seeks congressional approval of a treaty or national law which restricts traditional states' rights in order to advance foreign policy interests.

This distinction regarding where and how federal foreign relations disputes are adjudicated ties into the third related factor concerning the relative priority and resource commitment assigned a particular issue. Dispute resolution is not cost-free in any case. While the legal presumption in certain cases rests with the national government, the political presumption in virtually all cases favors NCGs which claim the goal of safeguarding or advancing local domestic interests. Hence, the Executive Branch must be willing and able to expend considerable time, attention and political capital to overcome this initial premise and to sustain its momentum through a cumbersome and multistage legislative process to attain a positive law that will pre-empt the claimed NCG authority.

This resource commitment cost forces the national government to respond cautiously to proliferating NCG involvement in foreign relations, choosing carefully the priority issues upon which to fight. Actions involving political issues are more likely to be challenged than economic ones. After the Executive Branch position on the unitary taxation issue was defeated in Congress and in the courts, the preferred path has been advance coordination and cooperation rather than conflict. The difficulty is in discovering how best to achieve this objective.

Institutional channels and process mechanisms

Formal institutional channels are slowly developing, aided by informal, process-oriented mechanisms, to facilitate dialogue, communicate advice, promote coordination and enhance intergovernmental cooperation on foreign relations issues. The first contemporary step occurred in 1978 when an invitation from President Jimmy Carter, a former governor of Georgia, led the National Governors' Association to create a new Committee on International Trade and Foreign Relations. Sporadic discussions turned into policy debates as well as follow-up lobbying on international issues.[20]

Similar institutionalized activities evolved in other interstate organizations, including regional governors' associations, the National Conference of State Legislatures, and groups representing city and county officials.

These forums provide channels to exchange information and viewpoints among NCG leaders and with US foreign policy officials. NCGs gained new importance on international issues, finding a place among the interest groups solicited and consulted during policy formulation, expressing collective NCG views before congressional hearings, and otherwise participating in national policy debates.

The most direct institutional channel to emerge for NCG input to national decision-making on foreign policy is the Intergovernmental Policy Advisory Committee on Trade (IGPAC). State, county and municipal leaders are appointed to provide advice to the US Special Trade Representative (USTR). This group did not meet early expectations as a significant influence channel, but its role and importance increased as GATT talks turned to subjects overlapping state government powers such as trade in services, public procurement and investment incentives.[21] Nevertheless, IGPAC's effectiveness may remain limited due to its restriction to trade issues and the diluted viewpoint that emerges from its broad NCG membership.

An even broader membership group that also includes representatives from national government institutions is the US Advisory Commission on Intergovernmental Relations (ACIR). This institution had not focused specifically on international issues until the beginning of this decade when the Commission studied state and local government involvement in foreign relations and adopted a set of recommendations to improve intergovernmental cooperation in this field.[22] The Commission recognized that the concurrent responsibilities of NCGs and national authorities for citizen welfare and economic well-being left room for NCG activities involving foreign policy.

The Commission itself is not an implementing body, but its recommendations propose a number of process-oriented steps to improve intergovernmental cooperation, including NCG representation on US delegations to international organizations, greater NCG involvement in the treaty-making process, and more education, training and personnel exchange programs. These steps could facilitate communication, promote mutual understanding and provide enhanced flexibility for avoiding or managing intergovernmental frictions.

The new federalist challenge

Managing intergovernmental tensions in US foreign relations will form a new test for the federal system through the end of this century. Various governmental units are gaining experience while sorting out prerogatives and priorities. Over the last decade the initiative fell to NCGs who expanded their interests and programs into the foreign policy realm. This thrust has now been institutionalized in numerous state executive and legislative offices and committees which formulate and oversee the states' foreign relations.

National authorities, slow to recognize and track NCG efforts, have responded sporadically as significant US policy positions were endangered. This reactive approach risks harvesting conflict from situations where early tensions are ignored until unacceptable friction develops. The national government's defensive stance has not yet been fully matched by a parallel emphasis on avoiding frictions by fostering a positive partnership with NCG authorities outside of trade promotion activities. Implementation of the ACIR recommendations could help develop more such cooperation and intergovernmental understanding.

One of the most challenging tests for the federal structure will be shaping a proper role for metropolitan foreign relations activities. Although legal creations of the states, these governmental units are not directly constrained by state authorities and often command significant resources and direct outreach capabilities to overseas interests. The collectively diverse yet individually narrower metropolitan constituencies offer fertile ground for promoting special interest positions and actions at odds with prevailing national policies. The free expression of grassroots opinion is fundamental to the healthy functioning of a democratic political system, yet NCG actions must reflect due consideration for their potential impact on official US foreign relations.

Finally, the ultimate test of the federal system will not rest solely on the resolution of potential conflicts, but also on the positive enhancement of democratic values. The United States remains a relatively insulated nation in terms of knowledge and appreciation of its international, interdependent responsibilities and commitments. More active involvement by NCGs in foreign relations can benefit the country and the world through developing a better informed and participatory electorate.

Foreign relations can no longer remain the restricted enclave for a national élite; its impact reaches into the everyday lives of all Americans and therefore becomes a legitimate concern for their representative institutions throughout the federal structure. As with domestic policy, a federal system can prove its value through promoting participation, experimentation and democratic involvement. The new federalist challenge is to shape a positive and productive state and local government role in US foreign relations for the twenty-first century.

Notes

1. John M. Kline, *State Government Influence in U.S. International Economic Policy*, D.C. Heath, Lexington, MA (1983), 15–21.

2. See surveys and other information released periodically by the National Association of State Development Agencies, Washington, DC, particularly the *State Export Program Database*.
3. The US Conference of Mayors sponsored the first joint investment effort overseas, organizing over 180 participants for an 'Invest in America's Cities' program held in Zurich, Switzerland in October 1981. See also *Exports and Economic Development: A Guidebook for Local Government Officials*, prepared by the US Conference of Mayors for the US Department of Commerce (July 1981).
4. *U.S. Export Weekly*, Bureau of National Affairs, Washington, DC, Special Supplement, 19 (30 August 1983).
5. 'Eximbank State and Municipality Pilot Marketing Program', presentation to the Advisory Board, US Export–Import Bank, 30 June 1987; and 'Eximbank, FCIA develop $10 million short-term credit insurance umbrella for CEFO', *Daily Commercial News and Shipping Guide* (31 March 1988).
6. For the latest statement on US policy, see 'United States foreign direct investment policy', Office of the Press Secretary, The White House, Washington, DC, 26 December 1991. Also see *Economic Report of the President*, US Government Printing Office, Washington, DC (February 1992), 201–8.
7. *Directory of Incentives for Business Investment and Development in the United States*, National Association of Development Agencies, Urban Institute Press, Washington, DC, (April 1991).
8. For example, see Norman Glickman and Douglas Woodward, *The New Competitors: How Foreign Investors are Changing the U.S. Economy*, Basic Books, New York (1989).
9. *United States Trade Barriers and Unfair Practices 1991*, Report by the Services of the Commission of the European Communities (15 March 1991), 53–6.
10. John M. Kline, 'Negotiating limits on unitary taxation in the United States', case 402, The Pew Charitable Trusts, distributed by the Institute for the Study of Diplomacy, Georgetown University, Washington, DC (1988).
11. John M. Kline, 'Doing business in South Africa: seeking ethical parameters for business and government responsibilities', Case Studies in Ethics and International Affairs, no. 11, Carnegie Council on Ethics and International Affairs, New York (1991).
12. Jennifer D. Kibbe, *U.S. Business in Post-Sanctions South Africa: The Road Ahead*, Investor Responsibility Research Center, Washington, DC (1991); and 'The last mile: US communities and South Africa', *Global Communities* (Winter 1991–92), 1–5, 8.
13. *Rudy Perpich, Governor of Minnesota et al.*, v. *Department of Defense et al.*, no. 89–542, Supreme Court of the United States 110 S. Ct. 2418, decided 11 June 1990. Also see 'Judge rips hole in Dukakis's suit', *Bulletin of Municipal Foreign Policy*, 2 (1988), 10–12.
14. 'Judge undermines Oakland NFZ law', and 'A tale of two courts', *Bulletin of Municipal Foreign Policy*, 4 (1990), 4–6, 22.
15. See various issues of the *Bulletin of Municipal Foreign Policy* during 1988–91, and *Global Communities* (Autumn 1991).
16. 'US–Nicaragua sister city briefs' and 'Sister cities gear up for Nicaraguan elections', *Bulletin of Municipal Foreign Policy*, (1989), 16–20 and 34–6, respectively.

17. Kline, *State Government Influence*, op. cit., 187–94.
18. 'Northern Ireland becomes new target for divestment' and 'More cities sign on to MacBride principles', *Bulletin of Municipal Foreign Policy*, 2 (1988), 36–7 and 3, (1989), 33–4, respectively.
19. John Kincaid, 'Rain clouds over municipal diplomacy: dimensions and possible sources of negative public opinion', in Earl Fry *et al.* (eds), *The New International Cities Era: The Global Activities of North American Municipal Governments*, Brigham Young University, Provo, UT (1989), 223–49.
20. Kline, *State Government Influence*, op. cit., 48–9; and John Kincaid, 'The American governors in international affairs', *Publius*, 14 (Fall 1984), 103–4.
21. Carol Conway, 'The coming of age of the IGPAC', *State International Policies*, newsletter of the Southern International Policy Network (1991) 5.
22. *State and Local Governments in the International Arena*, US Advisory Commission on Intergovernmental Relations, forthcoming.

7 The US States and foreign economic policy: federalism in the 'new world order'

Earl H. Fry

Federalism in the industrialized world has certainly been impacted by the monumental changes which have occurred in the international system over the past half-dozen years. Hopefully, the Cold War order which dominated the post-Second World War era is now defunct. Communism has been discredited as an ideology, the Soviet Union no longer exists, Germany has been reunited, and Eastern bloc institutions such as the Warsaw Pact and Comecon have been totally dismantled. The Western nations are the self-proclaimed victors of the Cold War, but even here it is difficult to ascertain whether NATO can continue to function effectively in the absence of a perceived Soviet threat to Western Europe, and whether the so-called 'West' will be transformed into three major trading blocs in Europe, North America and East Asia.

As conceived by former President George Bush, the post-Cold War era will lead to a new world order which will be opposed to imperialism and composed of independent, democratic, self-determining nation-states. This new order will bind nation-states together in regional and international institutions which will encourage free trade based on market forces, enshrine the Wilsonian concept of collective security, and promote common political objectives, especially the protection of basic human rights.[1]

Some would claim that the first victory in the new world order occurred in the Persian Gulf, when a collective security system either actively or tacitly approved beforehand by the five major global powers, thwarted the ambitions of a regional aggressor and restored Kuwait to the status of a nation-state.

In Europe, however, the tenets underpinning the new world order are already on shaky ground. According to the Bush administration, the new order should be predicated on a 'free and whole' Europe respecting territorial integrity. In an era when the twelve nations of the European Community are harmonizing policies in order to take advantage of growing regional and international economic interdependence, neighboring federal systems in the Soviet Union and Yugoslavia have disintegrated and some of the constituent units have continued to suffer civil strife and bloodshed.

The leading powers, especially the United States, are having a difficult time responding to these centrifugal forces. The Conference for Security and Cooperation in Europe (CSCE), which is composed of all the European nations plus the United States and Canada, has grappled with the demands for independence from subnational governmental units. Initially, the CSCE ignored the appeals for independence from Latvia, Lithuania, Estonia and several other former republics in both the Soviet Union and Yugoslavia, insisting on the integrity of the nation-state and arguing that any changes must be made peacefully, democratically and in an orderly fashion. On its own northern border, the United States also faces the specter of a new referendum on Quebec's independence from Canada. Washington's position in this case is that the United States favors the continued existence of the Canadian confederation, but it is a domestic affair of Canada and will be decided one way or another by the Canadian people through a peaceful, democratic process.

These examples illustrate that the post-Cold War international system, although offering many new opportunities for peaceful global exchanges, will also be very complex and at times vexatious. This chapter will focus specifically on the international economic activities of the states in the US federal system, whose objectives are much more modest than those of the former Soviet and Yugoslavian republics or even of neighboring Quebec. However, it will underscore the complexity of the contemporary international system as it emphasizes the growing role which subnational governments are playing in the global economic arena, and illustrates that it is increasingly more difficult to distinguish between 'foreign' and 'domestic' policy in federal systems of government.

The economic base of state governments

The major transformations which have occurred in the international system over the past decade have been matched by historic changes at the subnational government level. In the world today, there are over 180 sovereign nation-states and close to 300 federated or subnational governmental units. When the county and local governments and special districts are added to the equation, literally hundreds of thousands of subnational government entities are found in federal states. For example, the United States has more than 83,000 governments, an increase of 3,000 over the past decade. Among municipal governments, 195 US cities in 1990 had populations exceeding 100,000, an increase of twenty-nine since 1980. Many of these major cities have joined the state units in becoming actively involved in international economic activities.[2]

The capacity of US state and local governments to influence domestic and international commerce positively or negatively should not be underestimated. Among the twenty-five leading nations in the world ranked by gross national product (GNP), one could insert ten states; among the top fifty nations, thirty-three states; and among the top seventy-five nations, all fifty states. California is home to more than 30 million people, a population greater than that of Canada and Australia and three-quarters of the countries in Europe, and it enters the 1990s with a 717 billion dollar annual gross state product which would rank it as the eighth largest country globally.[3] New York is not far behind with its top ten ranking, and Texas produces more than twice as much as neighboring Mexico. These states are also important trading clients for many countries, with California ranking as Japan's second leading partner after the rest of the United States.

Furthermore, the annual budgets of states such as California and New York, which now exceed 50 billion dollars (including federal transfer payments), are surpassed by only a handful of national governments around the world. To put this in perspective, California's budget of 56 billion dollars in fiscal year 1991–2 is four times greater than the Philippines', a nation with 56 million people. At the municipal level, New York City's annual budget is bigger than all but two states and twice as large as that of the Philippines, and its long-term debt burden is greater than any other borrower in the United States except the US government.[4] Total state and local government revenues in 1990 were 801 billion dollars, with these non-central governments spending 674 billion dollars for the purchase of goods and services, compared with 424 billion dollars spent by the US federal government for similar purchases.[5] State and local governments account for 10 percent of all spending in the United States, employ one of every twelve workers, and build 20 percent of all structures.[6]

The impetus for international involvement

US state and local governments have rapidly expanded their international activities, primarily for economic reasons. Only four of the fifty states had opened an office overseas in 1970; twenty years later, forty-three states were operating 163 offices abroad, four-fifths of which were located either in East Asia or Western Europe. Annually, forty governors now lead at least one international mission in search of trade, investment and tourism opportunities, and states spent 92 million dollars on international economic programs in 1990, excluding investment incentive programs.[7] Many mayors of big cities also head international missions, and leaders of smaller cities can participate in the periodic missions sponsored by two umbrella organizations, the National League of Cities and the US Conference of Mayors. Almost 1,000 US communities have also teamed up with 1,850 municipalities in ninety-six countries through the sister city program.[8] Increasingly, these sister city alliances are used to strengthen economic linkages between the twinned municipalities.[9] Cities generally rely on their state offices, US embassies, and the 124 overseas offices of the US Foreign and Commercial Service to represent their economic interests abroad, but Tucson, Arizona has operated its own trade office in Taipei since 1987 and the Las Vegas Convention and Visitors Authority maintains three offices in Europe and Asia.

As I have discussed in detail in a previous article, there are a variety of factors which account for the rapid increase in state and local government involvement overseas.[10] Above all, the imperatives of complex global interdependence are pushing the non-central governments to be active participants at the international level. In the realm of foreign direct investment (FDI), the United States ranks as the number-one host nation in the world and more than four million Americans now work for foreign-owned companies situated on US soil. States and cities are spending hundreds of millions of dollars annually in programs and incentives in an effort to attract this direct investment to their areas of jurisdiction. Globally, the flow of FDI has increased tenfold in real terms from the end of the 1970s to the end of the 1980s.[11]

Because of the lack of economic diversity in several states and many municipalities, US direct investment abroad has received mixed reviews from non-central government leaders. Some consider that such investment is indispensable if US firms are to remain globally competitive, and believe that in the long run more jobs will be created locally by enterprises which have well-established international networks. Approximately 2,000 American companies have established 21,000 foreign subsidiaries in 121 countries, and these subsidiaries annually manufacture and sell abroad products worth about 700 billion dollars.[12]

Conversely, other non-central government leaders are convinced that American corporations are abandoning facilities in the United States for countries with cheap labor and minimal environmental and worker protection standards. In a vote at the 1991 annual meeting of the US Conference of Mayors, the delegates refused to approve a resolution supporting the proposed North American Free Trade Area (NAFTA).[13] These delegates feared that companies would eliminate high-paying jobs in urban areas and transfer the work to Mexico where wages and fringe benefits in the manufacturing sector are only one-sixth to one-seventh US levels.

In recent years, world trade volume has also easily outdistanced the aggregate growth in national economies, and one-fifth of global production is now linked to international trade.[14] Global trade in goods and services added up to about four trillion dollars in 1990, a thirteenfold increase in real terms since 1950.[15] Unfortunately, the United States experienced a staggering trillion-dollar merchandise trade deficit during the 1980s, but its performance is now improving significantly.[16] The US annual current account deficit finally dropped below 100 billion dollars in 1990, the lowest since 1983, and was unexpectedly low in 1991 because of increased export activity and special payments received from the allied nations for US participation in the Persian Gulf War. In addition, the United States has enjoyed five consecutive years of declining aggregate trade deficits with the other key industrial nations. Merchandise exports topped 389 billion dollars in 1990, and although Germany edged out the United States as the world's leading exporter, the US trade trend is encouraging.

Approximately 100,000 American businesses are now involved in export activity, but the US Census Bureau estimates that 3,600 firms account for over three-quarters of all merchandise exports.[17] State and local governments recognize that tens of thousands of small and medium-sized businesses are capable of entering or expanding export markets, and all of the states and many of the metropolitan governments have established assistance programs for these businesses. For example, California's Export Finance Office alone has issued almost as many loan guarantees to individual businesses as the Export-Import Bank of the United States has issued nationwide.[18] Collectively, state and local governments are spending much more on export promotion than the US federal government.

Globalization has also precipitated a major restructuring in many industries and a growing recognition in the United States of the implications of the internationalization of production. Robert Reich clearly illustrates this internationalization phenomenon in the following statement:

What's traded between nations is less often finished goods than specialized research, design, fabrication, management, marketing, advertising, consulting, financial and legal services, as well as components and materials.

When an American buys a Pontiac le Mans from General Motors, for example, he engages unwillingly in an international transaction. Of the 10,000 dollars paid to GM, about 3,000 dollars goes to South Korea for routine labor and assembly operations, 1,850 dollars to Japan for advanced components (engines, transaxles, and electronics), 700 dollars to the former West Germany for styling and design engineering, 400 dollars to Taiwan, Singapore, and Japan for small components, 250 dollars to Britain for advertising and marketing services, and about 50 dollars to Ireland and Barbados for data processing. The rest—less than 4,000 dollars—goes to strategists in Detroit, lawyers and bankers in New York, lobbyists in Washington, insurance and health care workers all over the country, and to General Motors shareholders all over the world.[19]

Even though the United States created approximately 20 million net new jobs during the ninety-two-month economic expansion which began in November 1982 and ended in July 1990, almost 2 million jobs were lost in the manufacturing sector. States and cities have all had to cope with the costs and benefits of restructuring. Detroit has been badly hurt by the downturn in the domestic automotive industry, whereas Marysville, Ohio, Georgetown, Kentucky, and Smyrna, Tennessee have profited from Honda, Toyota and Nissan building huge assembly plants in their localities. With the marked decline in international petroleum prices in the early 1980s, Houston lost 225,000 jobs in a five-year period. New York City once provided headquarters for one-half of America's thirty largest industrial firms. Today, only two remain.[20] Over the past two years, the New York City metropolitan area has lost 440,000 jobs out of a total of 8 million. During the same period, New Hampshire and Massachusetts both lost more than 10 percent of their total jobs, with the latter losing one-quarter of its manufacturing employment since the early 1980s.[21]

International tourism has also emerged as an increasingly important revenue source for many non-central governments. In 1991, an estimated 41.5 million foreign residents visited the United States and spent 57 billion dollars.[22] Approximately 20 percent of all the tourists in New York City are from other countries, and they annually spend more than 2 billion dollars.[23]

In addition, immigration is in the process of transforming several American states and cities. California had a net increase of 3.2 million new entrants into the state in the 1980s, and 2.3 million of these came from other countries.[24] During the same decade, New York City attracted 854,000 immigrants, mostly from developing countries.[25] One-third of all New York City residents are now foreign-born, up from one-fourth just a decade ago. Because of this immigration, New York City experienced a modest 3.5 percent population increase during the 1980s. Los Angeles added more people than any other US city during the past decade, and many of these new residents were immigrants. In both New York City and Los Angeles, the so-called 'white' population now constitutes a minority group.[26]

The US Immigration Act of 1990 also provides economic incentives for states to attract a special category of immigrants. This act establishes up to 10,000 annual investor-immigrant visas for foreign residents and their families willing to invest large amounts of money in US businesses and create jobs for Americans. Seven thousand of these visas require an investment of at least one million dollars, and 3,000 an investment of at least 500,000 dollars in high-poverty or rural areas. Municipal governments are interested in attracting the lion's share of these immigrants, and thirty-eight states now sponsor Enterprise Zone programs, most of which will qualify as investments in 'high-poverty' areas.[27]

There are several additional factors other than complex economic interdependence and the internationalization of trade, investment, tourism and financial linkages which help explain the growing global involvement of non-central governments. These would include the uneven distribution of economic gains in America's vast federal system, electoral considerations, significant growth in non-central governments plus an improved capacity to interact with international actors, and a willingness on the part of the national government to permit non-central governments to strengthen linkages abroad.[28]

On the other hand, this phenomenon in many respects is attributable to the traditional role of state and local governments which is to protect their revenue base and to safeguard the interests of the people whom they represent. The collective fiscal health of these non-central governments is currently the worst since the recession period of the early 1980s, with two-thirds of the states, two-fifths of the largest counties, and one-half of the major cities facing very serious financial challenges. Although forty-nine of the fifty states are required to balance their budgets each year, debt can be carried over from one year to the next in off-budget accounts. During the past decade, the off-budget debt of state governments actually doubled. In addition, even though the federal government provided in 1991 144 billion dollars in grants-in-aid to state and local governments, this represented only 17 percent of non-central government revenues, compared with 25 percent of total revenues in the late 1970s. The decline in federal assistance to municipalities is even more pronounced, with Washington providing 6.4 percent of total city revenues in 1991 versus 17.7 percent in 1980.[29] The problem is compounded further by the federal government's propensity in recent years to 'mandate' new responsibilities to state and local governments without transferring adequate funds to pay for these predominantly social-welfare programs. Moreover, the money which is made available by Washington has many strings attached and only a small portion can be used for economic development purposes. Indeed, 60 cents of each dollar of federal grant money are now earmarked for only two welfare programs — Aid to Families With Dependent Children and Medicaid (a health insurance program for low-income individuals and families) — versus only 40 cents for these programs in 1980.[30]

In spite of the myriad social problems faced at the state and local levels, the prospects for a big increase in federal funding to subnational governments are very dim. The US federal debt will approach four trillion dollars by the end of 1992, and annual interest payments on this debt now surpass 200 billion dollars. Proportionally, interest payments are the fastest-growing budgetary allocation of the federal government, and money spent on this debt liability is far greater than the allocations to state and local governments. Moreover, two-thirds of the budgetary allocations of a typical state are now earmarked for only three programs: welfare, Medicaid and corrections. Over each of the past two fiscal years, state governments have faced double-digit spending increases in both the Medicaid and corrections programs, putting severe stress on other budgetary allocations.

With rising costs associated with explosive increases in health-care costs, homelessness, AIDS, crime and infrastructure deterioration, state and local governments are facing major fiscal crises. Health care now absorbs 12 percent of America's GDP, far more than any other industrialized country. In spite of this huge expenditure, 34 million Americans are without health insurance and tens of millions of additional people have inadequate levels of insurance. The US infant mortality rate also ranks near the bottom of the industrialized countries, even though the US rate has been gradually improving. Many urban centers have a much higher rate than the national average, with New York City's a third higher and Central Harlem's two and one-half times higher.[31] Although estimates vary dramatically, homelessness has apparently increased significantly. Among these homeless are tens of thousands of people who are in desperate need of mental health care but who are now wandering aimlessly on urban streets. AIDS has afflicted hundreds of thousands of young people, a disease which was unknown less than two decades ago.

In terms of crime, the US inmate population doubled to more than one million during the 1980s, and the United States has the highest incarceration rate in the world. The average cost of incarcerating a juvenile now approaches 30,000 dollars per year, far more than the cost of educating a young man or woman at a prestigious university.[32] A recent report of the US Senate Judiciary Committee described the United States as 'the most violent and self-destructive nation on earth.'[33] Violent crime increased by 516 percent between 1960 and 1990, while the US population as a whole increased by only 41 percent.[34] The US murder rate is fifteen times higher than that of Japan and Great Britain, and more than one-half of federal prisoners are now serving time on drug-related charges.[35] Much of this crime is an urban problem, and minority groups have been especially decimated by lawlessness. Blacks are six times more likely to be murdered than whites, and one of every four young black males is on probation, paroled, or in prison, a higher percentage than is to be found in college.[36] Dropping out of school contributes to higher poverty and crime and welfare costs, at a time when one in four children under the age of six already lives in poverty. Municipalities such as New York City are experiencing an overall 33 percent school drop-out rate, with the rate among minority groups at times approaching 50 percent.[37]

Public infrastructure deterioration is frequently referred to as America's third great deficit (in addition to its government and current account deficits), with perhaps 50 billion dollars in added spending needed each year for modernization and repairs. Once again, much of the deterioration which has occurred in the public infrastructure is urban-based. Furthermore, the difficulty in paying for infrastructure and other improvements at the municipal level has been exacerbated by the flight of the middle class to the suburbs. Many of these people work in urban centers and take advantage of city services, but their contribution to the municipal tax base is minimal. The per capita income in America's largest central cities is now only 59 percent of their suburbs, whereas city–suburban income levels were roughly equal just two decades ago.[38]

How America copes with the problems of its urban centers will have a dramatic effect on US competitiveness in the twenty-first century. Whereas two-thirds of all Americans lived in rural areas in 1890, three of every four now live in metropolitan areas (a population exceeding 50,000), and more than one-half are concentrated in thirty-nine metropolitan areas having at least one million residents. Fully 90 percent of America's population growth during the 1980s occurred in these areas with more than one million inhabitants.

Great diversities in regional economic development and the constant need for additional revenues have prompted many states to develop their own industrial policies. Some observers now refer to the state governments as the 'dynamos' of the US federal system, and there is no doubt that their policies will have a growing impact during the 1990s upon US commercial relations at home and abroad.[39] Two dozen states are now directly involved in the venture capital game, committing in excess of 300 million dollars for projects over the past few years. State agencies also provide low-interest loans, help in securing private financing and technical managerial assistance. As an illustration, the Connecticut Product Development Corporation has invested more than 12 million dollars in approximately sixty small businesses. The state receives a 5 percent royalty on products sold by the companies backed by the venture capital.[40] The Connecticut state government has also entered into a controversial agreement to purchase 47 percent of the equity in Colt's Manufacturing Company, a major supplier of automatic weapons. Pennsylvania's Ben Franklin Partnership has provided over 80 million dollars for state-based technology projects, and the Massachusetts Technology Development Corporation has distributed more than 10 million dollars in seed money.[41] Over the past decade, more than 700 state and local governments have funded programs to help small companies bring new technologies to market.[42] Many states have also set up industrial parks, enterprise zones, business incubators and greenhouse projects to spur on economic development, with the latter program geared to the construction of special buildings to house new high-technology businesses.

Increasing the effectiveness of state-level programs

The following prescriptions should help subnational governments in the US federal system to adapt more effectively to the economic challenges facing them both domestically and internationally.

(1) An export partnership

In the export arena, national, state and local governments can do much more to facilitate US economic activity abroad. The United States is the world's leading trading nation, but it continues to suffer sizable trade deficits.[43] Moreover, a nation with less than a third of its population, Germany, actually exported more than the United States in 1990.

The US Department of Commerce estimates that at least 70,000 companies have products that are in demand worldwide, but that are not involved in exporting at this time. It is with these 70,000 enterprises that grass-roots support from local and state governments can provide big dividends. With more outreach efforts and preparatory work, all levels of government should be able to assist small and medium-sized firms producing competitive goods to tackle international markets. The first step should be to enter the Canadian marketplace and take advantage of the recently enacted Canada–US Free Trade Agreement (FTA). If the NAFTA is successfully implemented, then both Canada and Mexico will be prime export markets for US companies, forging a market with 360 million consumers and over a six trillion dollar annual production base. The state government of Texas has also inaugurated a useful program in cooperation with four municipal governments. This program establishes Export Assistance Centers which emphasize basic trade procedures for small and medium-sized businesses. The Department of Commerce in Texas estimates that every 44,000 dollars in goods or services shipped to foreign markets creates or retains 2.3 jobs in the state.[44]

At the municipal level, the Trade Development Alliance (TDA) of Greater Seattle has recently been created to promote export activity. TDA is patterned after European and Asian port-city promotion councils and is a collaborative project involving the Port of Seattle, the King County government, the Seattle municipal government, the Greater Seattle Chamber of Commerce, and a group of union leaders. It has four permanent staff members, a seventeen-member executive board, and a modest 310,000 dollar annual budget.[45]

Easily accessible 'one-stop' export centers should be started around the country, centers combining the resources of city, county, state and federal governments and the private sector. Moreover, state and local governments should not hesitate to use the services offered by the regional International Trade Administration offices and the US Foreign and Commercial Service offices located in many US embassies.

(2) Tourism cooperation

By the year 2000, tourism will probably be the largest industry in the United States. Almost exactly 500 years after Columbus's voyage, foreigners have rediscovered America, and cheap air fares and ground accommodations, particularly from a European and Japanese point of view, are prompting a tremendous increase in overseas visitors.

Once again, tourism is a win–win game for states and cities within close proximity to one another. City, county, state and federal governments, along with the Travel Industry Association of America and other related tourism, theme park and convention groups, must be more aggressive in their European, Asian, Canadian and Pacific advertising campaigns. The pooling of resources at the national and the state levels will provide significant economies of scale and should enhance tourism activity.

(3) The delicate investment dimension

Foreign direct investment is a touchy issue on Washington's Capitol Hill with new restrictions added in the 1988 Omnibus Trade and Competitiveness Act. However, FDI is generally welcomed with open arms in most states and local communities. On the other hand, export activity and tourism promotion can be a 'mixed-sum' game, meaning that subnational units can work together with all players potentially benefiting. As an illustration, some states already cooperate on a regional basis to promote tourism and also pool some of their exports, especially agricultural commodities. In contrast, both states and cities perceive the attraction of FDI as a 'zero-sum' game, with only one winner and the remaining players losers. States are now pitted against states in very costly investment incentive bidding wars, and more attention must be paid to the ramifications of this competition to attract investment from abroad. The vast majority of FDI will come to the United States without any incentives at all, but the nature of America's competitive federal system has convinced subnational leaders that incentives must be offered. Quite frankly, many incentives are simply a waste of taxpayers' money, and the federal government should work with the National Governors' Association, the National League of Cities, the US Conference of Mayors and related organizations to formulate new rules of the game which would de-emphasize direct cash incentives to foreign and domestic investors alike.

In addition, once incentives have been offered to a domestic or foreign investor, can they be recouped if the investor fails to carry through with his part of the bargain? Pennsylvania pieced together a big incentive package for Volkswagen, but the German firm has now closed its facility in that state. The Governor of West Virginia lodged a breach-of-contract lawsuit against the Newell Company for closing its plant in Clarksburg. The former owner of the facility, Anchor Hocking, had accepted a state government incentive package of subsidized loans worth 3.5 million dollars.[46] City officials in Norwood, Ohio also sued General Motors because of GM's plant closure in that city. City representatives claim that the municipality spent hundreds of thousands of dollars to improve railroad links to the GM plant, and that Norwood should be reimbursed and penalties exacted.[47] If incentives are to be offered in the future, both subnational governments and the investors must clearly spell out what their responsibilities are, and what the so-called 'clawback' penalties will be for non-compliance.

In the foreseeable future, it should be expected that FDI activity in the United States will continue to increase at moderate levels as foreign investors take advantage of favorable exchange rates and attractive equity and real estate prices. On the whole, this activity is healthy for the American economy and through the introduction of new technology, production, and marketing processes, should help to make the United States more competitive internationally. Subnational governments should also be expected to accelerate their own involvement in the international economy and will be enthusiastic supporters of most types of future FDI activity.

(4) Continuity and a long-term perspective

Numerous state and local government officials have expressed concern that periodic changes in executive or legislative leadership, or impatience on the part of the electorate, might shift the priorities of subnational governments away from the international arena.

These problems can be solved through the education process and through institutional continuity. Local residents must understand that significant changes in the international economic system do require some state and local government involvement abroad in order to protect the economic interests of the state or municipality. More than ever before, interdependence at the global level necessitates vigilance and policy planning at the local level. Furthermore, patience will be required, for the establishment of solid trade and other economic linkages generally takes years to achieve.

Moreover, state and local governments must create permanent institutions to cope with international trade, investment, tourism, and cultural exchanges, institutions which will survive the transition from one administration to the next. These institutions should be staffed by permanent civil servants who can gain expertise and provide the continuity and stability needed to survive most any change in political leadership. On the other hand, few programs will be eminently successful unless the elected representatives of the people enthusiastically support subnational government involvement in the international arena.

(5) Sensitivity at the national and grass-roots levels

Washington must be much more sensitive to the huge task faced by the states and cities in funding desperately-needed infrastructure improvements such as schools, roads, bridges, waste treatment plants, etc.

The much-heralded Tax Reform Act of 1986 has severely crippled state and local government participation in the tax-exempt bond market, and removed some of the advantages once offered to banks and insurance companies which purchase state and local government-issued bonds.[48] Further damage was done with the Supreme Court's decision in April 1988 to leave the future of the tax-exempt market solely in the discretionary hands of the US Congress. Faced with a drop in transfer payments from Washington, DC and limited access to the bond markets, state and local governments will need to generate revenues from other sources, with domestic and foreign direct investment and export and tourism promotion being prime candidates. Both Capitol Hill and the White House must show a better understanding of the plight faced by subnational governments, and comprehend the consequences which national policies are having on the financial well-being and viability of state and municipal governments.

At the other end of the spectrum, significant questions must be posed about the potential repercussions of state and municipal 'foreign policies'. In the very same week that President George Bush announced the lifting of US sanctions against South Africa, Mayor David Dinkins of New York City announced the tightening of municipal sanctions against banks which were willing to do business with South Africa.[49] Currently, there are over 140 state and local governmental units which sponsor sanctions against South Africa falling into four major categories: (1) laws requiring the divestiture or partial divestiture of public pension fund holdings in companies doing business with South Africa; (2) a prohibition on state and local governments using the financial services of banks doing business with South Africa; (3) a ban on the purchase of South African goods by state and local governments; and (4) restrictions on contracting out services to specific companies which continue to do business with South Africa.[50] The use of public-employee pension funds as a strategy for state and local governments to influence the behaviour of private companies listed on the US stock markets is a recent phenomenon. These public pension funds now hold over 300 billion dollars in corporate equities and control about 10 percent of the total value of companies traded on the New York Stock Exchange. The California Public Employees' Retirement System (CalPERS) alone has over 65 billion dollars in assets.

How many cities would have to adopt San Francisco's positions of maintaining sanctions against South Africa, providing sanctuary for illegal immigrants from Central America, and opposing the basing of nuclear-armed US warships at local ports, before people begin to wonder who speaks for

America in the foreign and defense policy arenas? Should cities be permitted to establish new sister city relationships or send envoys and material assistance to countries such as Cuba whose policies are currently at odds with those of the US national government? Should New York City and Newark have been permitted to deny Soviet UN representatives landing rights at their airports following the shooting-down of the KAL 747 passenger plane in 1983? Should state and city officials be permitted to order their law enforcement officers to desist from cooperating with federal officers tracking down illegal immigrants? Can 'civil disobedience' be tolerated from duly-elected state and municipal representatives of the people?

Constitutionally, it is clear that the people's elected representatives on Capitol Hill and in the White House have the authority to determine the nation's foreign policy, and this is backed up by the Supremacy Clause, Commerce Clause, Logan Act, and various court decisions including *Zschernig* v. *Miller*.[51] However, if the voters become disenchanted with the guns versus butter priorities of the White House or Capitol Hill, or the specific conduct of policy towards Eastern Europe, Central America, South Africa, or any other region, then they have the right to use the power of the ballot box to dump their elected representatives.

State and local government representatives should, of course, be able to express their opinions on a wide variety of issues, and more so today than at any other time because of the growing overlap of 'domestic' and 'foreign' policy issue areas. At its World Congress in Rio de Janeiro in 1985, the International Union of Local Authorities (IULA) issued a Worldwide Declaration of Local Self-Government. Article 10 of this declaration states that local authorities should have the right to belong to an international association of local authorities, and to maintain links with their counterparts in other countries for the purpose of interchange and cooperation and promoting international understanding. This is a perfectly logical demand in a shrinking world where so many problems will require regional and global cooperation before they can be resolved.

Voters in state and local elections must likewise be entitled to express their own opinions on a wide variety of issues through the initiative process. As an illustration, an initiative was passed by the voters in November 1986 instructing Seattle's municipal leaders to keep the sister city linkage with a Nicaraguan city out of politics. The voters also overturned a City Council resolution approving Seattle as a sanctuary city. Voters have in the past and should continue in the future to express their opinions on such issues as the nuclear arms race, environmental issues, and other related topics which have both domestic and international connotations.

On the other hand, state laws and municipal ordinances which impede the ability of federal officials, such as Immigration and Naturalization Service agents, to carry out their lawful duties will eventually prompt a

crackdown from both Capitol Hill and the federal court system. The ship-
ment of supplies by municipalities to nations at odds with US policy may
also precipitate a crackdown. In effect, state and local leaders should feel
free to speak out against what they consider to be injustices at home or
abroad, and pressure their elected representatives in Congress to echo their
point of view, but they should not cross the line which leads to civil
disobedience or an outright violation of US laws.

With this caveat in mind, American state and municipal governments
must continue to be actively involved in the international arena, especially
at a time when leading figures in both major political parties are reverting
back to the 'America first' philosophy of the pre-Second World War period.
Such a philosophy is blind to the trend toward greater global interdependence and the need for cooperation which transcends national boundaries.
Moreover, when carried to an extreme, the 'America first' proponents could
provoke a repeat of the highly destructive protectionist wars of the 1930s
which followed the enactment of the Smoot-Hawley tariffs by the US
Congress.

More inter-state and international cooperation should also be encouraged
among America's subnational governments. The New England Governors'
Conference, the Council of Great Lakes' Governors, the Mid-South Trade
Council and the Pacific Northwest Economic Region are among the organizations which facilitate greater cooperation among subnational units.
Canadian provincial and US state governments are also cooperating more
than ever. The New England governors meet with the eastern Canadian
premiers on an annual basis, and the western premiers and governors have
begun to invite one another to their annual regional conferences. With the
possible enactment of the NAFTA, linkages are now being forged between the
governors in the southern United States and northern Mexico.

In the economic sphere especially, US subnational governments have
much to do just to keep up with the torrid pace now being set by many of
their European, Japanese, and Canadian counterparts. European regional
and municipal governments, in particular, are now accelerating their activities as they prepare for the major changes envisioned in the European
Community after 1992. On the opposite side of the world, a city such as
Osaka has already created a mini-foreign policy apparatus.[52] One should
hope that many US states and cities will continue to be among the leaders
in forging strong economic and cultural ties abroad and in helping America
at the grass-roots level to prepare for the growing competition and interdependence of the twenty-first century.

In the academic arena, the notion of 'thinking globally and acting
locally', or 'glocalization', is just beginning to take root. State and local
government specialists have thus far had little contact with comparative or
international relations experts. There is much that they can learn from one
another as complex interdependence intensifies. Practitioners at the non-

central government level must also be included in this dialogue, for they will assume the leading role in coping with the very serious human problems outlined in this chapter. And finally, both government officials and academicians in the United States must cogently recognize that there is much to be learned from experiences in federal systems elsewhere in the world in terms of improving the quality of life for America's citizens, especially those who reside in major metropolitan areas.

Notes

1. See Tony Smith, 'Democracy resurgent', in Nicholas X. Rizopoulos (ed.), *Sea Changes: American Foreign Policy in a World Transformed*, Council on Foreign Relations, New York (1990), 152–60.
2. These figures are based on the 1990 census.
3. *Los Angeles Times* (18 June 1991) D1.
4. *New York Times* (5 March 1991), A1. New York City's long-term debt surpasses 22 billion dollars.
5. 'National income and product account', *Survey of Current Business* (March 1991), 11.
6. John E. Petersen, 'Local government spending can aid economy', *Deseret News* (3 March 1991), 16A.
7. *Governors' Weekly Bulletin* (30 March 1990), 1; and *Nation's Cities Weekly* (1 July 1991), 6. In 1989, governors from forty-one of the fifty-five US states and territories made eighty-two trips to thirty-five countries. Forty-eight trips were primarily to encourage exports and thirty-two to increase investment. Japan was the leading country visited, with nineteen trips, followed by thirteen trips to Belgium.
8. Wilbur Zelinsky, 'Sister city alliances', *American Demographics* (June 1990), 43.
9. ibid., 44–5. Zelinsky discusses in particular a business alliance between Louisville, Kentucky and Montpellier, France, and business linkages between Baltimore, Maryland and Xiamen, China, and Portland, Oregon and Sapporo, Japan.
10. Earl H. Fry, 'The impact of federalism on the development of international economic relations: lessons from the United States and Canada', *Australian Outlook: The Journal of International Affairs*, 43 (1989), 19–25.
11. *Economist* (22 December 1990), 44. At the end of the 1980s, the annual flow of FDI exceeded 100 billion dollars (measured in 1980 dollars).
12. *Wall Street Journal* (27 March 1991), A16; and the *New York Times* (26 February 1991), C2.
13. The US Conference of Mayors held its annual meeting in June 1991 in San Diego. See *U.S. Mayor* (1 July 1991), 8 and 11.
14. For example, world trade volume grew 5 percent in 1990, whereas the global economy grew only 3 percent.
15. *Economist* (22 December 1990), 44.
16. This trade deficit includes transportation charges and insurance fees associated with import and export activity. During the 1982–90 economic expansion, US

exports increased in real terms by 93 percent.

17. Martha E. Mangelsdorf, 'Unfair trade', *Inc.* (April 1991), 28.
18. Elliot King, 'Bridging the finance gap for mid-sized exporters', *Global Trade* (July 1989), 18. This statement was made by L. Fargo Wells, who was then executive director of the California Export Finance Office. The Export-Import Bank, of course, had far more money available to loan to businesses than its subnational counterpart in California. Through mid-1990, California's Export Finance Office had guaranteed 51 million dollars in loans generating 260 million dollars in sales. See the *Wall Street Journal* (7 November 1990), B1 and B2.
19. Robert Reich, 'The myth of "Made in the U.S.A."', *Wall Street Journal* (5 July 1991), A6.
20. *Economist* (1 June 1991), 19.
21. *New York Times* (15 December 1991), A1; and the *Economist* (29 July 1989), 55.
22. These are estimates of the US Travel and Tourism Administration made in a report issued on 13 May 1991. In 1990, 38.8 million foreign residents visited the United States and spent 51.1 billion dollars. Twenty-five million of these visitors came from neighboring Canada and Mexico. These tourists helped to provide the United States with a record 23 billion dollar surplus in trade in services in 1990.
23. In 1989, 25 million tourists visited New York City, with one in five being a foreign resident. Collectively, these tourists spent about 9 billion dollars in the metropolitan area.
24. *New York Times* (21 February 1991), A14.
25. These figures were compiled by the US Immigration and Naturalization Service.
26. New York City had 7.3 million people in 1990, with 43.2 percent being white, 25.2 percent non-Hispanic black, 24.4 percent Hispanic, and 7 percent Asian (see the *New York Times*, 22 March 1991, B1). Los Angeles had 3.5 million people, with 40 percent being Hispanic, 38 percent white, 13 percent black, and 10 percent Asian. These percentages, of course, would change significantly when the entire metropolitan area is considered. New York City ranked as the largest US metropolitan area in 1990 with 18 million people, and Los Angeles ranked number two with 14.5 million people.
27. *Wall Street Journal* (1 April 1991), B1 and B2.
28. All of these factors are explored in detail in Fry, 'Impact of federalism', op.cit.
29. *Wall Street Journal* (5 February 1991), A1.
30. *Fortune* (3 June 1991), 21.
31. *New York Times* (30 June 1990), sec. I, 11. The US rate dropped from 9.7 deaths per thousand in 1980 to 9.1 in 1990, but the United States still ranks 22nd in the world. The infant mortality rate among blacks is twice the level of whites.
32. In comparison, annual room, board and tuition at Harvard University is only 18,000 dollars. See William Raspberry, 'Prison costs more than Harvard', *Washington Post* (13 May 1991), A11.
33. *Washington Post National Weekly Edition* (8 April 1991), 25.
34. ibid.
35. According to the US Office of National Drug Control Policy, Americans spent an estimated 40 billion dollars on illegal drugs in 1990, compared with 50 billion dollars in 1989 and almost 52 billion dollars in 1988.

36. These estimates are made by the Sentencing Project, a non-profit organization headquartered in Washington, DC. See *Fortune* (3 June 1991), 182. According to a recent US Health and Human Services Study, more teenage boys die from gunshots than from all other natural causes combined. A black male teenager is eleven times more likely to be murdered with a gun than a white teenager. Moreover, the leading killer of young black males is young black males. See the *Washington Post* (14 March 1991), A1.

37. *Washington Post National Weekly Edition* (27 May 1991), 10.

38. ibid. (8 April 1991), 6. *Nation's Cities Weekly* (17 June 1991), 6.

39. In Neal R. Pierce, 'States: dynamos of the federal system', *State Government News* (December 1989), 23, the author asserts that the '1980s indisputably have been the decade of state governments. Those in doubt need only take a look at virtually any major domestic policy-making arena-welfare reform, early childhood care, education, environmental protection, homelessness, infrastructure, foreign trade promotion and health-care cost containment.'

40. *Christian Science Monitor* (20 November 1984), 37.

41. *Wall Street Journal* (9 November 1987), 27.

42. ibid. (4 October 1991), B2.

43. This includes insurance and transportation expenses.

44. Texas Department of Commerce, *Report* (July 1988).

45. *Nation's Cities Weekly* (1 July 1991), 7.

46. *Wall Street Journal* (8 March 1988), 1.

47. ibid., 26.

48. *Washington Post* (September 1988), H8.

49. *New York Times* (11 July 1991), A7. New York will withdraw municipal deposits from any bank conducting business with South Africa. In 1990, New York City held deposits in twenty banks with an average account balance of 250 million dollars.

50. Kathleen Sylvester, 'Keeping the pressure on South Africa', *Governing* (December 1991), 24–5.

51. *Zschernig* v. *Miller* was decided by the US Supreme Court in 1968. Oregon had passed a law denying a resident alien the right to inherit property in the state, if the alien's home country barred US residents from inheriting property. The Supreme Court ruled against Oregon's law because of the potentially adverse impact it might have on the central government's conduct of foreign policy.

52. The activities of non-North American municipalities were outlined for me by the former director of the International Union of Local Authorities, Mr Van Putten, in a meeting held at The Hague on 25 March 1988.

8 Quebec's international relations: a response to needs and necessities

Louis Balthazar

With its twenty-eight missions abroad, Quebec represents a unique case of international involvement for a federated state. This phenomenon is often related with Quebec's incessant striving to assert itself within Canada as 'a province unlike the others'. International relations are thus envisaged as one element of the conflict between Ottawa and the French-speaking province. Some would even go further and associate Quebec's international activity with the secessionist movement.

This chapter will question such an interpretation. Not that it can be proven completely wrong. Nobody would deny that Quebec's claims to international recognition have often taken place in an atmosphere of conflict. But to focus on the conflictual aspects of Quebec's policies would result in an incomplete and distorted picture of reality. The purpose of the following analysis is to stress the importance of non-political factors in the conduct of international relations by the province of Quebec so that we may conclude that foreign relations, even when they originate from a centrifugal province like Quebec, are potentially more cooperative than conflictual in the perspective of the whole country's foreign policy.

After a brief description of Quebec's international activities, particularly in the last thirty years, some tentative answers will be put forward to the question: 'Why did the province of Quebec resort to a foreign policy?' Some empirical findings concerning Quebec's objectives, means and actions abroad will be put forward to illustrate the main contention of this essay.

Quebec's foreign relations

For as long as it has existed, the province of Quebec has represented the homeland of the French Canadians and a political unit of its own. Great

Britain recognized this fact as early as 1774 by the Quebec Act. Given that specificity, the need was felt by Quebecers, at various times in their history, to establish their own relationships with the outside world. Even as a colony of Great Britain, French Canadian representatives, in an assembly that enjoyed very limited power, created a Quebec agency in London so that they could be heard directly in Westminster.

No sooner had Quebec become a province in the Canadian Confederation than representation abroad was envisaged. As early as 1868, a federal-provincial agreement was negotiated and signed on provincial foreign representation. In 1881, after Premier Adolphe Chapleau's trip to France, Hector Fabre was sent to Paris as Quebec's special agent. (He later represented Canada as well.) But when he died in 1910, he was not replaced. In 1911, an agency was created in London and in 1915, Quebec was also represented in Brussels. Both agencies were closed in the 1930s in the context of the Great Depression and of an inward-looking French Canadian nationalism. The only presence of Quebec abroad until the 1960s was a tourist and commercial office opened in New York in 1941.

Quebec's 'Quiet Revolution' in the 1960s brought the modernization and secularization of the French-Canadian province. Internationalization came about as a necessary corollary of a new concern for economic and social affairs on the part of the provincial government. The first manifestation of Quebec's new desire to establish foreign relations was above all cultural when a delegation was opened in Paris in 1961. But it was soon to be followed by a representation in London and the upgrading of the New York mission. There was nothing conflictual in the creation of those three delegations. Ottawa was even helpful in organising the new Quebec presence in Paris. Not only did the embassy provide its full collaboration but the first 'délégué général' (up to 1965) was the former director of the 'Maison Canadienne' for professors and students in Paris. In London, the Quebec representatives were granted diplomatic immunity (with the Canadian High Commission's blessing), and in New York it was more or less 'business as usual' in the dense transnational Canadian–American network.

Conflict erupted in 1965 for two main reasons. First, a rather doctrinaire declaration was produced in the form of a speech, in the month of April, by the Quebec Minister of Education, Paul Gérin-Lajoie (later to be referred to as Doctrine Gérin-Lajoie), claiming the legal extension of provincial jurisdictions to the international level. Second, in Ottawa, officers of the Department of External Affairs were increasingly concerned by Quebec's international activity. Not only was Canadian diplomacy still relatively young and proud of its new achievements since the Second World War but French Canadian officers were particularly jealous of their fragile but growing presence in Canadian foreign policy. There is reason to believe that in a more mature environment conflict would not have occurred. But in Canada there was plenty of pretention and pride at both levels of government.

Quebec had just concluded what was imprudently called a 'treaty' with France in matters of education (providing for academic exchange) and another one was to be signed later in 1965 dealing with cultural and artistic exchange. Ottawa felt threatened enough in its jurisdiction over foreign affairs to conclude immediately two umbrella-treaties with France to cover the French–Quebec agreements which were labelled as 'ententes'. As a reaction to this federal solicitude, the dynamic and ambitious Minister of Education, Paul Gérin-Lajoie, made a speech to the Montreal consular community in which he expressed his government's legal contention to negotiate international agreements in matters under its jurisdiction. He went even so far as to interpret international law's reference to the 'state of residence' as meaning the 'state of Quebec' for some consular activities pertaining to provincial jurisdictions. Quebec was relying on the silence of the Canadian Constitution (the British North America Act) on international relations for the good reason that in 1867 foreign policy was still the responsibility of the imperial government in London.

Ottawa could and did argue that common and universally admitted practice made the federal government the one and only spokesman for Canada and its provinces abroad and the only recognized sovereign Canadian government according to international law.[1] That debate was well publicized and gave way to numerous academic articles. But the few concrete problems that ensued were relatively easily handled.

The atmosphere of conflict was intensified and dramatized by the visit of French President Charles De Gaulle in 1967 and his famous exclamation from the Montreal City Hall's balcony: 'Vive le Quebec libre'. But this incident, for all the diplomatic tension created, did not add anything to the issue of Quebec's international relations. The Quebec government was more embarrassed than pleased by the statement and the relations between France and Quebec remained exactly as they were, except that the federal government was more determined than ever to keep Quebec within limits.

A good opportunity appeared when Quebec was invited 'alone' to an international conference on education in Gabon (under French recommendation). Ottawa took offense, broke diplomatic ties with Gabon and did not resume them until the small African state pledged its full recognition of Ottawa as an exclusive Canadian partner in return for generous aid. This was another incident that made much noise but changed very little in the nature of Quebec's international presence.

Much more important was the long and painful negotiation surrounding the status of Quebec in the new international organization created in Niamey (Niger) in 1970—'Agence de coopération culturelle et technique' (ACCT)—providing for a broad range of cooperation between countries where the French language is used. It was agreed that Quebec would obtain the status of a 'participating government' within the organization and that, although included in a Canadian delegation, Quebec representatives would participate in the proceedings and express the Quebec government's views on all matters pertaining to its constitutional jurisdictions.

Although that agreement took place in an atmosphere of conflict it finally represented a *modus vivendi* that was observed and worked successfully for two decades, except for a few occasional skirmishes. It was used as a model for another federal–provincial accommodation on the status of Quebec within a broader international organization, the 'Francophonie' or general association of French-speaking countries. Again, since 1985, Quebec has been a 'participating government' in an organization of sovereign states, as a specific part of the Canadian representation.

Some would have thought, back in 1970, that Quebec's foreign relations would be considerably reduced if not abandoned when Robert Bourassa became Premier of Quebec with a very federalist and pragmatic platform. Bourassa would put a stop to a silly 'flags war' and concentrate on sound management and economic matters. That did not keep him from opening new Quebec missions in Düsseldorf, Boston, Lafayette and Los Angeles, in Abidjan (within the Canadian embassy), in Beirut, Athens, Rome, Brussels, Tokyo and Port au Prince. Bourassa also reorganized the Department of International Affairs (then called Intergovernmental Affairs) to make it more of a central agency for external relations and he concluded large-scale agreements with France.

The Parti Québécois (PQ) came to power in 1976 and stayed until 1985. Although this party was devoted to bring about the independence of Quebec, it never received a mandate other than to form a provincial government. Amazingly enough, it did not significantly extend the range and intensity of international relations, except on the economic level. Contrary to expectations, Quebec's missions abroad were not used to promote the ideal of sovereignty.

In the 1980s, after the failure of the referendum on sovereignty and difficult years of economic recession until 1983, Quebec's international relations became more oriented than ever towards economic goals: providing outlets for mushrooming entrepreneurs and their small and medium-size firms; attracting investments in Quebec. This new orientation was so firmly adopted by the PQ government that the Liberal Party, coming to the helm in December 1985, did not have to modify, in any major way, Quebec's main international objectives. After thirty years, under many governments, at different times and in different settings, Quebec's foreign relations have become a well-entrenched phenomenon. Given the fact that other Canadian provinces have also entered the picture, it must be recognized that Canadian diplomacy is irreversibly federal–provincial.

Theoretical approaches

Why is that so? In the case of Quebec, in particular, why such a spectacular orientation? It is understandable that modernization brought about a desire among French Canadians to open windows, to establish communication and rapport with other peoples, and to set up a new presence in foreign lands. It is also obvious that Canadian foreign policy, at least before the 1960s, had not offered an appropriate picture of French-speaking Canadians, although they counted for more than 25 per cent of the total population. But why did not francophone Quebecers make themselves more visible at the centre, where real foreign policy is conducted? Why not rely on a bilingual and bicultural Canadian foreign policy?

Ivo Duchacek has pointed out two forms of participation for 'subnational territorial authorities':

1. Subnational units try to influence the decision-making process of the central government from *within* by means of various lobbying efforts directed toward the legislative and executive branches of the central government, or
2. They *bypass* the central government mechanisms by maintaining informal or formal direct trans-sovereign contacts with other neighbouring or distant foreign sources of power and knowledge. Such trans-sovereign interactions are often in harmony, but occasionally in direct competition or conflict with the broad aims and methods of the national center.[2]

And he went on to give many reasons that explain why central governments are so often bypassed to the point that sovereign boundaries have become permeable and sovereignties are 'perforated': the expansion of foreign policy to economic, social, cultural, environmental issue-areas, global and regional interdependence, the welfare roles of all levels of governments, vulnerability to distant events and emulation facilitated by modern communication.[3]

No doubt these factors have been at work in Quebec, especially the 'welfare role' of the provincial government that was rapidly expanded during the 'Quiet Revolution'. As many new programs were fashioned with the obvious intention of countering federal initiatives that were seen to be contrary to the Constitution's power distribution and threatening to the autonomy of the French-speaking province, a new, dynamic and ambitious bureaucracy was created in Quebec. Naturally, these civil servants were power-hungry and international relations appeared to them as attractive 'turf'.

Another factor related to the 'Quiet Revolution' must be mentioned. The atmosphere in Quebec in the 1960s called for rapid change. Élites, government officials and a good segment in the population became impatient. To rely on the slow, long-term transformation of Canadian diplomacy, as promising as it might be, was considered rather frustrating and not responding to urgent needs.

Of course, one must add to that the new nationalist fervour that accompanied the 'Quiet Revolution'. The government of Quebec kept rationalising its expansion and growing intervention by its alleged mandate to see to the emancipation of the French Canadian culture, thereby being endowed with a 'special' mission, requiring a 'special' status. As Premier Lesage was stating in 1964 that Quebec had become the 'political expression of French Canada', it was natural to extend that role to international representation. Hence, Quebec's international involvement first appeared in the context of the struggle between Ottawa and Quebec as to who represented best and with most legitimacy the French Canadian population. This seemed obvious in 1965 and throughout the late 1960s when Quebec was seeking to establish its international status and Ottawa was devoted to confine it as much as possible.

So much for the surface of the iceberg. So much for heavily reported political declarations. But, as the day-to-day practice of international relations was taking form in Quebec and in its missions abroad, other factors were at work, calling for a growing international dimension of the provincial government's activities. The factors, pertaining to the phenomena related above such as the porousness of borders, global interdependence, transnational relations, etc., could be clustered under two headings: adaptation and necessity. To respond to the need for adaptation is to adjust to structural and cyclical factors in the external environment, in the international system, in the world economy. For example, how could a government responsible for education (especially if education is seen as 'national' or at least culturally specific) not be concerned with educational exchange? How could it not consider labour relations in an international context? 'Necessity' is an even more stringent concept; it refers to structural imperatives for the functioning of the state. Even a provincial government cannot function in a vacuum; it has to take into account its international environment and, if it is jealous enough of its constitutional prerogatives, it will want to operate internationally on its own without relying on the federal government which may use this pretext to interfere in its junior partner's affairs.

Concern for status may not be separated completely from adaptation and necessity. But it does not account in itself for international involvement. In other words, adaptation and necessity are at work and make for a non-sovereign government's foreign relations even when 'status' factors are not operative. There were times in the history of Quebec's international relations when conflict with Ottawa did not exist and international activity was none the less very intense. It can even be said that the less conflict there was, the more international relations took place in an efficient manner.

But that does not account for Quebec's greater involvement than its sister provinces. Let us point out that the difference is smaller than one would expect between Quebec and other large provinces in the Canadian federation, such as Ontario, Alberta and British Columbia which are quite active internationally. They nevertheless operate a smaller network of missions. Another reason has to be found for Quebec's special role.

The concept of 'asymmetry' may be quite helpful in this context. It was well analysed and applied to non-sovereign governments' international relations by Renaud Dehousse who observed particularly well the Walloon community in Belgium as well as Quebec in this respect.[4] He defines asymmetrical systems as those that are composed of disparate political entities distinct by their situation, their attitudes and their interests. Canada is obviously an asymmetrical system as it represents a conglomerate of regional and relatively diversified economies. In such a complex situation, where the regulation of foreign investments, energy and commercial policies are seen so differently from one region to the other, national interest becomes an abstraction that does not really respond to any general interest.[5]

In that picture, Quebec has to be identified as the most asymmetrical region of Canada. Not only is it the sole province where the great majority speaks another language, but it is also the province that seeks the greatest degree of autonomy and its economic configuration and organization are also quite unique. As an important part of its population is seriously contemplating sovereignty, it is certainly the most centrifugal province.

Here, elements of status are intertwined with elements of necessity and adaptation and command a greater involvement at the international level. Because asymmetry allows more intense transnational activities, Canada offers the most striking example of transnational flows. There is no country where so many people are naturally more attracted by what is going on across the border than by what is going on in their own country. The North–South transactions often seem to be more natural than the Canadian East–West network. Quebec, given its feeling of isolation from the Canadian English-speaking network, is brought to seek communications abroad, even in the larger English-speaking North American network, which does not appear, rightly or wrongly, very different from the Canadian, but only more appealing.

Thus, asymmetry, necessity and adaptation may account more adequately for Quebec's international relations than any desire of its ruling élite to antagonize the federal government. Although conflicts between Ottawa and Quebec have been afforded great publicity, they do not explain the regular functioning of Quebec's foreign relations. Let us see how this may fit with an empirical picture of those relations.

An empirical picture

Together with a research group of the 'Centre québécois de relations internationales', we have undertaken a vast survey of Quebec's international relations during the last three decades. We have identified three operational indicators of these relations: the *objectives* as stated by decision-makers, the *means* that were made available to the pursuit of these objectives, and the *actions* that came out of the process.[6] The study was restricted to the Quebec government's apparatus, the state being considered here as an autonomous actor, submitted to a web of influences and constraints from the society and the international environment, but in possession of its own proper resources and capable of formulating its own proper objectives.[7] These were defined as the expression of a will on the part of responsible government officials toward an international target. We assumed a correlation between the frequency of an objective's formulation and its importance, according to what is referred to as the Baldwin principle.[8]

Objectives were classified in many ways according to issue-areas, targets (countries or regions), context and the particular government issuing them. The only source from which they were extracted is public speeches. Other public documents were neither sufficiently numerous nor available to constitute a reliable source. For reasons of economy, speeches were restricted to those of First Ministers (heads of government) and Ministers responsible for international relations: during the period 1960–85, this group included fourteen persons.[9] All their speeches, in the National Assembly (provincial legislature) and in other forums as well, were scanned and 1,509 objectives were retained.

The allocation of means and resources is already a step in the implementation of objectives. They allow a certain degree of control over the external environment. We may postulate with Bruce M. Russett that 'diplomatic staff is a measure of political attention'.[10] In addition to the personnel appointed to international relations, we have also examined public outlays. It turned out to be impossible to identify expenses directly related to international relations since not only the budget of the department immediately concerned but also those of many other departments such as Industry and Commerce, Education, Natural Resources, Agriculture, to name but a few, had international dimensions. We therefore opted to restrain our study to budgets allocated to missions abroad.

By actions on an international level, we could mean a great number of phenomena. Actions performed by a federated state include a certain participation in international organisations, the reception of foreign officials, official visits abroad, signature and ratification of international agreements, consular relations with foreign diplomats, exchange programs for students, teachers, civil servants and others. We have chosen visits abroad and international agreements as two reliable and typical indicators. We have identified 1,012 visits of government members (First Ministers or members of their Cabinets) outside Canada or to the seat of an international organization. Agreements amounted to 230 documents referred to officially by the Quebec government as 'ententes internationales'.[11]

It is not the purpose of this chapter to relate all the findings related with that research. It should be sufficient, in this context, to mention a few typical data to illustrate the nature of Quebec's international relations. Out of 1,509 objectives, 603 are related to economic and commercial ventures. This is a much higher number than for any other sector (politics and diplomacy: 115; culture and communication: 158; education and science: 138).[12] Economic objectives were especially frequent during the PQ mandate (339 out of 750).

When objectives are listed according to targets, the country that comes on top is the United States with 297 objectives, followed by France (230); 564 objectives were classified general or addressed to international institutions.

Those findings should not cause any surprise when one realizes that Quebec depends heavily on the United States for its exports, and for a large part of foreign investments. But they certainly attenuate the impression (often retained from the media as stated above) that Quebec's international relations are a highly politicized enterprise related to the search for a better status on the part of ambitious élites. Let us remember that the United States is a country that never gave the slightest encouragement to Quebec's political ambitions. It is also interesting to note that the PQ, the 'separatist' party, is the one that pushed more intensely for international activities on the economic front and particularly in the neighbouring country. During the Liberal tenure of Robert Bourassa from 1970 to 1976, 18.6 per cent of objectives were addressed to France and 7.6 per cent to the United States. With the PQ in power between 1976 and 1985, figures were inversed: 8.8 per cent to France and 16.7 per cent to the United States.

Data related to means and resources confirm this picture. Economic issues are given major consideration. Among professionals appointed abroad between 1969 and 1985, there are always 40 per cent or more who are assigned to economic areas. In fact, the number of professionals working in economic fields is growing with time. Here again, the United States is the country where the highest number of Quebec representatives are at work, between 23 and 30 per cent over the years. Although France has always been quite important as the launching ground for Quebec's diplomatic endeavour, there have been fewer Quebec professionals assigned there than in the United States since the late 1970s. The Paris 'Délégation générale' is the largest of all but it is the only one in France compared with seven Quebec missions in the United States, which hired thirty-six professionals in 1988–9, as opposed to twenty-four for France. The total for the whole world was then 134.

As for expenditure, a high proportion also goes to the US missions: some 30 per cent, that is 3.5 million Canadian dollars in 1984–5. This is a very small fraction of the total budget of the Quebec government but international relations counted for scarcely 0.1 per cent of that budget.

If we now turn to actions, we find that 428 of the 1,012 visits paid by Quebec officials abroad were dealing with economic matters. Some 264 took place in the United States. This is less than Europe as a whole (not counting France: 321) but more than France (207). Again, the PQ government is the one that was most active in the United States (158 visits in nine years).

It is true that the PQ government's interest in the United States had a political connotation. After the failure of René Lévesque's appeal to the Economic Club of New York in January 1977, when he dared compare his party's drive toward sovereignty to the American Revolution, the PQ government launched what was called 'Operation America'. The operation aimed at keeping Americans from actively and openly working against the sovereignty project. Many government ministers and the Premier himself, who had become more cautious, travelled to the United States with the mission of reassuring Americans as to the Quebec government's ideological orientation and the effects of an eventual secession. Because of that, it cannot be denied that Quebec's international relations were politicized to some extent and, consequently, in conflict with Canadian diplomacy.

But two factors attenuate this consideration considerably. First, it must be noted that, in spite of this political intention (which was rather negative in character not seeking support but rather neutralizing opposition), the proportion of visits that had economic implications was still quite high. In other words, Quebec was trying to persuade Americans that it would always remain a reliable economic partner. Second, after the failure of the referendum, at a time when the sovereignty project was put on the back-burner, so to speak, by the PQ government, visits to the United states were intensified. It seems reasonable to conclude that Quebec's relations with its neighbour were not immediately aimed at some political objective.

Finally, our analysis of international agreements does nothing but corroborate the highly non-political nature of Quebec's international relations. If we look at the 230 'ententes internationales' listed by the Quebec government, we find that sixty of them are economic in nature, seventy-four relate to education and science, and the great majority of these agreements were concluded in the 1980s (164), at a time when status-seeking was not a priority for Quebec.[13] Moreover, fifty-seven of these 230 were concluded with the United States, mostly with some American states. A high proportion, of course (thirty-eight out of fifty-seven), are economic and commercial, while the others pertain to technical matters related to transportation, the environment, energy, etc.

Let us now sum up the highlights of our empirical findings:

1. Objectives, means and actions are predominantly economic and commercial.
2. This was especially the case under a separatist government.
3. The United states is the most important target.

These three characteristics obviously allow for very little status-seeking on the part of Quebec and if they may entail some conflict with the federal government, it certainly does not appear at first sight. We must therefore conclude that adaptation and necessity have been much more instrumental in the development of Quebec's international relations and that asymmetry is the main factor to account for the intensity of that development.

Conclusion

This is not to say that status did not play a role in bringing about Quebec's international activity. Of course, it did. The events related above show it explicitly. And, as mentioned, the concept of status is implied in the notion of asymmetry. Obviously, Quebecers for a long time, rightly on wrongly, have not felt adequately served by Canadian diplomacy. They insist on representing a political entity of its own within (or without) Canada. That is certainly an important reason for them to seek an international representation. But that in itself is not the major ingredient in the course of Quebec's international dealings. The development of transnational relations and of regional transborder transactions coupled with an awareness of globalization and interdependence seems to be the main reason why Quebec has created and cultivated so many relations with foreign political entities.

There is no immediate and obvious reason why these relations would bring about conflict with Ottawa and Canadian diplomacy. In fact, it must be noted that the greatest part of Quebec's activities are conducted in harmony and cooperation with the federal government.

Actually, for the most efficient conduct of its foreign relations, Quebec needs to adopt a dual strategy: to make sure that Ottawa takes care of Quebec's interests and, at the same time, to pursue its own objectives, most of which are not detrimental to Canada as a whole.[14]

Notes

1. See Paul Martin, *Federalism and International Relations*, Ottawa, Queen's Printer (1965). For Gérin-Lajoie's speech, see *Le Devoir*, Montréal (14 and 15 April 1965) and André Patry, *Le Québec dans le monde*, Montréal, Léméac (1980). See also H.A. Leeson and W. Vanderelst, *External Affairs and Canadian Federalism: The History of a Dilemma*, Holt, Rinehart & Winston, Toronto (1973).
2. 'Multicommunal and bicommunal politics and their international relations', in Ivo D. Duchacek, Daniel Latouche and Garth Stevenson, *Perforated Sovereignties and International Relations*, Greenwood Press, New York/London (1988), 5. I prefer the word 'non-sovereign' to 'sub-national' to characterize Quebec's international relations for the good reason that many Quebecers do not consider Canada to be a nation but see in Quebec their 'national' government, without necessarily seeking full sovereignty for this 'national' political entity.

3. ibid., pp. 6–7.
4. Renaud Dehousse, 'Fédéralisme, asymétrie et interdépendance: aux origines de l'action internationale des composantes de l'État fédéral', *Études internationales*, 20 (1989), 283–309.
5. ibid., p. 295. Most Canadians would deny that as they would be prompt to say that the so-called 'national interest' corresponds to southern Ontario's interest. But even Ontario is often dissatisfied with Canadian foreign policy and watches over her own international interest.
6. The methodology of this research is exposed in detail by Louis Bélanger in a chapter of a book to be published in 1992 by the Centre québécois de relations internationales (Université Laval, Quebec City, Canada), 'Méthodologie: mesurer la politique étrangère du Québec'. I rely here on parts of this chapter.
7. See Stephen D. Krasner, *Defending the National Interest*, Princeton University Press, Princeton (1978), 10–20.
8. See A.L. Baldwin, 'Personal structure analysis: a statistical method of investigating the single personality', *Journal of Abnormal and Social Psychology*, 37 (1942), 163–83. Quoted by Louis Bélanger.
9. Although our study aimed at the period 1960–89, the mandate of Robert Bourassa (1985–9) could not be included. Thus, the fourteen authors of speeches were: Premiers Jean Lesage (1960–6), Daniel Johnson (1966–8) Jean-Jacques Bertrand (1968–70), Robert Bourassa (1970–6) René Lévesque (1976–85) and Pierre-Marc Johnson (1985); Ministers Marcel Masse, Gérard D. Lévesque, Oswald Parent, François Cloutier, Claude Morin, Jacques-Yvan Morin, Bernard Landry and Louise Beaudoin.
10. Bruce M. Russett, *Power and Community in World Politics*, Freeman & Co., San Francisco (1974), 71.
11. See Gouvernement du Québec, *Recueil des ententes internationales du Québec*, Québec (1984), and Ministère des Affaires internationales, *Ententes internationales, 1984–1989* (internal document).
12. Here is the complete list of sectors identified:

Political and diplomatic	115
Institutional and organizational	110
Culture and communication	158
Economic and commercial	603
Education and science	138
Immigration	21
Ecology and environment	17
Developing countries	40
Social affairs and labour	34
Quebecers' mobility	6
General	267

13. The agreements were thus categorized:

Political and diplomatic	21
Institutional and organizational	4
Culture and communication	25
Economic and commercial	60
Education and science	74
Immigration	2

Environment	10
Aid to development	2
Social affairs	9
Mobility	21
Urban planning	2
Total	230

14. This is well expressed in a document tabled by Quebec's Department of International Affairs in the fall of 1991: 'compte tenu du rôle joué par les ministères et organismes du gouvernement fédéral spécialisés en matière internationale, le gouvernement cherchera à s'assurer, d'une part, que ses intérêts, tels qu'il les définit lui-même, sont dûment pris en compte dans les politiques et programmes de ces ministères et organismes et lui assurent des retombées réelles appropriées et, d'autre part, qu'il est à même de jouer son rôle d'acteur international en sachant qu'il peut compter sur la collaboration effective du gouvernement fédéral.' *Le Monde pour horizon: Éléments d'une politique d'affaires internationales*, Gouvernement du Québec, Ministère des Affaires internationales (1991), 124.

9 Substate paradiplomacy: the case of the Ontario government

David K.M. Dyment

The province of Ontario has the second largest government in Canada and is the source of 37 percent of the federation's gross national product. Its interests are extensive and its pursuit of them in the international domain has resulted in an increasingly complex paradiplomatic policy process and attendant bureaucracy. Compared with Quebec, which has conducted an often high-profile pursuit of international contacts particularly within *la francophonie*, leading to friction with the central government, Ontario has a more congruent or symmetric relationship with Ottawa. Consequently, the expansion of its international activities has attracted less notice, yet it is more representative of substate paradiplomacy within federations.

Nevertheless, a sense that the central government is not directly serving their needs seems to be evident in both provinces. For Quebec, this is made clear in an article by Louis Balthazar[1] and would seem to be evident in Ontario as well—as one senior Ontario paradiplomat put it: 'We need our international activities, our interests are not pursued adequately by the federal government.'[2]

International relations have moved beyond questions of war and peace, and alliance building toward the jurisdictions and concerns of non-sovereign governments. The knowledge, skills and resources for some types of Canadian international activity are found only in provincial governments. As a former Ontario official described it, 'When such issues as commercial policy, energy, agriculture, industrial development are all matters of provincial concern it is not very difficult to see why the provinces have more than a yearning, indeed a responsibility to make an effective contribution.'[3]

Much of the content of the two provinces' international activities is similar, as are their origins at the level of global causal variables. At the level of causal variables operative within the federation there is a divergence. Ontario is said to have a symmetric, and Quebec an asymmetric, relationship with the federal government. Ontario's relationship, like that of most federated units, leads it to practice what can be called circumscribed diplomacy, or what is more commonly known as paradiplomacy. Paradiplomacy is understood as operating alongside the federal government's international diplomacy. Whereas this concept is useful, another dimension needs to be considered. Quebec, unlike most federated units, is said to practise protodiplomacy, which is understood as the 'proto', or first, stage of a process leading to recognition as a sovereign state.

These differences are explored in two figures. In Figure 9.1, the federal government surrounds or circumscribes Ontario's international activities. The degree of circumscription is not uniform but varies depending on the nature of the government with which Ontario is in contact. The Ontario government is satisfied for the federal government to be involved in its relations with foreign sovereign governments but less so in the conduct of its international activities with foreign substate governments, other Canadian provinces and major cities in Ontario. This relationship with the federal government is indicated by the changing thickness of the circle marked federal government.

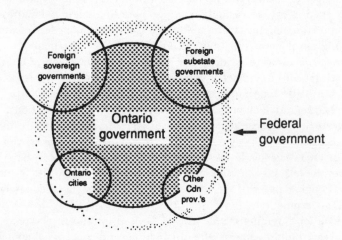

Figure 9.1 Circumscribed diplomacy of the Ontario Government

Showing the relationship the Ontario government is satisfied to have with the federal government in the conduct of its international activities with other governments.

In Figure 9.2, the Quebec government strives to ensure that there is no omnipresent federal government that circumscribes its international activities. In this model Quebec sees the federal government as ideally only an interceder in its relations with foreign sovereign governments, and then with notable exceptions such as in its relations with France. This relationship with the federal government is indicated by the three overlapping circles marked federal government, foreign sovereign governments and Quebec government.

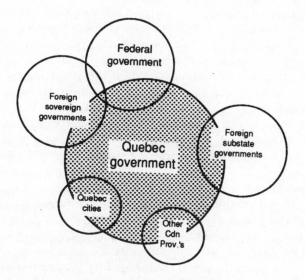

Figure 9.2 Protodiplomacy of the Quebec government

Showing the extent of the relationship the Quebec government strives to have with the federal government in the conduct of its international activities with other governments.

Para- or circumscribed diplomacy informs the nature of the Ontario government's international activities and is the context of this study. Further discussion will explore the historical development of Ontario's international relations bureaucracy before taking a more contemporary look at its staffing, budget, international agreements and international offices. Examination then moves to two areas of paradiplomatic activity— international development, and relations with foreign substate governments. Before concluding, dimensions of upstream and downstream vertical fragmentation are considered.

The paradiplomatic bureaucracy: a brief history[4]

Ontario's first presence abroad (like that of most Canadian provinces and Australian states) was an office in London, which by the 1920s had developed into Ontario House headed by an Agent General. After the Second World War its activities were significantly expanded to include the administration of an influx of immigrants from the United Kingdom and Europe to meet the growing needs of Ontario for skilled labour. And in 1945 a trade division in the Ministry of Industry and Tourism was created with responsibility for establishing foreign contacts and advising manufacturers on trade opportunities. During the 1950s expansion continued slowly with the opening of the province's second international office, in 1953, in Chicago, the establishment of an immigration section in the Ministry of Industry and Tourism in 1955, and the opening of a third office, in 1956, in New York.

The 1960s were a period of significant growth in the province's international activities: eleven new offices were opened, Ontario began to participate in Commonwealth Education Ministers' meetings, Commonwealth teacher exchanges, and agricultural and development projects in the Caribbean. In the late 1960s the province was represented in federal delegations to conferences of *la francophonie*. The 1970s were characterized by consolidation and a heightened level of organization in Ontario's international activities. Emphasis shifted to fewer but larger offices as twelve posts were closed and only two opened. With the establishment of the (super) Ministry of Treasury, Economics and Intergovernmental Affairs (TEIGA), in 1972, an External Activities Coordination Secretariat was established to—'[give Ontario's] international relations a distinct organizational focal point for the promotion of [its] interests with other countries . . . [by ensuring] a coordinated approach to the international activities of Ontario ministries.'[5]

When TEIGA was broken up in 1978 a separate Ministry of Intergovernmental Affairs (MIA) was established with an international relations division. Since then Ontario's international activities have continued to expand, supported by government policy statements such as: 'in international relations there is a parallel nature of federal and provincial competence and the growth of a role for the provinces is both normal and healthy.'[6] But its bureaucratic structure remained relatively unchanged until, in 1991, growing tension for leadership between the Office of International Relations of MIA and the Ministry of Industry, Trade and Technology (MITT) led to the International Office being transferred to MITT.

During the 1980s the government experienced increasing internal conflict in the conduct of its international activities. A consultant was hired in 1987 to address the management of these activities by the two ministries. His conclusion was that the province should develop a provincial version of the External Affairs Department as an agency of central control. This recommendation was not implemented, but a Deputy Ministers' Committee on International Relations was created to oversee, but not to direct and control. Ontario's international activities remained dramatically bifurcated and the province was left without a central agency of coordination and direction. The basis of MITT's power is the importance of trade in the mix of Ontario's international activities and the relative size and influence of the Ministry. MIA, which had a semi-official mandate to act as a central agency, was relatively small both in size and influence.

Tension inside international activities bureaucracies does not seem to be unique to Ontario; it is evident in most governments (state and substate) and stems from the division of international activities into two functions—trade and diplomacy. The resulting, largely separate, bureaucracies see their roles differently and tend to constitute different cultures that often have trouble communicating effectively with each other.[7] Addressing this problem, in Ontario, through the subsumption of the Office of International Relations into MITT may have two outcomes: the more obvious is that the importance of the perspective and activities of the Office will be diminished; however, it is possible with the Office housed in MITT, and perhaps liberated from the restraining influence of a protracted turf war with a stronger rival, that its functions may now have greater scope to develop.

The paradiplomatic-bureaucracy: staffing, budget, international agreements and international offices[8]

What is the scope of the Ontario government's international activities in terms of the number of ministries and staff involved, the amount of money they spend, the number of international agreements they are party to, and the number of international offices they have? In 1988 there were fifteen ministeries involved, with the equivalent of 510 person years; they spent $87 million; twelve ministries were party to at least forty-four agreements; and they had fifteen international offices representing six ministries. The cost of maintaining these offices represented about a quarter of total international activities expenditures, or over $20 million.

Sixty per cent of the $87 million was spent on commercial and economic activities and the remaining 40 per cent on activities relating to the environment, aid, education and culture. The cost of supporting these activities was equivalent to two-tenths of 1 per cent of the government's total spending. Ninety per cent of this spending was by six ministries: MITT, $34 million; Environment, $15 million; Colleges and Universities, $11 million; Tourism and Recreation, $10 million; Agriculture and Food, $4.5 million; and Intergovernmental Affairs, $3.7 million. The international agreements of the following three ministries constituted almost 65 per cent of the total: Environment, thirteen agreements; MITT, seven agreements; and Colleges and Universities, six agreements.

In 1990 the Ontario government had offices in seventeen cities; a year later it had offices in nineteen cities. In 1990, MITT was represented in seventeen cities, Agriculture and Food in seven, Culture and Communications in three, and MIA in three. In 1991 the average Ontario government post had 8.6 people and in 1989 the office with the most staff was Ontario House in London with twenty-seven. Ontario had almost 24 per cent of all provincial international offices and 23 per cent of provincial personnel abroad. Ontario's international offices represent almost 7 per cent of all Canadian offices and representatives abroad.

The largest portion of international activities personnel are involved in marketing, investment and tourism. A 1988 government report indicates 55 per cent, and a survey conducted by the author using the *Government of Ontario Telephone Directory* and the *Government of Ontario Kwic Index to Services* from the fall of 1990 would support this, with a figure of 44 per cent of staffing allocated to these functions. It seems clear, in the light of the figures presented in Table 9.1, that the total number of personnel involved in the conduct of international activities is in the range of 400–600 people. Table 9.1 also indicates that, if the international activities of Ontario Hydro's New Business Ventures Division are excluded, the province has approximately fifty civil servants abroad and 150 locally engaged staff. Using a figure of 500 Ontario government employees involved in international work, approximately 300 (or 60 per cent) are located in Ontario and the remaining 200 (or 40 per cent) are abroad.

Table 9.1 The Ontario government's international activities personnel

	1988 govt. survey	1990 author's survey	1990 author's survey, including Ontario Hydro*
Civil servants in Ontario	335	215	239
Civil servants abroad	41	56	90
Locally engaged staff**	134	183	294
Total	510	454	623

* For additional information on the New Business Ventures Division of Ontario Hydro, see the section of this chapter on international development.
** A ratio of 3.27 locally engaged staff to one Ontario civil servant abroad is used in this table as it is in: Government of Ontario, Ministry of Intergovernmental Affairs, *International Review Project, Phase One: Research Findings* (September 1988), 31.

A 1988 government report says that fifteen ministries were involved in international activities. The author's survey, admittedly for 1990, indicates that there are not fifteen but at least nineteen ministries involved in these activities. Four ministries not mentioned in the 1988 report are: Financial Institutions, Health, Natural Resources, and Treasury and Economics. The Ministry of Financial Institutions has an International Markets Unit. The Ministry of Health has an immigration officer. The Ministry of Natural

Resources is involved in a number of transborder issues and in the Jiagedaqi Forest Management Project in China. And the Ministry of Treasury and Economics has an International Economics Unit. That a government review of its international activities would not turn up at least four ministries with international activities illustrates the horizontal fragmentation and uncoordinated nature of the province's international activities, and underscores the lack of central agency control.

International development

The knowledge, skills and resources for some types of Canadian international activities are found largely in areas under provincial jurisdiction and increasingly the Ontario government, its agencies, universities, community colleges, and to a certain extent school boards have been involved in promoting international cooperation and technical assistance to developing countries. The first such example is probably an agreement in 1941 with Bermuda for the training of teachers. And later in the 1960s, when decolonization posed new economic and political problems for the international community, Ontario was involved in the Commonwealth's Columbo (development) Plan.

Some of the most striking examples of international cooperation and technical assistance to developing countries are the external projects of Ontario Hydro, one of the world's largest electric utilities. In 1984 Ontario Hydro created the New Business Ventures Division (NBV) to provide a more systematic and less reactive bureaucratic infrastructure to market Ontario Hydro's goods and services internationally. From 1961 to 1983, before NBV was created, Ontario Hydro was involved in twenty-one projects in the developing world with a total of 612 person years. During this period the pace of increasing involvement is seen in its association with three projects totaling 130 person years during the 1960s, eight projects equalling 312 person years in the 1970s, and in the early 1980s ten projects with a total of 168 person years.

NBV currently has about fifty managers, engineers and technicians in developing countries. In its first full year of operation it had revenues of $22 million, with a high of $55 million in 1988, and projected revenue growth to $100 million per year. In 1990 NBV was contracted to undertake new projects in Ethiopia, Kenya, Malaysia and Hungary and hosted visits to Ontario Hydro by representatives of thirty-nine countries.[9] A constant theme in Ontario Hydro's international activities is training. Measured in person years, from 1961 to 1984, only 12 per cent of projects did not have a training element. Some of NBV's projects involve Ontario's universities, one of which is in Kenya where it is working with York University and the Ontario Ministry of Energy to provide energy policy and planning assistance and training for the Kenya Ministry of Energy. At any given time there are five to seven Canadians, mostly from Ontario, working on this project in Kenya.

York University's participation in the above project is by no means an isolated case. The international projects of Ontario's universities are mentioned, between 1982 and 1988, over 220 times in the Association of Universities and Colleges newsletter *Canadian Universities in International Development*. Sometimes these projects involve all of a community's educational institutions, and not just its university, as is the case of a collaborative effort in Peterborough involving Trent University, Sir Sandford Fleming Community College and local school boards.

The international projects of Ontario's universities are a significant part of the international development assistance undertaken by the Ontario government, its agencies and institutions.[10] On the domestic side, the waiving of university fees for a significant number of foreign graduate students constituted most of the $11.3 million the government spent in 1988 on aid (aid spending in that year was reported as 13 per cent of the international activities budget).

Aside from Ontario Hydro and the province's universities there is, in non-governmental organizations (NGOs), a third significant locus of international development activity and expertise. There are, for example, over forty Ontario-based NGOs active in the development of sub-Saharan Africa that have formed a network whose headquarters is at the University of Guelph. They, with other groups, through the Ontario Council for international Cooperation (OCIC) have, since 1987, been lobbying the Ontario government to support financially Ontario-based NGOs involved in international education and development. In November 1989, Bill 77, An Act Respecting International Development, received a first reading. Under the provisions of the Bill international non-governmental development organizations would be able to apply to the Ontario government for funding.

The OCIC says 'That in light of the 1989 federal budget cuts to Official Development Assistance (ODA) and the potential future cuts to ODA, the time has never been more appropriate . . . to secure alternative funding.' The Bill is described as '[an] excellent tool for encouraging a matching grants programme in Ontario.'[11] Though the Bill has yet to be made law its adoption would formalize and expand a process of funding that is already in place; in 1988, for example, the International Defence and Aid Fund for South Africa raised funds for the first time from the Ontario government. And in 1989–90 Match International, a development organization for women, received grants from the Ontario Women's Directorate — an agency of the Ontario government — and the Ontario Ministry of Citizenship. In the area of funding, as in others, the Ontario government, its agencies and institutions are becoming increasingly involved in international development.

Relations with foreign substate governments

One of the traditional areas of research in the study of substate paradiplomacy is the transborder and overseas relations between the constituent
governments of different federations. Ontario's relations with adjacent US
state governments are particularly dense. These interactions are of two
types: direct and indirect.[12] In the latter case interaction is through input
into the mechanisms of the Canada–United States relationship. For
example, Ontario and Minnesota do not determine lake levels along their
shared border through direct interaction but through the International Joint
Commission.

The five provinces east of Ontario and the six New England states, in
1974, structured their 'direct' relationship through the formation of the
Conference of New England Governors and Eastern Canadian Premiers,
which meets annually and is supported by two secretariats, one on each side
of the border. To this point no other combination of jurisdictions have
replicated it although the Great Lakes states and Ontario have been
expanding their relationship.[13]

Ontario's interactions with US states constituted, in 1974, easily the
largest percentage of interactions of any province, over 29 per cent.[14] The
majority of these relations are with the eight Great Lakes states, and in
September 1991 Premier Bob Rae of Ontario began to explore the possibility of joining the Council of Great Lakes Governors and their Great
Lakes Protection Fund which supports projects to improve water quality in
the Great Lakes. If Ontario were to join, the Council's name would no
doubt be changed to reflect Ontario's membership. Quebec has also entered
into discussions with the Council, which are not as far along as those with
Ontario. Even if Quebec joined, the question arises as to the dynamic of
such an organization. At best it would have two Canadian and eight
American members, which could be quite different than the Conference of
New England Governors and Eastern Canadian Premiers with five
Canadian and six American members.

Though Ontario has yet to form an organization of coordination with its
foreign contiguous subnational neighbours, it has entered into increasing
close cooperation with them. For example: in 1989 the premier of Ontario
and the governors of the Great Lakes states agreed to provide $750,000 to
start up a joint 'North America's Fresh Coast' tourism campaign, which
two years later had attracted 13,000 tour groups from the United Kingdom;
in 1991 Ontario began negotiations with Great Lakes states to form a
regional crossborder solid-waste compact; and in 1992 the province was
considering a contribution of almost $25 million to the Great Lakes
Protection Fund. Ontario cities are also involved in the process of increasing
transborder cooperation with their counterparts in US Great Lakes cities
through such organizations as the international Great Lakes–St. Lawrence

Mayors' Conference, and Water Works—an organization that brings together regional political leaders and waterfront development experts.

The pace of increasing linkage between Ontario and US border states seems certain to quicken, as an Ontario Minister of Industry, Trade and Technology told a Chicago audience early in 1990:

If you consider the central portion of the North American continent as a single economic unit . . . you are dealing with perhaps the most powerful economic region on Earth. For all intents and purposes the FTA [Canada–US Free Trade Agreement] will create a borderless economy within that area. What I would like to suggest is a strategic alliance of sorts. We are already deeply involved with each other in this region. But we can strengthen those ties. We can improve our areas of cooperation.[15]

Though not as intensive as its interactions with bordering US states, the Ontario government also has relations with non-contiguous US state governments, and with the constituent governments of overseas federations. The most developed are with what is known as the 'Four Motors of Europe', a loose association of regions, each of which is an engine of its respective national economy. The regions in the association are: Baden-Württemberg in Germany, Rhône-Alpes in France, Lombardy in Italy, and Catalonia in Spain. Their objective is to foster economic and social interaction among themselves, and to a lesser extent with other subnational governments with similarly vital economies, such as Ontario. Cooperation between the four European subnational governments is a manifestation, evident in the European Community, of a shift in power from national to regional and supranational authorities.

Ontario's first relationship with a Four Motors member was with Baden-Württemberg in 1986. Since then Ontario and Baden-Württemberg have entered into numerous agreements, such as one to spend $1 million annually on joint scientific research and technological cooperation, and another involving the exchange, each year, of sixty students. Ontario signed its first agreements with Rhône-Alpes and Lombardy in 1989, and with Catalonia in 1990. In the context of these relations the province opened an office in Stuttgart in 1989 and the next year appointed a representative in Milan.

The Ontario Government became, in 1989, the first jurisdiction outside Europe to become an associate member of the Four Motors grouping. A year later the Four Motors Association held its first meeting in North America, in Toronto. Discussion centred on business, advanced education, training and research, the environment, and culture. At the gathering the five governments signed a 'Declaration of Partnership and Memorandum of Understanding on Cooperation' in which they agreed to take a number of initiatives, perhaps the most significant being an Interregional Business Centre in Toronto, to facilitate collective ventures and technology transfers among the five partners. In a joint press release at the end of the Toronto meeting they summarized the broad objectives of the relationship:

Because our jurisdictions are so alike, we will build bridges into North America for European business people, artists, students and researchers. In return the Four Motors will directly help Ontarians broaden their profitable contacts in Western Europe and the expanding markets of Eastern Europe.[16]

Ontario has relations with other contituent governments of overseas federations. The bureaucratic manifestation of its relationship with Jiangsu province in China can be seen in (at least) four Ontario government ministries: Intergovernmental Affairs, Culture and Communications, Natural Resources, and Colleges and Universities. The Ministry of Intergovernmental Affairs originally had responsibility for the overall direction of the agreement. The Ministry of Culture and Communications through its Arts Branch manages the Ontario–Jiangsu Cultural Exchange Agreement. The Ministry of Natural Resources is responsible for the Jiagedaqi Forest Management Project. And the Ministry of Colleges and Universities oversees the Ontario–Jiangsu Education Exchange Agreement which is administered by the University of Toronto/York University Joint Centre of Modern East Asian Studies.

The federal government: source of encouragement and restraint

There is evidence in earlier sections of this essay of horizontal fragmentation; we now turn to vertical fragmentation. As described at the outset, Ontario's international activities are within the purview of a federation, and vertical fragmentation is inherent in circumscribed diplomacy. An interesting element in Ontario's relationship with Ottawa is that the intervention of the latter can be both a source of encouragement and restraint.[17]

As we have seen, education is a vital tool of international development and as the central government has very little jurisdictional responsibility in this area it naturally looks to the most populous and wealthy province for expertise. One of the Canadian government's foreign policy objectives has been to develop its relatively good and historically privileged relationship with China, which, with over one billion people, is a potentially vast market. One of China's greatest needs, as a developing country, is for training and education. It seems clear that Ottawa has turned to Ontario to help provide them. This may, in part, explain Ontario's relationship with Jiangsu and the extent to which it has been developed, as well as the large number of Ontario universities and cities involved in projects with China.[18]

The federal government has encouraged the expansion of Ontario's international activities in at least two other cases. The Canadian Ambassador to France, Gérard Pelletier, is reported to have encouraged the provincial government to open its Paris office, and the Canadian Ambassador to Belgium, Lucien Lamoureux, is attributed with a request for Ontario to open an office in Brussels.[19] Both requests had as their object the creation of a counterweight to the large offices, in those cities, of the Quebec government.

The federal government can also act to restrain the development of Ontario's international presence, as in the case of the province opening an office in Washington, DC. In the early 1970s Ontario announced that it would open an office in the American capital. In response to protest from Ottawa, Ontario dropped the idea. Instead the province monitors and lobbies Washington by sending officials from Toronto and its office in New York on regular trips to the capital, and through consultants and law firms based there that it hires to keep abreast of, and report on, developments.

Cities

The forces drawing federated units into international activities are also working upon other subnational governments, such as cities. Larger urban centres, like many constituent governments of federations, have the resources to respond to these pressures and set up international activities bureaucracies. Toronto, Canada's largest city, and Ottawa, Ontario's second largest city and Canada's fourth largest urban area, are two such centres. Like other big cities they are moving toward '*[une] ère d'une stratégie globale d'intervention en matière de relations internationales [où ils se dotent] d'une armature institutionnelle adéquate.*[20]

The City of Ottawa, for example, in 1989, in response to its growing number of international activities, produced an International Relations Strategy, appointed a coordinator of international relations, and established an International Relations Liaison Committee. In the same year it budgeted $120,000 for its twinning relationship with The Hague. In the area of international development the city has been active in programmes in China, Nicaragua, and with Georgetown, Guyana with which it has had a relationship since 1965. In 1987 the city was host to the first Capitals of the World Conference, attended by participants from over eighty of the world's capital cities.[21]

This development is particularly striking in Toronto which in 1986 established an International Office. Two years later the city had a paradiplomatic staff of thirteen and an international activities budget of over $750,000. Toronto has been especially active in the areas of the environment and international development. It was chosen as the headquarters for the UN-sponsored International Council for Local Environmental Initiatives, which operates as a technical clearing-house for local environmental protection activities. In 1991, Toronto was host to the World Cities and Their

Environment Conference, which was the first worldwide municipal response to the Brundtland Report on the Environment. In the area of international development Toronto has had projects with cities in a number of countries; for example, with São Paulo alone it has had over sixty exchanges of staff, and signed three cooperation agreements involving such issues as urban planning, housing and public health.[22]

Toronto capitalized on its reputation as being exceptionally well run when, in 1990, it founded the Canadian Urban Institute, which is dedicated to helping large cities with urban management issues. In 1991 the Institute had a staff of eleven and a budget of almost one million dollars; during the next few years the staff is expected to grow to thirty or thirty-five. The Institute is particularly active in urban planning assistance to Third World cities, funded largely by the Ontario and federal governments.[23] Such projects are a clear illustration of municipal government taking the initiative to create vertical synergy with higher levels of government in external activities.

In the expansion of its international activities Toronto has hired many people from the Ontario international activities bureaucracy. And many of its senior people, since its emergence as a paradiplomatic player in the 1960s, were formerly within the federal Department of External Affairs. This hiring pattern has. by all accounts smoothed relations between the three levels of government.

It appears that each level of government has in turn become increasingly involved in international activities. This began with the the dominion government's increasing autonomy in the conduct of foreign relations from the imperial government through a process that ultimately led to sovereignty. Though a similar outcome for Ontario and its major cities seems unlikely there has, however, been some speculation that globalization may lead to the re-emergence of cities as independent states (as independent as any state can be).

The increasing realization that 'The nation state has become too small for the big problems of life, and too big for the small problems'[24] has in part driven the expansion of the Ontario government's international activities, and has to be considered *vis-à-vis* major cities.

New gravitational pulls are working on Toronto, global political and economic forces that are changing the relationships between cities and nations all over the world . . . '[The] traditional power of nation-states is eroding, and in its place there's a reversion to the city state as the organic unit of the new global economy. The process will be slowed by old, instinctive loyalties, and by institutional interests but it is . . . irreversible.'[25]

Major cities are becoming, and some argue always have been[26], the salient economic entities; whether they become the focuses of a postnational global economy and cut the cords of their parent states is another question.

The Greater Toronto Area, or GTA as it is commonly known, will according to present projections have a population of 5.4 million in 2011, in part fuelled by its absorption of 75 percent of immigration to Canada. The GTA is a behemoth that has, as a former senior GTA politician recently remarked, 'the ability to have more control over its own future and sort things out for itself. But there seems little will to take up that challenge.'[27]

The province's two largest cities are forcing a new dimension upon its international activities, downstream vertical fragmentation. Should the international activities particularly of Toronto be appreciated as part of the dynamic driving the growth of Ontario's, and indeed Canada's, international activities? And to what extent are the international activities of the province and its large municipalities symbiotic?

Conclusion

The basic premise of this study is that the interests of the Ontario government have drawn it into international activities, and that an attendant paradiplomatic bureaucracy has emerged to support these activities.

The impetus for Ontario and Quebec's international activities at the level of global causal variables is similar. However, at the level of causal variables operative within the federation there is a divergence which leads Ontario to practise circumscribed diplomacy, or what is more commonly described as paradiplomacy. Quebec, unlike most federated units, is said to practice protodiplomacy.

It is clear that the depth and breadth of the Ontario government's international activities are growing as economies, cultures and nations become increasingly interconnected and interdependent. Some of the once autonomous power of the nation-state over foreign policy is moving to transnational actors, such as international organizations and multinational corporations. It is increasingly understood that some of this lost power is also shifting to subnational, regional governments.

The sovereign state has become a multivocal international actor. This has resulted in often chaotic and segmented, or marbled foreign policy making. As the boundaries of political authority are buffeted, and percolated through, by transfrontier flows of contact caused by interdependence, the walls of national sovereignties remain standing, but become sieves, and international relations can be seen to take place among perforated sovereignties.[28] In Canada decentralization of central powers is accelerating this process.

Canada and its constituent governments are at the leading edge of a global reconfiguration of international relations where the once autonomous power of the nation-state over foreign policy is moving to subnational levels. In some respects the Canadian experiment is a global one; we have an obligation to demonstrate to the world that the maintenance of federal states and the development of substate paradiplomacy is sustainable.

Notes

1. Louis Balthazar, 'Quebec's triangular situation in North America: a prototype?', in Ivo Duchacek, Daniel Latouche and Garth Stevenson (eds), *Perforated Sovereignties and International Relations: Trans-sovereign Contacts of Subnational Governments*, Greenwood Press, New York (1988).
2. Interview with a former senior Ontario Government official.
3. Thomas Levy, 'Federal–provincial dimensions of state–province relations', *International Perspectives* (March/April 1976).
4. Much of this section draws from: Donald Stevenson, 'L'évolution des activités de l'Ontario dans le domaine des affaires internationales', a speech made to the Institut canadien des affaires internationales in Quebec City (2 March 1988); Ontario government, *Guide to the Holdings of the Archives of Ontario*, vol. 1; and Ontario government, *The Ministry of Intergovernmental Affairs: A History*, (January 1985).
5. ibid., 12.
6. Ian Scott, 'The provinces and foreign policy: form and substance in the policy making process', in Elliot Feldman and Priscilla Battis (eds), *New North American Horizons*, University Consortium for Research on North America, Boston (1988).
7. For a more complete treatment of relations between MIA and MITT during the 1980s, the Deputy Ministers' Committee on International Relations, and the ways in which the bureaucratic components of a government's international activities can be organized see: David Dyment, 'Substate para-diplomacy: the international activities of non-sovereign governments: the case of Ontario', paper presented at the Annual Meetings of the Canadian Political Science Association (1990).
8. Much of this section is drawn from the following sources: Government of Ontario, Ministry of Intergovernmental Affairs, *International Review Project, Phase One: Research Findings* (September 1988); Government of Canada, Department of External Affairs, 'Canadian Representation Abroad', valid to 12/7/91; *Government of Ontario Telephone Directory, Winter 1990/91*, valid to 20/12/90; and *Government of Ontario Kwic Index to Services, 1990/91*, valid to 15/11/90.
9. From material supplied by Ontario Hydro; and Bob Papoe, 'Hydro finds overseas jobs generate gains', *Toronto Star* (27 December 1989), E1.
10. The Association of Universities and Colleges of Canada, *Canadian Universities in International Development*, newsletter (June 1979 to Spring 1989) indicates that five universities are involved in over 50 percent of the international activities conducted by Ontario's seventeen universities. In order of descending number of references, they are: York University, the University of Ottawa, Carleton University, the University of Toronto and the University of Guelph.
11. From material supplied by the Ontario Council for International Cooperation.
12. Brian Hocking describes this as the distinction between primary and mediating

168   DAVID K.M. DYMENT

action. As primary actors regional governments act directly in the international system, and as mediating actors they are seen to influence the formulation of national policies. See Brian Hocking, 'Regional governments and international affairs: foreign policy problem or deviant behaviour?', *International Journal*, XLI (Summer 1986), 484.

13. Emery Fanjoy, 'A view from the inside: the conference of New England governors and Eastern Canadian premiers', *Canadian Parliamentary Review* (Autumn 1990).

14. Roger Swanson, *State/Provincial Interaction: A Study of Relations Between US States and Canadian Provinces*, prepared for the US Department of State (1974).

15. Paul Botts, *The Great Lakes Reporter*, Center for the Great Lakes, Chicago (January 1990). Much of the material in this section on Ontario's relations with Great Lakes states is from this newsletter.

16. David Rampersad, 'Current issue paper #110: Ontario and the "Four Motors" of Europe', Legislative Research Service, Government of Ontario (1990), appendix C. Material on Ontario's relations with the members of the 'Four Motors' is drawn largely from this article.

17. Panayotis Soldatos is credited by the late Ivo D. Duchacek as the originator of the term 'paradiplomacy'. The work of Elliot and Lily Feldman should also be acknowledged here, particularly as it concerns the influence of the Canadian federal government on provincial government international activities.

18. The Association of Colleges and Universities' newsletter *Canadian Universities in International Development* mentions, from 1984 through 1987, ten Ontario universities as having projects with China. The cities of Ottawa and Toronto have projects with Chinese cities; and Patrick Smith and Theodore Cohn mention in their paper, 'Municipal and provincial paradiplomacy and intermestic relations: British Columbia cases', presented at the Annual Meetings of the Canadian Political Science Association (1990), that CIDA has provided seven million dollars for Canadian cities to participate with their Chinese counterparts in human resource development projects.

19. From interviews with former senior Ontario government officials.

20. Pierre-Paul Prouix and Panayotis Soldatos, 'Quel profil international pour Montréal?', *Le Devoir* (10/11 February 1988).

21. From material supplied by the City of Ottawa.

22. See: Peter Kresl, 'Variations on a theme: the internationalization of "second cities"', in Earl Fry, Lee Radebaugh and Panayotis Soldatos (eds), *The New International Cities Era: The Global Activities of North American Municipal Governments*, Brigham Young University, Utah (1989): and Art Stevenson, 'The international activities of Canadian municipalities, the City of Toronto's international programs, an overview', paper presented at the Institute of Public Administration of Canada's 43rd National Conference (1991).

23. See: Richard Gilbert, *Metro Report*, Office of Metropolitan Toronto Councillor Richard Gilbert, Toronto (1991).

24. See: Daniel Bell, 'The future world disorder: the structural context of crisis', *Foreign Policy* (Summer 1977).

25. Elizabeth Grove-White, 'The eleventh province', *Toronto* (March 1990).

26. See: Jane Jacobs, *Cities and the Wealth of Nations: Principles of Economic Life*, Random House, New York (1984).

27. Richard Gilbert, *Metro Report*, Office of Metropolitan Toronto Councillor Richard Gilbert, Toronto (August 1991), 6.
28. See: Ivo Duchacek, *The Territorial Dimension of Politics Within, Among, and Across Nations*, Westview Press, Boulder (1986).

10 Triangular dynamics: Australian states, Canadian provinces and relations with China

George MacLean and Kim Richard Nossal

What prompts non-central governments like states, provinces and even municipalities to become international actors by projecting themselves beyond the boundaries of the nation-state? Commonly, the answer to this central question tends to be tautological: non-central governments project themselves into the international sphere because it is in their interests to do so. In other words, the propensity of these governments to project themselves into the international arena is a function of the interests, desires and capacities of the non-central governments themselves.

In this chapter, we argue that this assumption, which underlies so much of the burgeoning literature on subnational international activity,[1] provides us with an incomplete view of the dynamic that has led to such a proliferation of international activity by non-central governments in the last three decades. While we would not deny that a non-central government must have an interest in projecting itself beyond its national borders, we suggest that this is a necessary, but not a sufficient, condition for non-central government activity in the international sphere. Rather, we must look beyond the interests of the non-central government alone, and see the international activities of non-central governments as an essentially triangular phenomenon that involves two other governmental actors. These must include the central government which usually has constitutional responsibility for the foreign affairs of the nation; and the foreign central government (or non-central government) which is the target, or the object, of the non-central government's external interests.

There are two conditions necessary for the international *interests* of a non-central government to become international *activities*. First, and most obviously, the target state must be willing to entertain and sponsor the growth of relations with and between non-central governments. Without that willingness, the non-central government with international interests would find it impossible to operate in the international system. Second, the central government must be at least indifferent to the international activities of its own non-central governments. If the central government is opposed, tensions on two sides of the triangle will make the development of non-central government relations more difficult, if not impossible. In short, then, in looking at the dynamic of non-central government behaviour in the international system, we have to examine the interests and attitudes of all three sets of actors.

This dynamic is well illustrated in the case of relations between Australian states and Canadian provinces with China in the 1980s. In this chapter, we survey the rapid and dramatic increase in the relationships among the non-central governments in all three countries between the adoption by the Chinese government of the 'open door' policy in December 1978[2] and the abrupt break in relations that occurred after the Tiananmen massacre of June 1989. We demonstrate the degree to which most Australian states and Canadian provinces were indeed impelled by their parochial interests into an activist role in seeking expanded relationships with provincial governments in China. But we also argue that a fuller explanation for this dramatic increase would focus not so much on the interests of the non-central governments in Australia and Canada as on the interests of both the Chinese government in Beijing—and the provincial administrations—and the broader strategic interests of the central governments in Canberra and Ottawa which catalyzed the interest in China over the course of the 1980s.

Australian states

Over the course of the 1980s, an increasingly rich network of Australian contacts with China was developed at both the governmental and non-governmental levels.[3] Five of the six Australian states developed twinning arrangements with Chinese provinces: New South Wales with Guangdong, Victoria with Jiangsu, Tasmania with Fujian, South Australia with Shandong, and Western Australia with Zhejiang. The purpose of this section is to survey the growth in these relationships, focussing particularly on government-to-government interactions.

New South Wales

The NSW government was the first Australian state to establish formal relations with a Chinese province. Shortly after the adoption of the open door policy by China, the New South Wales government negotiated a twinning arrangement with Guangdong, which was signed on 1 September 1979. Shortly afterwards, high-level visits were arranged to cement the relationship: in 1980, the premier of New South Wales, Neville Wran, visited China, and a return visit was by paid by the Governor of Guangdong, Xi Zhongxun.[4] High-level visits were also paid to the state by officials of the central government in Beijing, usually as part of an official visit to Australia. Thus, for example, when Hu Yaobang, General-Secretary of the Chinese Communist Party, visited Australia in April 1985, he had a state luncheon with Neville Wran and held discussions with NSW officials.[5] Likewise, when Li Peng visited Australia in November 1988, he held talks with Nick Greiner about the development of NSW–Guangdong relations.[6]

While there was some attention paid to developing cultural links between the two jurisdictions—visits by orchestras and the development of a language skills exchange, for example—most of the focus was on increasing economic intercourse. Each government sponsored a trade fair in the other's capital in the early 1980s, and each subsequently sought to institutionalize negotiations over economic linkages by establishing a Joint Economic Committee which was charged with investigating joint venture possibilities in such areas as wool- and food-processing, and agriculture. In July 1982, Guangdong established an agency in Sydney to enhance trade and investment, not only displaying Guangdong products, but also offering services to business people in Australia interested in trade with China.[7] The two major joint projects undertaken were agricultural. New South Wales helped organize a Model Beef Cattle Farm on Hainan Island, which was designed to increase beef production by improving feed. The Guangdong government assisted in the establishment of lychee production at a state research station.

Victoria

When the Premier of Victoria, R.J. Hamer, visited China in August 1979, the Governor of Jiangsu province, Xu Jiadun, proposed a twinning relationship between their jurisdictions. A return visit by Xu to Victoria led to the signing in November 1979 of an umbrella agreement for the encouragement of exchanges in a number of different fields.[8]

Both trade delegations and high-level visits were a feature of the relationship. The Premier of Victoria, John Cain, visited Jiangsu in December 1983, a visit reciprocated by the Governor of Jiangsu, Gu Xiulan, in June 1984; the Vice-Governor of Jiangsu took part in Victoria's sesquicentenary in 1985; a number of other ministerial visits marked the relationship. As in other jurisdictions, central government officials from Beijing also played a part in encouraging Victoria's relations with China. For example, when Hu Yaobang visited in April 1985, he took the opportunity to open a Chinese consulate in Melbourne, specifically recognizing the growth in state–provincial relations.[9] Likewise, Li Peng's visit to Australia in November 1988 was the occasion for a state luncheon given by the Governor of Victoria and meetings with the Australia–China Business Cooperation Committee.[10]

As part of the Victoria–Jiangsu linkage, a range of activities designed to foster closer relations was launched, including exchanges of musical performers, arts and crafts fairs, sports teams, and even native animals for each other's zoos. Likewise, exchanges in post-secondary education were also encouraged. Twinning relationships were established between the Royal Melbourne Institute of Technology and the Nanjing Institute of Technology.

Not related to the Victoria–Jiangsu relationship was the development of a municipal twinning relationship between Melbourne and the northern port of Tianjin, which was signed in May 1980.[11] The exchanges between these two cities focused not only on commercial activities, such as the holding of a joint trade exhibition in Melbourne, Sydney and Brisbane in 1984, but also the development of exchanges between members of the city administrations and the municipal libraries. Moreover, the state government of Victoria became involved in a redevelopment program for the Port of Tianjin, assisting the Port of Melbourne Authority in its tender for work in Tianjin's redevelopment.[12]

Tasmania

The Premier of Tasmania, Doug Lowe, paid a visit to China in 1980; from this came the negotiation of a link with Fujian province, which was signed on 5 March 1981. However, it would appear that little developed from this formal relationship. An exchange of craftspeople from each jurisdiction was funded by the Australia–China Council in 1981,[13] but the links did not extend much beyond this. Exchanges were minimal and visits were few. And while other states saw their relations with China given a boost when high-level officials from the central government in Beijing visiting Australia included state capitals in their itineraries, a trip to Hobart was rarely included. For example, when Hu Yaobang visited in April 1985 and Li Peng in November 1988, neither leader paid a visit to Hobart. By 1985, two different observers of state relations with China would comment on the undeveloped state of the relationship.[14]

South Australia

By contrast, the South Australian government was slower than New South Wales, Victoria or Tasmania in developing links with a Chinese province.

But since the decision to twin with Shandong province in 1984, the two jurisdictions developed a strong relationship.[15] The decision to seek a special relationship with Shandong did not emerge until 1984, when Bruce Guerin, the director of the Department of the Premier and Cabinet visited China. But the twinning relationship took nearly three years to negotiate. Guerin's visit was followed in April 1985 by a visit by the South Australian minister of agriculture to develop cooperative plans for a farming project in northern Shandong. Two further visits—by Guerin to Shandong in September 1985, and by the Secretary-General of the Shandong government to South Australia in March 1986—were needed to finalize the Friendly Relationship Agreement. The agreement was not signed until April 1986, when the Premier, John Bannon, accepted an invitation to visit Shandong for a ceremonial signing with the Governor of Shandong, Li Chang'an. The ensuing relationship was marked by high-level and governmental visits, including a number of South Australian ministers travelling to Shandong and one vice-gubernatorial visit to South Australia.

As a result of the state–province relationship, sister relationships between other institutions also developed: the Royal Adelaide Hospital and Shandong Provincial Hospital explored developing a sister relationship over the course of 1987; dental and medical exchanges were initiated in 1987 and 1988. There were also exchanges in the field of education: in October 1985, a twinning agreement was signed between the University of Adelaide and Shandong University and Shandong Polytechnic Engineering University. High school exchanges involving both students and teachers began in 1986.[16]

Western Australia

Western Australia's major involvement with China in the 1980s was the $250 million investment that Chinese state enterprises had in CRA Mount Channar, a joint-venture iron ore facility in the state. This mega-project tended to attract considerable attention as a symbol of the burgeoning relationship between Australia and China in general. Thus, for example, when Premier Li Peng visited Australia in November 1988, a trip to Western Australia was included in the itinerary, with a trip to Mount Channar.[17]

Western Australia did develop a twinning relationship—with Zhejiang province in central China—but much of the focus of the state's linkages with China in the 1980s was focussed on the wider relationship. Thus, for example, on the occasion of Li's visit, Premier Dowding took the opportunity to announce a $5 million Western Australia–China Technical and Research Development Fund. Likewise, Western Australia participated in the China Skills Trainee Program, begun in May 1988. This was a two-year work experience in China and Australia for Australians. The year in Australia was paid for by Australian firms and governments, and the Overseas Relations Office of the Western Australian government paid for a placement.[18]

Queensland

The Queensland government, like other Australian states, was interested in developing closer relations with China. The Premier, Joh Bjelke-Petersen, visited China in March 1984, being received by the Chinese Premier, Zhao Ziyang. In June 1985, the Deputy Premier, Bill Gunn, led a trade mission to China to explore the possibilities for expanded trade.

However, Queensland's major involvement with China did not emerge through twinning; it was the only Australian state which did not develop a sister relationship in the 1980s.[19] Although Queensland was courted hard by officials from the provinces of Guangxi and Anhui, the government in Brisbane eschewed sister relationships. Rather, Queensland's involvement with China came primarily through state participation in development assistance projects to China established by the Australian Development Assistance Bureau (ADAB). State forestry officials helped manage a euca-lypt afforestation project, Dongmen State Forest Farm, in Guangxi and transfer skills and technology. A second ADAB project, centred in Beijing, involved state officials advising their Chinese counterparts on the use of agricultural chemicals, and training in the use of pesticides.

Canadian provinces

There was a comparable growth in relations between Canadian provinces and China. However, only four of Canada's ten provinces developed twin-ning relationships: Alberta with Heilongjiang; Saskatchewan with Jilin; Ontario with Jiangsu; and Quebec with Shaanxi.

Alberta

The relationship between Alberta and the north-eastern province of Heilongjiang represents the most involved set of Canadan provincial linkages with China. In the words of one observer, there was 'almost a perfect fit' between the two provinces: Heilongjiang has a climate and topography similar to Alberta; both provinces are their country's main supplier of oil.[20] The relationship began in 1980, developing from Chinese agricultural and oil missions to Alberta in 1978.[21] At the suggestion of the Chinese ambassador in Ottawa, the two provinces negotiated a twinning agreement that was signed in September 1981. This was designed to develop links in agriculture, petroleum and petrochemical technology, forestry, education, culture and recreation.

The twinning arrangement spawned an increase in visits between the two provinces: Chinese missions to Alberta rose from five in 1978–9 to fifteen in 1980–1, eighteen in 1982–3, thirty-three in 1983–4, thirty-five in 1984–5 and thirty-eight in 1985–6. Given the importance of petroleum interests to the provincial twinning, it is not surprising that petroleum experts from the Daqing, Gaotaizi and Zhongyuan-Wenliu oilfields regularly visited Alberta.[22] High-level visits were also common: in June 1983, the Minister of International Trade, Horst Schmid, visited China, followed in August by Alberta's Premier, Peter Lougheed; Intergovernmental Affairs Minister James Horsman visited Heilongjiang's capital Harbin and Beijing in June 1985.[23] On the Chinese side, Alberta was visited by Heilongjiang Vice-Governors Jing Bowen and Wang Lianzheng and the Secretary-General of the province's Education Commission visited Alberta, as did the Vice-Chairman of the People's Congress, Wang Jun, and the Minister of Agriculture, He Kang.[24]

Besides official visits, there was also a considerable flow of business missions between the two jurisdictions. For example, the 'Great Trade Show of China' was held in Edmonton in the spring of 1984, and in 1986 Alberta sponsored a provincial mission to Beijing and the Daqing oilfields, and took part in the 'Onshore China' oil show in Guangzhou.[25] Seventeen trade missions were scheduled to visit China in the first quarter of 1989 alone.[26]

The twinning at the provincial level was mirrored by an increase in ties between other institutions. In May 1985 Calgary was twinned with Daqing and in December 1985 the two provincial capitals, Edmonton and Harbin, were twinned.[27] Secondments and staff exchanges in municipal administration followed shortly thereafter. Exchanges of students and teachers were the primary feature of a twinning relationship between Lethbridge University and Harbin Teachers' University, formalized in October 1988.[28] Graduate students attending Alberta universities were to be sponsored by the Daqing oilfields. Albertan teachers taught English in Daqing, and academic exchanges took place between Heilongjiang University and the University of Alberta. Calgary General Hospital and Daqing No. 1 Hospital were twinned and established the Alberta–Heilongjiang Program for Advanced Medical Training. Edmonton's ETCOM Ltd. undertook to train Chinese telecommunications personnel.

Indeed, the relationship with Heilongjiang was so successful that Alberta explored the possibility of expanding links with other Chinese provinces.[29] It also sought to expand relations with the central government in Beijing: at the end of a visit to the Far East in November 1987, the minister of economic development, Larry Shabden, announced that Alberta would seek to post an agent-general in Beijing.[30] Another tangible sign of the province's presence in the Chinese capital was the establishment of an Alberta Petroleum Training Centre, originally slated to open in Beijing in late 1989.[31]

Saskatchewan

Although Saskatchewan's trade connection with China dates back to the massive grain sales of the 1960s and 1970s, the first formal contacts between the province and China did not develop until the late 1970s. From 1980 to 1982, Chinese farmers visited Saskatchewan to learn dryland farming techniques and to become acquainted with potash application. Saskatchewan also encouraged university twinnings between the University of Regina and the University of Shandong and participated in the federal government's PRC Scholars Program: thirty-eight scholars from China attended Saskatchewan universities. Finally, the province established the Saskatchewan–China Potash Agronomic Program in 1983.[32]

However, it was not until Alberta had signed a twinning arrangement with Heilongjiang that Saskatchewan was moved to forge formal ties with a Chinese province. Using the Alberta–Heilongjiang agreement as a model, Saskatchewan twinned with Jilin, a province whose topography and economy was not unlike that of Saskatchewan, in June 1984. This twinning evolved from initial contacts made by Saskatchewan's Department of Industry and Commerce, which established links with Jilin as part of what was, according to the Department of Intergovernmental Affairs, Saskatchewan's 'new Asian thrust'.[33]

Premier Grant Devine visited Jilin in 1983, which resulted in the signing of a protocol of friendship in January 1984. Devine's trip was reciprocated by the Governor of Jilin, Zhao Xiu, in June 1984. Saskatchewan Deputy Premier Eric Berntson followed up Premier Allan Blakeney's twinning ceremony with a June 1985 visit to Jilin.[34] Colin Maxwell, Minister of Advanced Education and Manpower, led a delegation to China in the fall of 1984 to establish educational exchanges with Jilin and Shandong province. And, as part of the Jilin twinning, a trade agency was established by Tourism and Small Business Minister Jack Klein and Yang Fu Chun, General Manager of China Jilin Province Foreign Trade Import and Export Corporation, to facilitate direct trade relations between the provinces. Saskatchewan was also given permission by the Chinese government to establish its own trade office, which opened in 1985.[35]

Ontario

Ontario government's relations with China date from the early 1970s. In 1974, Ontario welcomed its first Chinese trade delegation and in 1976 a Chinese technology and product marketing delegation visited the province. Throughout the 1970s China was Ontario's second major customer in Asia after Japan. By the early 1980s, primary exports of synthetic resins and fibres, steel bars and rods, wood pulp, tobacco leaves, telecommunications equipment, auto parts and industrial machinery were resulting in 'particularly rapid growth' in exports to China, which in 1984–85, for example, rose 136 per cent.[36]

Despite the growth in trade links between Ontario and China in the 1970s and early 1980s, it was not until the mid-1980s that the Ontario government moved to formalize a relationship with a Chinese province. In 1984, Jiangsu was selected as the appropriate twin, and the Minister of Industry and Tourism, Frank Miller, was dispatched to China on a fourteen-day visit in July and August 1984 to lay the groundwork for the provincial twinning.[37]

The twinning arrangement was signed in November 1985 by Premier David Peterson and Gu Xiulan, the Governor of Jiangsu province. The twinning marked a rapid increase in Ontario's relations with China in general and Jiangsu in particular. Ontario signed a five-year trade and technology agreement with China, and formed a 'China Section' in the Ministry of Industry. In 1985, over $2.25 million was spent promoting trade with China, and over 100 trade missions from China visited Ontario. Within a year, Ontario had five full-time provincial representatives stationed in China, and Beijing had a trade representative in Toronto.[38]

The twinning also catalysed the growth in Ontario–Jiangsu relations. The most tangible manifestation was the construction of the Ontario–Jiangsu Science and Technology Centre. This joint project was designed not only to provide a permament site for the exhibition of Ontario technology, but also to provide a locus for Ontario's technology transfer and training program in China.[39] Not surprisingly, one of Ontario's representatives in China was stationed in Nanjing, Jiangsu's capital.

The provincial initiative spawned the growth of other relationships, both governmental and non-governmental. In 1986, Toronto twinned with Chongqing in an economic and cultural program.[40] Under this umbrella arrangement, Harbord Collegiate Institute in Toronto twinned with Chongqing No. 1 Middle School; York University's Osgoode Hall with the Southwest Institute for Political Science and Law; the Ontario College of Art with Sichuan Fine Arts Institute; the Hospital for Sick Children in Toronto with Chongqing Paediatric Hospital; and Norman Bethune College at York University with the Sichuan Foreign Languages Institute.[41]

High-level visits included a visit by Peterson to Nanjing in October 1986, reciprocating Gu's earlier visit to Ontario. While in Jiangsu, Peterson was pressed by Nanjing University for the development of links with either York University or the University of Toronto (or both), and by the Jiangsu Academy of Agricultural Sciences for links with the University of Guelph. Indicating his optimism for the future of the relationship, Peterson indicated that, in his opinion, an Ontario minister should visit Jiangsu at least once a month.[42]

Quebec

The Quebec Ministry of Intergovernmental Affairs decided in 1980 to formalize its relationships with China. An educational accord was signed in March 1980, and later that year the Chinese Vice-Premier, Bo Yibo, met with Quebec's Finance Minister, Jacques Parizeau, to discuss economic relations between the two governments. At the same time, there were ongoing university exchanges between Fudan University and the Université de Montréal, and in 1981 Quebec instructors and equipment were placed in the Peking Language Institute. Finally, in recognition of the importance of the China market, the ministry formed a 'China division' in order to study the economic and technological potential for Quebec in China, and even began printing Chinese-language versions of Quebec economic reports in 1981.[43]

Indicative of the growing relationship between Quebec and China were the high-level visits that began in the mid-1980s. In January 1984 Chinese Premier Zhao Ziyang visited Quebec to identify areas of cooperation and to discuss a science and technology agreement between Quebec and its Chinese twin, Shaanxi. After this visit, the Quebec government and the Chinese Association of Science and Technology signed an agreement in February 1984 outlining the development of Quebec–China relations from primarily agricultural and educational matters to those of technology and industry. There were also visits from Forestry Minister Yang Zhong, Foreign Affairs Minister Wu Xueqion, and a Beijing-sponsored cultural mission.[44] In 1984, the premier, René Lévesque, led a delegation of officials and business leaders to Shanghai in 1984 to develop inter-provincial ties.[45] It was during this trip that Bernard Landry, Minister of Foreign Trade, secured a $1 million contract for Hydro-Québec International to study the feasibility of developing a dam on the Three Gorges River. The four-day trip to China included a meeting with Premier Zhao, who described Quebec as 'good partners rather than [commercial] partners'.[46]

Other twinnings and formal arrangements also deepened the relationship. In May 1985 Montreal Mayor Jean Drapeau took advantage of the warm relations between Quebec and China to twin with Shanghai.[47] In the field of education, Concordia University became the first western university to set up a joint doctoral program with a Chinese institution. The agreement with

Nanjing Institute of Technology saw Ph.D. candidates in electrical and computer engineering spend part of their residency at the other university, eventually earning a Concordia degree.[48] Likewise, the Université du Québec à Trois Rivières also set up a joint program with the University of Heilongjiang in the pulp and paper sectors.[49]

With education, science and technology, and twinning agreements in hand, the intergovernmental affairs ministry appealed to Quebec businesses to assist in the 'modernization' of Chinese industry, notably in energy, transportation and communications. Bernard Landry, the then minister of international relations, announced in July 1985 that the provincial government was willing financially to assist Quebec firms interested in doing business with China.[50] To promote its links with China, Quebec received visits from Science and Technology Minister Song Jian, Energy Minister Qian Zhengying, Ambassador to Canada Yu Zhan, and Chinese president Li Xiannian.[51] In 1987 Agriculture Minister He Kang came to Quebec to discuss agricultural reforms for Shaanxi, Civic Affairs Minister Cui Nai Fu met with Quebec's Ministry of Health and Social Services, Shanghai Deputy Mayor Ni Tianzeng met with Drapeau to renew the ties between the cities, and Ambassador to Canada Zhang Wen Pu and Lin Han Xiong paid formal visits to Quebec.[52] In 1988 Pierre Macdonald, Minister of External Trade and Technological Development, led a business delegation to China; Health and Social Services Minister Thérèse Lavoie travelled to Beijing and Shanghai. In the spring of 1989, Jean Doré, mayor of Montreal, visited Shanghai and Jean Pelletier, mayor of Quebec City, visited Xian. During Pelletier's stay, a twinning agreement between the two cities was signed. In 1988, Quebec was visited by Chinese Vice-Premier Tian Ji Yan, the Vice-Governors of Hunan and Hubei, the Vice-Minister of Industry, the Vice-President of China's State Planning Committee, a delegation from the Chinese Institute of Foreign Affairs and Tian Jinyn, Deputy Minister of State for the People's Republic.[53]

British Columbia

Like Queensland, British Columbia developed no formal twinning relationship with a Chinese province; but also like Queensland, linkages with China rapidly developed during the 1970s and 1980s. While trade with China expanded dramatically in the early 1970s,[54] it was not until November 1979 that the BC government sponsored its first trade mission to China.[55]

High-level visits also marked the relationship in the mid-1980s. The premier, William Bennett, visited China in 1984, calling British Columbia 'Canada's window' to China, and stressing the need for closer relations.[56] Later in the year, Forestry Minister Thomas Waterland and Energy Minister Stephen Rogers led trade missions to China.[57] By late 1984 the

Ministry of Industry and Small Business Development was reporting a 'most significant recent development' in the 'rapid advance in trade with the People's Republic of China.' The missions in 1984 led the province to send a special delegation to Shandong in 1985 to consolidate ties with that province.[58] For their part, the Chinese were interested in British Columbia's hydro-electric technology: the president of the Bank of China, Jin Dequin, met with Bennett and BC Finance Minister Hugh Curtis in October 1984 to discuss possible funding arrangements for the proposed Three Rivers hydro-electric dam on the Yangtze river.[59] This was followed by a visit by China's President, Li Xiannian, to Vancouver in July 1985.[60] British Columbia placed three full-time trade representatives in China, while Beijing opened a commercial office in Vancouver, one of three of its kind in Canada.[61]

Notwithstanding this activity, however, British Columbia showed little interest in formal twinning arrangements. While a dairy pact between British Columbia and Liaoning province was signed in 1985,[62] the high-level visits of 1984 and 1985 produced no formalized bilateral relations. An official mission from Shaanxi province in 1985 encouraged British Columbia to look to it for increased investment and technological relations; the government in Victoria forged no formal ties with a Chinese province and indeed stated explicitly in 1986 that there were 'no plans for any'.[63]

However, twinning arrangements proved to be popular with municipalities and other institutions in the province. In the mid-1980s, the Port of Vancouver twinned with the Port of Dalian, Vancouver with Guangzhou, and Victoria with Suzhou. Simon Fraser University and Jinan University in Guangzhou province formally twinned in 1981.[64] However, while municipal, business and educational links with China grew during the 1980s, formal provincial affiliations were not actively pursued.

Other Provinces

In sharp contrast to the activities of British Columbia, Alberta, Saskatchewan, Ontario and Quebec, none of Canada's five other provinces—Manitoba, New Brunswick, Newfoundland, Nova Scotia and Prince Edward Island—demonstrated comparable interest in China in the 1980s. The Manitoba government organized a number of trade missions to China in the mid-1980s in an attempt to move from primarily agricultural-based trade to machinery and technology agreements with China.[65] But rather than focus relations on a particular province, Manitoba's activities in China were 'focused on a sectoral basis', according to Dennis Cleve of the Manitoba Department of Industry, Trade and Technology.[66]

The response in Atlantic Canada was even more cautious. In October 1984, Nova Scotia received a Chinese delegation exploring possibilities for increased trade with the region.[67] After this trip, Chinese officials expressed interest in educational and fisheries programs and suggested that a twinning arrangement could be set up with Halifax.[68] Nova Scotia reciprocated this visit in summer 1984 with a government-sponsored business trip to China.[69] In New Brunswick, the only linkages with China were institutional, between the University of New Brunswick and New Brunswick Telephone. Brian Peckford, former premier of Newfoundland, visited China in January 1986 but no firm agreements were reached between governments.[70]

Conclusions

When one examines the relations between Australian states and Canadian provinces with China in the 1980s, one cannot but be struck by the high degree of international activity of these non-central governments directed towards China. One cannot also help being struck by the similarities in the experiences of non-central governments in both Australia and Canada. And indeed the different levels of activity of the various states and provinces tends to confirm the importance of looking at non-central government interests as the necessary but insufficient condition for international activity. Those states and provinces which lacked the interest to press for expanded relations either kept their relationships with China at a minimal level—for example, the four Maritime provinces in Canada or Tasmania in Australia—or simply did not formalize the relationship through twinning, as was the case with both Queensland and British Columbia. On the other hand, other jurisdictions eagerly sought to expand links as much as possible.

Yet if one looks at the China policies of these non-central government relationships in isolation, one will miss an essential part of the explanation for the increasing involvement with China in the 1980s. Rather, to understand these linkages, one should see them as evolving within the framework of interests of other actors.

First, developing non-central government-to-government relations with China was firmly in the interests of both central governments in Australia and Canada. Both governments over the course of the 1980s had their different reasons for developing and maintaining warm and friendly relations with China.[71] For the Liberal/National government of Malcolm Fraser, the reasons were primarily strategic and bound up in Cold War rivalries between the United States and the Soviet Union: China was seen as pivotal in the attempt to constrain the expansion of Soviet influence in the Far East. For the Labor government of Bob Hawke, by contrast, the relationship assumed a more symbolic importance. Not only was it part of the Labor legacy from the early 1970s; it also carried the symbolism of signifying Australia's new Asian thrust, developing what Stephen FitzGerald, a former Australian ambassador to Beijing, would criticize as a national love affair with China.[72] Indeed, Hawke once described the relationship with China as exceeded in importance for Australia by no other.[73]

For the Liberal goverment of Pierre Trudeau the steady growth of the relationship with China was in part the natural outgrowth of the historical relationship based largely on the grain trade; in part the natural outgrowth of the prime minister's own initiative in 1968 and 1969 in securing Canadian recognition of the People's Republic of China; in part the desire to use relations with China to diversify Canada's trading relationships; and in part a desire to give expression to the notion that Canada is a 'Pacific nation'. For the Progressive Conservative government of Brian Mulroney, the relationship with China, while not as important symbolically, was none the less embraced as warmly partly for its strategic value, and partly because of the economic opportunities it offered.

In short, the burgeoning relationships at the subnational level directly complemented central government interests. To the extent that non-central government activities spurred trade—and there is some evidence to suggest that they did[74]—such activities were to be welcomed, particularly when the China trade in the 1980s usually ran in Australia's and Canada's favour.[75] And to the extent that non-central government activities deepened the strategic/political relationship between China and the West, such activities were also to be welcomed, particularly by policy-makers in Canberra and Ottawa who tended to believe that heightened economic linkages would also lead to improved human rights in China.

Nor should we forget the final side of the triangle—the Chinese interest in non-central government relationships. In particular, it is worthwhile recalling that during the 1970s and 1980s, the central government in Beijing evinced a general interest in expanding contacts of all sorts with the West. The encouragement of ties, particularly formal ties, between non-central governments was a natural outgrowth of that concern. In some cases, it was a crucial element of the strategy. For example, improving links with post-secondary institutions in Canada meant focussing on the provincial governments, which have jurisdiction over education under the Canadian constitution. Likewise, Australian state and Canadian provincial jurisdiction over aspects of economic development made them natural targets of the Chinese strategy.

But it was more than merely the interests of the central authorities in Beijing that was driving these linkages with non-central governments abroad. What we refer to in the singular as 'the Chinese interest' is in fact a plurality of interests, even if the pluralism of the Chinese unitary system differs considerably from the pluralism inherent in the federal systems in both Australia and Canada. Thus we also have to consider the interests of provincial administrations in the development of foreign linkages. In this case, as in Australia and Canada, the interests of the centre in Beijing complemented the interests of China's provincial governments. Linking with western jurisdictions and institutions directly provided provincial administrations with access to western technology, education, investment and trading opportunities that was relatively unimpeded by the central authorities.

For both levels of government, then, there was a complementary interest in seeking to expand foreign contacts. The strategy preferred by the Chinese, it is clear, was the twinning arrangement. While calls for sister relationships with non-central governments had been first bruited by Zhou Enlai in the early 1970s, it was not until the emergence of Deng Xiaoping and the open door policy in 1978 that the search for twins became more pronounced. Thus, while only six twinning arrangements were concluded between 1973 and 1978, a total of 137 twinning relationships were negotiated by the Chinese between 1979 and 1984. By 1985, of China's twenty provinces, only Yunnan did not have a provincial twin; otherwise, there were 143 Chinese twinning arrangements in place with jurisdictions in twenty-one countries on six continents.[76]

In sum, the rapid expansion of non-central government links with China in the 1980s—and the equally rapid contraction of these links after Tiananmen in 1989—provides an illustrative example of the need to examine more than merely the interests of these non-central governments in projecting themselves abroad. We suggest that equally important are the interests of the other points of what must be seen as a fundamentally triangular relationship.

Notes

1. This has been a persistent analytical theme in the literature over the last two decades. See, for example, Ronald G. Atkey, 'The role of the provinces in international affairs', *International Journal*, 26 (1970–1), 249–73; Elliot J. Feldman and Lily Gardner Feldman, 'The impact of federalism on the organization of Canadian foreign policy', *Publius*, 14 (1984); Brian Hocking, 'Regional governments and international affairs: foreign policy problem or deviant behaviour?', *International Journal*, 41 (1986), 477–506; Earl Fry, 'The impact of federalism on the development of international economic relations: lessons from the United States and Canada', *Australian Outlook*, 43 (1989), esp. 19–25; Kim Richard Nossal, *The Politics of Canadian Foreign Policy*, 2nd edn, Prentice-Hall Canada, Scarborough, Ont. (1989); Annemarie Jacomy-Millette, 'Les activités internationales des provinces canadiennes', in Paul Painchaud (ed.), *De Mackenzie King à Pierre Trudeau: quarante ans de diplomatie canadienne*, Les Presses de l'Université Laval, Québec (1989), 81–104; Hans J. Michelmann and Panayotis Soldatos (eds), *Federalism and International Relations: The Role of Subnational Units*, Clarendon Press, Oxford (1990).
2. The desire to open the Chinese economy to the west was part of the Four

Modernizations (in agriculture, industry, national defence, and science and technology) embraced after the death of Mao Zedong. The open door policy is usually dated to the decisions of the Third Plenum of the 11th Central Committee in December 1978, which sought to restructure China's economy by encouraging production to satisfy basic human needs rather than the statistical targets of central planners; focusing development to improve production rather than merely expand it; allowing the expansion of the non-state sector; and opening a hitherto closed economy to the international marketplace. For discussions, see Andrew Watson and Xin Luolin, 'China's open-door policy in historical perspective', *Australian Outlook*, 40 (1986), 91–9; Jonathan D. Spence, *The Search for Modern China*, Hutchinson, London (1990), 653ff.

3. For an overview, see E.M. Andrews, *Australia and China: The Ambiguous Relationship*, Melbourne University Press, Melbourne (1985), 224ff.

4. Australia, Australia–China Council, *Annual Report* (1980), 2.

5. *Australian Foreign Affairs Record*, 56 (April 1985), 309–11.

6. 'Visit to Australia by Chinese premier', ibid., 59 (November 1988), 508.

7. J.Y. Wong and D.L. Michalk, 'New South Wales and Guangdong', in H.A. Dunn and Edmund S.K. Fung (eds), *Sino-Australian Relations: The Record, 1972–1985*, Centre for the Study of Australian Asian Relations, Griffith University, Nathan, Qld (1985), 262–71.

8. Michael A. Pointer, 'Victoria and Jiangsu', in Dunn and Fung (eds), *Sino-Australian Relations*, op. cit., 249–61.

9. *Australian Foreign Affairs Record*, 56 (April 1985), 309–11.

10. 'Visit to Australia by Chinese premier', ibid., 59 (November 1988), 508.

11. Australia–China Council, *Annual Report* (1980), 2.

12. Pointer, 'Victoria and Jiangsu', op. cit., 258.

13. Australia–China Council, *Annual Report* (1981–2), 9.

14. See the assessments of the Tasmania–Fujian relationship in Wong and Michalk, 'New South Wales and Guangdong', op. cit., 264; and Edmund S.K. Fung, 'Queensland and China', in Dunn and Fung (eds), *Sino-Australian Relations*, op. cit., 284.

15. 'South Australia's overseas links', *Australian Foreign Affairs Record*, 59 (June 1988), 243.

16. 'The relationship between South Australia amd Shandong Province', ibid., 59 (June 1988), 255–6.

17. 'Visit to Australia by Chinese premier', ibid., 59 (November 1988), 508.

18. Australia–China Council, *Annual Report* (1988–9), 16.

19. Edmund S.K. Fung, 'Queensland and China', in Dunn and Fung (eds), *Sino-Australian Relations*, op. cit., 272–87.

20. Wayne Gooding, 'Alberta and Heilongjiang find relationship a close fit', *Financial Post* (13 July 1985), S19; Alberta, Department of Federal and Intergovernmental Affairs, International Division, *An Overview of Alberta-Heilongjiang Relations* (October 1991), 3. The Daqing oilfields in Heilongjiang province produce over 50 per cent of China's petroleum.

21. Alberta, Department of Economic Development and International Trade, *1978 Alberta Exports* (May 1979), 9.

22. In 1985–6, for example, Alberta received visits from a science and technology commission; Changshu Research Institute of Mining and Metallurgy; Xian

Jiatong University School of Management; Heilongjiang Academy of Sciences; and a delegation from the Daqing oilfields. Alberta, Department of Federal and Intergovernmental Affairs, *Thirteenth Annual Report to March 31, 1986*, 22.

23. Stanley Oziewicz, 'Alberta given boost by Premier in China', *Globe and Mail* (30 August 1983), 12; Lois Bridges, 'Industry hopes Orient trip will help trade', *Financial Post* (20 August 1983), 7; also John Davidson, 'The Pacific Rim: trading with the Rim', *Alberta Report*, 12 (April 1985), 16.

24. Alberta, Department of Federal and Intergovernmental Affairs, *Sixteenth Annual Report to March 31, 1989*, 45.

25. Alberta, Department of Federal and Intergovernmental Affairs, *Fourteenth Annual Report to March 31, 1987*, 37.

26. Alberta, Department of Economic Development and Trade, *Annual Report 1989–1990*, 15.

27. Jude Carlson, 'Peeking into Daqing', *Calgary Herald* (27 October 1985), D1.

28. Alberta, Department of Federal and Intergovernmental Affairs, *An Overview of Alberta–Heilongjiang Relations* (October 1991), 2.

29. A mission was dispatched to Sichuan in February 1987 to explore twinning with that province; representatives were also sent to Fujian and Guangdong in 1988. Alberta, Department of Federal and Intergovernmental Affairs, *Fifteenth Annual Report to March 31, 1988*, 22; *Sixteenth Annual Report to March 31, 1989*, 39, 41.

30. Shabden argued that this was necessary because Alberta was being 'outhustled' in China by Quebec, Ontario and British Columbia. Kathy Kerr, 'Offices in Asia vital: ministers', *Calgary Herald* (4 November 1987), A7.

31. Alberta, Department of Federal and Intergovernmental Affairs, *Sixteenth Annual Report to March 31, 1989*, 39, 41. The Centre was eventually opened in 1992.

32. Saskatchewan, Saskatchewan Intergovernmental Affairs, *Annual Report, 1982–83*, 9, 7, 13.

33. Saskatchewan, Department of Industry and Commerce, *Annual Report, 1974–75*, 1.

34. Canada, Department of External Affairs, *Report of the Department of External Affairs, 1984–85*, 32; 'Trade agency agreement signed', *Provincial Pulse*, 2 (November 1985), 567; John Schreiner, 'Grain farming progress worries Saskatchewan', *Financial Post* (13 July 1985), S17.

35. Saskatchewan, Saskatchewan Economic Development and Trade, *Annual Report, 1984–85*, 8; *Annual Report, 1985–86*, 4.

36. Ontario, Ministry of Trade and Tourism, Industry and Trade Analysis Branch, Policy and Priorities Division, *Exports and Imports by Countries, Commodities and Industries*, 1974, 1976, 1984; also Ministry of Industry and Tourism, *Ontario Industry Trade and Tourism Review* (July 1974), 17.

37. Ontario, Ministry of Industry and Trade, *Ontario Business News* (July–August 1984), 3.

38. Andrew Cohen, 'Opportunity abounds for Ontario', *Financial Post* (13 July 1985), S18.

39. Ontario, Ministry of Industry, Trade and Technology, *How to Do Business in China* (Toronto, 1987), 13, 27; James Rusk, 'China visit takes premier to see "twin" in Jiangsu', *Globe and Mail* (4 October 1986), A9; '"Trade through technology" Ontario plan for Jiangsu' *Financial Post* (17 November 1986), 40.

40. Susan Pigg, 'Toronto may soon twin with China's largest city', *Toronto Star* (11

May 1985), p. A8; Andrew McIntosh, 'Some Canadian provinces link with Chinese counterparts', *Globe and Mail* (17 March 1986), C20.

41. Sean Fine, 'Toronto, Chongqing will promote trade', *Globe and Mail* (31 October 1986), A17.

42. James Rusk, 'Peterson calls China a market worth developing', *Globe and Mail* (6 October 1986), A11.

43. Québec, Ministère des Affaires intergouvernementales, *Rapport annuel* (1981–2), 40–1 (1982–3), 33–4. Also Ministère de l'industrie et du commerce, Bureau de la statistique du Québec, *Annuaire de Québec: 1979–80*, 827.

44. Québec, Ministère des Affaires intergouvernementales, *Rapport annuel: 1983–84*, 41, 85.

45. R.B. Byers (ed.), *Canadian Annual Review of Politics and Public Affairs* University of Toronto Press, Toronto (1987), 240. Lévesque argued that he was unable to go earlier because Secretary of State for External Affairs Jean Chrétien had denied him authorization for the trip. Chrétien denied this charge.

46. 'Lévesque winds up Chinese tour with hydro-dam contract', *Montreal Gazette* (6 October 1984), A5; 'Lévesque returns from Asian trip', *Canadian News Facts*, 18 (October 1984), 3142.

47. Ingrid Peritz, 'Pact is Montreal's entry into Asia: mayor,' *Montreal Gazette*, 15 May 1985, A4.

48. 'A first: Concordia and China set up joint doctoral program', *Montreal Gazette* (13 March 1987), A3.

49. Andrew McIntosh, 'Some Canadian provinces link with Chinese counterparts', *Globe and Mail* (17 March 1986), C20.

50. Daniel Drolet, 'Quebec to help firms crack Chinese market', *Montreal Gazette* (18 July 1985), A4.

51. Québec, Ministère des Relations internationales, *Rapport annuel: 1985–6*, 54, 93, 94. Li met with the ministers of foreign trade, forestry, communications, cultural affairs, agriculture and transport. Daniel Drolet, 'Chinese to talk trade in Quebec City', *Montreal Gazette* (17 July 1985), A4.

52. Québec, Ministère des Relations internationales, *Rapport annuel 1986–1987*, 49, 96–7.

53. Québec, Ministère des Affaires internationales, *Rapport annuel: 1988–1989*, 43–4.

54. British Columbia, Department of Industrial Development, Trade and Commerce, Economics and Statistics Branch, *Summary of Economic Activity in British Columba* (1972 and 1974); Department of Industrial Development, Trade and Commerce, *1973 Annual Report*, 98.

55. British Columbia, Ministry of Industry and Small Business Development, Economic Analysis and Research Bureau, *China Economic Overview: A British Columbia Perspective*, by Madeline Cox, Vancouver, (1981), vii.

56. Ian Mulgrew, 'B.C. Premier to visit China; trade relations may expand', *Globe and Mail* (23 January 1984), 8.

57. John Schreiner, 'Trade missions helpful: B.C. firms build up their links,' *Financial Post* (13 July 1985), S18.

58. British Columbia, Ministry of Industry and Small Business Development, *British Columbia Facts and Statistics*, Vancouver (1984), 78; British Columbia, Ministry of Intergovernmental Relations, *Annual Report: April 1, 1985 to March 31, 1986*, 11.

59. Rod Nutt, 'China ponders B.C. investment', *Vancouver Sun* (4 October 1984), D9;

James Rusk, 'Canadians may have inside track if Chinese hydro project proceeds', *Globe and Mail* (27 April 1988), B14.

60. Ingrid Peritz, 'Drapeau's back from the Orient with image as a salesman intact', *Montreal Gazette* (27 May 1985), A1.

61. David Steward-Patterson, 'Canada sees dramatic climb in manufactured goods sales', and 'Both countries receiving benefits from business, cultural exchange', *Globe and Mail* (17 March 1986), C3, C9.

62. *Vancouver Sun* (10 July 1985), A14.

63. Rod Nutt, 'Opportunity knocks in Shaanxi province', *Vancouver Sun* (20 July 1985), C6.

64. Larry Pynn, 'SFU, Chinese agree on exchange program', *Vancouver Sun* (6 October 1981), A11.

65. Manitoba, Department of Industry, Trade and Technology, *Annual Report: 1983–84*, 9; Andrew Allen Tuck, 'Future of Manitoba exports centre on technology', *Financial Post* (13 July 1985), S17.

66. Andrew McIntosh, 'Some Canadian provinces link with Chinese counterparts', *Globe and Mail* (17 March 1986), C20.

67. David Abbass, 'China seeks N.S. trade ties', *Chronicle Herald* (20 October 1984), 15.

68. David Abbass, 'China shows interest in N.S.', *Chronicle Herald* (21 February 1985), 14.

69. Marianne Tefft, 'Atlantic firms learn to deal Chinese style', *Financial Post* (13 July 1985), S17.

70. Andrew McIntosh, 'Some Canadian provinces link with Chinese counterparts', *Globe and Mail* (17 March 1986), C20.

71. For surveys of the development of the relationships with China, see Paul Evans and Bernie Frolic (eds), *Reluctant Adversaries: Canada and the People's Republic of China, 1949–1970*, University of Toronto Press, Toronto (1991); Edmund S.K. Fung and Colin Mackerras, *From Fear to Friendship: Australia's Policies Towards the People's Republic of China, 1966–1982*, University of Queensland Press, St. Lucia (1985); Andrews, *Australia and China*, op. cit.

72. In a highly critical speech given in November 1989, FitzGerald termed Australia's attitude towards China since 1972 an 'Alice in Wonderland approach': see his 'Australia's China', *Australian Journal of Chinese Affairs*, 24 (1990), 315–35.

73. 'Visit to Australia by Chinese premier', *Australian Foreign Affairs Record*, 59 (November 1988), 509.

74. In a related study of Canadian provincial trade patterns with China in the 1980s, we show that spurts in provincial trade with China inexorably followed such activities as trade missions and high-level visits.

75. China was Australia's ninth largest customer, importing AUS$1.3 billion in 1987–8 and $1.2 billion in 1988–9 (2.8 per cent of Australia's exports). Moreover, trade ran in Australia's favour: Australia imported $851 million in 1987–8 and $1.03 billion in 1988–9 (2.2 per cent of total imports). Canadian trade was likewise lucrative: exports had risen from CDN$1.4 billion in 1987 to $2.6 billion in 1988 (2 per cent of total exports); imports had risen from $812 million to $955 million in the same period (0.07 per cent of imports). Australia, Australian Bureau of Statistics, *Foreign Trade, Australia: Comparative and Summary*

Tables, 1988–89, Canberra (1990). Canada, Department of External Affairs and International Trade, *Annual Report 1988/89*, Ottawa, Supply and Services Canada (1989), 50–1.

76. All figures from Wong and Michalk, 'New South Wales and Guangdong', op. cit., 263.

11 Federalism and cultural diplomacy in Canada and Australia

Robert J. Williams

In international relations, as in human relations, image and perception can exert a powerful influence. Foreign policy is driven by national interests, but perceptions—at home and abroad—play an important part in the capacity of any country to pursue permanent interests. Image cannot substitute for substance, but a positive image can help to create a climate more conducive to achieving substance, just as a negative image can act as a brake on getting things done.[1]

This study examines the management of the international cultural activities of Canada and Australia. In the former, the federal government and those provinces which are active in international cultural relations operate unilaterally; moderate levels of cooperation and consultation take place on request. In the latter, fragmented federal activities have been drawn into a corporate consultative process which indirectly has the effect of weakening the capacity of the states to act independently in international cultural relations.

The discussion takes as given the complexity and extensiveness of interstate contacts in the modern world. It also understands international priorities, practices and targets as an extension of domestic policy and politics, which includes the operational arrangements of the federal system itself and the roles played by the system's non-central units. We know, too, that the overall international agenda of federal states is confounded by jurisdictional ambiguity and by potential rivalry among the non-central units.

The traditional mechanisms of—and priorities in—interstate dealings have changed in the latter part of the twentieth century. Conventional diplomacy, in the sense of private, official-level intelligence gathering and bilateral persuasion, coexists with extensive public and private contacts with political decision-makers, opinion-leaders and the public at large, created and reinforced by the relative ease of transportation, innovations in personal means of communication, migration and even tourism. Out of this change comes a greater concern, as Gareth Evans put it, for 'image and perception'.

On the one hand, successful interstate relationships require trust and accurate knowledge: 'Stereotypes are one barrier to understanding. They are often deep-seated and unconscious . . . The best way to combat stereotypes is by contrary evidence.'[2] At the same time, there has evolved a recognition that a nation's external policy interests 'are most successfully pursued through the development of well-rounded, *multifaceted* relations based on mutual benefit.'[3] Cultural relations have therefore become an alternative to force or bravado in modern external policy since cultural contacts contribute to the achievement of policy goals by cultivating favourable impressions. Artistic, intellectual, performing and sporting talents participate in bilateral dealings since they serve as symbols of desirable national qualities such as creativity, respect for human achievement and 'excellence'. As the Australian Department of Foreign Affairs told the Committee on Administrative Review in 1976:

Cultural relations promote mutual understanding and assist in the furtherance of foreign policy objectives. The whole thrust of diplomacy is to advance the national interest by negotiation of political, economic and defense issues. By promoting mutual and reciprocal understanding through cultural programs, we create an atmosphere in which these objectives can be more hopefully pursued. In short, if we are to work with and achieve results from people very different from ourselves, we must understand them and they must understand us.[4]

The systematic involvement of government in cultural policy (broadly defined) is a fairly recent phenomenon in both Canada and Australia, with responsibility and funding shared between the federal government and the non-central (and municipal) governments. Because of the ambiguity of constitutional provisions for matters traditionally thought to be 'cultural'[5] and the involvement of individual creators, community groups, service providers, commercial enterprises and not-for-profit organizations, the net result is a situation 'probably as complex as any to be found in fields of joint . . . activity'[6]. Overlap occurs particularly in the development of facilities and audiences, in direct support for the artistic community and in international cultural activities.

The latter is, in part, one 'result of a supportive infrastructure that allows artists to develop reputations which grow from local through to a national level' and which can then be used by the country 'to present the face of its cultural legacy and identity to the world.'[7] It may be understood as the extension of domestic policy support for the cultural sector's quest for excellence and its search for wider markets and audiences. *International cultural relations*, in other words, amount to 'a foreign cultural policy'[8] which seeks to foster 'co-operative relationships between cultural and educational institutions and individuals so that nations can interrelate intellectually, artistically and socially.'[9]

However, international cultural activity can have another goal: the promotion of 'image and perception' for the country itself. Here cultural resources are deployed as part of a strategy to support the achievement of broader international objectives which have been previously defined through normal foreign policy-making channels. This 'cultural foreign policy' is better described as *cultural diplomacy*: 'the application of culture to the direct support of a country's political and economic diplomacy.'[10]

This distinction between ends and means is not always easy to make in the 'real world' but both practices can be found in official statements on international cultural activities in both Canada and Australia.[11] These two processes are complicated in a federal state by the fact that the provinces and states have become direct and significant actors on the international scene (which includes a cultural relations role) and by the potentially competitive stances of the non-central units with each other and with the national government in these activities.[12]

There are two pertinent points which emerge from this situation. The first is that the provinces and states have enhanced their international status by expanding from their traditional external priorities (commerce, trade and general economic activity) into more complex and competitive areas of technology transfer, investment and industrial cooperation. To achieve success, the provinces and states must compete with one another as well as other jurisdictions; 'culture' is recognized as an important weapon in the quest to carve out a distinctive image in these competitions. The two federal governments, at the same time, have redefined their priorities to recognize that 'commerce, trade and economics are also political and diplomatic in character'[13] and, therefore, trade policy and trade promotion (in which culture is part of the 'bait') have been elevated to much higher status than in the past. The activities of the two levels of government, then, are taking place in a highly competitive environment in which cultural resources are important.

This leads to the second point: governments in both countries have recognized that commerce does not occur in a vacuum and have developed very similar strategies to assist in marketing themselves and their interests through culture.[14] In a recently issued information package on Canada's international cultural programmes, the Canadian Minister of External Affairs and International Trade asserts that

To seize new opportunities and take on new challenges [in trade], we must break through cultural barriers. International Cultural Relations is the modern arm of traditional diplomacy that allows us to lay the groundwork for Canada's foreign policy and trade interests. Nations that understand each other are more inclined to trade with each other.[15]

In the case of Australia, the Minister of Foreign Affairs and Trade argued that his country needed

to be concerned about what other nations think of us for the good reason that the images which others carry of us influence their attitude towards us—not only in the general sense, but also with regard to our security requirements, to our goods and services, to our appeal as a place to invest in, to migrate to, to visit and so on.[16]

The provinces and states, for their part, have developed an enhanced international presence through cultural contacts, although their programmes may not parallel those being pursued by the national governments. Quebec, of course, led the way in this area as far back as the mid-1960s, and continues to give high priority to the francophone world in its international cultural relations.[17] Other Canadian provinces have followed suit, albeit with a different agenda. Alberta, for example, has attempted to enhance its trade position in Asia by signing twinning agreements with non-central governments in China, Japan and Korea which feature a heavy cultural and educational component, while South Australia has a twin-province agreement with the Campania region of Italy and supported extensive community-based exchanges with communities in Texas when both states shared the same centennial year. Many other Canadian provinces and Australian states—as their financial and marketing capabilities have allowed—have also used international cultural programming on the assumption that cultural ties will increase their influence abroad and heighten their competitive economic advantage.

International cultural activity is a fairly recent element of the bilateral relationships of both countries, dating only from the 1960s; it was stimulated by internal political crises in Canada and by external challenges in Australia.[18] A common operational concern stems from unresolved issues in domestic politics which may hamper the successful selling of an image abroad: what are the 'images and perceptions' which are actually being promoted externally?[19] Of crucial importance, too, is the determination of which aspects of culture are relevant abroad and where they might command interest and respect.[20] Unfortunately, the direct role of the subnational units is often downplayed or ignored in describing the work of the national units in cultural relations.[21]

Australia's international cultural activities have been the responsibility of a large number of federal departments, agencies and special bilateral foundations which are serviced by the Department of Foreign Affairs and Trade (DFAT), as well as some not-for-profit enterprises such as Musica Viva. The lead unit in *international cultural relations* has been the Australia Council, whose international activities have been traditionally client-driven in most of its programmes (although its expenditures on international activities have been only about 4 per cent of its total support for the arts since 1987–8). The lead unit in *cultural diplomacy* is the Cultural Relations branch of DFAT which is guided largely by geopolitical priorities. Some measure of coordination has been achieved in recent years through the creation of interdepartmental committees for overseas information and international cultural activities.

The international cultural roles of the states are much less developed; in the eyes of federal, state and territorial ministers, international cultural relations tops the list of the Commonwealth's spheres of interest in culture.[22] Some states have little or no international activity, while in others particular institutional links (for example, between the New South Wales State Library and the Tokyo City Library) serve as major vehicles for an international profile. Sister-state, or twinning, agreements are important structures for cultural exchange; without the recognition these agreements bring, however, the states are usually resigned to sending applicants for financial and logisitical support off to federal agencies or DFAT. There are also very extensive intermunicipal programmes, especially involving the larger state capitals (for example, in 1990 Melbourne had at least six formal sister-city agreements). Here, as in the case of the state-level twinnings, cultural relations are explicitly used as an adjunct to the real or potential economic link which is being recognized. It also appears to be the case that state activity is heavily influenced by the personal preferences of the premier (insiders suggest, for example, significiantly different perceptions of the value of cultural exchanges between premiers Wran and Greiner of NSW) and the minister responsible for the arts and the capacity of the state ministry to be an active participant.

The experiences of NSW and Victoria are interesting in this regard, in particular their management of formal relations with China. In the former, a sister-state agreement was signed with Guangdong province in 1982 and a series of modest (but clearly export-driven) tours and exhibitions went to China in the first three or four years. Overall responsibility for these contacts was vested in an economic committee which was located in the Department of Overseas Trade. It had very little interest in culture and essentially waited for the Ministry of the Arts to take the initiative. In Victoria, on the other hand, a sister-state relationship was established with Jiangsu in 1979 and is monitored through the Victorian government's China Advisory Committee, an interdepartmental body working out of the Department of Premier and Cabinet. Cultural exchanges are a very important part of this work and the Ministry of the Arts maintains an active role in the overall programme through a Cultural Relations Subcommittee of VGCAC which explores potential incoming and outgoing activities. The different approaches taken to managing this relationship demonstrate the way domestic policy and administrative styles influence the practice of international cultural relations by the Australian states.

In March 1990, the Australian government announced the creation of the Council for Australia Abroad as the major body to promote public diplomacy.[23] Its responsibility is to articulate policy and to coordinate the delivery of cultural relations programmes, including cultural exchanges.[24] The Council itself is composed of the Minister of Foreign Affairs and Trade, plus the secretaries of seven major departments, the chairs of the four existing bilateral foundations (with China, Japan, New Zealand and Indonesia), the executive heads of ten government agencies (including the Australia Council), and eight members of the public.[25] The essential purposes of the CAA include replacing the two interdepartmental committees with a single forum and, as a consequence, bringing the activities of bodies as diverse as Austrade, the Australian Sports Commission and the Australia–Indonesia Institute into direct contact with one another so that a sharper focus can be maintained in cultural relations and resources can be more effectively used.

The states are involved in a formal way with the CAA through their membership in the Cultural Ministers Council, a permanent body which brings together annually ministers with responsibility for the arts in the Commonwealth and the six states (plus the two territories and New Zealand). The CAA's second tier is composed of designated senior officials of the bodies represented on the Council and it is here that the bulk of the work in developing public diplomacy will take place. As a contribution to that process, CMC agreed, at its 1990 meeting, to the creation of a working group to frame a coherent strategy for international cultural relations and in 1991 it endorsed a framework to be developed in consultation with the CAA and other relevant parties.[26] Among the proposed objectives for international cultural relations are

— promoting Australia's complex and distinctive cultural identity;
— enhancing the potential of the arts and cultural activities to complement economic and trade policy;
— promoting the value of cultural exchange in assisting the professional development of artists and arts organizations.

These objectives, worked out in a consultative process involving federal- and state-based interests, will essentially integrate the programmes of the two levels of government into a common strategy for cultural diplomacy.

It should also be noted that within the federal arena a fundamental realignment of international cultural relations has been launched — one which no doubt takes its impetus from the articulation of 'national imperatives' in external relations through the Council for Australia Abroad. The Australia Council, after extensive internal study (including the acknowledgement that the Council's support for international activity was dramatically out of line with that of other agencies), will now devote upwards of 50 per cent of its 1992–3 international budget in the Asia–Pacific region (as opposed to approximately 10 per cent in 1989–90).[27] The era in which international cultural relations are strategically important for Australia has arrived.

In organizational terms, the Canadian Department of External Affairs has traditionally had primary responsibility for outgoing international cultural programming, but it has long been expected to promote several different objectives in those activities. The Massey Report of 1951 advocated a more vigorous international cultural program as a way of combating the 'very widespread' ignorance concerning Canada in other countries. More significantly, the Report concluded that an international cultural programme, managed by External Affairs, would contribute to the 'development of Canadian cultural life' and was encouraged on that basis.[28] External has also always worked with a politically sensitive agenda. When an international cultural programme was first implemented in the years between 1963 and 1967, it was in response to domestic politics rather than foreign policy since it affirmed Canada's bicultural and bilingual characteristics and responded directly to Quebec's international initiatives, which were themselves focused largely in the cultural field. Later, External Affairs began to describe itself more explicitly as an extension of the domestic cultural infrastructure: 'The Department of External Affairs provides an international arm to domestic programs which support and encourage the growth of the arts in Canada.'[29] Similar themes began to appear in formal cultural programme guidelines adopted for the Department and were widely circulated in various reports, briefs and brochures, especially those issued between 1977 and 1981.

The same message—that international cultural relations are as much about cultural and political ends as foreign policy—is repeated in the 1991 information package:

The objectives of International Cultural Relations (ICR) are to give international exposure to outstanding Canadian achievements in the arts, scholarship and sport; to strengthen the sense of national identity through pride in those achievements; to promote Canada as a unique, competitive and sophisticated nation; and to further foreign policy and trade interests by extending knowledge and understanding of Canada.[30]

The reality is somewhat different since the officials in External Affairs who managed ICR have, for the most part, been outsiders to the cultural field and were, as career foreign service officers, most interested in promoting activities which would benefit the Department's diplomatic goals (not to mention their own careers). Two consequences emerge: first, the priorities in programming and targets have tended to accentuate the federal vision of Canada (bilingual and bicultural), one which is not shared with enthusiasm in all parts of the country.[31] Secondly, the bulk of the efforts have been concentrated in Europe where, historically, defence, immigration and trade priorities have been at the forefront. This relative neglect, in cultural terms, of the north Asian world prompted several provinces to make their own efforts to establish contacts. Thus, the three Alberta twinning agreements noted earlier, as well as agreements signed with Chinese provinces by Saskatchewan and Ontario, are a reflection of different economic and investment priorities which these provinces, and others, have chosen to pursue unilaterally.

Despite an explicit recognition that international cultural activities 'enhance the federal–provincial partnerships',[32] Canadian experience suggests a policy and operational separation between the federal government and those provinces which continue to support international cultural activities. In principle, all provinces (including Quebec) cooperate with EAITC's programme as their own resources allow.[33] The Department does not hold regular consultations on its cultural programmes with the provinces, although provincial representatives are often involved in Mixed Commission meetings for various cultural agreements and the like.[34] Since the 'international arm to domestic programs' does not have direct links to the domestic cultural community, consultations between External Affairs and provincial ministries for culture (and the Canada Council) occur virtually on a daily basis as applications for support are processed in Ottawa and the provincial capitals. The only geographic sector in which consultation has occurred formally in recent years involved China, especially after 1989. Liaison is more likely to occur in the field where some of the provinces maintain offices with cultural attachés. Beyond this, EAITC and the relevant provinces operate in parallel, pursuing goals set unilaterally.

The provinces themselves, despite regular meetings of ministers responsible for cultural affairs, have never discussed the development of a common strategy in international cultural activities and certainly, as long as Quebec pursues its own agenda, they are unlikely to do so. In a highly decentralized federation such as Canada, it is not surprising that cultural relations are designed and operationalized unilaterally by the provinces, in isolation from one another.

The parallel nature of federal and provincial international cultural relations in Canada can be demonstrated by a brief overview of the external cultural activities of the province of Ontario. Its activities have remained very much in the shadow of the federal and Quebec governments and the rationale for what is sponsored has not been widely communicated,[35] but for all intents and purposes Ontario operates, on a smaller scale than Ottawa to be sure, an international cultural relations programme. It has a designated operational unit in Toronto, officers in the field, formal international cultural exchanges, and a set of objectives to be met through cultural contacts.

The Ontario Ministry of Culture and Communication (MCC) has offered programmes and services to promote Ontario internationally since the early 1980s.[36] In 1986, an External Cultural Activities Unit was formed with a threefold mandate:

1. to increase professional growth and market opportunties for Ontario's artists, their work, and the rest of the province's cultural community;
2. to advance the province's broad economic objectives by using cultural resources as a tool for enhancing Ontario's image abroad;
3. to increase Ontarians' exposure to, and appreciation of, the culture of other countries by hosting the work of foreign artists.

The major method of serving these objectives is through a grant programme called Arts Abroad, which sees MCC making relatively small dollar grants which served primarily as leverage for funds from other sources (including Ottawa). MCC also places cultural attachés in Ontario's overseas offices (presently Paris, London and New York) to ensure the cultural richness of Ontario is brought to the attention of the host jurisdiction.

As a unit operating within the province's culture ministry, ECAU integrates these (albeit modest) activities into the domestic programmes of MCC and serves as a single focus for linkages to the Ministry of Industry, Trade and Technology, now the lead actor in Ontario's foreign policy.[37] It is significant to note that MCC has a designated officer to coordinate the cultural component of Ontario's involvement with the European regional grouping known as 'the Four Motors of Europe'.[38] Cultural initiatives form an important component of Ontario's interregional relations.

A lingering issue for the Canadian cultural community has been the appropriateness of EAITC as the lead unit for international cultural relations. Historically, the Canada Council, the Department of Communications and several operating agencies such as the NFB, CBC and the National Museums have spent resources outside Canada in support of the cultural sector with little regard for the foreign policy implications of the activity. One of the key recommendations on ICR by the Federal Cultural Policy Review Committee (Applebaum-Hebert) Report of 1982 was the creation of an independent agency to promote Canadian cultural and academic interests internationally, one which would 'do more than merely support Canada's foreign policy objectives'.[39] Few of the Report's recommendations ever appeared to be seriously considered for the government's policy agenda, so it was a surprise to most people (including the Canada Council and major cultural posts overseas) that the 1992 federal budget announced that EAITC's international cultural programme would be shifted to the Canada Council.[40] This move, which was part of a series of agency reorganizations, should enhance the linkages between international cultural programmes and the domestic cultural community in the way Applebaum-Hebert had sought, that is through bureaucratic specialization. The critical question is whether EAITC, freed of its obligations to fund international cultural relations, will continue to consider cultural programming a priority in its foreign policy strategy and in the operation of its posts abroad.

To achieve success in the international trade and investment market, both central and non-central governments are using 'culture' to create a positive image for themselves. As a result, international cultural activity has become an extensive and complex dimension of modern foreign relations. This study has examined some ways in which such international cultural relations have been managed within the context of jurisdictional ambiguity and competitive governmental interests in two federations.

Australia has responded to the challenge to bring form and purpose to international cultural relations—a particularly difficult task given that such concepts sit so uneasily with the creative forces inherent in the cultural field—by creating a coordinating body which brings the diverse national operating units and, indirectly, the states into an integrated planning process. As a result, Australia can expect over the next few years to achieve an international cultural relations strategy which overcomes federalism.

In Canada, international cultural relations have historically been determined as much through the domestic cultural and political agenda as foreign policy priorities. Programmes are designed and operationalized unilaterally by Ottawa and the provinces, largely in isolation from one another. Even in 1992, the capacity of ICR to contribute to serving Canada's international interests is hampered by uncertainty over the allocation of bureaucratic responsibilities within the federal government and also by debates over the legitimacy of federal jurisdiction over cultural matters *per se*.[41] Until that question is resolved, the management of Canadian international cultural activities will continue to be hindered by federalism.

Notes

1. Senator Gareth Evans, 'Australia and Asia: the role of public diplomacy', *Australian Foreign Affairs and Trade: The Monthly Record*, 61 (1990), 135.
2. J.M. Mitchell, *International Cultural Relations*, Allen & Unwin, London (1986), 17–18.
3. Evans, op.cit., 136, emphasis in original.
4. Quoted in R.P. Throsell, 'Toward a multicultural society: the role of government departments and officials in developing cross-cultural relations in Australia', in Stephen Bochner (ed.), *The Mediating Person: Bridges Between Cultures*, G.K. Hall, Boston (1981), 265.
5. See Marcel Caya, 'The dilemmas of cultural management in a federal state', and K.R. McKinnon, 'Australian cultural policy issues', in R.L. Mathews (ed.), *Public Policies in Two Federal Countries: Canada and Australia*, Centre for Research on Federal Financial Relations, Canberra (1982), 242–5 and 249–52.
6. Joan Rydon and Diane Mackay, 'Federalism and the arts', *Australian Cultural History*, 3 (1984), 95.
7. Keith Kelly, 'Why is federal responsibility for culture an issue?', Canadian

Conference of the Arts briefing paper, Ottawa (1991), 16.

8. CAPPA (Confederation of Australian Professional Performing Arts), Submission to the Inquiry into Commonwealth Assistance to the Arts by the House of Representatives Standing Committee on Expenditure (1985), 27.

9. Mitchell, op.cit., 81.

10. *ibid.*

11. See Robert J. Williams, 'International cultural programmes: Canada and Australia compared', in Andrew Cooper (ed.), *Canadian Culture: International Dimensions*, Centre on Foreign Policy and Federalism and the Canadian Institute of International Affairs, Waterloo, Ontario and Toronto (1985), 83–111; 'Culture in the service of the state: Canadian and Australian international cultural policy', *Australian–Canadian Studies*, 5 (1987), 49–60; 'The provinces and Canadian international cultural activities: the contribution of Ontario', *Canadian Issues/Thèmes canadiens: Practising the Arts in Canada/La Pratique des arts au Canada*, XII (1989), 83–92.

12. Williams (1989), op.cit., 86.

13. Elliott Feldman, 'The impact of federalism on the organization of Canadian foreign policy', in Tom Keating and Don Munton (eds), *The Provinces and Canadian Foreign Policy*, Canadian Institute of International Affairs, Toronto (1985), 38.

14. See, for example, Victoria, *Mapping Our Culture: A Policy for Victoria*, Victorian Ministry for the Arts, Melbourne (1991), 18.

15. *International Cultural Relations/Relations culturelles internationales*, External Affairs and International Trade Canada (EAITC), Ottawa (1991), 1.

16. Evans, op.cit., 136.

17. An overview of the development of Quebec's role is found in Claude Ryan, 'The origins of Quebec's cultural diplomacy', in Cooper (ed.), *Canadian Culture*, op.cit., 59–68. Another perspective on Quebec's cultural links, both general and specific, is found in Alfred Olivier Hero, Jr. and Louis Balthazar, *Contemporary Quebec and the United States, 1960–1985*, Center for International Affairs, Harvard University and University Press of America (1988), 224–31, 253–9.

18. Williams (1985), op.cit., 89–97 and (1987), op.cit., 52–7.

19. Michael Lee, 'The projection of Australia overseas: the origins of the Council for Australia Abroad', *Australian Journal of Public Administration*, 50 (1991), 38 and 42–4.

20. One perspective on this issue is found in Federal Cultural Policy Review Committee (FCPRC), *Report*, Department of Communications, Ottawa (1982), 319–22.

21. Les Rowe, 'Cultural relations: working creatively for maximum effect', *Backgrounder*, Department of Foreign Affairs and Trade, Canberra, 2 (November 1991), 6–9 and EAITC (1991).

22. Cultural Ministers Council, Communiqué Sixth Meeting, Rotorua, New Zealand (1990), 3.

23. Evans, op.cit., 140.

24. Lee, op.cit., 41–2.

25. Lee, op.cit., 39.

26. Cultural Ministers Council, Communiqué Seventh Meeting, Hobart (1991), 3.

27. Bryce Hallett, 'Australia Council targets Asian cultural exchange', *Weekend*

Australian (5–6 October 1991), 5.

28. Williams (1987), op.cit., 55.
29. *Cultural Relations with Foreign Countries: A Description of the Cultural Affairs Division,* Department of External Affairs, Ottawa (1977), 2.
30. EAITC (1991), 2
31. Andrew F. Cooper, 'Roots and directions: functional and geographical aspects of Canadian cultural diplomacy', *Canadian Issues/Thèmes canadiens: Culture, Development and Regional Policy,* IX (1988), 17–31.
32. EAITC (1991), 1
33. It is relevant to note, as Louis Balthazar does elsewhere in this volume (chapter 8), that Quebec has become much less confrontational *vis-à-vis* Ottawa in its international activities in recent years. Outside major centres like Paris and London, it relies on the financial and logistical resources of External Affairs and limits itself to a watchdog role to ensure that Quebec's interests are being considered.
34. Robert J. Williams, 'Canadian cultural agreements: "essentially political documents"' *Journal of Canadian Studies/Revue d'études canadiennes,* 22,4 (1987), 65
35. Williams, op.cit. (1989).
36. ibid.
37. The Ministry of Intergovernmental Affairs had operated an Office of International Relations to provide analysis and advice on Ontario's relations with foreign jurisdictions, but its responsibilities were shifted to MITT in 1991.
38. See David Rampersad, 'Ontario and the "four motors" of Europe', Current issue paper #10, Ontario Legislative Research Service, Toronto (1990).
39. FCPRC, op.cit., 336–40.
40. Christopher Harris and Kate Taylor, 'Canada Council to become super-agency', *Globe and Mail* (26 February 1992), C1.
41. The possibility that the federal government might 'devolve' its role in the cultural field to the provinces or possibly just to Quebec provoked much controversy in 1991. See Kelly, op.cit., *passim.*

International trade policy and the role of non-central governments: the recent Canadian experience

12

Derrick G. Wilkinson[1]

As a number of other chapters in this volume describe, non-central governments (NCGs) are increasingly important players in international affairs. Until recently NCG activities at the international level centred on trade and investment promotion, including tourism, as well as cultural affairs. By the 1980s, however, NCGs had also begun to take an active interest in trade policy.[2] It is this more recent interest which, from the point of view of the province of Alberta, this short essay will address. In particular it will review the primary reasons for NCG interest in trade policy, how these interests are pursued by the Canadian provinces, and how these present arrangements could be improved.

There are two main reasons for NCG interest in trade policy. The first is because increasingly the development and behaviour of the international trading system is of crucial importance to the economic well-being of the region under the jurisdiction of the NCG. In the case of the province of Alberta, for example, exports account for about 25 per cent of the provincial GDP. By way of comparison, Germany is at about 30 per cent, the United States is at about 5–10 per cent, and the OECD average is of the order of 15–20 per cent.

Given such an export-oriented economy, then, the Alberta government is naturally keenly interested in the prevention of any trade-restricting measures, as well as the development of any regional or sectoral arrangements which may affect their exports. In light of the increasingly rapid evolution of the international trading system over the past twenty years or so, this can be understood as a logical concomitant activity to the more traditional activities in trade promotion and development; clearly an efficient and effective trade promotion and development program can only be undertaken with the guidance of a close understanding of the commercial realities of the target market. Thus the gathering and analysis of trade policy intelligence is an increasingly important aspect of NCG activity. At the same time, the benefit–cost ratio of such a program will be increased in some positive relation to the degree of trade liberalization existing in the target market. Accordingly, to the extent possible, the government of Alberta seeks to ensure the greatest possible degree of trade liberalization in the relevant commercial regimes.

The second, more recent, reason for NCGs becoming active in the field of international trade policy is that it is taking a growing interest in the activities of NCGs. International trade policy has traditionally been concerned with the actions of national governments, focusing by and large on the so-called border issues—mainly border charges, such as tariffs, and quantitative restrictions on the international trade in goods. Recent developments in the global economy, however, have, amongst other things, brought into focus the increasing role played in the international trading system by NCGs; as border concerns, especially tariffs, have declined in importance to international trade, and production is increasingly globalized, what had hitherto been considered to be largely domestic issues, including the actions of NCGs, are being seen as ever more important determinants of international competitiveness and trade, and as such within the bailiwick of international trade policy.

But while the international trade policy-makers seek to establish obligations which affect the activities of NCGs, in Canada only an informal facility to influence the nature of those obligations is yet available to the provinces. This is notwithstanding the fact that matters under provincial jurisdiction can only be implemented by act of the provincial legislatures; the federal government can enter into whatever international obligations it wishes to, but it can only implement those aspects which fall under its own jurisdiction.

Before proceeding to describe the Canadian federal-provincial arrangements and where improvements could be made, it may be useful to review briefly a few of the new provisions in the draft Uruguay Round GATT agreements, which illustrate some trade policy developments of concern to NCGs.

1. Article XXIV. 12 of the GATT requires each contracting party to 'take such reasonable measures as may be available to it to ensure observance of the provisions of' the GATT by the subnational authorities within its territory. This is a reasonable and quite acceptable provision. However, in an interpretative note on this article in the draft Uruguay Round final text it adds that 'each party is fully responsible' for observance by subnationals of all provisions of the GATT. This is of great concern

because of the possibility of a misinterpretation of the respective authorities of federal and provincial governments in Canada for implementation. The federal government argues that 'responsibility' only means 'accountable', whereas the provinces are concerned that it may be interpreted as meaning 'responsible for acting'.

2. The new GATT subsidies rules also contain a provision which is unacceptable to NCGs. To impose a countervailing duty on a product, in response to its benefiting from a subsidy, in general it must be demonstrated that the subsidy was 'specific' to the recipient industry,[3] and that the subsidy caused injury to the competing industry. Under Article 2.2 of the new GATT code on subsidies and countervailing duties, however, assistance provided by NCGs will automatically be deemed to be 'specific' even if that same assistance would be considered to be generally available if provided by a central government. This clearly impairs the ability of the Canadian provinces to meet their constitutional responsibilities in the area of economic development, and causes an unacceptable change in the relationship of provincial versus federal assistance measures by making one automatically more vulnerable to countervailing duty action than the other. And when about 75 per cent of your trade goes to the United States, as in the case of Alberta, and given the growing predilection in the United States for the aggressive use of their trade laws, this is no small concern.

3. The new GATT Services agreement (GATS) provides a further example of the growing encroachment of the international trade rules into areas of provincial jurisdiction. It contains a number of provisions which affect the rights and responsibilities of the provinces to regulate services in areas under provincial jurisdiction—the licensing of professionals, for example. And as the GATS contains the same provision as Article XXIV.12 of the GATT, the federal government is again undertaking to be 'fully responsible' for the observance by the provinces of obligations which are under exclusive provincial jurisdiction.

4. Finally, the new draft Agreement on Technical Barriers to Trade is also of concern to provincial governments. After reiterating the standard Article XXIV.12 language,[4] paragraph 3.3.2 provides that 'parties shall ensure that technical regulations of local governments on the level directly below that of the central government are notified in accordance with the provisions of Article 2 . . .' By this, the federal government assumes an obligation to act with respect to provincial governments that is in excess of the normal Article XXIV.12 requirements; in effect, to take action with respect to the provincial technical regulation development process. Furthermore, Article 3.5 provides that 'parties are fully responsible under this agreement for the observance of all provisions of Article 2. Parties shall formulate and implement positive measures and mechanisms in support of the observance of the provisions of Article 2 by

other than central government bodies.' Thus again the federal government is assuming international trade policy obligations with respect to areas of provincial jurisdiction.

These issues are but four amongst many. Some of the concerns being addressed in protocols on the treatment of foreign direct investment, for example, fall within the jurisdiction of the provinces in Canada. Likewise the relationship between international trade policy and environment policy—another area of growing international interest—relates critically to matters under provincial jurisdiction, including natural resource base management, as well as raising the possibility of more unnecessary restrictions on international trade. Both the Canada–US Free-Trade Agreement (CUSTA) and the North American Free-Trade Agreement (NAFTA) also contain numerous provisions affecting areas under provincial jurisdiction, and contain even more onerous 'extent of obligations' clauses than GATT article XXIV.12.[5]

To summarize, then, NCGs are taking a growing interest in international trade policy both because it affects directly the export performance of their economies as well as, in the case of the Canadian provinces, the scope for carrying out their constitutional responsibilities including local economic management. In rising to these challenges the provinces—and it is widely recognized that the province of Alberta has been prominent in this—have sought both to work with the federal government as well as to influence directly developments in the international trading system.

The largest part of the Alberta government's international trade policy activity is by way of working with the federal government. So it will be useful at this point to turn to a description and evaluation of the federal—provincial arrangements in place in Canada for international trade policy development and management. These were established largely within the context of, and for the purpose of negotiating the CUSTA.[6] They arise from an agreement by the prime minister and the ten provincial premiers meeting in Halifax in November 1985 to the principle of 'full provincial participation' in trade negotiations.

In March 1986 the provinces put forward an eight-point proposal to substantiate this commitment. This essentially provided for the close participation of the provinces in the establishment of the negotiating mandate and in the conduct of the negotiations, acknowledging of course that Canada would be represented by a single Chief Negotiator, and a full exchange of information. In the event, what was achieved was only an arrangement for consultations, not much different from that established at the same time for the private sector. Over the course of the negotiations there were numerous federal–provincial meetings of first ministers, ministers, as well as officials. Although this consultative arrangement retained for the federal government full control of all aspects of the negotiations, and as such were rather less than full provincial participation, they were useful.

In addition to the verbal exchanges and correspondence associated with these consultative arrangements, the provinces also developed position papers on many of the issues under negotiation to ensure that the federal government was fully aware of provincial concerns. Sometimes these were done by a single province, sometimes jointly. For example, the four Western Provinces Ministers Responsible for Trade Negotiations jointly developed papers on a number of issues, including natural resource-based products and dispute settlement.

These consultative arrangements have been carried over into the Uruguay Round of Multilateral Trade Negotiations, (MTN) and the NAFTA negotiations. Overall, as noted, they have proven to be useful. A number of problems exist, however, principal amongst which is that they are informal. Both the institutional and the procedural aspects are entirely at the behest of the federal government. This, in the view of the provinces, is unsatisfactory.[7] Such an important aspect of the federal–provincial relationship should not be at the whim of ministers and/or senior public servants. Accordingly the need was seen by the provinces for a formal federal–provincial agreement providing for a structured, regularized arrangement that would facilitate full provincial participation in trade negotiations. At the 1988 Annual Premiers Conference hosted by Quebec the provinces decided to pursue such an agreement.[8]

To be absolutely clear, the provinces neither sought to usurp, nor would view as desirable to usurp, the federal responsibility for Canada's external relations.[9] Rather, the provinces argued that

it is both necessary and desirable to establish a framework between the federal and provincial governments to facilitate communications and to ensure that the rights and interests of all parties are effectively observed so as to permit Canada to meet its international trade policy obligations.[10]

The provinces argued that, at a minimum, such a federal–provincial agreement would need to provide formally for a joint ministerial-level body to provide trade policy direction and leadership, under the chairmanship of the federal government, as well as a facility for the direct participation of the provinces in any dispute settlement procedures whenever matters of provincial responsibility and interest are at issue. To work effectively, this body would need to be supported by a federal–provincial officials-level group and an information distribution system that is rather less arbitrary than that in place now.[11]

Over the course of 1988–9 the provinces proffered five draft agreements. Regrettably the federal government proved to be quite inflexible, focusing exclusively on consultations. Ottawa put forward to the provinces only one draft agreement. Essentially this entailed an open-ended provincial commitment to provide information to the federal government without making any corresponding federal commitments. Ottawa offered very little in the way of developing a formal mechanism for giving federal-provincial ministerial direction to trade negotiations or for meaningful participation by the provinces in the settlement of disputes which directly affect their practices or interests. All the federal proposals for consultations were worded in conditional language such as 'where appropriate', 'if necessary', 'if invited', 'where useful', and so on, leaving it to the federal government to determine all conditions without agreeing to any intrinsic provincial rights. A deadlock resulted and in August 1989 the negotiations were effectively suspended.[12]

So consultative arrangements are all that are in place. As to information regarding the trade policy activities of the Canadian government, it is distributed to the provinces to the extent that specific arrangements have been made. Provincial officials are not vetted by the federal government and are sometimes refused information because 'it is not available to the public'. Thus the present system is *ad hoc*—at times frustrating, at other times good. The information exchange during the NAFTA negotiations, for example, has been very good, with draft chapters being made available to the provinces on a strictly confidential basis even during the critical final stages of the negotiations.[13] But clearly if the provinces are to be able to make a useful and substantial contribution they will need to be kept fully and regularly informed as a matter of right.

It was in part to address this information gathering issue that, in 1990, the Alberta government retained the services of a Senior Trade Policy Adviser at their London office. Amongst other things this enabled the Alberta government to supplement the federal–provincial information flow. Being in closer proximity to Geneva for the MTN and other GATT issues, to Paris for the OECD, and to Brussels for European Community trade developments often facilitates the obtaining of information for Edmonton more quickly than it could be delivered through the federal–provincial information flow system. Having someone based in London also enables Alberta at times to be alerted to trade policy developments of which the federal government has not yet informed them.

The provinces are also beginning to act more directly outside of Canada. A London-based trade policy adviser, for example, is able to discuss informally trade policy issues with the Canadian officials in Europe, as well as with officials of European governments, the European Commission and various international organizations on a more regular, ongoing basis than would otherwise be feasible. Obviously these meetings and discussions would not entail negotiations in any sense. But it does enable Alberta better to ensure that their views are conveyed fully and frequently to the appropriate officials.

These ongoing exchanges are in addition to those which occur when provincial ministers and senior officials visit. In this regard, Alberta's Minister Responsible for Trade Negotiations attended all of the ministerial meetings, in Uruguay, Montreal and Brussels, of the current round of GATT negotiations. Similarly, during the autumn of 1991, Alberta's Minister of Agriculture paid a useful visit to Geneva to discuss with officials there the current state of the MTN. He met with senior GATT officials, senior negotiators from the EC, the United States and Australia, amongst others, in addition to the Canadian team. Subsequently both the Alberta premier and provincial treasurer have visited Europe and met various government ministers and officials, as well as the Canadian and Secretariat officials at the OECD.

In working with the federal officials, both in Canada and abroad, it has been my experience that, within the constraints within which they work—the Official Secrets Act, for example—usually they are quite forthcoming and helpful. But, as already noted, it is based primarily on the individual professional relationships that are developed.

Clearly, in the final analysis, the federal government must be the one that represents Canada as a whole. However, it is also reasonable to suggest that the Canadian position on matters of concern to the provinces should only be arrived at with the full participation of the provinces, especially in areas of exclusive provincial jurisdiction. Substantiation of the principle of full provincial participation by an agreement such as the one proposed by the provinces during 1988–9 would rectify to a large extent the present overly assymmetrical relationship. It would also enable Canada to undertake international obligations in areas of sole provincial or joint jurisdiction with greater confidence that those obligations will be fully implemented and observed by the provinces.

As already mentioned, in Canada, while the federal government can enter into any international obligations they wish, they can implement those obligations only as far as they are matters of federal constitutional responsibility. This has given rise to concern in some quarters, such as the European Community, about the enforcement of international obligations at the subnational level. It is felt that there is an asymmetry between the obligations undertaken by unitary states and those by federal states: that firmer assurances can be given by unitary states than by federal states that obligations undertaken with respect to a wide range of current trade policy issues will be fully respected. This has potentially important implications for the ability of trade policy negotiators to compare concessions, and so for the further development of the international trading system.

Of course NCGs should not look to escape international disciplines. Strong, predictable international trade rules are, after all, of the greatest benefit to those with small export-oriented economies. Rather, they need to develop the means to participate responsibility in the development of those rights and obligations. Given this, the question of enforcement at the subnational level could be resolved quite easily. In exchange for a formal federal–provincial agreement substantiating the principle of full provincial participation in Canada's international trade policy decision-making, wherever it relates to provincial issues, the provinces could undertake to implement any resulting international obligations by signing an annex to the agreement binding themselves.

This is not quite as odd a suggestion as it might at first appear. The legal problems would not appear to be insurmountable, given the will and the imagination. Such provincial signatures would not be enforceable at the international level because the provinces do not have international standing. However, they would carry significant political and moral weight. If necessary, they could also be reinforced by providing in the federal–provincial agreement for domestic enforcement in the Supreme Court. Moreover, this approach could provide greater assurance to Canada's trading partners than the 'extent of obligations' clauses being agreed to by the federal government.

There are also a number of precedents. During the 1970s this approach was taken in the case of the Canada–US Northern Natural Gas Pipeline Agreement, and in a statement of intent regarding provincial liquor boards during the Tokyo Round GATT negotiations. More recently, the European Energy Charter provides a precedent.

At the Charter-signing conference on 16–17 December 1991 in the Hague, nine of the twelve republics of the former USSR signed this international agreement. The signatures of these republics, and the Interstate Economic Committee, were, as the chairman of the Preparatory Conference said, inspired by a desire to enable those who bear political responsibility for the implementation of the Charter to participate and to confirm by signature their commitment to implementation. He made clear that this decision to sign does not influence or prejudge questions relating to the status of the signatories under international law, and the United States expressed their view that signature of the Charter has no implications whatsoever with respect to recognition of sovereignty or statehood of the republics.[14]

Of course, comparisons between the Canadian provinces and the emerging former Soviet republics are in most respects neither close nor appropriate. None the less, it would seem that when necessary signing of international agreements, whether directly or in an annex, by the relevant political authorities, even when those political authorities do not have international standing, may be a viable means of ensuring the implementation and observance of those agreements. The quid pro quo, of course, is that such subnational political authorities must be able to participate fully and responsibly with the federal government in the development and ongoing management of those agreements.

Notes

1. The author wishes to acknowledge the invaluable contribution of Helmut Mach, Executive Director, International Trade Relations, Alberta Department of Federal and Intergovernmental Affairs, Edmonton, Aberta. Mr Mach was instrumental throughout the history considered in this study, and originated a number of the ideas proffered here. The views expressed here are personal and do not necessarily reflect those of the government of Alberta.
2. Trade policy encompasses the development and management of the international regime of trade rules and norms within which international trade and investment occur.
3. This excludes generally available government assistance such as infrastructure, law enforcement, etc.
4. Paragraph 3.3.1 provides that 'Parties shall take such reasonable measures as may be available to ensure compliance with the provisions of Article 2 with the exception of the obligation to notify as referred to in paragraphs 2.9.2 and 2.10.1.'
5. Article 103 of the CUSTA provides that 'the Parties to this Agreement shall ensure that all necessary measures are taken in order to give effect to its provisions, including their observance, except as otherwise provided in this Agreement, by state, provincial and local governments.' Nowhere in the Agreement is it 'otherwise provided'. The NAFTA reiterates this 'all necessary measures' obligation.
6. A good review of the development of these arrangements is provided by Douglas M. Brown, 'The federal–provincial consultation process', in P.M. Leslie and R.L. Watts (eds), *Canada: The State of the Federation, 1987–88*, Institute of Intergovernmental Relations, Kingston, Ontario (1988).
7. Some of the smaller provinces, with fewer resources to devote to international trade policy issues, have expressed less dissatisfaction than those, including Alberta, who have a more active interest in this area.
8. As host of the conference which gave rise to the initiative, Quebec took the lead in developing draft agreements. These drafts were then circulated to the other provinces for consideration and revision. Consensus drafts were then forwarded to the federal government.
9. The Preamble to the final draft, Draft 5, of the 'Federal–Provincial Agreement on Managing the Canada–United States Free-Trade Agreement', proposed by the provinces on 8 August 1989, hereinafter Draft 5, begins 'Whereas the Government of Canada is responsible for international trade negotiations . . .' As well, Article 1 clarifies that the scope of the agreement is limited 'to matters of exclusive provincial jurisdiction, shared jurisdiction or of major interest to a province as determined by that province.'
10. From the Preamble to Draft 5.
11. These were the essential provisions of Draft 5.
12. Subsequently Alberta has been the strongest proponent of a formal federal–provincial agreement, and has taken the lead in trying to restart negotiations.
13. This did not occur during the final stages of the CUSTA negotiations, when the information flow from the federal government effectively ceased.
14. According to an informal account provided to the author by one of the participants.

13 Policy phases, subnational foreign relations and constituent diplomacy in the United States and Canada: city, provincial and state global activity in British Columbia and Washington*

Patrick J. Smith

Nation-state centric notions of international relations no longer hold. Traditional distinctions between domestic and foreign policy have given way to 'intermestic' definitions which merge the two,[1] and newer explanatory ideas such as interdependence have themselves been superseded by policy conceptions 'beyond interdependence'[2] to a Borderless World.[3] Managing foreign relations in this new global order has been altered irrevocably. As the scope of international relations has expanded dramatically at the approach of the twenty-first century, so too has the capacity (though generally not the formal authority) of national governments to exercise foreign policy jurisdictional exclusivity been limited. This has created what the Chinese refer to as 'dangerous opportunities' for 'hybrid international actors',[4] particularly those of a subnational—state/provincial and municipal—governmental variety.

This shift in national capacity is partly explained by the growing realization that national economies have become substantially premised on the economies of a nation's major city regions.[5] For some it has meant that the 'traditional boundaries between countries . . . [have] become increasingly

---

* All references to $ are in US$, except those referring specifically to B.C. which are in Canadian $.

meaningless . . . cities [have] become independent of their countries and deal directly with other parts of the world, [and] city and regional interests . . . will be far more important than national and provincial economic policies.[6]

This study traces the development of subnational global policy-making—and policy-making capacity—in the United States and Canada through analysis of a series of policy phases. It examines the international policy activities of state/provincial and municipal (Vancouver/Seattle) actors in the State of Washington and the Province of British Columbia. While not entirely new, the global policy thrust of these 'constituent' actors[7] has expanded rapidly, both in terms of extent and type:

(a) in *extent*, for example, between 1944 (when the first Canadian city was twinned) and 1967, only nine Canadian municipalities had twinned themselves with non-Canadian communities. Over the past twenty years, this pattern has accelerated considerably to include several hundred such formal subnational international exchanges.[8] In the United States, there are currently over 900 cities with more than 1,600 sister city affiliations, most of this extension since the mid-1970s.[9]

(b) in *type*, more importantly, as the number of subnational governments involved internationally has grown, so too have the types of global activity and exchange; initially, often cultural and educational, these shifted to more strategic, business-oriented forms and now show distinct signs of an emerging global policy phase.

As such, the development of differing forms represents a maturing of such subnational paradiplomacy. This article traces and compares the development of subnational internationalist policy-making in different jurisdictional settings in the Pacific Northwest of North America through a series of policy phases:

(i)   an *ad hoc* phase, indicative of relatively immature policy intent and capacity, running, in early instances, through the 1940s and continuing into the 1960s and early 1970s;

(ii) efforts to develop a more *rational* approach to such international activities in the latter 1970s and early–mid-1980s;

(iii) the development of a more *strategic* subnational internationalist policy position in many jurisdictions in the late 1980s; and,

(iv) a *global* policy stance—a potential and developing fourth phase, and a more prescriptive policy alternative beyond earlier iterations.

Each policy phase has reflected a series of choices by the appropriate subnational governmental actor and a different set of policy objectives. Each also has represented different policy implications for senior jurisdictions. The shift from incremental to more rational forms—and then to more

mature rational responses—has also been reflected in a growing institutio-
nalization of the subnational global policy-making process.

The settings

Washington

Located in the north-west corner of the United States, adjacent to British
Columbia, Washington State ranks twentieth of the fifty United States in
both size (68,192 sq. mls.) and population (4,866,692 (1990)). Divided by
the Cascade Mountains, nearly two-thirds (65 per cent–3,163,498) of the
state population resides in ten of thirty-nine counties in the Seattle-centred
Puget Sound Basin.[10]

Seattle (pop. 516,259, in King County, pop. 1,507,300 (1990)) and
Tacoma (pop. 158,900, in Pierce County, pop. 530,800) are two of the three
state cities with over 100,000 residents. Together with Everett/Snohomish
County (pop. 381,600) immediately to the north and the state capital,
Olympia/Thurston County (pop. 142,200) to the south, these four metropolitan counties make up 54.7 per cent of Washington's population. The Puget
Sound metropolis elects sixty-four of ninety-eight State Representatives
(65.3 per cent) and thirty-one of forty-nine State Senators (63 per cent). It
also returns five of eight US House Representatives.[11]

The state economy has been centred around manufacturing, forest products, fishing and agriculture: almost one-third of manufacturing is in aero-
space production, much of this with Boeing Aircraft (34.5 per cent of all
manufacturing); forest products account for 20.3 per cent and food products
an additional 11 per cent. Together with agricultural trade, particularly
with the Asia–Pacific region, aircraft, wood products, metals and fish products accounted for $30 billion in state exports in 1989–90. The Pacific
location also encouraged $21 billion in foreign imports. Eight of the state's
top ten importing countries are Asia–Pacific-based; seven of its major cus-
tomers are also from the Pacific region. In both categories, Canada ranked
as Washington's second most important trading partner, behind Japan
($21.8 billion to $7.59 billion in 1989–90). Current international exports
account for 24 per cent of gross state product in 1990, 'twice the U.S.
average and higher than any other U.S. state'.[12]

Seattle/King County accounts for 31 per cent of the state population. The
city lies at the heart of the nineteenth largest metropolitan region in North
America. Its economy is made up of 20 per cent manufacturing (primarily
transportation/aircraft, wood products, electronics, agricultural/food production, etc.) and 80 per cent non-manufacturing (e.g. 24 per cent retail, 25
per cent service sector, 12.3 per cent government, and between 5 and 7 per
cent for each of finance/insurance/real estate, transportation/public utilities

and construction). The US military is also the second largest employer in the Puget Sound region (accounting for 60,000 of 1,136,400 regional jobs). Seattle's port had $28 billion in import/export business in 1990.[13]

British Columbia

On Canada's Pacific Coast, British Columbia is Canada's third most populous province (pop. 3,282,061 (1991 census)), representing approximately 12 per cent of the total Canadian population. It is also Canada's third largest province (948,600 sq.km.), slightly larger than the states of Washington, Oregon and California (or just smaller than France, Germany and the BENELUX low countries—972,687 sq.km. combined). Yet despite this size, 83 per cent (approximately 2.7 million) of the provincial population reside in 149 incorporated municipalities encompassing less than 1 per cent of provincial territory.[14]

Over half (1,795,287–54.7 per cent) of the citizens of the province reside in the 'Lower Mainland', comprising four regional districts along the Fraser River adjacent to Vancouver. This 'Lower Mainland' is bounded on the south by the US border (with Seattle only 100 miles to its south), on the north by mountains which extend virtually without interruption to Alaska, and on the east by similar mountain ranges, and its western extremity, where the city of Vancouver is situated, by the Gulf waters of the Pacific Ocean. In Jacobs' terms, this 'Lower Mainland' forms one coherent 'city region'. Politically, the region elects just over half (50.7 per cent) of the seventy-five Members of the Legislative Assembly of the Province.

The Vancouver metropolitan area is largely represented by the Greater Vancouver Regional District—a functional amalgam of eighteen municipalities and three electoral districts, covering just under 3,000 sq.km. at the mouth of the Fraser River. This GVRD represents a little under half (1,542,744 million—47 per cent) of the provincial population, and eight of the twelve largest (over 50,000) local authorities in the province. The 1991 Canadian census confirmed the Vancouver Census Metropolitan Area, with a population of 1,602,502 (49.9 per cent of BC's population), as the third largest in Canada (and the twenty-ninth largest in North America). The city of Vancouver's population is 471,844, compared to Seattle's 516,259.[15]

The BC economy has been substantially based on resource extractive forestry, mining and fishery industries. It has had a limited manufacturing component. The economic base of metropolitan Vancouver, on the other hand, is increasingly service-oriented, with a strong base in personal and corporate services. Combined with a significant internationalist population (e.g. over half the public school population of Vancouver has English as a second language), a more interdependent—and internationally oriented—regional economy (e.g. Vancouver has been designated as one of two

Canadian International Banking Centres), and its Pacific port location (the Port of Vancouver is the second busiest port in North America), the City/Region economic outlook has become substantially internationalist.[16]

The policy implications of these factors for national governments as well as for the state/province and their major cities are apparent in constituent global policy-making in both countries.

City cases

That cities have become significant global actors contradicts not only many of the traditional views about the natural order of governance—where, constitutionally, foreign policy-making has been a primary responsibility of national governments—but also runs counter to the fact that in both North American federations local authority derives from a senior level of government: 'at common law, and under the constitution, Canadian and American local governments . . . are . . . "tenants at will" of the provinces or states.'[17] In the American institutional setting there may be more opportunity for such intergovernmental policy play; in Canada, senior constitutional authorities have been more prone to see any significant policy divergence as conflictual. And whether in Margaret Thatcher's metropolitan Britain or in British Columbia's school governance, such perceived policy conflict is not without some jurisdictional danger.[18] Instances of senior governmental exercise of their 'nuclear option'[19] serve as reminders to local authorities about 'when, how and where . . . [senior] governments exercise their will against their recalcitrant or innovative children.'[20]

What has been most intriguing about the global activities of North American municipal governments to date is how little conflict local international policy innovations have engendered.[21] By tracing different policy phases of the global activities of Vancouver and Seattle, policy lessons from this North American experience may be drawn.

Vancouver

(i) The ad hoc *policy phase: 1940s–1970s*

The first sister city established in North America was through Vancouver's 1944 twinning with the (then Soviet-allied) city of Odessa. The local rationale was rooted in humanitarian assistance to a war-devastated sister port. There was also, and continues to be, a cultural link between the Jewish communities in both cities. Cold War relations after 1945 limited further contact, but the sister city link was never broken.[22]

Vancouver added the sister cities of Yokohama in 1965 and Edinburgh in

1978. In each instance, the incremental pattern was the same: intense initial involvement by parts of the community creating pressure for formal municipal linkages to be established, followed by considerable periods of relative neglect. The basis of these early international exchanges for Vancouver was substantially cultural and educational. The incremental phase was, as Vancouver Alderman Libby Davies stated, 'never a set program; it was just a matter of evolution.'[23] As such, this policy phase was consistent with Federation of Canadian Municipalities (FCM) objectives for such twinnings: to provide direct contact between diverse peoples to foster international understanding, to expand contact between homelands of new Canadians and Canadian communities, to develop an appreciation of foreign culture, history and traditions, and to develop better perspectives on problems/opportunities at home.[24]

The most significant dimension of the incremental phase was the sporadic nature of Vancouver's global exchange. Depending on the interest of a particular mayor, or city councillor, or on the interest of a particular—usually cultural—segment of the community, there would be brief bursts of interaction followed by more extensive periods of inactivity. For some, this was an entirely natural situation; for others, particularly city officials, by the end of the 1970s, this was increasingly 'not enough'.[25]

(ii) The rational policy phase: 1980–1986

In 1980, Mike Harcourt was elected as Vancouver's mayor, with substantial leftist support. During his three terms (1980–6), Harcourt sought to put the city's internationalist links on a less *ad hoc* basis. Apart from active participation in the FCM and in the discussions of 'Big City' mayors, Harcourt promoted the case of Vancouver as Canada's Pacific Gateway. As a result, the city's international focus began to shift to a more economic rationale.

This involved work with the new (1984) Conservative federal government to establish Vancouver as one of two Canadian International Banking Centres, and to strengthen Vancouver's Pacific Rim links. The Yokohama/Japan link was revitalized under Harcourt and in 1985 Guangzhou, China was added as a sister city, drawing on the significant Cantonese base in Vancouver. Guangzhou's increasing ties to the Hong Kong region were an additional consideration. This was consistent with the more rational policy phase; as expressed by the city's Economic Development Manager, 'your sister city program has to focus on something.' That something in this first rational phase was 'on economics' with a 'Pacific focus'.[26] This was evident in the 1986 choice of Los Angeles as Vancouver's US twin. Despite proposals for many other US relationships, Harcourt pushed for Los Angeles because of business opportunities, particularly in the film industry. In this, the mayor had local Board of Trade support.

The more rational phase II policy stance was also reflected in both the organization and funding of city international initiatives between 1980 and 1986: prior to 1980, there had been no obvious organizational centre for this activity; and prior to 1982, budgetary allocations had been *ad hoc*, like the organizational base. In 1982, Harcourt had City Council establish an annual budget for Vancouver's International Program; initially set at $30,000, this grew to $100,000 (out of a total city budget of $300 million) by 1985. Despite the apparently limited nature of city funding, when private sector multipliers (such as hosting dinners, arranging air travel, etc.) and senior governmental grants (such as travel funding for cultural/artistic groups to participate abroad) were added, the impact of this city seed funding was considerably greater. Organizationally, day-to-day staff responsibility for Vancouver's global activities was shifted to the City's Economic Development Office, with protocol placed in the City Clerk's Office; there was involvement by the Mayor's Office as program needs dictated. More importantly, the Harcourt initiatives of this second policy phase contained the seeds—and some of the fruit—of the third, and emerging fourth, phases of the City's international policy-making: the third—strategic—phase reflected a more obvious business focus; the fourth—global—phase contained a broader, more prescriptive orientation, emphasizing city contributions on issues such as foreign aid, world peace and the environment. Under Harcourt, for example, Vancouver was designated a Nuclear Weapons Free Zone, reflecting a city view that issues such as peace and disarmament were clearly within the city's policy purview; in addition, Harcourt was instrumental in federal foreign aid initiatives such as the Canadian International Development Agency (CIDA)-funded/FCM-administered China Open Cities Program, Africa 2000 and the Municipal Professional Exchange Project. The very success of this more rational city diplomacy under Harcourt highlighted the limitations of the incremental phase with its emphasis on formal sister city links. The confluence of increased interdependence, a pro-active, internationalist mayor and senior governments with coincident Pacific policy goals—all created important global opportunities for Vancouver. Yet with Harcourt's departure to lead the official (leftist New Democratic) opposition in the province, the October 1986 election of a new (rightist Social Credit) provincial government,[27] and the November 1986 election of a business-backed Vancouver mayor, Gordon Campbell, the way was paved for a redefinition of the rational policy phase.

(iii) The strategic policy phase: 1987–1990

The strategic policy phase undertaken by Campbell involved a 'quiet moratorium' on additional sister city links and a new emphasis: 'a sister city rationale for the 1980's must recognize that in addition to friendship, economic and cultural opportunities must be reinforced. It is vital that governmental and non-governmental institutions coordinate their efforts to optimize their economic benefits'.[28] To ensure this policy goal, Campbell had Council create a Sister City Commission and five sister city Citizen Committees. This was followed by a major policy review which produced the Strategic City program in August 1987. Amongst its key policy goals were flexibility (as opposed to the formal requirements of more twinnings), stronger business links (as opposed to a mixed range of relationships, with business often a limited priority), access to foreign cities that act as gateways to significant national and regional economies and that could provide a discernible niche for Vancouver business, with the potential for generating frequent contact between a considerable number of Vancouver and overseas business people, and centres where such activity accorded with federal priorities. Except for the early established Edinburgh and Odessa twinnings, all other cities considered by Vancouver were in the Pacific Rim, each with cultural components to complement economic exchange.[29]

Perhaps the most innovative dimension of the strategic city policy thrust was the idea that without any formal designation by Vancouver, there was no necessity to even let the targeted city know of its place in Vancouver's international policy. This also allowed Vancouver to add other collateral cities to its strategic plan; for example, Yokohama is Vancouver's Japan link, but the city seldom went to Yokohama without economic development/cultural stops in neighbouring Osaka and Tokyo. Neither was designated as part of the main strategic city plan, yet both met the strategic criteria.

The 1988 Strategic City program budget was $92,000 plus a one-time $200,000 city grant to Yokohama's International Exposition. This city seeding again illustrated the impact of multipliers: the city grant was matched by the federal government and the province. With this start-up, the Vancouver–Yokohama Society was able to raise an additional $1 million—a total of $1.6 million for one international event. When budgetary restraint returned at the end of the 1980s, cutting the city's strategic city spending by two-thirds, many of the global links had reached the self-standing take-off point. The mayor continues to remain the most significant door-opener and official city involvement is considered essential despite this more limited municipal expenditure.

By the end of the 1980s the policy environment was shifting, however; other policy dilemmas were emerging which placed the city's strategic policy considerations in a much broader setting. Economic considerations remained important, but city activities related to concerns identified by the Brundtland Report,[30] and the summer 1992 United Nations Conference on Environment and Development and local studies on preserving livability now were becoming integral parts of city constituent diplomacy.

(iv) The global policy phase: the 1990s and beyond

Soldatos' definition of an 'International City' substantially corresponds to Vancouver's *strategic* definition: a primarily economic focus, with key cultural components.[31] The policy reality of the 1990s and beyond suggests an altered and expanded city international role, however. In no one city in North America could it be argued that a fully coherent *global* policy stance exists. The experience of Canadian and American cities like Vancouver and Seattle suggests the likely characteristics of this emerging global policy phase. It would contain the following elements:

1. *A world peace/disarmament component.* Much of the impetus for city-based twinnings grew out of the experience of the Second World War. In Europe, Canada, Japan and the United States, promotion of world peace through improved international understanding *via* people-based exchanges began in the decade following 1945. It continued into the 1950s and 1960s, but by the 1970s it was beginning to take on a different, more business-oriented, direction. In the 1980s, the original purpose began to be reasserted. The 1983 designation of Vancouver as a Nuclear Weapons Free Zone, the city's long-standing support for the Canadian peace movement, and the 1986 designation of Vancouver as a United Nations 'Messenger of Peace' city on 'the principle that cities represent local powers in the service of peace',[32] all reflected this aspect of the emerging global policy. In Vancouver, this emphasis has continued despite a shift in municipal administrations.

2. *A foreign aid component.* For Vancouver, there are roots in its 1944 humanitarian aid to war-ravaged Odessa; and in the 1980s, Harcourt initiatives within the FCM for federally funded, city-based aid through programs such as the Municipal Professional Exchange are case points. Neighbouring Saanich's Africa 2000 assistance to Zomba, Malawi is another good case example.[33]

3. *A global ecological component.* In Vancouver, the 1960s debate/defeat of freeways, and its long-standing commitment to preservation of regional farmland were forerunners for broader city environmental concerns. Greater Vancouver's 1991 review of its Livable Region Plan, 'Choosing Our Future', under the Chair of Vancouver Mayor Gordon Campbell, with its emphasis on such policy concerns as air and water quality, waste treatment/disposal and preservation of greenspace and arable land, suggests city recognition of its potential to contribute to such global issues as planetary warming.[34] The international city-based Urban Carbon Dioxide project, with Toronto as a member, 'hopes to develop a blueprint for the rest of the world to follow' in dealing with CO2 gases; 'with their power over zoning and land use, transportation and building approvals, cities have their hands on the levers which can turn down the

global warming tap.'[35] More importantly, here as in other policy fields, cities are no longer prepared to wait for senior governments to act. The global city links developed over fifty years are being applied to policy initiatives on recycling, automobile-alternative transportation, newer waste-disposal forms, etc. The policy push is for preserving livability in cities and globally. In Vancouver, aspects of each of these global components currently exist. In October 1990, for example, the City Council released 'Clouds of Change', a report containing thirty-five recommendations on atmospheric change; many were outside the formal jurisdiction of the city, but their inclusion indicated Vancouver's determination to deal with air quality and other environmental problems in the region irrespective of where authority resided.[36]

Seattle

(i) The ad hoc policy phase: 1950s–1970s

The first American city twinning was in 1945; Seattle's formal international activities commenced in 1951 when the city helped organize the first Japanese–American Conference of Mayors and Chambers of Commerce Presidents. Now held biennially, this conference has sought to strengthen Japanese and US (particularly West Coast) city ties. In 1957, in response to President Dwight Eisenhower's 1956 'People to People' policy, and in reflection of its significant Japanese/Asian population (over 11 per cent of the city), Seattle twinned itself with the Japanese port city of Kobe. In 1963, Seattle became the first city in the United States to arrange a Soviet twin, the Uzbekistan capital of Tashkent in Central Asia. This initiative came to be reflective of Seattle's international initiatives, not always in keeping with senior governmental definitions of preferred policy choice, but indicative of the city's outward-looking, liberal traditions. The city's active Peace Committee was a major mover in this 'Great Power' city-to-city initiative; and the ongoing involvement of local Project Ploughshare members helped construct the city's Seattle–Tashkent Peace Park.[37] In 1967, the Norwegian port of Bergen was added, a development from the fact that Seattle has one of the largest Scandinavian populations in the country. In 1977, the Israeli City of Beer Sheva became a sister city to Seattle. The Bergen and Beer Sheva twinnings were primarily based on cultural/educational exchanges, the former being awarded the Sister Cities International 'Best Program' award in 1970, the same year Seattle elected Wes Uhlmann, a Scandinavian-American Mayor. When Uhlmann left city office in 1978 Seattle had four sister city links. The basis of these early links corresponded with traditional 'people-to-people' cultural/educational exchanges.

(ii) The rational policy phases: 1978–1992

City Mayor Uhlmann was replaced by liberal Democrat Charles Royer in 1978. From a base of four sister cities, Royer developed ten additional city international linkages. As an active participant in the National League of American Cities and an important opponent of the Reaganomic presidency, Seattle's international activities under Royer ranged from peace-based and humanitarian concerns to tourism/business promotion. The Seattle policy phases under Charles Royer are not quite as neat as Vancouver's, but aspects of rational, strategic and global phases are identifiable.

Rational dimensions   One of the major contributions of Mayor Royer's three four-year terms, apart from a significant expansion of the city's international paradiplomacy, was in organization and funding. By 1986, Seattle had nine additional sister city relations: Mazatlan, Mexico (1979), Nantes, France (1980), Christchurch, New Zealand (1981), Mombasa, Kenya (1981), Chonging, China (1983), Limbe, Cameroon (1984), Managua, Nicaragua (1984), Galway, Ireland (1986), Reykjavik, Iceland (1986). To coordinate this activity, Royer created an Office of International Affairs within his Executive Office. Its 1988 budget was $230,000, with a Director, a federally funded Pearson Fellow, two program coordinators (on Economics and Community Programs) and an Administrative Assistant. Under Royer's administration one additional city was added in 1989 — Taejon, Korea. This significant extension in the number of sister cities reflected the city administration's international policy objectives. The range of additional city commitments to Central America, Africa, Europe, China and Korea, Iceland and New Zealand under Mayor Royer was indicative of local cultural communities, politically active local groups, increasing business potential and an internationally oriented mayor.

Strategic dimensions

Several of the early twinnings under Charles Royer began to include a more obvious economic dimension. By the time of the creation in 1986 of the Office of International Affairs, the traditional cultural/educational aspects of such municipal paradiplomacy had expanded to include a clearer international business and trade objective. Not unlike Vancouver, the natural orientation of Seattle's Pacific location continued to impact on the city's international policy focus. This strategic policy definition and Pacific Rim emphasis has extended into the term of Democratic Mayor Norm Rice, first elected in 1990. Apart from the Korea link established by Rice's predecessor in 1989, Kaohsiung, Taiwan and Cebu, Philippines were made sister cities in 1991, and Surabaya, Indonesia in 1992. All emerged from important business links in Seattle, assisted by the Trade Development Alliance, created in early 1991. The Surabaya link started with an invitation from the Provincial Governor of East Java via the US Consul General in the East Java capital. Seattle drew on its citizens with Indonesian interest and links and created a Seattle–Surabaya Sister City association, with the expectation that considerable trade opportunity and interest in cultural exchange might flow from the link.[38]

The Trade Development Alliance was created with roughly equal funding of $75,000–80,000 each from the city of Seattle, King County, the Port of Seattle (a state agency), and the Chamber of Commerce. Its 1992 budget of $346,000 is also supplemented by approximately $15,000 via individual business memberships of $100. Rather than supplant the city's sister city activities, the Alliance (with a staff of five, under the Directorship of the former Director of Intergovernmental Relations for Seattle) seeks to make the city/county trade connection more obvious. Apart from completing a study of Greater Seattle/King County's commercial relationships to determine whether they were particularly different from the state as a whole—they are not—the Alliance has sought to build on the region's strong European connections. (Direct air links from Seattle to Europe are the same distance as to Tokyo, and the ethnic make-up of Greater Seattle contains significant communities with strong European backgrounds.) The city sister city program has links with Norway, France, Ireland, Italy (Perugia—1991), Hungary (Pecs—1991) and Poland (Gydnia—1992), and the Alliance has been keen to expand its European trade opportunities in the context of Europe 1992 and the significant changes in Eastern Europe. The more strategic emphasis undertaken by the Trade Development Alliance has sought to identify the top target markets and intends to focus on these, recognizing that there are limits to what any city/region can do. The metropolitan region's markets reflect both a Pacific Rim and European focus: Japan is the top trading partner, with Korea, China/Hong Kong, Taiwan and Australia in the 'top ten'; Canada ranks second or third, with the other strategic markets for Seattle/King County being the United Kingdom, Germany, France and the Netherlands.[39]

As with Vancouver, the city of Seattle has also felt the necessity of limiting its own direct expenditures for its sister city programs. The 1992 International Affairs budget was set at $186,000, a cut of $44,000 from 1988 levels; the total Seattle City budget proposed for 1992 was $1,309,247,602. At the same time, the Office of International Affairs also became a Division of the Office of Intergovernmental Relations within the Mayor's Office as of 1992. Its staff include a Director, a Community Program Coordinator, and an Administrative Assistant shared with the Intergovernmental Relations program—effectively half that at its highpoint under Charles Royer, though this reflects more the economic realities of post-Reaganomic cities in

America rather than any declining city commitment to its international programs.[40]

The final reflection of a more strategic rational policy phase was the passage of Resolution 28362, establishing a sister city affiliation policy for the city on 13 May 1991. Seattle's direct contribution to sister city organizations is very limited—$900 annually to each. Any additional funding for sister city activities is community-based. In large organizations like the Seattle–Tashkent Association, with a membership of 400–500 that is easier than associations that have had as few as twenty members. The affiliation policy now seeks to place a minimum membership requirement of thirty and to establish specific criteria for formal city affiliation, including a proposed twelve-month budget and comprehensive work plan. (At least one sister city association—with Izmir, Turkey—is not city-recognized, although it was established in 1988.) These criteria provide some basis for limiting the extention of such formal recognition by the city. They also recognize the increased significance of economic considerations: any new sister city affiliation with Seattle must 'be the center of significant educational, cultural or political resources which offer Seattle's citizens significant exchange opportunities' or 'be or have the prospect of being a major trading partner or [with] some other major economic aspect that is similar to or complementary to the economic character of Seattle.'[41] The policy also now restricts Seattle twinnings to cities with no other US city affiliations or to cities in countries where Seattle has no existing sister city links.

Global dimensions   Seattle's global emphasis in its international activities overlapped with the end of the traditional *ad hoc* phase and the emergence of its current, more strategic phase. This different policy positioning was at least partly a product of jurisdictional rainclouds over its municipal diplomacy.[42] As Kincaid has demonstrated, there have been a broad range of traditional foreign policy intrusions by municipalities in the United States. These have been predominantly *liberal* and therefore generally in opposition to national/presidential foreign policy responses. The nadir of this foreign policy dimension for Seattle was *vis à vis* the Reagan Central American policy. Under Charles Royer, Seattle had designated itself a 'City of Sanity' and created a Citizens' Commission on Central America. In 1984, in a municipal digital salute to the Reagan White House, the city made Managua, Nicaragua a sister city. Whether it was a way of speaking back to a presidency that had cut urban programs dramatically or not, it did represent a city initiative 'totally based on politics'.[43] The sister city initiative provided a formal basis for 'frequent visits to Nicaragua enabling citizens from all walks of life to see schools, churches, hospitals, and other areas of interest, and to experience first-hand the inspiration and love of the people of Managua'.[44] While reflective of a strong local sentiment in opposition to Ronald Reagan's foreign policy, the sister city initiative tried to emphasize that

the role of local government at the international level is clearly distinguished from the role of the federal government. National security, national foreign policy . . . and related matters . . . are outside the jurisdiction of the City of Seattle . . . The educational benefits and enhanced international awareness in the local community resulting from a sister city program and other international exchanges are . . . a direct responsibility of city government. These distinctions between city and federal responsibilities at the international level seem well enough defined at the present time.[45]

The Citizens' Commission on Central America was seen by some to have missed this sister city distinction and to have strayed significantly into national foreign policy-making. The ensuing struggle resulted in an initiative being placed on the ballot in late 1986. The initiative called for the disbanding of the Commission on Central America on the grounds that the City 'should not meddle in foreign relations.'[46] On 8 December 1986, Initiative 30 was passed and the Commission dissolved. The Managua link remained, however, partly on the rationale that such exchanges are 'people-to-people' rather than government-to-government. This rationale has also allowed city twinnings in both China (1983) and Taiwan (1991).

It is arguable that the early, and successful, challenge to this global aspect of Seattle's international activities truncated the city's global policy phase. It did not eliminate it. The city extended its Tashkent links with the local peace movement central to these exchanges; its Mazatlan Sister City Association has adopted three orphanages in the Mexican city, raising funds in Seattle for clothing, medicine, food and toys and to provide vocational training for older orphanage children; the Mombasa, Kenya exchange has allowed for books and school supplies to be sent from Seattle, providing magazine subscriptions for the Mombasa library, the hosting of Crossroads Africa health professionals and the donation of an emergency aid car to the African city; and the Limbe, Cameroon city link has provided aid such as pharmaceuticals for the Limbe Clinic and a medical aid van presented in Limbe by Seattle Mayor Charles Royer in 1988.[47]

On the environmental policy front, Seattle's development of bus technology, its encouragement of recycling, its programs to put limits on the one-passenger private automobile user, etc. all reflect a city-based agreement with the ecological components of an earth strategy where urban livability is central.

City lessons

It is only a small step for a significant number of major cities in the world to move to the adoption of a rational global city policy position. Through national and international organizations like the Federation of Canadian Municipalities/Sister Cities International and the International Union of Local Authorities, the potential for significant policy diffusion in municipal internationalism is high. Whatever the outcome of this extension in forms of local governmental international activity, it seems likely to limit the capacity of senior national governments to impose their jurisdictional wills as easily as in the past. Policy-making in the age of the global city will be more complex; it will produce different policy choices. Globalization has meant that the emergence of the global city will occur with or without senior governmental support.

Provincial state cases

Just as municipalities are 'creatures' of senior authority, provinces and states are not. As such, their potential to challenge nation centric foreign policy-making would appear greater. The British Columbia and Washington cases suggest that such challenges are long-standing but relatively limited. Provincial constitutional interpretations on trade and commerce powers were early examples resolved by judicial review.[48] More recent international policy-making at the provincial/state level suggests less *ad hoc* responses. The main policy shifts here appear to be from incremental and rational, and to a combined global/strategic phase.

British Columbia

The incremental phase: 1900–1970

In the 1950s and 1960s public servants in the province of British Columbia had to get permission from the Premier's Office to make out of province phone calls. Premier W.A.C. (Wacky) Bennett was his own Minister of Finance, and probity and prudence were his administrative watchwords. It also reflected a very personal style of politics. External interaction in such a setting was limited. The provincial tradition of strong premiers and weak structures allowed for some spectacular international forays, though this was not the norm. The most outrageous BC intervention into foreign relations was the provincial purchase of two submarines built in Seattle for the Chilean government immediately prior to the outbreak of the First World War. With war imminent, an American declaration of neutrality and resulting trade embargo likely, and provincial fears of lack of adequate defence for the Pacific Northwest, BC Premier Richard McBride requested that Ottawa arrange for the British Admiralty to purchase the subs. When an answer from senior authorities was not received fast enough to satisfy the BC Premier, he arranged to have the subs inspected at sea five miles offshore. They were found to be war-ready—apart from all the manuals being only available in Spanish. McBride then sent the head janitor of the BC Parliament Buildings to Seattle with the $1.15 million payment arranged under his signature and without legislative approval. When Ottawa sent a telegram stating, 'Prepare to purchase submarines. Wire price' a day later, McBride responded with a fine three-word put-down of the federal government: 'Have purchased submarines.' For three days, the BC government owned the two subs. It took that long for an angry national government to arrange for the British Admiralty to take possession. With war soon declared, the vessels remained to defend BC. They saw no action, though at one point McBride took over complete control of coastal defence.[49] Under W.A.C. Bennett (1952–72), the province exerted pressure on national policy discussions with the United States on a range of issues such as the negotiations over the Columbia River Treaty through direct international action and *vis à vis* the province's constitutional powers.[50] The generally *ad hoc* policy pattern remained the W.A.C. Bennett norm.

The rational phase: 1972–75, 1975–86

The election of a leftist New Democratic government in 1972 represented the arrival of rational approaches to policy-making. Apart from beginning to develop central agencies beyond the rudimentary structures that have served BC since 1870,[51] Premier Dave Barrett made a number of excursions into international relations.[52] With an overt nationalist emphasis, three cases stand out as illustrations:

(i) The BC–US Natural Gas dispute, where the province took control of the resource through the creation of a crown agency, raised foreign (that is US) prices in a series of quick stages by more than 300 per cent in two years, producing Ottawa consternation, US government anger and Washington state outrage. It also produced some US retaliation— for a short time—on Canadian access to American aviation fuel.[53]

(ii) The Trans-Alaska Pipeline (TAPS) dispute, where again the Barrett government intervened to oppose an American plan to transport Alaskan oil by ship to Washington state. BC's policy involved efforts at direct provincial access to President Nixon (these failed because of Canadian government intervention) and an alternative provincial plan unveiled in Washington DC without prior Ottawa consultation. This failed to get Ottawa support and Barrett was criticized by the senior authority for breaching foreign relations protocol. BC's reponse was to suggest 'laxity and timidity' on the part of Ottawa.[54]

(iii) The BC attempt to have the Columbia River Treaty and the High Ross Dam agreement renegotiated: Barrett called the mid-1960s Columbia River Treaty 'the biggest skinning since the selling of Manhattan Island'.[55] He failed to get Ottawa to renegotiate a better deal. Threats of American retaliation and lawsuits were part of this policy discourse.

Consistent with the Barrett government's more rational provincialist/nationalist goals, BC also sought to redirect its trade away from the United States to the Pacific Rim. Here there was a shift of 10 per cent from the United States to Japan between 1972 and 1974, Barrett's last full year in office.

In 1975, the NDP was replaced by the rightist Social Credit government of Bill Bennett. Between then and 1986, the son of the former BC Premier W.A.C. Bennett built on the preliminary, more rational structure initiated by Barrett, including a significant expansion of the Premier's Office, related Cabinet support structures and the creation of an Office and then Ministry of Intergovernmental Relations. Bennett also emphasized a Global Economic Strategy—for example, through the expansion of provincial trade missions in Europe and the Pacific, under a Ministry of Economic Development—rather than seeking stronger US regional ties. Bennett's *bunker* internal policy style, particularly between 1983 and 1986, led to his resignation[56] and the October 1986 election of his Social Credit successor, Bill Vander Zalm.

The policy gambling phase: 1986–1991

Vander Zalm represented a dramatically different policy style from the truncated pose of his predecessor. Policy gambling, uncertainty and a return to one personality government were the key descriptors,[57] but under his administration several key international initiatives arose that reflected a developing strategic/global position:

(i) The Canada–US Softwood Lumber Dispute: under Vander Zalm, BC took a stronger stance on developing US regional links ('We really are one region with much in common').[58] To do so, the province cooperated with other western Canadian provinces and US states to create the Pacific Northwest Economic Region (BC, Alberta, Washington, Oregon, Idaho, Montana and Alaska), a grouping of 16 million people and US $300 billion in gross regional product. This alliance has sought to sell the region and its products as one—whether to Europe or the rest of the global market. In 1989, BC and Alberta were also accorded 'honorary status' at the Western Legislative conference (WLA is a formal grouping of US western states). Despite this subnational international cooperation, the 1986–7 softwood lumber dispute strained Canada–US and subnational relations. BC's interventions ran counter to the federal government position; BC's offer of concessions on stumpage cut Ottawa's negotiation stance. This was followed by direct BC–American talks at the regional level, unilateral BC proposals, Ottawa getting American agreement to prevent BC from making its case directly to the US government and, finally, to a voluntary 15 per cent Canadian duty to keep the tax benefits in Canada.[59]

(ii) BC's interventions on west coast fishery issues—from arguments over driftnet fishing to landing rights under the Canada–US Free Trade Agreement—recognized federal paramountcy but sought a mediating role in national positions through international coalition-building. These stances were partly a reflection of provincial frustration with a perceived Ottawa neglect of BC concerns.[60]

(iii) Perhaps the most significant provincial initiative under Vander Zalm was the provincial response to the December 1988 Gray's Harbour, Washington oil spill. The loss of 1,048,740 litres of Alaskan crude became BC's worst coastal environmental problem. It resulted in international protests and lawsuits, provincial criticism of the federal government's response, and ultimately direct substate attempts at solutions. Initially, this involved a Joint BC–Washington State Committee. When the Exxon Valdez spill occurred in Alaska one day after this initial agreement, Premier Vander Zalm travelled immediately to Alaska and got that governor's signature to create a four-partner Task Force (Washington, Oregon, Alaska and BC).[61] (California subsequently joined.)

This subnational Task Force was created despite Ottawa's objections. BC's response was best expressed by the then Environment Minister, John Reynolds: 'They are looking more at the diplomatic old stand-by rules of what you should do. We can't afford to worry about what some diplomat in Seattle thinks or a bureaucrat working for the federal government. We're concerned about spills and we're going to work with our American neighbours.'[62] Despite Department of External Affairs objections, BC concluded the Task Force Agreement; this Task Force has more recently had discussions on offshore drilling issues and alternative regional sitings for oil landing.

The strategic–global phase: 1991 and beyond

In April 1991, affected by conflict of interest charges over the sale of his Christian Theme Park, Fantasy Gardens, to a Taiwanese businessman, Vander Zalm resigned. Apart from the already noted global efforts, his international legacy included efforts to ignore a Canadian limit on South African trade. In October 1991, former Vancouver Mayor Mike Harcourt led the leftist NDP to provincial power. Rather than immediately recall the BC legislature, Harcourt (a) led an extended trade mission to Japan, Hong Kong and other Pacific Rim countries; (b) travelled to New York City to meet US/international money managers, including Standard and Poors, the BC bond rater; (c) participated in international economic meetings in Davos, Switzerland, with other European trade stops such as to London. All these early provincial initiatives reflected a strong strategic element. At the same time, the very first Cabinet decisions were environmental—such as preservation of farmland, stronger controls on international pulp and paper companies, on resource extractive industries and land use. Given the past Harcourt record in Vancouver, this combined strategy is likely to continue as the major policy focus of the BC government. BC's Georgia Basin initiative which combines environmental and economic development policy choices with its US neighbours, and broader subnational regional efforts on the Portland, Oregon, Seattle, Washington and Vancouver, BC corridor are indications of future policy direction. Indications on Canadian constitutional matters also suggest a provincial stance designed to be more constructive in federal–provincial matters. That may have an impact on future BC international efforts. The recent past supports a conclusion that provincial foreign relations will exhibit an increasing independence.

Washington

The Incremental phase: pre-1970s

Under post-war Washington State Governors Arthur B. Langlie (Republican, 1949–57) and Albert Rosalini (Democrat, 1957–65) there appears little official state interest in Canadian linkages. The emerging Boeing economic giant in Seattle and the impressive defence establishment in the Puget Sound region meant that state interest and involvement in foreign policy and international trade issues were high. Such outward-looking trade links were furthered by agricultural and lumber product state economies all affected by world markets. Most Washington—Canadian relations during this period were through federal agencies such as Agricultural Departments, Trade and Commerce Departments and trade-related local consulates, Coast Guard agencies, etc.

The rational phase: 1970s

Under Governor Dan Evans (Republican, 1965–77) state decisional structures became more reflective of rational policy models. Evans's early political efforts involved largely unsuccessful attempts to update the state's antiquated tax system.[63]

Under the Evans administration, there were also 'serious efforts to communicate' with BC.[64] Despite the lack of formal structures or channels for such subnational communication, there were three Cabinet-level meetings between the Washington State Governor, BC premiers and related ministers/officials. These meetings allowed BC direct access to state decision-makers on such policy problems as the High Ross Dam. It also provided a basis for several formal agreements between BC and Washington state:[65]

(i) Under Governor Evans, a 'Letter of Understanding On Civil Emergency Planning and Cooperative Emergency Arrangements' was formally signed in October, 1968.
(ii) In March 1972, both Washington and British Columbia passed equivalent legislation on Reciprocal Enforcement of Maintenance Orders to support each other's jurisdiction. (Such efforts have been extended to include exchange of information on motor vehicle violations in either jurisdiction, with attendant penalties.) As Mitrani and Rutan have argued, 'in essence this serves as a "treaty" or compact for the two intermediate level governments whose federal jurisdictions have reserved treaty power unto themselves.'[66]
(iii) In 1975, and subsequently, Washington State and BC passed reciprocal in-state/in-province tuition legislation.
(iv) In May 1976, BC and Washington signed a 'Memorandum of Understanding For Fire Suppression' to ensure cooperative fire protection along the international border.
The Evans terms also saw the development of a more outward policy style generally for the state.

The policy uncertainty phase: 1977–1981 (and 1981–1985)

Republican Governor Dan Evans retired and was replaced by Democrat Dr Dixy Lee Ray (someone close in policy style—and length in office—to the BC Vander Zalm model of a decade later). Brilliant, outspoken and unpredictable, Governor Ray had served as the dynamic Director of Seattle's Pacific Science World, raising funds and driving around the region in a Jaguar equipped with a Paris taxi horn.[67] Her single term in office ended in a successful Democratic challenge to her candidacy in the subsequent election. During her term, Governor Ray's interest in BC and

Canada seemed limited to criticism of policies on tourism and the environment and negative reaction to BC/Canadian commentary on American policies. The primary policy position of Dr Ray's term in Olympia was the promotion of nuclear power, both in the state and nationally. Though not the initiator, Governor Ray promoted the state plan to build five nuclear generating plants. One was completed and two half-built when the system collapsed in the early 1980s in a $22-billion failure. The state still spends $20 million annually to maintain the two partially constructed sites.[68]

Ray's primary defeat in 1980 allowed Republican John Spellman to take the Governor's seat. A former King County Executive, Spellman arrived in time to have to manage the early 1980s recession. One of his noteworthy acts was to appoint former Governor Dan Evans to fill the vacant Henry 'Scoop' Jackson US Senate seat when Jackson died. Evans was re-elected until retirement in 1990, and served as a strong promoter of international trade, the Canada–US Free Trade Agreement, etc.

The strategic–global phase: late 1980s–1990s

Booth Gardiner (Democrat, 1985–92) has represented more recent international policy orientations. A former mayor of Tacoma and family member of the corporate Weyerhaeuser Forest Products, Adams has represented liberal social views with a hard economic management stance. Since his election, both within the Governor's office and the state legislature, there have been numerous state initiatives of a global sort. These include BC, Alberta, Oregon and Washington proposals on 'Cascadia', a regional proposal to preserve and promote the area through public/private cooperation. In Washington, this includes efforts such as those by State Senate Vice President Alan Bluechel, from Kirkland. According to Bluechel, 'regions will be able to exploit their own assets and become major players in the world economy . . . In the changing world, economics are taking a front seat to political boundaries . . . We have no interest in political union or anything pertaining to the politics of either country except to make it easier for us to work together. The political entities are irrelevant.'[69] Equivalent efforts, such as by Fraser Valley Tory MP Bob Wenman to seek a United Nations designation of Puget Sound as a special environmental region, promote parallel BC views.

Not all activity in the region, however, is reflective of this new, largely positive, subnational internationalism. Recent battles between US Puget Sound area governments and Victoria, BC over sewage treatment—or the lack of it—and the city's dumping into the ocean waters have involved efforts from American local governments to the State of Washington and the US State Department to protest via Ottawa to the BC government to get Victoria city to act that suggest that old-style diplomacy still has its place.

Provincial–state lessons

Provincial and state international activities have generally been longer standing, more economically focussed, and less varied than their municipal counterparts. As such they have offered little serious conflict with national authorities. The increasing indication that these *intermediate* jurisdictions are becoming more pro-active in their policy stances, and prepared to engage in formal global exchanges, even over national governmental objections, supports the contentions of the interdependence thesis.

Conclusions

Examples such as the proposition of the Second Foreign Minister of Singapore for a Pacific League of Cities based on the Thirteenth—Fifteenth Century Hanseatic League model to promote mutual regional interest across national boundaries, or the actions of the French and Italian cities of Menton and Ventimiglia seeking to operate as if the border that separates them does not exist, or the UN Rio Earth Summit suggestion of a $600 billion bill to relieve the planet of population and development stress with Agenda 21 proposals on poverty, health and other ecological plans, all support the conclusion that foreign relations reality in the twenty-first century will include subnational involvement. The trick may be to ensure that such subnational foreign activity is more often complementary than conflictual—and not with national priorities alone. In that we will 'live in interesting times'.

Notes

1. Bayless Manning, 'The congress, the executive and intermestic affairs', *Foreign Affairs*, 55 (1977), 306–24.
2. James MacNeill *et al.*, *Beyond Interdependence: The Meshing of the World's Economy and the Earth's Ecology*, Oxford University Press, Oxford (1991).
3. Kenichi Ohmae, *The Borderless World: Power and Strategy in the Interlinked World Economy*, Harper Business, New York (1990).
4. Brian Hocking, 'Regional governments and international affairs: foreign policy problem or deviant behaviour?', *International Journal*, 41, 2 (Summer 1986), 483.
5. Jane Jacobs, *Cities and the Wealth of Nations: Principles of Economic Life*, Random House, New York (1984).
6. Michael Y. Seelig and Alan F. Artibise, *From Desolation to Hope: The Pacific Fraser Region in 2010*, Board of Trade, Vancouver (1991).
7. John Kincaid, 'Constituent diplomacy in federal polities and the nation state: conflict and cooperation', in Hans J. Michelmann and Panayotis Soldatos (eds), *Federalism and International Relations: The Role of Subnational Units*, Oxford

University Press, New York (1990), 54–75.

8. Patrick J. Smith and Theodore H. Cohn, 'Municipal and provincial paradiplomacy: British Columbia cases', Canadian Political Science Association paper, Victoria (June 1990).

9. Sister Cities International, Virginia (1991).

10. *Washington Yearbook*, Sisters, Oregon (annual).

11. ibid.

12. Seattle, *Datasheet* (1992).

13. ibid.

14. H. Peter Oberlander and Patrick J. Smith, 'Governing metropolitan Vancouver', in Donald Rothblatt and Andrew Sancton (eds), *Metropolitan Governance in North America*, University of California, Berkeley/Institute of Governmental Studies, Berkeley, California (1992).

15. Statistics Canada, *1991 Canadian Census*, Ottawa (1992); and Seattle, *Datasheet* (1992).

16. See Theodore Cohn, David Merrifield and Patrick Smith, 'North American cities in an interdependent world: Vancouver and Seattle as international cities', in Earl Fry, Lee Radebaugh and Panayotis Soldatos (eds), *The New International Cities Era: The Global Activities of North American Municipal Governments*, Brigham Young University, Provo, Utah (1989), 73–117.

17. Victor Jones, 'Beavers and cats: federal–local relations in the United States and Canada', in H. Peter Oberlander and Hilda Symonds (eds), *Meech Lake: From Centre to Periphery*, University of British Columbia/Centre For Human Settlements, Vancouver (1988), 89–90.

18. Patrick J. Smith, 'Local-federal government relations: Canadian perspectives, American comparisons' in ibid., 127–38.

19. Patrick J. Smith, 'Regional governance in British Columbia', *Planning and Administration*, 13, 2 (Autumn 1986), 1–20.

20. Victor Jones, 'Beavers and cats', op.cit., 91.

21. Patrick Smith and Theodore Cohn, 'Municipal and provincial paradiplomacy', op.cit.

22. Patrick Smith, 'The making of a global city: fifty years of constituent diplomacy—the case of Vancouver', *Canadian Journal of Urban Research*, 1 (June 1992), 90–112.

23. Interview, Vancouver Alderman Libby Davies (6 October 1988).

24. Federation of Canadian Municipalities, *A Practical Guide to Twinning*, Ottawa (1988).

25. Interview, Sid Fancy, Manager, Economic Development, City of Vancouver (27 October 1989).

26. ibid.

27. Patrick J. Smith, 'Déjà vu all over again? policy gambling and restraint revisited in British Columbia', in Andrew Johnson, Stephen McBride and Patrick Smith (eds), *Continuities and Discontinuities: The Political Economy of Social Welfare and Labour Market Policy Making in Canada* (forthcoming, 1993).

28. Interview, Janet Fraser, Executive Assistant, Vancouver Mayor Gordon Campbell (30 September 1988), and Interview, Vancouver Mayor Gordon Campbell (17 October 1988).

29. Patrick Smith, 'The making of a global city', op.cit.

30. Gro Harlem Brundtland, *Our Common Future*, World Commission on Environment and Development, United Nations, New York (1987).
31. Panayotis Soldatos, 'Atlanta and Boston in the new international cities era: does age matter?', in Earl Fry *et al.* (eds), *The New International Cities Era*, op.cit., 39.
32. United Nations, 'Messenger of Peace' designation, City of Vancouver (1986).
33. See P. Smith and T. Cohn, 'Municipal and provincial paradiplomacy', op.cit. for a discussion of the Saanich, BC program.
34. Greater Vancouver Regional District, *Creating Our Future: Steps to a More Livable Region*, GVRD, Burnaby (September 1990).
35. See for example, 'Cities join to fight global warming', *Toronto Star* (13 June 1991), A10.
36. City of Vancouver, *Clouds of Change*, Vancouver (October 1990).
37. Project Ploughshares is a non-governmental international aid agency.
38. Interview, Tsering Ottuk, Office of Intergovernmental Relations, Division of International Affairs, City of Seattle (25 February 1992).
39. ibid., and information provided from the Trade Development Alliance, February 1992.
40. Interview, T. Ottuk, op.cit.
41. City of Seattle, *Resolution 28362: Sister City Affiliation Policy* (13 May 1991).
42. See John Kincaid, 'Rain clouds over municipal diplomacy: dimensions and possible sources of negative public opinion', in Earl Fry *et al.* (eds), *The New International Cities Era*, op.cit., 233–49.
43. Interview, Seattle city staff, February 1992.
44. City of Seattle, *Passport to Sister Cities: Managua, 1984* (1984).
45. T. Cohn *et al.*, 'North American cities in an interdependent world', op.cit., 97.
46. City of Seattle, *Initiative 30* (8 December 1986).
47. City of Seattle, *Passport to Sister Cities*, various: Mazatlan, Mombasa, Limbe.
48. For example, see Peter Russell, *Leading Constitutional Decisions*, McClelland & Stewart, Toronto (1973).
49. See Margaret Ormsby, *British Columbia: A History*, Macmillan, Toronto (1958); and Martin Robin, *The Company Province: The Rush for Spoils, 1871–1933*, McClelland & Stewart (1972).
50. Neil Swainson, *Conflict Over the Columbia*, McGill-Queen's University Press, Montreal (1979).
51. See Paul Tennant, 'The NDP government of British Columbia: unaided politicians in an unaided cabinet', *Canadian Public Policy*, 3 (1977), 367–82; and Walter Young and Terence Morley, 'The premier and the cabinet', in T. Morley *et al.*, (eds), *The Reins of Power: Governing British Columbia*, Douglas & McIntrye, Vancouver (1983).
52. James P. Groen, *Provincial International Activity: Case Studies of the Barrett and Vander Zalm Administrations in British Columbia*, M.A. thesis, Political Science, Simon Fraser University, Burnaby, BC, Canada (1991).
53. ibid., 82–99.
54. ibid., 100–25.
55. ibid., 124–53.
56. Patrick J. Smith and Laurent Dobuzinskis, 'The bloom is off the locus: job creation policy and restraint in British Columbia', in J.S. Ismael (ed.), *The Canadian Welfare State: Evolution and Transition*, University of Alberta, Edmonton

(1986), 212–44.

57. P. Smith, 'Déjà vu all over again?', op.cit.
58. J. Groen, op.cit., 192–217.
59. ibid.
60. ibid., 224–64.
61. ibid., 218–44.
62. ibid., 234.
63. Nard Jones, *Seattle*, Doubleday (1972), 225.
64. Carol Mitrani and Gerard Rutan, *Washington State/British Columbia Governmental Interactions, 1979*, Western Washington University, Bellingham (1980), 71.
65. See ibid., 71–80.
66. ibid., 71.
67. N. Jones, *Seattle*, op.cit., 6–8.
68. C. Mitrani and G. Rutan, *Washington State/British Columbia Governmental Interactions*, op.cit., 72.
69. Canadian Broadcasting Corporation, Vancouver, *Evening News* (October 1991).

14 Federation and *Länder* in German foreign relations: power-sharing in treaty-making and European affairs[1]

Uwe Leonardy

Historical background

With the exception of two very different periods Germany has always been, throughout its constitutional history, either a confederation or a federation of the states located within its changing territorial boundaries. Even the two exceptions need to be qualified, though, albeit for different reasons. During the first of these periods, between the final dissolution of the Holy Roman Empire of the German Nation under the pressure of Napoleon in 1806 and the promulgation of the Imperial Constitution of 1871, there existed numerous sovereign monarchies and republics conducting their own sovereign foreign relations. Even during this period, however, there existed between some or all of these states links of a confederal, quasi-federal or even federal character, such as the German Confederation (*Deutscher Bund*) of 1815–66, the German Customs Association (*Deutscher Zollverein*) of 1833–71, and the North German Federation (*Norddeutscher Bund*) of 1867–71, the immediate predecessor of Bismarck's Empire.[2] The second period, Hitler's so-called Third *Reich* of 1933–45, represented an interruption rather than an exception to constitutional history since not just federalism[3] but also any form of constitution as such had ceased to exist.

In the course of this constitutional history, nothing marked the character of the institutional system more clearly as it fluctuated between confederacy, federalism and unitarism than the way in which the conduct of foreign affairs was organised constitutionally between the component parts of the German state and the community constituted by them. The declining Holy

Roman Empire and the predominantly confederate phases of the nineteenth century were both characterised, for example, by the growing monopoly of the states in foreign affairs. The institution of a fully fledged federal system in the Imperial Constitution of 16 April 1871[4] established, however, that foreign relations were a matter both for the federation (*Reich*) and the member states (*Bundesstaaten*). The Emperor represented the *Reich* under the usual terms of international law and treaty-making powers, but Article 11 of the Constitution[5] failed to give the *Reich* an exclusive competence in the conduct of foreign affairs. The states were thus able to maintain, without restriction, active and passive diplomatic relations with foreign powers. Some of them, in particular the larger ones (e.g. Bavaria, Württemberg, Saxony and Baden), therefore kept the legations they had established before the creation of the *Reich* in at least partial operation.

The Weimar Constitution of 11 August 1919[6] was still organised on federal lines, but was much more strongly unitaristic. The functions of the formerly powerful *Bundesrat* in domestic affairs were substantially curtailed in the case of its successor, the *Reichsrat*. Externally, foreign affairs became an exclusive competence of the *Reich*. The states (now termed, for the first time, *Länder*) were thus denied their previously extensive rights in foreign affairs. The *Länder* did keep treaty-making powers in matters lying within their own, now much more restricted fields of legislative competence, but these powers were now made subject to the consent of the *Reich* under the terms of Article 78 of the republican constitution.[7]

Current constitutional bases

The Basic Law of the Federal Republic of 23 May 1949[8] attributes powers and functions in foreign affairs to federation and *Länder* in two different fields (the latter of which would not have been conceivable for its predecessors in constitutional law).

Article 32 of the Basic Law regulates the traditional domains of foreign relations and treaty-making powers. It thus remains confined to the field which, in Montesquieu's terms, had been the 'federative power' of participation, as a sovereign member of the community of nations, in the shaping of the outside world. However, in keeping with the German federal tradition, and in a much stronger form than in the Weimar Constitution, Article 32 allows for the shared exercise of sovereignty by the *Länder* as partners of the federation, granting them independent rights both in matters where their interests are affected and within their fields of autonomous legislative competence:

(1) Relations with foreign states shall be conducted by the federation.
(2) Before the conclusion of a treaty affecting the special circumstances of a *Land* that *Land* shall be consulted in sufficient time.

(3) In so far as the *Länder* have power to legislate, they may, with the consent of the federal government, conclude treaties with foreign states.

In addition to Article 32, and for the first time ever, Article 24 of the Basic Law also makes provision for the (relatively) new need not just to exercise, but also to transfer and restrict sovereign powers:

(1) The federation may by legislation transfer sovereign powers to international institutions.
(2) For the maintenance of peace, the federation may enter into a system of mutual collective security; in doing so it shall consent to such limitations upon its rights of sovereignty as will bring about and secure a peaceful and lasting order in Europe and among the nations of the world.
(3) For the settlement of disputes between states, the federation shall accede to agreements concerning international arbitration of a general, comprehensive and obligatory nature.

The first paragraph of Article 24 was composed with a view to the aim of 'a united Europe' as laid down in the Preamble to the Basic Law. Against this background it has become known as the 'power of integration'. Since the scope of the sovereign powers transferable under it is not restricted solely to those of the federation, Article 24's relevance for federal–*Länder* relations has grown constantly ever since the Treaty of Rome was signed in 1957. Seen together with the implications of Article 32, the two fields of both international and supranational power-sharing and power-transfer have thus had a strong impact on the development of these relations and the institutional structures through which they are conducted.

Treaty-making powers and foreign relations (Article 32 of the Basic Law)

The wording of Paragraph 3 of Article 32 allows room for two different interpretations of the question of treaty-making powers in the fields of exclusive competence of the *Länder*. On one side, the *Länder* maintain that this power resides exclusively with them and that the transformation of obligations arising from such treaties into internal German law is also a matter of their exclusive competence. On the other, the federation insists that it has a concurrent competence in this field of the treaty-making power, irrespective of the allocation of corresponding functions in the area of transformation. This dispute[9] has never been settled legally, but a mode of practice has been developed in a way typical of German federalism which allows both sides to hold to their respective views without disturbing the conduct of business.

The basis of this arrangement, laid down in the so-called Lindau Agreement of 14 November 1957,[10] is the assumption by the *Länder* that the federation acts on their behalf when negotiating or signing foreign treaties which either partly or wholly regulate matters of their competence. In exchange for empowering the federation to act on their behalf, the *Länder* have secured for themselves wide-ranging rights of participation which deny the federation the right to sign such treaties without previously securing their unanimous consent. As will be shown below, the institutional structures built on these principles have worked successfully and without serious disruption ever since the Lindau Agreement came into force.

The still unresolved legal question underlying the exercise of treaty-making powers in fields of *Länder* competence has, however, a second aspect which would seem to prove that the view held by the *Länder* is the correct one. Even if the federation had a concurrent treaty-making power in fields of *Länder* competence, it could never claim the internal legislative power to transform treaty obligations into domestic law, since this would allow it to break into any internally exclusive domain of the *Länder* by way of international treaty-making. This would obviously unbalance the federal structure to an unjustifiable extent.[11] The *Länder* consider this line of reasoning to be a central, underlying component of the Lindau Agreement. In doing so they correctly maintain that the treaty-making power cannot be legally separated from the power of transformation. As the latter, however, clearly resides with them, the assumption must logically be correct that the federation needs their mandate to exercise the treaty-making power in fields of *Länder* competence. The Lindau Agreement thus clearly reflects the *Länder* interpretation of Article 32, Paragraph 3 of the Basic Law.

In matters of foreign affairs concerning relations with political and/or administrative counterparts below the level of the nation-state, the *Länder* have always considered themselves free of constitutional restriction. Their right to communicate directly with foreign regions, provinces or autonomous communities was indeed confirmed in one of the first decisions of the Federal Constitutional Court.[12] Under the terms of Paragraph 1 of Article 32 it is clear, however, that this right does not extend to a right of the *Länder* to maintain diplomatic missions of their own. This clearly marks a difference to the Imperial Constitution of 1871 and continues the tradition established by the Weimar Constitution. Nevertheless, political representatives of the *Länder* have frequently regarded themselves as entitled to maintain informal relations, below the level of formal diplomacy, with foreign states. There is nothing in the Basic Law to bar them from doing so as long as the principle of federal loyalty or comity (*Bundestreue*), which obliges federation and *Länder* to mutual consideration, is not disregarded.[13] This means in particular that any political guidelines set in foreign relations by the federation must not be counteracted by such contacts.

The power of integration (Article 24 of the Basic Law)

The competence of the federation to 'transfer sovereign powers to international institutions', particularly to the European Community, refers undisputedly to the transfer of both federal and *Länder* powers. As such, this power of integration[14] has increasingly come to be seen as 'the open flank of the federal order'.[15]

In order to guard this open flank, the *Länder* have attempted to secure rights of participation, wherever possible, in the exercise of the federal government's functions in the organs of the European Community, above all in the Council of Ministers. Prior to 1986 the rights of the *Länder* in this field lacked detailed legal foundations.[16] However, the *Länder* successfully insisted on a clause which provided such foundations in Article 2 of the Statute of Ratification of the Single European Act in 1986. As the content of this Article is the basis not only of subsequent practice in EC matters, but also of current deliberations on constitutional reform in this field, it is worth quoting it in full:[17]

(1) The Federal Government shall inform the *Bundesrat* irrespective of Article 2 of the Statute of Ratification of the Treaties of 25 March 1957 for the Foundation of the European Economic Community and of the European Atomic Community of 27 July 1957 . . . fully and at the earliest possible moment of all projects within the scope of the European Community which could be of interest to the *Länder*.

(2) Prior to its consent to decisions in the European Community which concern either wholly or through individual provisions matters of exclusive legislative competence or the essential interests of the *Länder*, the Federal Government shall give sufficient time and opportunity for the *Bundesrat* to state its opinion.

(3) The Federal Government shall take this opinion into account in the negotiations. In so far as the opinion concerns matters of exclusive legislative competence or the essential interests of the *Länder*, the Federal Government may only deviate from it for unavoidable reasons of foreign or Community policy. Otherwise it shall include the concerns of the *Länder*, presented through the *Bundesrat*, in its considerations.

(4) In case of a deviation from a *Bundesrat* opinion on a matter of exclusive legislative competence of the *Länder* and otherwise on request, the Federal Government shall convey the decisive reasons for such a deviation to the *Bundesrat*.

(5) If opportunity for comment is to be given to the *Bundesrat*, representatives of the *Länder* are to be included . . . in the negotiations within the consultative bodies of the Commission and the Council insofar as this is possible for the Federal Government.

(6) Details of information and participation shall be reserved for agreement between Federation and *Länder*.

Such an agreement arising from Paragraph 6 of the above was subsequently signed by the federal government and the governments of the

Länder on 17 December 1987,[18] and the Standing Orders of the *Bundesrat* were amended accordingly by a new chapter on 'The Procedure in Matters of the European Community' on 10 June 1988. Despite this, the conduct of 'foreign' relations in the EC, which the *Länder* no longer consider to be 'foreign' in substance within the framework of a supranational organisation, still needs to be modified further in favour of the *Länder* if their role as constituent parts of the federal system is to be protected sufficiently. The current debate on this issue will be examined below, following a review of the organisational structures through which the *Länder* participate in treaty-making and integration policy.

Practice and institutions

The exercise of Länder influence on foreign treaty-making

The central institution in the operation of the Lindau Agreement is the Permanent Treaty Commission of the *Länder*. It meets monthly and consists of civil servants from the *Länder* Missions to the federation in Bonn (one from each of the sixteen Missions). Their function is to communicate demands of the *Länder* concerning draft treaties of the kind described above to the federal government and to coordinate their recommendations both within and between the *Länder* (the function of coordination within the *Länder* is mostly performed by the cabinet offices, which then convey the results to the Missions). The proceedings of the Treaty Commission, assisted by a permanent secretariat in the Bavarian Mission, generally commence with the examination of a draft treaty or agreement conveyed to it by the Foreign Ministry or by any other federal ministry negotiating or intending to negotiate terms with a foreign power or international organisation. In some cases, however, the secretariat of the Commission may itself approach the federal government with the demand to be informed of negotiations which have become known to the *Länder*.

The examination initially focuses on whether the draft under review falls under the terms of Point 3 or Point 4 of the Lindau Agreement. Under the regulations in Point 3, the participation of the *Länder* in the preparation of treaties touching upon any of their exclusive competences must be sought by the federation 'as early as possible, but certainly before final agreement is reached on the treaty text.' The consent of all the *Länder* must be secured before obligations created by the treaty achieve validity under international law. The legislative process of ratification, beginning with the treaty being sent to the *Bundesrat*, does not normally start in these cases before the federal government has asked for the consent of the *Länder* to be given. The position of the *Länder* is thus particularly strong in this field. The Lindau procedure ensures that any demands made by the *Länder* for the alteration of, or amendment to, the treaty text can be taken into account at a sufficiently early stage in the negotiations with the foreign power or international body concerned. As most of these cases concern cultural affairs (such as the mutual recognition of diplomas or other educational matters), a representative of the Secretariat of the Permanent Conference of (*Länder*) Ministers of Culture in Bonn almost always takes part in an advisory capacity in the deliberations of the Permanent Treaty Commission. The Commission then decides on an opinion to be conveyed to the federal ministry in charge. If the solution then reached by the federal ministry appears to be unsatisfactory to the Commission after further consultation by its members of the relevant departments of their respective governments, the original opinion or a modified version of it may need to be restated. In any event a final evaluation is given by the *Länder* through the Commission whenever the conclusion of the treaty is pending. The Commission then decides whether it should raise objections to the treaty being signed—if need be by the threat of non-ratification—or whether a recommendation for approval should be given to the *Länder* cabinets. As the suggestions of the Commission are in most cases taken on board by the federal government, a recommendation for approval is given in the overwhelming majority of cases. Although the recommendation of the Commission must be unanimous the *Länder* cabinets are, however, not bound to it. Despite this, there has only been one case out of a total of 2,201 draft treaties and other settlements reviewed in both categories of the Lindau Agreement between 16 July 1958 (when the Commission first met) and 1 January 1992 in which the consent of a *Land* cabinet was withheld after its representative in the Commission had contributed to a unanimous recommendation for approval.[19]

After all the *Länder* cabinets have conveyed their consent to the federal government, the formal process of ratification can begin, which means that the document of ratification may be deposited. The process of legislative approval of ratification (under Article 59, Paragraph 2 of the Basic Law) may also begin earlier and run in parallel to the Commission's deliberations. Normally, however, it does not do so, and in any case the process cannot be completed before proceedings are closed in the Commission and the consent of the *Länder* cabinets is granted.

Point 4 of the Lindau Agreement refers to treaties 'which touch upon the essential interests of the *Länder*' without necessarily being relevant to any of their exclusive competences. In cases of this type, the *Länder* must once again be informed 'as early as possible about the proposed conclusion of such treaties so that they can voice their demands in due time.' Although the procedure of communication between the Treaty Commission and the Federal Government is the same under Point 4 business as under Point 3, the position of the *Länder* is weaker under Point 4. Nevertheless, under the principle of federal comity the federal government is still obliged to take into account the opinion of the *Länder* and normally does so as far as it can in the course of negotiations.

The institutional structure of the Permanent Treaty Commission, set up according to Point 4, section 2 of the Lindau Agreement as 'an interlocutor for the Foreign Office or the otherwise competent departments of the federation', has proved to be an effective and succesful *practical* compromise in bridging the *legally* irreconcilable interpretations by federation and *Länder* of Article 32, Paragraph 3 of the Basic Law. There has thus been no reason to call in the Federal Constitutional Court to settle the dispute.

The Lindau Agreement was subsequently complemented by arrangements made in the so-called 'Kramer-Heubl Paper'[20] of 5 and 26 July 1968 (supplemented by detailed provisions set out on 31 October 1968) with regard to the participation of representatives of the *Länder* in foreign relations. These covered the following:

— the position and functions of representatives of the *Länder* in international negotiations of the federation 'including those in supranational organisations';
— the procedures for inclusion of such representatives;
— and the definition of cases in which such participation shall take place.

The Kramer-Heubl Paper is based on the principle that any representative of the *Länder* taking part in international negotiations of the federation has the position of a government representative of the Federal Republic, acting on a mandate of the federation, *vis-à-vis* the foreign partner. Its rules are highly complicated and in some parts the Paper is only able to state that federation and *Länder* 'agree to disagree'. Moreover, the Paper has become outdated in many respects. In particular, developments concerning the 'supranational organisations' mentioned above—the formerly distinct European Communities (Coal and Steel, Common Market and Atomic Energy) have meant that much of this Paper has only marginal relevance today. It does not need, therefore, to be discussed in depth.

Internal participation in European integration

In its place a whole range of institutions has been set up since the foundation of the EEC by both the *Bundesrat* and the *Länder* themselves concerning European Community business under the 'power of integration'. As was stressed above, Community matters can no longer be considered a part of foreign relations in the classic meaning of the term. The institutionalised European policy process within the framework of the EC has long since evolved into just another species of internal policy conducted on the supranational rather than the national level. There can hardly be any doubt that it will continue to do so within the increasingly state-like and federalised framework of the forthcoming European Union. For this reason it will be sufficient here to restrict the discussion of institutions and practice in this area to a few central points[21] and to point out the main differences which distinguish this field from that of *Länder* participation in 'classic' foreign relations. These differences relate to procedure and—following from the procedural aspect—organisation.

As has been shown, the central guideline of the operation of the Permanent Treaty Commission is that of unanimity. Up until the ratification of the Single European Act (SEA) in 1986, this was also the case in EC matters in so far as they were dealt with outside the *Bundesrat* structure in a complicated and increasingly unsatisfactory system of horizontal, so-called 'Third Level' coordination among the *Länder* in cooperation with the federation (known as the Maußer Procedure of 1977). The changes initiated by Article 2 of the Statute of Ratification of the SEA (as reproduced above) led, however, to the abolition of this system in favour of the complete incorporation of EC matters, including *Länder* coordination, into *Bundesrat* business. Since the *Bundesrat* is part of the 'Federal State' within the three levels of the federal–*Länder* relations (Whole State, Federal State and Third Level),[22] this meant that EC affairs were now wholly subject to majority-voting procedures irrespective of whether or not they impinge on exclusive *Länder* competences. This represents the essential difference in procedures in EC affairs compared to those in 'classic' foreign relations.

The organisational differences in the conduct of EC business follow on from this. The *Bundesrat* has now absorbed almost all the institutions of horizontal *Länder* coordination in EC matters. The only remaining Third Level institution in this area is the Permanent Observer of the *Länder* in Brussels, whose office was set up as early as 1957 by the *Länder* Conference of Economics Ministers, and who still reports to the *Länder* rather than the *Bundesrat*, in particular on meetings of the Council. His role as a liaison institution with the Commission has, however, been increasingly assumed by the liaison offices which the *Länder* have individually set up in Brussels since the initiation of procedures under Article 2 of the SEA Ratification Act in 1986–7.

Although EC matters have recently been incorporated increasingly into the sphere of *Bundesrat* business, it should not be assumed that there was no involvement of the *Bundesrat* in Community affairs prior to the SEA. The *Bundesrat* was, after all, the first of the two legislative chambers to institute a Committee for EC matters directly after the ratification of the Treaty of Rome in 1957. The *Bundestag* only followed suit as late as 1991.[23] The *Bundesrat* and its committee system consequently discussed no less than around 6,000 items of draft EC secondary legislation between 1957 and 1 January 1992.[24] The main purpose of the rules incorporated into federal law by Article 2 of the SEA Ratification Act was to enhance the weight of its comments on such draft legislation (although *Bundesrat* comments made under the terms of the Ratification Act of the Treaty of Rome had already begun to have a growing political impact).[25]

The SEA Act did, however, lead to the establishment of an entirely new institution in 1988. In order to secure its ability to react quickly and flexibly enough to proposed new EC legislation, the *Bundesrat* set up, by amendment to Standing Orders,[26] a so-called Chamber for European Community Matters, and empowered it to act on its behalf in cases of urgency and/or confidentiality. Doing so without simultaneously amending the constitution itself was legally contested at the time, but has not been challenged since.[27]

The most effective step taken in the SEA Act was, however, the inclusion as of right of *Länder* representatives appointed by the *Bundesrat* in the German delegations to working groups of the Council and Commission. This clearly marked the incorporation of *Länder* coordination concerning EC matters—normally undertaken outside the level of the federal state at the Third Level of direct horizontal cooperation—into *Bundesrat* business, i.e. into the level of the federal state. This measure has resulted in the membership of *Länder* representatives in more than 300 working groups of the Council of Ministers and Commission in Brussels.

Perspectives for reform

Proposals for the improvement of the positions of *Bundesrat* and *Länder* both in the field of foreign relations generally and in the area of European integration in particular are currently central topics in discussions on the amendment of the Basic Law. These began in the *Bundesrat*'s Commission on Constitutional Reform in April 1991 (concluded in May 1992) and were subsequently continued in the Joint Constitutional Commission of *Bundestag* and *Bundesrat*.[28] The deliberations of the Joint Commission on both the transfer of sovereign powers and the sharing of rights and functions in European affairs have been shaped mainly by the need to prepare the constitution for the amendments which will arise from the forthcoming Statute of Ratification of the Treaty on the European Union of 7 February 1992 (the so-called Maastricht Treaty).

Treaty-making

In the domain of 'classic' foreign relations (Article 32 of the Basic Law), the recommendations of the *Bundesrat* Commission to the Joint Commission focus on:

— stating the right of the *Länder* to cooperate with foreign states, regions

and other institutions without infringing on the conduct of foreign affairs by the federation;
— and incorporating the essentials of the Lindau Agreement into the constitution itself.[29]

This field had not yet been discussed in detail in the Joint Commission by the parliamentary summer recess of 1992. However, against the background of the long-established and essentially uncontroversial practice in this area, it can be expected that the debates to come before the conclusion of the Commission's work by 31 March 1993 will be characterised by general consensus.

Preparing the Basic Law for the European Union

In the field of the 'power of integration', however, the demands of the *Länder* not only for the consolidation of, but also for increases in, their rights of participation in European matters have aroused politically heated and legally intricate debates between 'federalists' and 'centralists', which have in part cut across party lines.

In the first months of its deliberations in the spring and summer of 1991, and at the risk of neglecting the already discernible implications of the emerging Treaty on European Union, the *Bundesrat* Commission had focused its reformist energies on the power of integration in Article 24 of the Basic Law. It aimed to secure:

— a requirement for the *Bundesrat*'s consent to any legislation transferring sovereign powers to the EC;
— a constitutional guarantee for *Bundesrat* and *Länder* participation in EC matters to secure a 'substantial influence' in areas of their own competence and of their 'essential interests';
— the right of the *Länder* to conduct their own relations with the EC, including the maintenance of missions of their own at EC institutions;
— the possibility for the *Länder* themselves to transfer their own sovereign rights to other international organisations and to institutions of interregional cooperation.[30]

The *Länder* only fully realised at the time of the establishment of the Joint Commission in January 1992—which coincided with the close of negotiations on the Maastricht Treaty—the potential constitutional impact of the Treaty. This would have far-reaching effects both in terms of the emerging federal structure of the forthcoming European Union and on the whole constitutional structure of the Federal Republic itself. Stimulated by a Lower Saxon initiative in autumn 1991,[31] the *Länder* now increasingly insisted that the Treaty on European Union and all its future alterations should, since they represent indirect amendments to the Basic Law, be subject to the same two-thirds majorities required in both *Bundestag* and *Bundesrat* for direct amendments to the constitution. This demand was justified by the fact, increasingly recognised not only by the *Länder* but by the parliamentary parties in the *Bundestag* too, that the European Union would have severe implications for both the federal and other fundamental values enshrined in the Basic Law. There exists a general consensus that both the emergence of a federalising European Union with a state-like structure and the definition of Germany's constitutional place within it will require legal safeguards. These are needed not only to underpin the Union's institutional development, but also to protect Germany's own triad of fundamental political values as laid down in the clause of non-amendability in Article 79, Paragraph 3 of the Basic Law: the protection of human rights, the democratic principle and the federal system.

In concrete terms this would mean that transfers of sovereign rights in the fields of both federal and *Länder* competence would require the *Bundesrat*'s consent by a two-thirds, not just an absolute, majority (similarly in the *Bundestag*). Following on from the Lower Saxon initiative mentioned above, the other SPD-governed *Länder*, along with the SPD *Fraktion* in the *Bundestag*, declared this to be an essential demand. The federal government, originally reluctant because of FDP and Foreign Office opposition, finally accepted this demand following pressure from the parliamentary *Fraktion* of the CDU and, in particular, from the Bavarian CSU and its State Cabinet in Munich.

The main controversy in the discussion of the constitutional reforms necessitated by the Maastricht Treaty centred, however, on the unanimous aim of the *Länder* to enhance their rights of participation in European secondary legislation in two ways.[32] Firstly and with regard to their influence on internal German policy-making prior to voting in the Council of Ministers, they insisted that *Bundesrat* comments should be 'decisive' and thus binding on the federal government in all matters which have their legal 'centre of gravity in the legislative competences of the *Länder*, in the establishment of any *Länder* authorities which might be required, or in their administrative procedures.' Secondly, and concerning negotiation and voting in the Council itself, the *Länder* demanded that 'the exercise of rights vested in the Federal Republic of Germany as a Member State of the European Union shall be transferred by a representative of the *Länder* nominated by the *Bundesrat* if the centre of gravity of the issue at stake concerns legislative competences of the *Länder*.'

In the latter area of acting directly in the Union's institutions, the *Länder* case was supported by Article 146 of the Maastricht Treaty, which now provides that 'the Council shall consist of a representative of each Member State at ministerial level, authorised to take binding decisions for the government of that Member State.'[33] This wording—amended with a clear view as to the demands of the German *Länder* and other comparable European regions—opens up the possibility for ministerial-level representation of the *Länder* in the Council, whereas before only national government members had been admitted.

The issue of the *Bundesrat*'s right to make 'decisive comment' in internal European policy-making procedures is, however, more controversial. The *Länder* have been confronted with a range of *political* accusations to the effect that they were trying to change the federation into a confederation. The *legal* disputes over this issue are thus likely to continue.

The political negotiations ended, however, with the federal government incorporating these central aims of the *Länder* into its own bill (partly modified by some compromise formulae which need not be discussed in detail here).[34] A point which ought to be made, though, is that the reason for all these controversies was in no way grounded in any hostility of the *Länder* to the Maastricht Treaty or even to the European Union as such (as has mistakenly been suggested in some foreign, especially British, quarters). On the contrary, the matter at stake was and remains a straightforward and even natural contest over power-sharing within a federal state which is itself growing into the *fully accepted*, new, federal structure emerging above it.

The awareness and the acceptance of this process has reached such a level that a new article of the Basic Law devoted to the European Union is to be created. It will 'house' in particular provisions in the field of federal-*Länder* relations as discussed above. But it will also contain German policy aims for the democratisation and federalisation of the Union as well as safeguards for the Basic Law's fundamental values against European encroachment. The location of this article will be the same—Article 23—as the provision which legally paved the way for German unity and which had to be deleted after its achievement. The new Article 23 will now, it is to be hoped, pave the constitutional way for European unification.

Article 24, which has been the *sedis materiae* of the power of integration up to now, will remain so, but only with respect to the transfer of sovereign functions to international bodies other than the European Union (since the latter is ever less an international body as such, and ever more a state-like structure). Within this narrower scope of Article 24, the details of federal–*Länder* power-sharing still remain to be discussed. However, it has already been decided in principle that the revised Article 24 will contain a clause entitling the *Länder*, too, to transfer sovereign rights of their own to bodies of interregional, cross-frontier cooperation in neighbouring foreign states.[35]

A Europe with, rather than of, the Regions

The latter point is not directly concerned with the much-mentioned but little-understood concept of a 'Europe of the Regions', which can only be dealt with briefly here.[36] An especially significant development in this respect, located outside the constitutional framework of the Federal Republic, is the new Regional Committee established by Articles 198a–198c of the Treaty on European Union. The Regional Committee will have a decisive impact on the (external) role of the *Länder* in the future development of European integration. However, while the process of integration, in most of its aspects, is no longer part of the realm of foreign relations, the question of federalisation, especially the regional concept, still needs to be clarified. In particular, the misunderstandable notion of a 'Europe *of* the Regions' should be replaced by the aim of a 'Europe *with* the Regions' since the latter offers a clearer indication of what is required. The eventual dispersal of foreign relations within a unified Europe cannot sensibly be equated with the dissolution of the national Member States into their regional sub-units. This would merely lead to an extreme centralisation at the European level by virtue of the myriad opportunities for a 'divide and rule' strategy which would exist with such a large number of units. Instead a regionalisation of the Member States undertaken *together with* a federalisation of the relations between the Member States would produce a doubly federalised structure, in which autonomous rights in external relations would be far better protected than in any centralised system.

To sum up on both power-sharing in treaty-making and regional participation in European affairs, it is worth recalling Bismarck's maxim when outlining his philosophy of federalism in 1869, shortly before the creation of the 1871 federation. In the *Reichstag* of the North German Confederation he suggested that the centre should not have more power 'than is absolutely necessary for the cohesion of the whole and for the effect presented to the outside.'[37]

Notes

1 For details see K. Reuter, *Praxishandbuch Bundesrat*, C.F. Müller Juristischer Verlag, Heidelberg (1991), 51–60.
2 Gesetze zur Gleichschaltung der Länder mit dem Reich, 31 March 1933 and 7 April 1933, *Reichsgesetzblatt*, I, 153, 173; Gesetz über den Neuaufbau des Reichs, 30 January 1934, *Reichsgesetzblatt*, I, 89.
3 Gesetz, betreffend die Verfassung des Deutschen Reichs (*BGBl des Deutschen Bundes*, no. 16, 63); reprinted in H. Triepel, *Quellensammlung zum Deutschen Reichsstaatsrecht*, Verlag C.L. Hirschfeld, Leipzig (1901), 1–20.
4 Triepel, op. cit., 6.
5 Verfassung des Deutschen Reichs, *Reichsgesetzblatt*, 1388. Reprinted in G. Anschütz, *Die Verfassung des Deutschen Reichs*, 8th edn, Verlag Georg Stilke, Berlin (1928).
6 G. Anschütz, op. cit., 235–41.
7 Grundgesetz für die Bundesrepublik Deutschland, *Bundesgesetzblatt*, 1. An English

translation as amended up to 23 September 1990 is available in: Press and Information Office at the Federal Government (ed.), *Basic Law of the Federal Republic of Germany*, Press and Information Office of the Federal Government, Bonn (1991).

8 Described in detail in Maunz-Dürig, *Kommentar zum Grundgesetz*, Art. 32 RdNrn. 29–41, 9–17.

9 Verständigung zwischen der Bundesregierung und den Staatskanzleien der Länder über das Vertragsschliessungsrecht des Bundes, in ibid., Art. 32 RdNr. 45, 9–17. See further ibid., Art. 32, 1–2; C. Hirsch, *Kulturhoheit und auswärtige Gewalt*, Duncker & Humblot, Berlin (1968); W. Busch, *Die Lindauer Vereinbarung und die Ständige Vertragskommission der Länder*, dissertation, University of Tübingen (1969).

10 Cf. Maunz-Dürig, op. cit., Art. 32 RdNrn. 32–34, 10–13.

11 Bundesverfassungsgericht, *Amtliche Entscheidungssammlung* (BVerfGE), 2, 266.

12 BVerfGE, 1, 299 (315); 4, 115 (141).

13 H. Blanke, *Föderalismus und Integrationsgewalt*, Duncker & Humblot, Berlin (1991), especially 227ff.

14 K. Reuter, op. cit., 635.

15 See R. Hrbek, 'German federalism and the challenge of European integration', in C. Jeffery and P. Savigear (eds), *German Federalism Today*, Leicester University Press, Leicester/London (1991), 88–92.

16 Gesetz zur Einheitlichen Europäischen Akte vom 19. Dezember 1986, *Bundesgesetzblatt* vol. II (1986), 1102.

17 Reproduced in Bundesrat (ed.), *Handbuch des Bundesrates für das Geschäftsjahr 1991/92*, C.H. Becksche Verlagsbuchhandlung, Munich (1991), 157–61.

18 ibid., 117–21.

19 This case concerned the Bavarian government's refusal to consent to the European Agreement on Violence and Misbehaviour of Spectators at Sports Events of 19 August 1985, which the Treaty Commission had recommended, after hesitation by the Bavarian representative, for approval on 18 September 1985. On 3 December 1985 the Bavarian Cabinet then declared that the proposed measures could and should be taken without the Agreement and that the administrative effort caused by it would, therefore, not be justifiable. The Agreement was consequently not presented to the *Bundesrat* for legislative approval of ratification.

20 Named after the then Plenipotentiaries of Hamburg (Senator Kramer) and Bavaria (Minister Heubl) in Bonn, who had negotiated the agreement with the federation on behalf of the *Länder*.

21 For further details see Hrbek, op. cit.

22 See U. Leonardy, *Working Structures of Federalism in Germany: At the Crossroads of German and European Unification, Centre for Federal Studies Research Papers in Federalism No. 1*, Centre for Federal Studies, Leicester (1992); U. Leonardy, 'The working relationships between *Bund* and *Länder* in the Federal Republic of Germany', in C. Jeffery and P. Savigear, op. cit., 40–62.

23 On the need to establish such a committee, see U. Leonardy, 'Bundestag und Europäische Gemeinschaft: Notwendigkeit und Umfeld eines Europa-Ausschusses', *Zeitschrift für Parlamentsfragen* (1989), 527–44.

24 5,572 by the end of 1990. See Bundesrat, op. cit., 287.

25 Article 2 of that Act, passed on 27 July 1957 (*Bundesgesetzblatt* (1957), II, 755), gave both *Bundestag* and *Bundesrat* the right to be informed regularly by the federal government 'on developments in the Council' of the European Economic and Atomic Communities.

26 §§ 45b–45h. See Bundesrat, op. cit., 119–21.

27 Current proposals in the Joint Constitutional Commission of *Bundestag* and *Bundesrat* are directed at anchoring the Chamber in Article 52 of the Basic Law.

28 For further details on the establishment and functions of both Commissions, see U. Leonardy, *Working Structures*, op. cit., 32ff.

29 Kommission Verfassungsreform Bundesrat, *Kommissions-Drucksache*, 12 (neu) (18 March 1992).

30 Kommission Verfassungsreform Bundesrat, *Kommissions-Drucksache*, 5 (7 October 1991).

31 Even before the Maastricht Treaty had arrived on the political agenda, Lower Saxony had organised a podium discussion in the State's Mission in Bonn on 'The Basic Law and the European Community—Do we Have to Adapt our Constitution?' on 3 October 1989. The debate was unfortunately not published, but a verbatim transcript is available from the Mission.

32 Gemeinsame Verfassungskommission, *Kommissions-Drucksache*, 7 (neu) (26 June 1992), as adopted by the Joint Commission on that date on the basis of the rapporteurs' recommendations on the topic 'The Basic Law and Europe' of 24 June 1992 (which were the result of lengthy negotiations between the *Länder*, the federal government and the parties in the *Bundestag*).

33 *Treaty on the European Union*, Office for Official Publications of the European Communities, Luxembourg (1992), 64.

34 Accepted by the Federal Cabinet on 21 July 1992. The text of the bill is identical to that approved by the Joint Commission. See ibid.

35 Such cooperation has hitherto only been possible on the basis of treaties concluded under the rules of the European Framework Agreement on Cross-Frontier Cooperation between Territorial Authorities of 21 May 1980. See BVerfGE 2, 369 on the treaty-making power of the *Länder* concerning administrative matters within their own competence.

36 For further details see U. Leonardy, *Working Structures*, op. cit.

37 Speech of 16 April 1869 reproduced in H. Kohl (ed.), *Die politischen Reden des Fürsten Bismarck*, vol. 4, 1868–1870 (1893), cited in Blanke, op. cit., 383.

The United States and the European Single Market: federalism and diplomacy in a changing political economy

15

Michael Smith

The construction of the European Community's Single Market Programme (SMP) has given rise to considerable debate in the Community and its member countries about the nature of federalism and the extent to which this can be married with the demands of markets both within the EC and more globally. It seems clear that the SMP and the subsequent Maastricht agreements of 1991 embody a form of 'federalism' which is at least mixed, and which is distinct from the classical models of the genre.[1] The Community of the 1990s and the next century will thus bring together elements of aggregation and disaggregation, integration and devolution, which guarantee a continuing state of tension, creative or otherwise.

The purpose of this study, though, is not to examine the SMP and the development of the Community as ends in themselves. Rather, it is to focus on the problems faced by those who have to deal with the Community, and who desire to gain access to, or to influence the process of policy-making within the EC. In particular, the study will explore the issues that arise when a federal system—the United States—attempts to deal with the complex and multilayered evolution of the European Single Market, and to gain a purchase on the distinctively European form of diffusion and aggregation of power. Just as in the case of the EC, the United States has seen recent debate about the nature of the federal system and the federal process, but it is clear that the departure point for the discussion is different on the two sides of the Atlantic. At the same time, the changing nature and impact of the global political economy has formed a significant factor in both the European and the American debates. As a result, the American federal system confronts the EC and the SMP in the context of a changing—some would say transformed—policy agenda.[2]

The main part of this essay will thus explore the ways in which the US federal system and policy process has approached the SMP, in the framework of a changing political economy. The argument is essentially twofold. In the first place, the traditional agenda of US policies towards the Community has been supplemented by a new agenda arising partly from the development of the US and EC political economies, and the coexistence of these two agendas raises new problems for policy-making and implementation. In the second place, the traditional diplomacy of American policies towards the Community has been supplemented by a new diplomacy which gives an enhanced standing and role to institutions and actors outside the Washington establishment. To put it simply, the interaction of a changing political economy and policy agenda with the internal structures of the American federal state raises important questions about the development of policy-making and diplomacy in federal systems. The Single Market Programme provides an explicit and concentrated test of the issues. Whilst the study does not attempt to resolve the questions thus raised, it does try to sharpen them and define an agenda for further investigation.

The traditional agenda of US–EC relations

The European Community has posed a challenge for US policy-making and diplomacy from the outset. Although it is possible to view the EC as essentially a product of US hegemony as applied within Cold War Europe, this version ignores or downgrades much of the complexity which has always attended US–EC relations. Both the European Coal and Steel Community and the subsequent European Economic Community expressed challenges to American policy as well as the working out of the post-war (US-dominated) order. As the 1960s and 1970s unfolded, the points of pressure and tension between the transatlantic 'partners' became more apparent, and many of those areas of tension remain in the 1990s.[3] Essentially, the traditional agenda surrounding these issues can be seen as threefold: trade policy, industrial policy and high technology. Each of these areas has seen and continues to see characteristic tensions and forms of interaction.

Perhaps the most enduring and irritating focus of US–EC tensions has been that of trade policy. At the outset, the Community required what many Americans could and do see as an act of self-sacrifice: the acceptance of discrimination at a regional level through the customs union and the Common External Tariff (CET). Acceptance of this deviation from multilateralism was facilitated by the surrounding context of the Cold War and alliance politics, and by the perception that the growth of a large European market could work to the advantage of US multinationals. Since the mid-1960s, though, there has been a litany of US complaints against the Community, arising partly from purely external trade practices and partly from the external consequences of the Community's internal development, such as the implementation of the Common Agricultural Policy (CAP).[4]

From the point of view of this study, the trade policy agenda in US–EC relations has possessed a number of key features. First, it has existed within the broad multilateral framework established during the immediate post-war years and reinforced by successive rounds of GATT negotiations. Second, within both the United States and the Community, trade policies have generated a good deal of legislative attention and activity; they have not only been matters for a technical policy élite, they have also involved legislators, lobbies and lawyers on a large scale. Third, the trade policy framework has not only been a means of handling trade issues and trade disputes; it has also been imbued with a broader and symbolic political significance within the context of the Cold War and US political economy. Although the United States and the Community have frequently come to blows, the tensions have been within an understood set of conventions and expectations.[5]

Alongside the trade policy agenda, there has arisen a set of issues relating to industrial policies in both the United States and the EC. The established version of these industrial policy issues is simply summarised: the Community has increasingly come to pose a threat to an ailing United States because of the vigour of its presence in the industrial policy field. Many Americans would also add the fact that EC industrial policies rely heavily upon intervention and subsidies which feed through into unfair trade policies. As a result, since the early 1970s, there has been a set of US–EC tensions focused on the attainment of industrial competitiveness and the defence of entrenched industrial positions. Good examples of this conflict-zone can be found in the steel industry, which has been a constant source of US–EC friction since the late 1960s, and which in the US case has led to a series of legal actions against either the Community or EC producers.[6] The incidence of industrial nationalism, of intervention and protectionism has been seen by the Americans as a constant feature of EC policies, although the harshness of their judgements has been conditioned by the prevailing state of the American economy. As with trade policies more strictly defined, though, the conflicts have been kept within bounds for much of the history of US–EC relations.[7]

Linked to both trade and industrial policies has been a third area of US–EC friction: that of high-technology policies. The establishment of the Community was accompanied by the hope that it would form a framework for the emergence of new high-technology industries, which would benefit from the economies of scale and the technological dynamism generated through the growth of the Community more generally. Interestingly, for much of the early history of the EC, the beneficiaries of the growing market were often US high-technology companies, led by the likes of IBM. It was apparent that the 'infant industries' of the Community would need additional help, and this led to programmes both at the Community and at the national level. One of the earliest such programmes was that for the development of the European Airbus, which has been a thorn in the flesh of the United States ever since. Later initiatives such as those in information technology (ESPRIT) and communications technology (RACE) caused additional frictions. In some ways, the issues raised were akin to those in the broader industrial policy area, but there were some particular features of the high-technology disputes between the United States and the Community—not least the fact that they raised important issues of national security and national prestige which could surface at times of international tension.[8]

This necessarily brief discussion of some aspects of US–EC relations in areas of traditional dispute has identified a number of salient features. One of the most important is the role played by context: the existence of the multilateral framework and the Cold War has been vital to the course of US–EC trade and industrial relations. Another is the way in which the Community has challenged US predominance in a number of sensitive industrial and commercial areas, but without fundamentally challenging the broader framework: indeed, the broader framework can be seen as an important support to the EC challenge in many instances. Finally, and perhaps most important for this essay, the focus on national policy measures and on competition at the level of governmental authorities has been a central feature. It is from this that there emerged a characteristic form of US–EC diplomacy, and thus of US policy-making on EC issues, during the 1960s and 1970s.

The diplomatic process

The diplomatic process through which US–EC relations have been handled for much of their history can be characterised by three central qualities: intergovernmentalism, institutionalism and the downgrading of subregional interests. The typical image of the transatlantic relationship on matters arising from the traditional agenda has been a form of intercontinental interaction, with Brussels and Washington cast in the roles of partners or rivals. How far this image ever really expressed the whole of the relationship is clearly open to question, but it is important to explore its implications for US diplomacy.

The first central feature of US–EC diplomacy as practised in the United States has been intergovernmentalism. In other words, the US federal government has been given or has taken the responsibility for aggregating and representing the interests of those Americans attempting to influence the Community or being affected by it. In a way, this is the natural outcome of the traditional agenda as described earlier: the focus on trade policy issues and the trade policy framework meant that the main arena for debate and the framing of actions would be Washington. To be sure, this meant not only successive administrations but also the Congress. The constant congressional sniping at trade policy-makers from the very outset of US–EC relations is a notable feature of the United States' EC policy process, but it was very much contained within the federal framework. To be sure also, the restructuring of trade policy responsibilities played a significant role in the US approach to the GATT and the Community in the GATT context: when trade agreements passed out of the ambit of the State Department to the office of the US Trade Representative (USTR) during the 1960s, this reflected not only a recognition of the importance of such agreements in themselves, but also a move in the broader institutional process within the federal government. But the focus was Washington, the specialists and the special interests were concentrated there and this continued to be the case into the 1980s. Where industrial or high-technology issues were at stake, the policy process was little different: Washington was where redress could be sought and influence exercised. Thus the steel industry complaints against the Community were and are handled through the federal trade policy machinery, and the semiconductor lobbyists are to be found assiduously working the Hill.[9]

The intergovernmentalism of the policy process extended to the implementation of trade and industrial policies. The US negotiators in the GATT were and are federal officials, with the addition of some industry representatives. The role of USTR in combating the EC's industrial policy misdemeanours is central, alongside that of the International Trade Commission. Successive agreements to regulate the disputes in such areas as steel, the Airbus or semiconductors have been reached through essentially governmental negotiations, influenced but not pervaded by the industrial or sometimes the regional lobbies.[10]

Alongside this focus on intergovernmentalism, there has gone a strong focus on the primacy of the multilateral framework in the handling of US–EC relations. As already noted, this has the status of a symbolic or even an ideological commitment, to which both the US government and the Brussels Commission pay obeisance. Although there are breaches of specific rules and conventions, the purpose of the framework is not only to express the commitment in general but also to provide general mechanisms of dispute settlement. There is, in short, a strategic commitment to multilateralism, and this has operated from the outset of US–EC relations despite challenges within the US political system or from US industry. In this context, the calculation of gains and losses from the relationship with the Community has been not only in terms of material exchange, but also and often more persuasively in terms of continuing adherence to the multilateral ideal. The supporters of multilateralism within the federal government, centred on the USTR and the State Department, have always been able to rely on the power of their ultimate appeal to the open world economy, in the face of challenges from others in the Treasury or Commerce.[11]

Finally, the traditional approach to issues in US–EC relations has expressed a downgrading of subregional interests. In a way, this is simply the other side of the focus on intergovernmentalism already noted, but it is important to highlight it here. The federal government is seen as aggregative and as representing the interests of all regions within the United States for the purposes of US–EC relations. Clearly, there are issues with a strong regional flavour such as agriculture or steel, which will colour the responses of government at the federal level. But as already noted, the federal level is what counts. It is there that the negotiating mandates are decided, there that the legislative and other outcomes are ratified, and there that the diplomatic relations are conducted. The clear sectoral and other variations in policy-making and implementation reflect not so much regional or state influences as the nature of the issues, not so much the spatial dimension as the pulling and hauling within and between branches of the federal government.

Presented thus, the essence of US–EC relations appears to be firmly within the tradition of the 'federative power', with the federal authorities clearly and wholly responsible for the formulation and the conduct of policy. But it is questionable whether this has ever been the whole story: there have always been important private and regional contacts between Americans and the Community, at the level of Brussels and national governments as well as purely private or commercial transactions. There has always been an important link between the development of the Community and the activities of US corporate concerns, particularly in the area of foreign direct investment (FDI). There has always been an awareness in the United States of the ways in which the multilayered character of the EC can be exploited as a means of increasing access or leverage.[12] The argument in this essay, though, is that the Single Market Programme in the context of the world economy of the 1990s provides both a transformed agenda and a transformed policy process to produce a new diplomacy. This is the focus of the next two sections.

The new agenda of US–EC relations

The new agenda in US–EC relations is the product of a combination of factors. First, in terms of the argument in this study, there is the SMP itself. This has brought on to the international agenda a number of sectors and issues that were previously insulated from international attention, either because of their inherent characteristics or because of conscious policy choices on the part of governments or other groupings. It has also promised to make the EC a more potent competitor for American industry and commerce in a wide range of sectors. In this way, the SMP has intersected with the often intense debate in the United States itself about the achievement of competitiveness and the maintenance of effective regulation in a global economy—a debate which has raised important issues of governance in a federal system. But this in its turn cannot be separated from the changing nature of the world economy: this has produced interdependence and interpenetration at levels unprecedented in the development of the international system, to the extent that according to some interpretations there is no such thing as a national economy in the typical advanced industrial society. Linked to this change in the world economy, there is a series of challenges to the multilateral framework and to international institutions, which have also been affected by change in the world political order, particularly in Europe. Although the SMP has acted as a catalyst for changes in US policy-making and diplomacy, it cannot be divorced from these other contextual factors.[13]

The first area of challenge posed by the SMP is that of *market access*. As already noted, one of the ways in which the SMP was conceived within the EC was as a lever to provide more strength for the Community and its exporters; this concept was broadly defined, to include not only exporters of goods but also the providers of services and potential direct investors. To put it very simply, the SMP could be seen as a source of influence over others (particularly the United States and Japan) whose markets were the target of European activity. The ways in which this influence could be achieved were several: the promotion of access through multilateral negotiations, the use of reciprocity provisions in specific sectors, the offering of rewards for good behaviour, including 'honorary European' status, in the case of specific 'outsider' enterprises. In general, these aims were expressed in terms of the promotion of openness and multilateralism, particularly related to the Uruguay Round of GATT negotiations.[14]

None the less, the SMP approach to market access has posed a number of problems for US industries, and a number of these are closely linked to the nature of US federalism. In the first place, it was far from clear in the early days of the SMP that the United States was in a position to respond to demands for access and reciprocity. As an example, the EC's Draft Second Banking Directive is perhaps the most striking. In this instance, the Directive offered a version of reciprocity which challenged the essentially state-based banking system of the United States, by apparently offering access to the EC market only in so far as access could be offered in the United States. Coming at a time of intense concern in the United States itself about the financial services industries, the Directive made a considerable impact. At the federal level, the Department of the Treasury was prominent in expressing its opposition, and the atmosphere was confrontational for several months during 1988 and 1989. But it was also notable that the debate about the Directive interacted with congressional and other debates about the future of the US banking system. Thus, leaders of the banking industry were to be found attempting to prod congress and state authorities into modifying the US system, on the basis that otherwise Americans could not compete with the Community.[15] It was apparent that, in important ways, the federal system inhibited the United States' ability to respond quickly and effectively, and this perception has influenced subsequent debate not only in banking but in other service sectors.

Another area in which the SMP has connected with 'domestic' concerns in the United States has been that of *competitiveness*. This is not the place to rehearse the extensive discussion in the literature and the political arena of the ways in which the United States might restore its international economic muscle, but it is important to note that many of the central elements in the debate concern the federal system. The notion espoused by Fred Bergsten and others of 'competitive interdependence', and the related discussion of regional competitive advantage, have not only raised questions about the ways in which state-based and federal programmes can be brought into coordination; they have also intersected with concern about the competitive advantages conferred on Europe by the SMP.[16] It has been apparent that the impact of this factor is differential: state authorities have often been more aware of competitive opportunities, and better able to respond quickly, than the federal government. Defensiveness at the federal level has often been contrasted with promotional and entrepreneurial behaviour at the regional or the local level. Calls for 'industrial policy' at the federal level have often missed the point that state governments with specific sectoral concerns have been able to penetrate the Community and establish fruitful relationships both in terms of exporting and outward investment and in terms of attracting investment from EC concerns.[17] At times also, this has strongly conditioned state orientations towards US trade policies, which continue to be legislated at the federal level while having important regional and state-level impacts.

An issue closely connected with the intersection between the SMP and US competitiveness policies is that of *regulatory policy*. One of the key elements in the SMP is the attempt to approximate regulatory structures and regulatory standards in the large market. Here again, as in the case of market access more generally, there are important points of contact with the US federal system. The question of technical standards and certification procedures has attracted considerable attention, partly because the US system is decentralised, relying on industry mechanisms and on state-based regulation. Linked to this is the vexed question of public procurement, where the SMP promises (or threatens) to establish Community-wide procedures for bids to public authorities, even in the so-called 'excluded sec-

tors' of public utilities. The Community's provisions are based in considerable measure on the mechanisms in place within the United States, with the
crucial difference that many of the US procedures are established and
applied at state level. The so-called 'buy American' legislation, giving
preferential terms to US suppliers, is thus not within the domain of US
federal authorities, and this has caused a number of significant frictions as
the Community has attempted to lever open American bid procedures.[18]
This is an area of distinct ambiguity both within the Community and the
United States, but it clearly raises questions for further investigation given
the importance of 'competition between rules' in the emerging global
economy.

The discussion so far indicates that the emerging agenda for US economic
policies in the 1990s has been focused at several points by the impact of the
SMP. Another area of sensitivity, and one which brings together a number
of strands, is that of *national security*. In the United States, there has been
increasing attention to the linkage between economic and technological
competitiveness and national security; indeed, one feature of the debate has
been the way in which the label 'national security' has been attached to
industries or sectors in which there is perceived to be a competitive challenge either from the EC or from Japan. One central characteristic of the
national security domain, as traditionally conceived, is its concentration at
the federal level, with the undisputed pre-eminence of the Executuve
Branch and of the Pentagon. But it has become increasingly apparent that
national security policy has major industrial and employment implications
at the regional or the state level. As a result, the debate has increasingly
involved local and state authorities in areas traditionally the preserve of
federal authorities. The SMP has in part fed this debate, although it would
be wrong to overstate its impact. The potential development of Community
policies for the defence industries, added to the existing EC intervention in
high technology, bears the seeds of further tensions, especially given the
shrinkage in the US defence procurement field as a result of the 'peace
dividend'.[19]

Much of what has been said so far indicates that the 'new agenda' of
US–EC relations in the context of the SMP reflects the impact of *economic
interpenetration* on the global scale. As a result of the increasing linkage
between economies in the industrial world, there has arisen a high degree of
market and technological interdependence, which at times means that it is
difficult to discern the boundaries of so-called 'national' economies. From
the point of view of the SMP, an interesting example is furnished by the
automotive industries. Because of the pressure to equalise competitive conditions in the Community, it has been necessary to bring together the widely
varying national approaches to trade in cars and components, in particular
where Japan is involved. The problem is that given the growth of interpenetration, this is not simply an EC–Japan problem. One of the most in-

triguing results has been a growing attention to the treatment of production by Japanese 'transplants' in the United States; as a result, the US federal authorities have become involved, but so also have state authorities in Ohio, Tennessee and elsewhere.[20]

In this context, it is significant that the consequent growth of policy interdependence has become connected to fundamental changes in political structures in the EC, but not in the United States. Two difficulties follow. First, it is increasingly difficult to see how the costs and benefits of economic policies can be aggregated at the national level, and this has led to an increasing focus on regional or subregional authorities. In the US case, this is sensitive terrain, given the broader issues attending the development of federal–state relations; whilst in the EC the debate has been accommodated within a broader reappraisal of the macroeconomic and political structures, partly prompted by radical political change in the 'new Europe' since 1989, the Americans have not yet reached that point. Some might argue in the context of the early 1990s that this American reluctance to engage in fundamental structural debate is a good thing, but it is clearly an important distinction which means that the breadth of the agenda is different in the EC from that in the United States. The second consequence is linked to the first: the difficulty of representing the increasing range of regional, subnational and sectoral actors with interests demanding attention at the international level. We have seen that the role of the federal government and particularly that of the USTR is pivotal, given the traditional concentration of legislative and diplomatic capacity at the federal level. But the SMP, as a symptom of broader economic change, challenges such a comfortable conception of the diplomatic function.[21] This leads to consideration of the 'new diplomacy' which has emerged in the handling of US–EC relations.

Towards a new diplomacy?

Much of what can be said about the emergence of a 'new diplomacy' in US–EC relations is implicit in the preceding discussion of the new agenda. It should therefore not be necessary here to reiterate the issues attaching to market access, to competitiveness, to regulatory policy, to national security, and to the growth of interpenetration. It is also important once again to underline the fact that the SMP has acted as a catalyst and a focus as much as an independent variable in this process of change. The focus here will thus be on four aspects of diplomacy broadly defined, which carry important implications for the evolution of American federalism in the 1990s. These are: the proliferation of diplomatic and quasi-diplomatic channels; the contrast between 'strategic' and 'tactical' diplomacy; the importance of sectoral issues; and the position of domestic federalism as a stake in diplomacy at the international level.

A first characteristic of the new diplomacy is a rapid growth in the range of channels available for interaction between the United States and the EC. One of the tenets of theories of 'complex interdependence' is the proliferation of channels for interaction between societies, and the US–EC relationship can be seen as one of the most highly developed examples of this phenomenon. But the situation is given an additional twist by the existence in the United States of a federal structure with an explicit division of powers between the centre and the state level. It has already been noted that this creates difficulties of representation. What should be added here is that in the case of the EC, there has been a quite spectacular growth of American state-level representation within the Community. Whilst this representation is to be found in several Community member states, there is evidence that the need to influence events in Brussels has become an increasing factor in the location of state missions. There has grown up a process of lobbying by state representatives in the EC, and perhaps as significantly, of lobbying by the EC representatives in the United States at state level. Whilst this has not supplanted the activities of federal authorities or of industry associations, the map of US–EC diplomatic contacts has been materially redrawn during the past decade. The implications for federal–state relationships in the United States itself are still unclear, but the *domaine réservé* of international trade and financial policies has at least been questioned.[22]

The second aspect of new diplomacy is the increased salience of the distinction between 'strategic' and 'tactical' diplomacy. In a sense, this distinction has always been a feature of US–EC relations: at the same time as the multilateral system has been an object of negotiation in the GATT, there have been important disputes and diplomatic processes taking place within the framework, often with subtle connections to the structural level. What appears to be happening now is that the proliferation of state-level contacts between the United States and the Community has introduced a new factor into the linkage between the strategic and the tactical. Whilst the federal government dominates at the level of the strategic framework, it is clear that state authorities, often associated with clusters of industrial partners, have a significant input into the tactical level. On issues such as the European Airbus, the beef hormones dispute, or the promotion of inward investment, it is not always to be taken for granted that the federal government has the best information or the capacity to respond on a day-to-day basis. Those with more effective regional awareness and sensitivity to nuance may be the best equipped. The SMP, and the associated moves towards the promotion of regional or trans-European networks in a number of areas, may well enhance this embryonic division of diplomatic labour; but if they do, the issue of aggregation and representation is likely to become particularly sensitive for the United States.[23]

The foregoing implies that alongside the distinction between strategic and tactical diplomacy, US policies towards the SMP and the evolving EC underline the distinction between 'high politics' and 'sectoral politics'. The sectoral specialisation of many US states, and the explicitly sectoral orientation of many EC policies, means that the salience of relations at the federal or Community level may be altering. The inherently multilevel nature of many sectoral issues, and the need for management of the interactions between public and private bodies, may mean that the appropriate mechanisms for US diplomacy are no longer those of the Washington bureaucracy. In addition, the ability of the federal trade policy machinery to legislate in such a way as to provide the basis for coherent diplomacy may also be changing; in voting on the 'fast track' authority for GATT negotiations, there have been distinct fault-lines between northern/eastern and southern/western groupings. What this means when it comes to the practice of trade diplomacy is still unclear, but the questions raised are none the less significant.[24]

Finally, it is apparent that the SMP has focused attention on the ways in which domestic federalism can become a stake in diplomacy. It was noted earlier that such measures as the Draft Second Banking Directive not only aroused debate about the challenge to US interests, but also enabled participants to get on to the agenda discussion of the federal banking structure itself. In the same way, the US–EC interaction in matters of standards or public procurement has raised the question of federal–state linkages by making these a part of the transatlantic discourse. One interesting subplot in this area concerns the issue of representation and voting rights in international bodies, where it is often the case that EC members are separately represented whilst adhering to common policies and positions. Thus, in the International Standards Organisation, it has been noted by Americans that the EC effectively has twelve votes. Whilst the significance of this kind of argument can be exaggerated, it is apparent that representation is a potential problem of international as it is of interstate diplomacy for the United States. The coexistence of competences at the federal and state level in the United States also raises issues of implementation: even if the United States and the Community can agree on issues in such areas as public procurement, can the Americans guarantee implementation, given the role of state bodies who might not accept the agreements reached at the strategic level?

Conclusion

As noted at the beginning of this chapter, the conclusions take the form of questions rather than answers. The argument has centred on the growth of a new policy agenda and a new diplomacy in US–EC relations: a process which has been focused and partly driven, but not created by the Single Market Programme. It has also been argued that this process intersects with and reinforces a number of characteristics in contemporary US federalism. As a result, that federalism itself has become both a stake and an issue in the diplomacy of US–EC relations, focusing questions of aggregation, representation, coordination and implementation. Having explored these areas, albeit in a preliminary way, what further questions demand attention in the next phase of investigation?

One important issue relates to the *scale of diplomacy*. It has been noted here that the perception of costs, benefits, interests and influence varies at different levels of the federal system, and that the SMP focuses this in certain sensitive areas. By doing so, it raises the broad question of the 'politics of scale', and the decision to participate in or defect from federal government diplomacy.[25] The ability of the federal government to aggregate, and the pressures for disaggregation of the diplomatic effort, form a potentially fruitful area for further investigation.

A second question concerns the *style of diplomacy*. In a number of areas, it has been apparent that the ways in which diplomacy towards the EC and the SMP has been conducted depend upon who is conducting it. One of the key elements here is the extent to which diplomacy is politicised and symbolic as opposed to 'quiet' and technical. The pressure is clearly on the federal government to play the political game and to focus on issues of high principle, often for less than noble reasons, but state authorities do not have the same imperatives; in addition, their links to strategic clusters of industries may dictate a policy of quiet diplomacy rather than a political stance. It is not clear to what extent this is a pervasive and tangible distinction, but that in itself makes the case for further enquiry.

A third area for investigation is the *direction and targets of diplomacy*. This essay has pointed out the ways in which diverse channels and levels of diplomatic activity are central to the US–EC relationship. In order to take this general point further, it is important to focus on two central characteristics. First, research can ask pertinent questions about processes of 'internalisation' and 'externalisation': that is to say, about the ways in which aspects of domestic federalism become items on the international agenda, and on ways in which items on the international agenda become injected into the dialogue of domestic federalism. By looking at these relationships in specific sectors or issue areas, it should be possible to say something interesting about the processes of economic and political interpenetration touched on in this essay.

Finally, it is important to deal with questions of *articulation and aggregation*. In other words, the argument here has suggested that the expression of interests and their collective pursuit is not a process to be taken for granted in US–EC relations. The linkages between policy arenas and between items on the agenda have changed and are changing, and it is clear that the calculus of policy formulation has to be reassessed in this light. The assumption that the 'federative power' is sufficient to express the needs of American citizens and enterprises in the international economy has never been more than a handy metaphor; in dealing with the Community, it is often positively misleading. By exploring the mechanisms of articulation and aggregation in particular issues areas or in relation to particular federal–state relationships, research can identify significant variations and relate them to policy outcomes.

What is clear on the basis of the argument here is that the relationship between US federal and state authorities is challenged by the process of US–EC relations, and that this has important implications for domestic and international policy making. This essay has only begun to suggest what these implications might be, but it has hopefully highlighted the variety and dynamism of the processes involved, as well as their connection to broader issues of the world political economy.

Notes

1. For an excellent review of the comparative federalist dimension, see Alberta M. Sbragia, 'Thinking about the European future: the uses of comparison', in Alberta M. Sbragia (ed.), *Europolitics: Institutions and Policymaking in the 'New' European Community*, Brookings Institution, Washington, DC (1992), 257–91.
2. For a more detailed review of the US/EC policy agenda, see Michael Smith and Steven Woolcock, *The United States and the European Community in a Transformed World*, Pinter for the Royal Institute of International Affairs, London (1993), especially chapters 1–2.
3. See Michael Smith, '"The devil you know": the United States and a changing European Community', *International Affairs*, 68(1992), 103–20.
4. See Gary Clyde Hufbauer, 'An overview', in Gary Clyde Hufbauer (ed.), *Europe 1992: An American Perspective*, Brookings Institution, Washington, DC (1990), 1–64.
5. See for example, Steven Woolcock, *Market Access Issues in US–EC Relations: Trading Partners or Trading Blows?*, Pinter for the Royal Institute of International Affairs, London (1991); and Hufbauer, 'An overview', op. cit.
6. See, for example, Patrick A. Messerlin, 'The European steel industry and the world crisis', in Yves Meny and Vincent Wright (eds), *The Politics of Steel: Western Europe and the Steel Industry in the Crisis Years (1974–1984)*, Walter de Gruyter, Berlin (1986), 111–36; Loukas Tsoukalis (ed.), *Europe, America, and the World Economy* Oxford, Basil Blackwell (1986) particularly chapter 2, Robert Crandall, 'The EC–US steel crisis', 17–49.
7. A path-breaking study of the industrial policy issue is William Diebold, Jr., *Industrial Policy as an International Issue*, McGraw-Hill for the Council on Foreign Relations, New York (1980). See also Stephen S. Cohen and John Zysman, *Manufacturing Matters: The Myth of the Post-Industrial Economy*, New York, Basic Books (1987), particularly part III.
8. See Michael Smith, 'The European Community, the United States and high technology: old issues and new dimensions', *European Trends*, 2 (1989), 49–57.
9. See Steven Woolcock et al., *International Trade in the Post-multilateral Era*, Harvard

University Press, Cambridge, MA (1986); I.M. Destler, *Making Foreign Economic Policy*, Brookings Institution, Washington, DC (1980); I.M. Destler, *American Trade Politics: System Under Stress*, Institute for International Economics, Washington, DC (1986).

10. Destler, *American Trade Politics*, op. cit., chapter 7, has a good discussion of the pressures.

11. ibid., which points out the forces working for change in the 1980s.

12. See Smith and Woolcock, *The United States and the European Community in a Transformed World*, op. cit., chapter 2; Michael Smith, *Western Europe and the United States: The Uncertain Alliance*, George Allen & Unwin, London (1984), chapter 5.

13. See Smith and Woolcock, *The United States and the European Community in a Transformed World*, op. cit., especially chapter 1.

14. See Woolcock, *Market Access Issues in EC–US Relations*, op. cit., especially chapter 2.

15. See Carter H. Golembe and David S. Holland, 'Banking and securities', in Hufbauer, *Europe 1992: An American Perspective*, op. cit., 65–118. For a later treatment stressing opportunities for the United States, see Raymond J. Ahearn, 'US access to the EC-92 Market: opportunities, concerns and policy challenges', in *Europe and the United States: Competition and Cooperation in the 1990s*, Study Papers Submitted to the Subcommittee on International Economic Policy and Trade and the Subcommittee on Europe and the Middle East of the Committee on Foreign Affairs, US House of Representatives, US Government Printing Office, Washington, DC (June 1992), 177–92.

16. See C. Fred Bergsten, *America and the World Economy: A Strategy for the 1990s*, Institute for International Economics, Washington, DC (1988); Hufbauer, 'An overview', in *Europe 1992: An American Perspective*, op. cit.

17. See, for example, Caroline Click, 'Virginia is poised to service the Single Market', *Europe* (October 1991), 28–30; Wolfgang Weltz, 'From Ohio to Brussels: the U.S. states enter the international marketplace', *Europe* (November 1989), 14–15.

18. See Raymond J. Ahearn, 'U.S. access to the EC-92 Market', op. cit. For sectoral studies, see Peter F. Cowhey, 'Telecommunications', in Hufbauer, *Europe 1992: An American Perspective*, op. cit., 159–224; Woolcock, *Market Access Issues in EC–US Relations*, op. cit., *passim*.

19. See Theodor W. Galdi, 'The European defense industry: responses to global change and European integration', in *Europe and the United States, Competition and Cooperation in the 1990s*, op. cit., 239–56.

20. See Alasdair Smith and Anthony J. Venables, 'Automobiles', in Hufbauer, *Europe 1992: An American Perspective*, op. cit., 119–58; James P. Warrack and Daniel T. Jones, 'European automotive policy: past, present, and future', in *Europe and the United States: Competition and Cooperation in the 1990s*, op. cit., 193–213.

21. See Sbragia, 'Thinking about the European future', op. cit.; Joseph Greenwald, 'Negotiating strategy', in Hufbauer, *Europe 1992: An American Perspective*, op. cit., 345–88.

22. See Weltz, 'From Ohio to Brussels', op. cit.; Hugh O'Neill, 'The role of the States in trade development', in Frank J. Macchiarola (ed.), *International Trade: The Changing Role of the United States*, Proceedings of the Academy of Political Science, 37

(1990), 181–9.

23. See O'Neill, 'The role of the States in trade development', op. cit. For an important study of the role of State Development Agencies (SDAs), see Frances H. Oneal, 'State government responses to EC-92: a survey of State Development Agencies', in Dale Smith and James Lee Ray (eds), *The 1992 Project and the Future of Integration in Europe*, M.E. Sharpe, Armonk, NJ (1992). Oneal concludes that 'the SDAs may ultimately play the leading role in U.S.–European economic policy making.'

24. See, for example, 'The fast track West', *The Economist* (1 June 1991), 36.

25. The idea of the 'politics of scale' is developed in Roy H. Ginsberg, *Foreign Policy Actions of the European Community: The Politics of Scale*, Lynne Rienner, Boulder, CO (1989). Its essential premise is that levels of cooperation between actors are influenced by the desire and capacity to share the costs of action, thus achieving 'economies of scale'.

16 Shaping a federal foreign policy for Europe

Christopher Hill

If we go through the looking glass after contemplating the burgeoning external relations of the units in federal systems, we come to the mirror-image question of the extent to which groups of states are capable of putting together a single foreign policy system. And since the European Community (EC) is far and away the most advanced grouping in this regard it will be of some relevance to study the experience of its collective diplomatic activity known as European Political Cooperation (EPC). Perhaps in comparing existing federal states with the EC we will be able to observe a process of convergence, whereby subnational units gain some autonomy just as fully fledged nation-states give some of it up in a confederal arrangement. Alternatively, the trends might lead the two sets of entities to pass each other unknowingly as they head in opposite directions, like ships in the night. It is conceivable that the individual member-states of the EC Twelve might end up with *less* international distinctiveness than a Quebec or a Florida.

This would by definition be the case if the EC were to develop into a single state with only one seat at the United Nations. If such a scenario is still quite difficult to envisage it is only imaginable at all on the basis of a federal United States of Europe, where the separate units retain their identity and considerable capacity for independent action. A unitary, centralised Europe, along the lines (say) of the French system, would never even get on to the drawing board.

This chapter seeks to examine what a federal foreign policy, if achieved by the EC, would look like. In doing so, it addresses the question of the dynamics of the present process: to what extent are elements of federalism already present in the system, and what federalist potentialities exist for future exploitation? Particular attention will be given to the impact of the

Single European Act (SEA) and the Treaty of Maastricht which have both (even if the latter remains unratified) raised the profile considerably of efforts to create a common European foreign policy.

The cooperation of states

Ever since the European Economic Community came into being in 1958 it has had external relations of one kind or another, and diplomats in non-member countries have accordingly (and increasingly) puzzled over 'who speaks for Europe?' While the Brussels Commission is far more than a service secretariat it hardly enjoys plenipotentiary status. The rotating President of the Conference of Foreign Ministers[1] often does technically speak for the Twelve as a whole, notably in the UN General Assembly in September each year, but on all policy matters he is merely enunciating a painfully agreed collective text. On certain important issues, indeed, what the President says will be belied by the actions or unilateral counter-statements of his colleagues, and on others it will have proved either imposs-ible or undesirable to find a common position. Here the separate nation-states make the running. It is thus not surprising that outsiders are puzzled as to whom to approach when they wish to negotiate with 'Europe'. There is no European foreign policy or foreign policy process, and yet it is arguable that the Community produces 'foreign policy actions'.[2]

It must be said at the outset, therefore, that the primary characteristic of European attempts to harmonise their foreign policy positions is that they are precisely acts of 'political cooperation', meaning that independent states make discretionary judgements and particular compromises about how far they will work together. The process is not legal, and it is not integrated in the sense of a merger between national diplomatic processes. There is not even a constitutive document for a future European foreign policy process, since the Title III of the Single Act and Article J of the Maastricht Treaty do no more than codify existing intergovernmental practices and lay down general desiderata about the way in which consultations should evolve into commonality. The sole restriction on national powers, through the extension of majority voting into foreign policy, is so heavily hedged around with qualifications that it has little more than symbolic significance. In short, there is at present no federal European foreign policy and no mechanism by which one could be produced.

The consequence of this is that the traditional nation-state structures remain solidly in place. All twelve are individually members of the UN and other international organisations. They all have their own foreign ministries and networks of embassies abroad (admittedly some far more extensive than others).[3] Accordingly, even if some diverge less frequently from the consen-sus than others, and have fewer purely bilateral ties of importance, they all have identifiable national foreign policies. Some of the smaller states indeed, such as Ireland, have acquired more of a distinctive profile in international relations since joining the EC and participating in EPC.

In parallel to the activities of the traditional diplomatic corps, which will hardly give up its career paths, traditions and politico-bureaucratic perspectives without a long fight, are the even stronger vested interests of the national defence ministries and their associated systems. Whereas diplomats have only small constituencies which they can appeal to for support, officials in defence ministries can look to their national arms producers and ancillary complexes as well as to their own military to defend the idea of a national defence policy. In the EC the five big states (Britain, France, Germany, Italy and Spain) plus the Netherlands are significant arms producers, while all the others bar Ireland and Luxembourg have armed forces with useful but limited roles, usually involving specialisation at sea or in the air.[4] These would only be relinquished when the state itself was absorbed into a large European entity, that is at one second to midnight on the clock of federalist advance.

The same is true of the extensive systems of national commercial support and cultural projection. It is sometimes overlooked in the welter of enthusiasm for the common-then-single European market that the member-states are still deadly rivals for shares of that market, and even more so for shares of the markets in the wider world. That governments cannot always do a great deal to determine the success of private enterprises does not stop them from being expected to do so by the voting public and by making persistent efforts to rig the terms of trade. Just as 'foreign policy' therefore is steadily expanding its scope into the area of economic interdependence, so there are created new and potentially significant further barriers to the creation of a common European foreign policy: the states need foreign policy to influence the management of international economic policy in their own particular direction.

None of this means that EPC is of no significance, or that it has not changed the conduct of national foreign policy. The history of the phenomenon since 1970 shows that it has made remarkable progress in terms of both procedure and substance. Moreover it remains an unprecedented and unparalleled experiment in group diplomacy within the international system. Nothing else has ever aspired to, let alone achieved, the level of coordination represented by EPC. Institutionalised joint working now occurs at all levels from that of embassy Third Secretaries to that of Foreign Ministers, and the topics covered range from the International Conference on the Middle East to human rights in Guatemala. All states in the world coordinate their external relations in some form with partners, both geographical and ideological. But only the EC-12 do so systematically, comprehensively and more or less exclusively. Their process is unusual in every respect, but particularly its intensiveness and resilience. These qualities have ensured that national foreign policies have been coloured by the experience of participation, and that a degree of convergence has taken place (some of which might have occurred even without EPC).

Yet however intense and regular a process of consultation becomes it remains intergovernmental so long as the entities exist as independently recognised states. To be sure, independence or even sovereignty may be challenged by the consequences of such activity—this is *le défi communautaire*—but until their extinction there is always the possibility of disregarding particular lines of policy, and even of withdrawal from the whole system. This will continue to be the case so long as the states control the resources behind foreign policy. It was a lesson painfully learned by the House of Commons and the États-Généraux that, until tax-raising powers had been taken permanently away from them, the English and French monarchies would always find ways of evading parliamentary attempts to spread the responsibilities of government more widely.

It is revealing that the European Court of Justice, the final arbiter over the interpretation of Community law and the degree of supranationalism present in it, has been allowed no place in EPC. The nature of any obligation is an inherently contestable matter, but what is not in doubt is that in the area of foreign policy the member-states are only under a treaty obligation to 'define and implement a common foreign and security policy'.[5] This is vague and unenforceable. So long as they do not officiously flout agreed positions the states will not come under serious pressure to conform in every aspect of a policy (indeed, in some respects national variations are a useful way of running hares and/or deflecting responsibility), let alone to channel all national concerns through the collective system. Moreover until the Single Act set up a tiny, circumscribed Secretariat in 1987, EPC did not possess a single institution of its own, unless we count the important direct telex link between foreign ministries known as COREU. The national foreign ministries ran COREU and EPC in general, and nothing existed as a counter-weight, with a structural bias towards the collectivity, as the Commission did in the area of treaty-based activity.

It was hardly surprising, therefore, that in 1990–1 the Gulf crisis and the war which followed showed that there was considerable life left in national diplomacy, whether security-related as in the German and Belgian concerns to avoid military deployments, or in the traditional pursuits of mediation, as prominently practised by France. This was for the negative reasons outlined above—the EPC system does not yet possess the power of constraint—but also because almost all the twelve member-states are still live political systems, with powerful domestic imperatives being brought to bear in clamorous national policy-making processes. The interests and values underlying these systems are certainly converging, but they are not identical and they still produce dramatically disparate results under conditions of stress.

The integrationist renaissance of the mid- and late 1980s did little to change all this, although it awakened wild expectations in the bosoms of those whose idealism was more powerful than their reading of legal texts. In both the Single Act and the Maastricht Treaty the provisions for foreign policy cooperation are shot through with intergovernmentalism. In the former, EPC was kept as a strictly separate activity from EC external relations. In the latter, the two have been nominally brought together but the policy-making process will remain largely bifurcated and there is no sense in which 'European foreign policy' (whatever that may be) is now a Commission responsibility, or even in which it is genuinely 'communautaire'. On the face of things the national governments most jealous of their high policy privileges have won the day, and federalism is no nearer breaching the walls of classical foreign policy than it was in the days of General de Gaulle.

The potential detonators of a federal foreign policy

Yet politics is never a static business, and it is unwise to judge its character solely on the basis of practice at one time, or a written agreement which may actually be in the process of constant reinterpretation. That is why it is important to read between the lines of Maastricht and the Single Act, and to identify trends and possibilities as much as codified procedures and norms which largely represent the political realities of the present and the past. And reading between these lines, we can see that those who wish to carry the process of European integration forward rapidly, but who have been frustrated by the slower ships in the convoy, have none the less been able to place certain seeds in the process which have the potential to grow into the elements of federalism. To change the metaphor, over the years a number of small charges have been inserted at key points of the EPC structure, which, if detonated effectively at the right times, have had the potential to bring down the intergovernmental structure and make possible its transformation along more federalist lines. In this respect EPC is not analogous to a normal inter-state alliance or intergovernmental organisation (IGO). It has at least seven distinctive characteristics:

(i)   The first of these is the well-known *coordination reflex*, perhaps more often aspired to than achieved. This denotes the presumed tendency of the member-states (a) to react to external stimuli by collective consultations (b) primarily with each other, thus possibly breeding a sense of common identity and purpose. Occasional setbacks have inevitably occurred but the trend has been towards this kind of fraternalism. The fact that outsiders like the United States and Japan have increasingly been concerned at their exclusion from the conference rooms of the Twelve testifies to the reality of the reflex. EPC has produced an expectation that the Europeans should and will work as one, and to some extent also an instinct to do so.

(ii) The other side of this coin is the personal sense of *collegiality* which has grown up among the key personnel involved in EPC, namely at the political level, the foreign ministers, and at the official level, the political directors and their assistants, the correspondents. Since the founding Luxembourg Report of 1970 these principals have always met more frequently than they were strictly required to, and now they come together far more often than does a national Cabinet. On one occasion in recent years the British Foreign Secretary Douglas Hurd calculated that he had met his French opposite number on seven occasions within fifteen days, and in five different cities.[6] No one would suggest that such togetherness leads to national interests being sacrificed—there are plenty of other bodies to remind the EPC players of their main loyalties—but the frequency of the contacts and the continuity of the personnel do create that sense of solidarity which professionals in any field tend to develop through expertise and the feeling that outsiders do not understand the complexity of issues. At the very least the sense of a European perspective and set of collective interests seems to have developed *alongside* the persistently pressing national concerns. Such a development can also be observed in other groupings, NATO for example, but they are always less intense in their pattern of interactions.

(iii) We have already referred to *COREU*, as something which is not quite an EPC institution in its own right. But it is, none the less, an extraordinary and significant phenomenon. COREU is the direct telex link which since 1973 has connected the foreign ministries of the EPC member-states with increasing facility, by-passing the laborious business of communication through embassies. More than 10,000 messages a year flow back and forth between the Presidency and the other member-states, which represents a formal process of sophistication and exclusivity—almost a match, in multilateral terms, for the especially close networks which exist more easily in such bilateral relationships as those between Paris and Bonn or Washington and London. Indeed, it provides an intimacy of the kind to be found in a single well-oiled national administration, although were a federal Europe to be created it would not, of course, be necessary. Chancellor Kohl does not want a COREU to talk to the *Länder* about foreign policy, nor President Bush one to liaise with the states of the Union.

(iv) The fourth distinctive characteristic of EPC is that it has added a *crisis consultation mechanism* to its repertoire since the London report of 1981.[7] Within 48 hours, at the request of any three foreign ministers a full meeting of Community foreign ministers can be held to discuss emergencies like Iraq's invasion of Kuwait (Maastricht upgrades this by providing for a meeting at the request of the Presidency, of any one state or of the Commission). In practice, it is not so easy. Aggressors tend to make their moves in the depths of the summer and Christmas holidays when ministers are not easily available, and reluctant members can always delay serious discussion if they so wish. Still, this innovation went a long way towards remedying the slow reaction time which had been all too evident a weakness in EPC during the late 1970s. It thereby helps to foster the sense of oneness and in-house decision-making (as opposed to occasional contacts between autonomous units), which is the prerequisite of making the system ready for federalism.

(v) The involvement and increasing role of the *European Commission* is another element of the process which could be seen as proto-federal. From the mid-1970s its presence at EPC meetings had become increasingly accepted, until the London Report legitimised Commission participation and therefore tacitly acknowledged the practical convergence of the traditional realm of state foreign policy and the external relations under Brussels' care.[8] This was the precursor of the Single Act's specification of the requirement of 'consistency' between the two strands of the EC's role in the world, and Maastricht's ultimate recognition that they had to be fused into a single system, albeit one which was fundamentally intergovernmental in character. By the late 1980s practice had evolved to the extent that the Commission was routinely accepted without comment as part of the 'Troika plus one' formula,[9] and the undoubted expertise present in Directorates I and VIII, together with the Secretariat-General of the Commission, was more readily acknowledged and drawn upon by national foreign ministries than it had been a decade before. The old sense, that a Brussels interest in foreign policy was both impertinent and subversive, has been replaced by a cautious recognition that foreign policy is a team effort in which Commission personnel (and representations) abroad might be able to work in a complementary way with national diplomats. This is a prerequisite, if not a harbinger, of the creation of a federal foreign policy.

(vi) Both a cause and an effect of the procedural improvements in EPC has been the aspiration to speak with one voice. As a cursory observation of recent crises shows us, the Twelve have regularly failed to live up to the expectation. Equally no one doubts the change that has taken place over twenty years in producing a common statement analysing the international scene every year through a statement in the UN General Assembly, in holding together through complicated negotiations in the Conference on Security and Cooperation in Europe (the CSCE), and in speaking to important outside states through the Presidency. This is not only a question of the Troika, interesting diplomatic innovation as that has been. Among others in the 1980s the two superpowers, Japan, Australia and India all recognised the EC's collective actorness in foreign policy by seeking a privileged dialogue with EPC, while other regional organisations with the basic capacity to engage in political discussions developed extensive bloc-to-bloc relations with the Community. These were sometimes through EPC, and sometimes through the Commission. Often there would be a 'mixed' quality to them, and the line between intergovernmentalism and treaty-based activity became ever less sharp.[10] This was symbolised by the TransAtlantic Declaration of November 1990, which provided for meetings between the United States President on the one hand and the two 'Presidents of Europe' on the other, that is the President of the Council of Ministers and the President of the Commission. It was not wholly surprising when, during the first such meeting in April 1991, most of the press coverage focused on Presidents Bush and Delors, to the exclusion of the nominally more significant European representative, Prime Minister Jacques Santer of Luxembourg. The Community is being treated increasingly as a single entity by outsiders, and even as a synonym for 'Europe'. That specialists would support neither of these claims hardly matters in terms of practical international relations. It is the half-informed men (mostly men) of affairs with the broad brush who tend to create the big picture.

(vii) Thus when we look closely at EPC we see that there is more going on than can be explained by a static intergovernmentalist interpetation. If the 'common market' is becoming a single market, then one step behind national foreign policies are moving from coordination towards a common European foreign policy. They have not yet arrived at that point, let alone at that of a *single* policy,[11] but there is a *sense of development*. Indeed, it can be argued that the way in which EPC has been set up and developed has created a *ratchet effect*. Right from the beginning, each constitutive report contained within it the seeds of its successor until the Single European Act formally provided for a formal five-year review of progress, which the Maastricht negotiations then anticipated. The subsequent treaty provides for a further reassessment of how to go forward, in 1996. Like the previous six characteristics we have examined, this is not federalism *per se* but it certainly provides some of the means by which a federal foreign policy could be produced. And it reveals the thinking behind the forces which have carried foreign policy cooperation forward. Although the British and Danes have favoured more effective diplomatic coordination, they alone would hardly have brought EPC to the brink of supranationalism. That has been achieved because genuinely federalist forces have come to see the advantages of pushing on foreign policy cooperation, after years of opposing it as a Gaullist ramp. It is to their recent impact that we should now turn.

The Single Act and Maastricht: further thin ends of the wedge

If there were already contained within the basic EPC structure certain elements which could be regarded as seeds of a future federal foreign policy, the two major acts of European constitutional amendment which were tabled in 1986 and 1991 sought to advance their growth quite significantly. In general they did not succeed. Britain's Prime Minister John Major rightly regarded it as a negotiating success that he was able to restrict the provisions for a Common Foreign and Security Policy to a separate intergovernmental 'pillar' of the Maastricht Treaty, just as EPC had been fenced off from the rest of the Single Act in the almost wholly autonomous Title III, Article 30.[12] But the price of this holding of the line was the concession of further small redoubts to those who wished to make a qualitative leap forward in foreign policy integration. These largely technical concessions have been barely noticed (although the progress on defence cooperation attracted considerable attention in the Danish referendum campaign), but they provide significant foundations on which to build if the political climate turns again in favour of the federalists (and who in the early 1980s would have predicted their recent successes?).

Innovations

(i) Maastricht itself built on the modest foundations of Title III of the Single Act. It provided for further discussion of *institutional developments*, designed to go beyond the 1986 innovation of a small *Secretariat for EPC*. This last created a pentagonal network in the Council of Ministers building in Brussels (representatives of the Presidency, plus its two predecessors and two successors) and was the first institution to exist for EPC alone. Given the uncertainty about the fate of Maastricht, the Secretariat is at present in a state of suspension, but until the Danish referendum negotiations were well advanced on expanding the Secretariat to include representatives of all twelve member-states and to locate it in the Secretariat of the Council of Ministers. This would be accompanied by the harnessing of the Political Committee (the official powerhouse which runs EPC at just below ministerial level) to COREPER (the Committee of Permanent Representatives) which is the main official policy-making level for the Community proper. Thus EPC would be all but fully integrated administratively with the supranational Community institutions, and the apparently intergovernmental nature of the CFSP pillar significantly challenged. States would still hold the whip-hand, as they do across the board in the EC, but no one would be able to pretend any longer that the formulation of a common European foreign policy was impossible on the grounds of institutional fragmentation.

(ii) Changes have also been proposed in *nomenclature* over recent years, although they have been cautiously drafted. At present 'EPC' and 'the external relations of the Communities' still hold the field. If Maastricht is ratified they will pass into history in favour of the 'common foreign and security policy'. It will be noted that this clumsy phrase (and acronym—the French PESC and German GASP are far more euphonious) is precisely chosen to avoid any commitment to a 'common foreign policy' let alone a 'European foreign policy'. The United States and other federal systems, after all, do not talk of their 'common foreign and security policies' but only of their 'foreign policies'.

The phrase 'CFSP' is artificial and the absence of 'defence' could not be more marked. But it does contain for the first time an element of singularity in that there is explicit reference to the existence of a *common* foreign *policy*, and to the linkage with security questions. Conversely, the odd use (in this context) of the terms 'political' and 'cooperation', which both underplayed the international relations content and led to confusions between foreign policy and what Interior Ministers met to discuss, is quietly put to rest. This is part of a ground-clearing with psychological effects, in making it more difficult for publics and politicians to think backwards to the time when European foreign relations were *not* conceptualised as 'common' and involving matters of security.

(iii) It has also only been in the last five years that EPC has even acquired a *legal basis*. First, in the provisions of the Single Act relating to EPC (half a distinct treaty, half an amendment of the Treaty of Rome), a formal obligation was entered into for the first time, but only that to consult.[13] This was of symbolic but not juridical or practical importance, as Title III's separateness from the rest of the SEA was accompanied by an explicit statement that it was not to be subject to the rulings of the European Court of Justice. It could, however, no longer be argued by the traditionalists that EPC had little to do with the Community proper, or (even) that non-member states might conceivably hope to join it.

Second, the CFSP provisions explicitly brought EPC into the centre of the Community's activities, even if they did so on the basis of the metaphor of the temple with three pillars rather than that of the organic tree.[14] Any change in one part of the overall system is now bound to have effects in the others, and there is less room for confusion both inside and outside the Community as to the importance of the attempt to produce a common foreign policy.

(iv) The practical accompaniment of the legal evolution has been the provision for the *institutional merger of EPC with the Communities external relations*. To some extent this is deceptive. The Commission is no European Foreign Office, and the twelve national diplomatic services are still robustly independent. Moreover as we have already seen,[15] the attempt to create even a single service structure through COREPER and the Secretariat of the Council of Ministers has not yet been achieved. Even with a green light for Maastricht, it will take time to implement. Yet there has been a significant shift of both aspiration and practice since 1987. The concern with mere 'consistency' or coordination, which the Single Act prescribed, has been superseded by a more relaxed pursuit of interchange and cooperation between the various institutions, Community, EPC and even national. It is not that effective coordination has been fully achieved. Between economic and political external policies it can never and perhaps should never be so, as the bureaucracies of individual states demonstrate daily. But there is now a more general acceptance of the futility of EC citizens (as they will be if Maastricht is ratified) not pulling together in a testing international climate, whichever budget their salary is ultimately paid from. A common agenda for external policy is gradually emerging between Brussels and the member-states, and with the new provisions for the Commission to have the right of initiative and for foreign policy actions (in principle) to be funded from the Community budget proper, we are getting closer to the notion of a single actor with a coherent decision-making process and a single pool of resources.

(v) For a unitary system to be achieved in full would require supranationalism in foreign policy. And indeed the principle of *majority voting* was introduced by the Maastricht Treaty. It was hedged around with so many safeguards that it will be almost impossible to use on anything but trivial matters of implementation, but the Rubicon has now been crossed. This is in fact why the provision was included, when everyone involved knows that as it stands it is virtually inoperable. Its importance lies as a marker for the future, in the idea that there is nothing inherently unsuitable about foreign policy (as many would assert) as an area in which to extend the well-tried Community method of decision-making. It was surprising that Britain, whose objections are fundamental, did not veto its presence in the Treaty, and the only explanation can be that a trade was done against some other point of principle. It is a concession that London might live to regret, as federalists will undoubtedly seek gradually to extend the scope of majority voting in foreign policy, and they are now more likely to be able to do so by traditional technocratic means without having to resort to grand constitutional debate.

(vi) The last significant innovation of the CFSP part of the Maastricht Treaty constitutes potentially the biggest federalist detonator of all, namely the *breaking of the taboo on relating EPC to defence*. While EPC was divorced from things military, and had to make a virtue of necessity with its 'civilian power', it was difficult to see the point of arguing for a qualitative leap into supranationalism. But now that the Maastricht

Treaty talks about 'the eventual framing of a common defence policy, which might in time lead to a common defence' (Title I, Common Provisions), the pendulum has swung the other way. It is difficult to see how a serious defence policy could be implemented without the capacity to make rapid decisions. This could only be done by creating a federal system (indeed it is one of the ultimate rationales for a federal state) or, where individual sovereignty survived, by conceding even more supra-nationalism than exists already in the area of trade policy. Moreover the effective recognition that the revived Western European Union is more an embryonic EC defence arm than a rival to the Community (despite the careful fudging of the Treaty's language) means that a significant amount of the institutional and military infrastructure necessary for a European defence policy is now in place. The plans for a Franco-German Corps are still a long way from a single European army, but it is now feasible to imagine the creation of an integrated high command of coordinated national forces—as, indeed, NATO has shown to be possible.

Conclusions: the threshold of choice

The discussion above has attempted to show both that the European Community's present foreign policy system is still intergovernmental, and that it contains certain federalist possibilities (called here 'detonators') which have been inserted into the system. The distribution of these detonators is mostly haphazard; it represents the outcome of a continuing struggle between those who wish to create a single European foreign policy and those who wish EPC to remain as a framework for achieving certain diplomatic economies of scale between national diplomacies. But their accumulation has reached a point which is well beyond the normal dialectical incorporation of opposite possibilities which exists in any human endeavour. In the foreign policy sphere, as in several others, the European Community is now on the brink of making a choice for or against federalism.

This is not to say that the choice cannot be evaded. At the time of writing the turmoil inside the Community seems to make non-decisions and playing for time the most likely option. But this cannot work for long. Now that institutional evolution has reached the brink of a transformation of intergovernmentalism, with key concessions having been made such as those on defence and majority voting, there is every encouragement for frustrated federalists to return to the charge again and again in more favourable circumstances. This will occur unless there is some major constitutional debate on what the Community is to be, and in this particular context on what its objectives in world politics should be, which will settle the issue for a generation. Such a debate could go either way, but it will have to be accompanied by practical decisions on institutions and resources, if destructive wrangling is not to continue *ad infinitum*. To some extent the present debate on Maastricht (revealingly *post hoc* in most countries) is providing the necessary catalyst, but foreign policy has not been the central issue, and as we have seen the CFSP promises major change only to stop tantalisingly short of it.

The alternative is for the various players in the struggle to try to determine Europe's destiny by more indirect but no less fundamental means. On the federalist side this could be done by fostering the steady integration of the Commission's external relations with those considered by the traditional intergovernmentalist method, and in particular by collapsing the various institutional arrangements into a single system. Those relating to the CFSP Secretariat and to diplomatic missions in third countries (e.g. the new states of the old USSR) are the most obvious candidates.

On the 'cooperation' side, the British have been playing the strongest card for four years now, through pushing forward on the question of the enlargement of the Community. They—and many dispassionate observers—take the view that the entry of even four new members would make agreement on integrationist advance almost impossible. This would be particularly true in the area of foreign policy, where the most likely new members, the old EFTA (European Free Trade Area) countries, have distinctive attitudes to international relations (often neutralist) that seem likely to be at odds with those of Britain and France, the leading factors in EPC. It is true that this strategy has its risks; enlargement might complicate decision-making so much that the Community was *compelled* to take the great leap forward. On the other hand it would certainly alter the balance of power in the EC between cooperators and integrators, centre and periphery, if one considers that the historical dynamo of integration has been the grouping of the original Six (France, Germany, Italy and the Benelux countries). With the significant exception of Spain, new entrants have either lacked the size to provide a real boost to federalism (Ireland and Portugal), or have been something of a millstone, whether political (Britain, Denmark) or economic (Greece).

As has been often observed, we have at present in the European Community a strange but dynamic hybrid. It is based (and here we can generalise across the board, beyond foreign policy) on a system of mixed competences with states and Community institutions jostling for influence. Agreements signed with outsiders, and participation in international organisations often display this element of 'mixity'.[16] In most federal models foreign policy is the one area where mixity should certainly disappear in favour of a central government with monopoly powers over external representations, defence and treaty-making. But the Community makes its own models. Even if, at the current crossroads, a federal choice is made, it is difficult to envisage the complete disappearance of the long-standing national traditions of diplomacy. The laxest of federal state systems (say Canada) does not provide for the kind of autonomy in international affairs that states like Britain or France, even assuming they were on good terms with the idea of European unity, would expect.

While national foreign ministries might be absorbed into some Brussels equivalent of Foggy Bottom, and national embassies closed or relabelled, the separate sets of interests, commitments and perspectives will not go away overnight. If Alberta is thinking about acquiring a foreign policy, and Quebec already has one of sorts,[17] then a federal Europe will have to coexist with twelve Quebecs, and in spades. The alternative is to imagine that the act of constituting a united Europe would inherently create (or demonstrate) a harmonisation of international interests between the separate states sufficient to obviate any need for independent activity. This seems little more than idealism.

The European Community is caught up in two kinds of flux: its own internal development, which has become unbalanced with the speed of recent changes, and the turmoil in wider Europe consequential on the collapse of communism. Yet it is unlikely to be be able to deal with the new demands and uncertainties on the basis of the technocratic incrementalism that has been its preferred historical path. This is particularly so because external expectations of the Community are now at an unprecedentedly high level, and endless failures of foreign policy will follow on from an inability to settle on a working pattern of collective diplomacy, whether it is to be intergovernmental or integrated. The political compromises of the Maastricht Treaty may serve in the short term, but in the long run a better-drafted constitution based on a clearer fundamental decision will be necessary. Otherwise we shall witness more Yugoslavias, where more is expected of the Community than it can deliver, and where member-states proceed at different speeds or even in different directions. We cannot say that federalism necessarily represents the end-point of the debate which has to take place on a European foreign policy, but the questions a federalist view raises can hardly be evaded for much longer. Conversely, a federalist 'solution' which ignored what is happening with the subnational components in existing federal states, and the evident need for some form of subsidiarity principle in external relations, would nurture the seeds of its own early destruction.

Notes

1. This term has been used to distinguish the meetings of foreign ministers in Political Cooperation from their meetings as the Council of Ministers, the Community's legislative body under the Treaty of Rome. In practice the distinction has been gradually blurred over the years but it will only formally disap-

pear if the Maastricht Treaty is ratified.

2. The concept is Roy Ginsberg's, in his *The Foreign Policy Actions of the European Community: The Politics of Scale*, Lynne Rienner Publishers, Boulder, CO (1989). Even this step down from the notion of an EC foreign policy may claim too much.

3. A systematic analysis of the variation for the Nine in the 1970s is provided in Christopher Hill and William Wallace, 'Diplomatic trends in the European Community', *International Affairs*, 55 (January 1979). The greatest deviation then was 119, between Luxembourg's ten missions and France's 129.

4. For data on armed forces, see *The Military Balance, 1990–1991*, Brasseys for the International Institute for Strategic Studies, London (1991); on arms production, see Michael Brzoska and Peter Lock (eds), *The Restructuring of Arms Production in Western Europe*, Oxford University Press, London (1992); and Harald Bauer, Michael Brzoska and Wilfred Karl, *Coordination and Control of Arms Exports from EC Member States and the Development of a Common Arms Export Policy: Study Prepared for the European Parliament, Directorate General for Research*, University of Hamburg, Institut für Politische Wissenschaft, Working Paper 54 (1991).

5. Maastricht, Article J.1. This again assumes the ratification of the Maastricht Treaty. If ratification does not take place the obligation will be even weaker—simply that to consult. But the author takes the view in any case that the Common Foreign and Security Policy (CFSP) element of the treaty is *de facto* likely to hold, unlike the common currency provisions, precisely because of its more limited and realistic character.

6. Cited by William Wallace in his review article, 'No tinkering please; we are British', *The World Today*, 48, 8–9, (August–September 1992).

7. For details, see Alfred Pijpers, Elfriede Regelsberger and Wolfgang Wessels (eds), *European Political Cooperation in the 1980s: A Common Foreign Policy for Western Europe?*, Martinus Nijhoff, Dordrecht (1988) 63–4, 122–3, 158–9. Also Christopher Hill, 'EPC's performance in crises', in Reinhardt Rummel (ed.), *Toward Political Union: Planning a Common Foreign and Security Policy in the European Community*, Nomos Verlagsgesellschaft, Baden-Baden (1992), 139–50.

8. See Simon Nuttall, 'Where the Commission comes in', in Pijpers, Regelsberger and Wessels (eds.), *European Political Cooperation in the 1980s*, op.cit., 104–17.

9. The Troika is the system, commonly used from the late 1970s, whereby the Presidency country was assisted by representatives of the preceding and succeeding presidencies when it engaged in special missions to third countries. The 'Troika plus one' refers to the Commission having joined in with the process after 1983. See Simon Nuttall, *European Political Cooperation*, Oxford University Press, Oxford (1992), 19.

10 For an innovative survey and analysis of these developments, see Geoffrey Edwards and Elfriede Regelsberger (eds), *Europe's Global Links: The European Community and Inter-Regional Cooperation*, Pinter, London (1990).

11 In conceptual terms 'cooperation' means the coordination of separate national positions, 'common' means separate states holding (by convergence) very much the same positions, and 'single' means the existence of one decision-making process and one set of policy outputs. The parallel between foreign policy and the developing common/single market then holds fairly well.

12 The author has analysed the provisions of these two documents, in greater detail

than is possible here, in 'Article 30: European political cooperation', in Ami Barav (ed.), *Commentaries on the Single European Act*, Oxford University Press, Oxford (forthcoming) and in 'The European Community: towards a common foreign and security policy?', *The World Today*, 47, 11, (November 1991).

13 Rosa Maria Alonson Terme, 'From the draft treaty of 1984 to the Intergovernmental Conferences of 1991', in Rummel (ed.), *Toward Political Union*, op.cit., 269–88.

14 These images originated with discussion of the Luxembourg 'non-paper' of April 1990. The temple with its separate, parallel, pillars allows foreign policy and internal affairs to be accommodated within the overall structure while remaining intergovernmental. The federalists preferred the idea of the Community as a single organism, with various activities branching out from the supranational trunk, but they could not persuade the British and the Danes. See Richard Corbett, 'The Intergovernmental Conference on Political Union', *Journal of Common Market Studies*, XXX, 37 (September 1992); and Finn Laursen and Sophie Vanhoonacker (eds), *The Intergovernmental Conference on Political Union: Institutional Reforms, New Policies and the International Identity of the European Community*, Nijhoff, Dordrecht (1992).

15 In (i) of this 'Innovations' section.

16 See Joseph H.H. Weiler, 'The external legal relations of non-unitary actors: mixity and the federal principle', in David O'Keeffe and Henry G. Schermers (eds), *Mixed Agreements*, Deventer, Kluwer for the Europa Institute, Leiden (1983).

17 See Elliot J. Feldman and Lily Gardner Feldman, 'Canada' in Hans J. Michelmann and Panayotis Soldatos (eds), *Federalism and International Relations: The Role of Subnational Units*, The Clarendon Press, Oxford (1990).

Index